Drumsville!

Drumsville!

THE EVOLUTION
— OF THE —
NEW ORLEANS BEAT

ROBERT H. CATALIOTTI
FOREWORD BY HERLIN RILEY

Louisiana State University Press ▐▐ Baton Rouge

This book was published with support from the New Orleans Jazz and Heritage Foundation
and the Threadhead Cultural Foundation.

Published by Louisiana State University Press
lsupress.org

Manufactured in Canada
First printing

Designer: Michelle A. Neustrom
Typeface: Sentinel
Printer and binder: Friesens Corporation

Front cover images, *left to right:* Warren "Baby" Dodds (New Orleans Jazz Museum),
Earl Palmer (New Orleans Jazz Museum), Ed Blackwell (copyright © Mosaic Images), and
Zigaboo Modeliste (Brenda Ladd). New Orleans skyline and drum courtesy iStock.

Previous page: Female congregants playing tambourine and drums at the St. Philip Church of God in Christ,
1956. Photo by Ralston Crawford. Loaned by Ralston Crawford Photography Collection, Tulane University
Special Collections, Tulane University; New Orleans, LA. Accession number RC000209.

Back cover images, *left to right:* Drummer figure on congo drum (New Orleans Jazz Museum),
sketches of instruments played in Congo Square (Maryland Center for History and Culture), The John
Robichaux Orchestra of New Orleans (Hogan Jazz Archive Photography Collection), and
Warren "Baby" Dodds's drum set (New Orleans Jazz Museum).

Library of Congress Cataloging-in-Publication Data

Names: Cataliotti, Robert H., 1955– author. | Riley, Herlin, writer of foreword. | Kunian, David, writer of
    afterword.
Title: Drumsville! : the evolution of the New Orleans beat / Robert H. Cataliotti ; foreword by Herlin Riley ;
    afterword by David Kunian.
Description: Baton Rouge : Louisiana State University Press, 2022. | Includes index.
Identifiers: LCCN 2021062546 | ISBN 978-0-8071-7760-0 (cloth)
Subjects: LCSH: Drum—Louisiana—New Orleans—History. | Drum set—History. | Brass bands—Louisiana—
    New Orleans—History. | Music—Louisiana—New Orleans—African influences. | Music—Louisiana—New
    Orleans—European influences. | Congo Square (New Orleans, La.)
Classification: LCC ML1035 .C36 2022 | DDC 786.9/190976335—dc23
LC record available at https://lccn.loc.gov/2021062546

I'd been playing it and noticing that after you played this kind of beat for a while—the people seemed like they changed.

—James Black

Dedicated to all the drummers—past, present, future—
for keeping the New Orleans beat alive

Contents

5. BRASS BAND DRUMMING AND THE EMERGENCE OF THE DRUM KIT "A Drum Revolution" 39

4. IMPROVISED PERCUSSION INSTRUMENTS "It Sounded All Right" 29

3. EUROPEAN INFLUENCE "Rattle-Te-Banging Away" 23

2. LEGACY OF CONGO SQUARE The Source Point 7

1. WELCOME TO DRUMSVILLE! The Evolution of the New Orleans Beat 3

INTRODUCTION The Rhythms That Have Informed Music Worldwide, by Greg Lambousy 1

FOREWORD The New Orleans Groove, by Herlin Riley IX

6. TRADITIONAL JAZZ *"From the Bottom Up"* 51

7. MODERN JAZZ, RHYTHM & BLUES, AND FUNK *"The Beat, the Beat, the Beat"* 70

8. EXTENSIONS AND VARIATIONS *Passing It On* 131

AFTERWORD *History, Power, Ecstasy, and Existential Funk, by David Kunian* 211

ACKNOWLEDGMENTS 213

NOTES 215

INDEX 224

ents

Foreword

THE NEW ORLEANS GROOVE

Every natural event in life happens in rhythm. The sun rises and sets each day. Seasons change every few months. Every twelve months we celebrate a new year, and babies are born nine months after conception. These are only a few examples of long-term *rhythms*. When musical instruments are played, specifically drums, we witness the execution of short-term rhythms. Although different percussive instruments may have different sounds, the shared characteristic of these instruments is that they're played to create rhythm. The *Drumsville!* exhibit at the New Orleans Jazz Museum, from which this book was born, is a physical manifestation of some of the instruments, people, and documents of the rich and historical legacy of New Orleans rhythms.

All music starts with rhythm! Rhythm is the first component of a musical statement. In early civilizations, when a person sang or chanted, they did it in rhythm. When a person uses body parts as percussive instruments (clapping hands, stomping feet, slapping the chest, thighs, or feet, as is done in the hambone or gumboot dance) it's done in rhythm. The primary function of the drums is to provide the rhythmic foundation (groove) for a musical melody. All other instruments play rhythms, but their primary musical function is for playing musical melodies and harmonies. When a melodic instrument plays a note and then changes to another note or attacks the same note again, regardless of duration of time that passes between the notes, this is the execution of rhythm. Whenever a melody is sung or played on an instrument, it is played with a rhythmic integrity that shapes the melody and expresses a musical coherence. Some rhythms follow a consistent pattern or succession, and some rhythms are liberal and free. Rhythm is a sequence of sounds or events. The duration of time between the sound or event defines the rhythm. In music, when a sequence or pattern of sound is repeated, this repetition defines what musicians call a time signature.

The oldest musical instrument in the world, after the human voice, is the drum or some form of percussion. This book pays homage to the cultures of Native American Indians, Europeans, and African descendants who played the drums and percussion instruments while shaping the musical and rhythmic culture of New Orleans. It acknowledges the invention of the drum set and the drummers who helped shape the concept of playing the drums for the past 100-plus years.

Since the art form of jazz music and the drum set were invented in New Orleans, it is most fitting to recognize the city and its drummers who played and still are playing this important musical instrument. Many of these drummers were contributors to the development of jazz music and have influenced musical styles around the world, consciously and sometimes unconsciously, as the groove evolved from one musical style to the next.

New Orleans is unique and significant when it comes to improvised music. The city's musicians were some of the first people to alter traditional marches by syncopating the rhythm and melodic structure of the music without changing the main melodic identity of the songs. Some of the most influential and innovative pioneers of improvised music were born in New Orleans, including Louis Armstrong, Sidney Bechet, Jelly Roll Morton, and Baby Dodds. Improvisation in New Orleans is a whole cultural experience. This book delves into the lives of enslaved African Americans in Congo

Square. As an African American drummer, I feel strongly that the concept of improvisation is directly associated with our African forebearers who expressed themselves through their music and dance in Congo Square. They used their creativity and imaginative spirit to entertain, create and exchange goods, and bask in some moments of fun before being subjugated again. Musically speaking, the African-derived rhythms that were cultivated in Congo Square served as the foundation of many musical genres that are associated with New Orleans, such as ragtime, brass band, Mardi Gras Indian chants (call and response), jazz, rhythm and blues, funk, zydeco, and gospel music.

Drumsville! peeks into the lives of many of New Orleans's most influential drumming pioneers, as well as many of the current drummers who are the guardians of the city's rich rhythmic culture. It is very important to tell the narrative of the history of New Orleans drumming because the core rhythms that have evolved into becoming second line, funk, R&B, jazz, pop, or whatever contemporary style of music you can think of, were born out of the expressive rhythms of Congo Square. As a drummer and native of New Orleans, I feel a deep sense of pride of being part of a drumming lineage that is unique and significant to the world.

Because of the festive and social nature of the people of New Orleans, one of the shared characteristics of most of the featured drummers in *Drumsville!* is an expressed sense of community and camaraderie. One of the things that stands out in the book is the stories of drummers getting together to practice and share information with each other. These impromptu jam sessions are fun, respectful, giving, void of jealousy, and one of the most beautiful experiences to be a part of.

The book also explores the lives of drummers who were born outside of New Orleans and who were greatly influenced by the infectious grooves that were born in the Crescent City. New Orleanians have a welcoming spirit that makes every visitor feel at home. Sometimes visitors come for vacation or a particular trip and ultimately acquire a home and become residents.

The art of jazz and improvisation is a living, breathing experience that makes the future of the New Orleans groove an ever-evolving entity. Although there may be subtle changes to the groove, I think the bass drum will always be the *heartbeat* of the New Orleans groove. It is very important to recognize and preserve cultural traditions. Those traditions are the substance that give us our identity as a community of people. However, as we recognize and celebrate those traditions, we should be open to accepting their evolution, so long as the evolution or expansion is still connected to its roots. As a drummer, I'm proud to have been raised in New Orleans and its culture. I'm also honored to be one of the keepers of the beat.

Herlin Riley
Preeminent New Orleans drummer

Drumsville!

Introduction

THE RHYTHMS THAT HAVE INFORMED MUSIC WORLDWIDE

Drumsville! The Evolution of the New Orleans Beat has been one of the New Orleans Jazz Museum's most visited exhibits. It stands to reason, since New Orleans is known for the rhythms that have informed music worldwide, from jazz to bounce and beyond. The museum has an incredible collection of storied artifacts related to New Orleans drumming traditions. In the exhibit, our curator, David Kunian, and music scholar, Robert H. Cataliotti, tell this story through the lives of the drummers who helped shape the tradition and the artifacts in our collections and those that have been provided on loan. In preparation for the exhibit, and later for the book, Cataliotti conducted a wide range of oral histories with drummers and has combed archives for documents and interviews with drummers who have since passed.

Of the drummers who are no longer with us, the collection features the drum sets of Baby Dodds, Earl Palmer, Cie Frazier, Minor "Ram" Hall, and James Black, among others. Papa Jack Laine's bass drum and early top-mounted drum pedal, as well as a 1908 Ludwig bass drum pedal on loan to us from Stanton Moore, help illustrate the beginnings of the drum set. In addition, many of the city's living legends provided their own drums and other percussion equipment to enhance the exhibit. The *Drumsville!* companion book tells the stories of these influential drummers, the origins of the drum set, which has become omnipresent in combos around the world, and the far-ranging reach of the New Orleans beat as it has evolved.

The New Orleans Jazz Museum is fortunate to have the best of current New Orleans drummers performing on a regular basis in its Balcony Concert series, Jazz Foundation of America series, a variety of festivals, and in educational programs such as the Trombone Shorty Academy mentorship program, where Herlin Riley shares his drumming expertise and life experiences with advanced students.

Exhibits are necessarily limiting—there is only so much gallery space. The subject of New Orleans drumming is vast, and we felt it important to tell the story in more detail. We hope this is the beginning of more in-depth research on the topic as a whole. In addition to this book, the *Drumsville!* exhibit will travel in various forms and expand to a virtual field trip that will tie into a new series of web pages devoted to drummers and drumming in New Orleans.

With both the *Drumsville!* exhibit and this book, the Jazz Museum continues to promote New Orleans's ongoing cultural renaissance by providing diverse resources for musicians and music lovers of all languages and nationalities and fully exploring America's quintessential musical art form in the city where jazz was born.

Greg Lambousy
Director, New Orleans Jazz Museum

Opening night of *Drumsville!* exhibit, November 8, 2018. Herlin Riley on drum set jams with Treme Brass Band, with Vernon Severin on snare, and Revon Andrews on trombone. Photo by R. Cataliotti.

1

Welcome to Drumsville!

THE EVOLUTION
OF THE NEW ORLEANS BEAT

On November 8, 2018, opening night of the *Drumsville! The Evolution of the New Orleans Beat* exhibit at the New Orleans Jazz Museum, the culminating performance featured the Treme Brass Band jamming with Herlin Riley on the drum set. As the performance reached a crescendo, snare drummer Vernon Severin declared: "All these drummers that came through New Orleans ain't never had drum night. We got drum night tonight!" *Drumsville!* is a celebration of "all these drummers" and the history of drums and drumming in New Orleans—past and present. The exhibit and this book, which is a companion to the exhibit, are intended to be representative rather than comprehensive. The sheer number of exceptional drummers who have come through the city is mind-blowing. The sense of tradition has been and is so strong among drummers that the lineage from generation to generation is traceable in remarkable detail. The acknowledgment of "all these drummers," both those whose names are known, and there is extensive documentation of them, and the anonymous drummers reaching back into the eighteenth century who contributed to the evolution of the New Orleans beat, is beyond the scope of what could be included in the exhibit or this book.

For more than a century, the drum set has been pervasive throughout popular music. It is almost a given that in whatever type of band—jazz, blues, rhythm and blues, gospel, rock, funk, country, zydeco, polka, reggae—there will be a drummer behind a drum set. Few people ever question where the instrument came from. Likely the youngest instrument in popular music, the drum set is an American invention. New Orleans played a central role in the development of the drum set, and the city's drummers have been particularly influential on its evolution and how it is played. The most renowned aspect of the New Orleans drumming legacy is the second-line rhythm, which emerged from brass band parades and can be traced back to the bamboula and other dances performed in antebellum Congo Square. New Orleans drummers adapt this distinct rhythm to many musical contexts, including brass bands, traditional and modern jazz, Mardi Gras Indian chants, rhythm and blues, rock and roll, and funk.

Perhaps what is most striking upon entering the *Drumsville!* exhibit is the full wall across from the entrance covered by a black-and-white photograph of members of the St. Philip Church of God in Christ taken in 1956 by the renowned modernist artist and photographer Ralston Crawford. It features a child, Bonnie Mae Jackson, playing a tom-tom, Sister Bertha Jackson Pooler playing cymbals with a tambourine resting on the seat behind her, and Mother Mamie Felix playing a bass drum. In other photos taken that day, Ernest Matthews is seen on the bass drum and Brother Octave Delmont is playing guitar. Joining the percussionists, the whole congregation is clapping their hands, and there was surely some foot stomping going on, generating an explosive rhythmic groove in that little church in the Treme neighborhood just across from Congo Square, where people of African descent drummed and danced more than a century earlier. During the 1960s, drummer Shannon Powell grew up on St. Philip Street next door to the church. As a child, he was drawn to the rhythms of the congregation:

> One time, they even had the police looking for me, and I was in the church because I was fascinated by what the tambourine sounded like [that] I'm hearing come out of the church. It was a powerful, powerful rhythm, and I didn't know what was going on. I really wanted to be in there. I wanted to see. I heard people hollering and screaming and testifying and singing, you know. So, I just said to myself, "I gotta get in there. I gotta get in there." And, at the same time, I was afraid, too. I was like, "Wow" because every time I was peeping I would see these women, and they'd be jumping around, and they'd be speaking in tongues. It's a wonderful thing they was celebrating, you know, but the music and the tambourine playing that they were doing, it was so syncopated. And, these people, mind you, they never went to school for music or nothing like this. It was all coming straight from the heart.[1]

Today, Powell incorporates those rhythms into his drumming. Often one of the highlights of his live performances is when he takes a solo and breaks out a tambourine and beats out a call-and-response with his bass drum constructing a straight-from-the-heart groove that takes his audience back to those childhood visits to St. Philip. Likewise, when drummer Herlin Riley toured the *Drumsville!* exhibit he was enthralled when he saw the photo of the drumming in St. Philip: "That's very familiar to me, and for myself, when I see this kind of image, it takes me back to my childhood." He was raised in the Guiding Star Spiritual Church, where his grandfather Deacon Frank Lastie played drums, along with another congregant, Mother Lewis, who played the bass drum. For Riley, who today is another master of the tambourine/bass drum groove, the picture evokes the spiritual power of the rhythms that he felt, a power that is infused in his drumming: "And, that inner thing, whatever that is, has permeated me and allowed me to play music with that kind of conviction and that kind of commitment, you know, because I know the power of the music, the power of rhythms, and the power of the repetition of the rhythms. There's a certain power there that's a part of that. And, being in church, you feel that."[2] This photo of these everyday folks surrounded by percussion instruments speaks directly to how the culture of New Orleans is immersed in drums and rhythm.

Shannon Powell performing at Jazz Roots II, 1976. Courtesy of the New Orleans Jazz Museum. Accession number 1978.118(B).0096.

If there is any place in the world that should be called Drumsville, it's New Orleans. The name Drumsville comes from the title of a 1961 album recorded by Earl Palmer, one of the city's most widely renowned drummers. On *Drumsville,* Palmer highlights his spectacular technique and grooves through instrumental rerecordings of a dozen of the smash R&B and rock and roll hits that had been propelled by his signature beat and changed the course of modern popular music. The New Orleans beat is the foundation upon which so much American music is built. Drumsville has been home to some of the greatest musicians to pick up a pair of drumsticks. Their grooves run deep, and the evolution of the New Orleans beat goes on. Welcome to *Drumsville!*

Titos Sompa and Bichini Bia Congo Dance Theater Company performing at a Maafa ceremony in Congo Square, honoring the victims of the transatlantic trade in enslaved persons, 2018. Photo by R. Cataliotti.

2

Legacy of Congo Square

THE SOURCE POINT

Congo Square is *the* source point for Drumsville. From the founding of Louisiana, Africans and people of African descent drummed throughout the region, and by the early decades of the nineteenth century, their tribal dance and drum circle Sunday-afternoon gatherings were concentrated in Congo Square. A combination of music and dance, spiritual rituals, marketplace, socializing, and tourist attraction, Congo Square performances brought together enslaved people who came directly from Africa; others came through the Caribbean. African people born in the Americas joined in the mix, and the gatherings attracted both the enslaved and free people of color. In addition, Native Americans—who had their own festivals in the area prior to colonization—and Caucasian people whose origins were in Europe and the United States were drawn to the festivities. As Freddi Williams Evans asserts in *Congo Square: African Roots in New Orleans* (2011): "The principal instrument among them was the drum, which musicians used to summon others to the Square."[1] They played percussion and stringed instruments that were re-created from their homelands and constructed from the materials at hand. Polyrhythms, syncopation, and pulse beats that were played there are the heartbeat of the musical forms that evolved in New Orleans and provide a link to the Afro-Caribbean diaspora and ultimately back to Africa. The music they made was founded on African-based cultural retentions that interacted with and absorbed elements of the cultures they encountered, and the rhythmic heritage that was passed down from Congo Square laid the foundation for the New Orleans beat.

THE AFRICAN DIASPORA AND NEW ORLEANS

It is important to understand that Africa is not monolithic. There are many different tribal cultures, languages, and belief systems throughout the continent, and the trade of enslaved people fostered interactions between African people of different backgrounds. Those types of interactions certainly took place in Louisiana, but the waves of Africans that arrived there were more ethnically homogeneous than in the thirteen British-American colonies. As detailed in Gwendolyn Midlo Hall's *Africans in Colonial Louisiana*

The Bamboula, engraving by Edward W. Kemble created to accompany George W. Cable's article "The Dance in Place Congo," *Century Magazine,* February 1886. Courtesy of the New Orleans Jazz Museum. Accession number 1978.118(B).00195a.

(1992), during the era of initial French rule, captured Africans were largely taken from Senegambia. When the Spanish took control, new arrivals came primarily from Caribbean colonies, such as Jamaica, Martinique, Saint-Domingue, and Cuba, rather than directly from Africa. And the dominant tribal group arriving during this period was the Kongo. The trafficking of human beings brought individuals from numerous African "nations" to Louisiana, including Wolof; Bambara; Mandingo; Fulbe; Nard; Ganga; Kissy; Susu; Mina; Fon; Yoruba; Chamba; Igbo; Ibibio; Kongo/Angola; Makwa; and others, each of them contributing distinctive rhythms to the musical synthesis taking place in Congo Square.[2] New waves of Africans and African-descended people arrived in Louisiana after the revolt that overthrew French rule in Saint-Domingue in 1804 and again in 1809–10, when refugees from Saint-Domingue who were expelled from Cuba sought refuge in New Orleans. After the Louisiana Purchase, and particularly with the ban on the international trade of captive Africans by the United States in 1808, the domestic trade increasingly brought enslaved African Americans from the Upper South to the city.[3] All these people from these backgrounds came together in Congo Square and laid the foundation for the New Orleans beat.

RE-MEMBERING AFRICAN RETENTIONS

Many of the African people who were caught up in the transatlantic trade in enslaved persons transmitted their history, culture, and values through oral tradition rather than through writing. Enslaved Africans fought to hold on to their identities and survive, resist, and transcend the horror of slavery. The Sunday gatherings in Congo Square were a regular outlet that enabled Africans from diverse origins and people of African ancestry to recognize that their distinct oral traditions shared a number of elements. African-based creative expression is both aesthetic and functional. Western or European-based art often emphasizes the aesthetic aspect; this means the focus is on creativity, artistic self-expression, and audience or viewer enjoyment. African art certainly embraces this aesthetic aspect, but often it is also functional; it serves an extended or multilayered purpose; it accomplishes something beyond the usual role as entertainment. Often African art exhibits feature objects like hair picks, stools, utensils, and musical instruments. They are beautifully rendered (aesthetic), *and* they work (functional). The dual purpose—aesthetic and functional—was also characteristic of creative expressions in the oral tradition. The Congo Square gatherings displayed sophisticated creative expressions. At the same time, they provided relief from the drudgery of forced labor, an outlet for economic advancement, and a public forum for spiritual belief rituals. The drumming and dancing affirmed the humanity and the distinctive tribal identities of the participants and connected these identities to each other, enabling them to foster a sense of community. The expressions provided an outlet to critique and mock their oppressors.[4] The gatherings gave them something that was all their own.

Three central creative elements that were common to many of the different African cultures were the "building blocks" for the oral traditions that developed in the different locales of the diaspora.[5] They were in evidence in Congo Square:

- Call-and-response is a performance technique where a leader is in dialogue with a group. It is pervasive in African-based oral expression. In the context of music, the audience often becomes part of the performance, like second-liners, the dancing crowd who respond to and follow a parading brass band. Call-and-response also has a symbolic function in African-based creative expression. It represents the role of the artist as a spokesperson for the community—an individual/communal duality.
- Improvisation is spontaneous creativity. It is a key element of many oral traditions. In Western- or European-based expression, a primary emphasis is often placed on a static or authoritative text, but much African-based performance places a premium on improvisation. The ultimate example of improvisation is the solo in jazz. The musician takes a basic text (a rhythmic pattern, melody, or a song's chord changes or harmonic structure) and plays creative variations—completely new and original—on it.
- Rhythmic sophistication is found in such techniques as the central or "pulse" beat, the interaction of multiple rhythms or "polyrhythms," and "syncopation," a seductive accent on offbeats that provides a propulsive effect. There are three essential elements in music: melody, rhythm, and harmony. In African-based music, rhythm is the dominant element. African rhythms also manifest a spiritual dimension, an ineffable power that is easy to feel but hard to describe.

Oral traditions are often absorptive; they incorporate new elements that are encountered. So, Africans who arrived in various "New World" locations, like New Orleans, began to

Drummer figure on congo drum, Congo, twentieth century, wood and natural fiber. Loaned by Norma Wolff Collection of African Art, Southern University at New Orleans. Photo by Grace Patterson. Courtesy of the New Orleans Jazz Museum.

Caption image labels:

Kalimba
Loango people, twentieth century
Metal, wood, and natural fibers
Loaned by Wolff Collection, Southern University at New Orleans-
Center for African and African American Studies.

Shakers
Twentieth century
Raffia and wood
Loaned by Wolff Collection, Southern University at New Orleans-
Center for African and African American Studies.

Traditional African percussion instruments. *Top left:* kora, possibly Senegal, twentieth century, wood, natural fibers, patina; *top right:* slit gong, Luba people, Congo, twentieth century, wood and natural fiber; *bottom left:* kalimba, Loango people, Congo, twentieth century, thumb piano over sounding board, Lamellaphone, metal, wood, and natural fibers; *bottom right:* shaker, twentieth century, raffia and wood. Loaned by Norma Wolff Collection of African Art, Southern University at New Orleans. Photo by Grace Patterson. Courtesy of the New Orleans Jazz Museum.

distinctively "re-member" their African roots based on where they arrived and what and whom they encountered there. To "re-member" implies that they not only *recalled* their past but also *reassembled* those three building blocks—call-and-response, improvisation, and rhythmic sophistication—and melded them to their new situations to produce new oral traditions that were rooted in the African oral traditions they were trying to retain.

"Re-membering" of the African oral tradition cultural retentions of call-and-response, improvisation, and rhythmic sophistication have resulted in distinct but related expressions throughout the diaspora. And, Congo Square in New Orleans was crucial to the nurturing of this re-membering process because it ultimately became the only locale during slavery times in North America where African people were allowed to publicly and regularly gather to practice their rituals and perform their traditional dance and music, especially their drumming. They interacted with and absorbed elements of the cultures they encountered to create the distinctive sound and style that would transform creative expression worldwide. As Gwendolyn Midlo Hall asserts, "They turned inhospitable swamplands into a refuge for the independent, the defiant, the creative 'unimportant' people who tore down barriers of language and culture among peoples throughout the world and continue to sing to them of joy and the triumph of the human spirit."[6] Congo Square was the epicenter of this cultural transformation.

THE NATIVE AMERICAN PRESENCE: "WOULD YOU DANCE?"

Located outside the colonial city's ramparts (today's Rampart Street), the area that has come to be known as Congo Square was a grassy plain that was close to a portage between the Mississippi and Bayou Choupic that was regularly used by the region's Native Americans.[7] In his *History of New Orleans* (1922), John Smith Kendall explains that "before the foundation of the city the Indians celebrated in this vicinity their corn feasts, commemorated in 'La Fete du Petit Ble,' the first dramatic composition ever written in Louisiana."[8] So, it is likely that the locale had a profound significance for indigenous people who lived in the region prior to the arrival of the French and Africans. When looking at the legacy of drums and percussion in Congo Square, it is important to recognize the first people who laid down beats in the region. Contemporary New Orleans drummer Grayhawk Perkins, who is of Choctaw and Houma Nation descent, is a teacher, historian, and performer of traditional Native American culture, as well as the leader of the Grayhawk Band, which melds blues, funk, folk, and rock with tribal rhythms and themes. Perkins describes the traditional instruments that were used:

> When you go back, I guess, to Natives before anyone else came here, the drum wasn't the most important thing as far as rhythm would go. The people here were Southeastern people, and the only known what we call official drums that we had before Europeans or Africans were the water drums. They were made with cypress knees, and they were filled with water to get the different sounds from it, but most of the rhythms that were done in the dances were done with rattles and voices . . . It's funny because even in the Muskogean Nation or Choctaw Nation, we have water drum songs, but most of the songs that we call stomp songs or traditional songs that are social songs, dances that were only done with a rattle or only done with a water drum, are now done in certain areas with what looks like a parade drum that they [use to] keep a beat. That didn't come along until later on.[9]

Both the rattles and the water drum used by Native people in the region are described in the writings of French colonists. In 1718, Antoine-Simon Le Page du Pratz was present when Chief Framboise and about forty members of the Chitimacha tribe arrived at the newly settled city of New Orleans to negotiate a treaty with the colony's governor, Jean-Baptiste Le Moyne, sieur de Bienville. The Chitimacha, according to Shane Lief and John McCusker in *Jockomo: The Native Roots of Mardi Gras Indians* (2019), approached chanting and shaking rattles called "chichicois," described by Le Page du Pratz as "a gourd pierced with two holes, for inserting a short stick, with the lower end serving as a handle. They put pebbles inside to make a sound; in the absence of pebbles, they put in dry beans or kidney beans. It is with this instrument that they keep the beat while singing."[10] At a ceremony held at Fort Maurepas (Biloxi) in 1699, André Pénigaut observed both a chichicois and a water drum: "They have another instrument too, made of an earthen pot in the shape of a kettle, containing a little water and covered with a deer skin stretched tight across the pot mouth like a tambour, this they beat with two drumsticks, making as much noise as our drum."[11]

Native Americans in Louisiana, like people of African descent, adapted and absorbed from the people with whom they came in contact. This is evident in the Choctaws' use of the parade drum, which is called the "Choctaw drum." Modeled on the militia drum used by European and American troops during the eighteenth and nineteenth centuries, the body is made from hollowed sourwood, black gum, or tupelo gum. The rims are made from

Grayhawk Perkins with buffalo horn rattle. Based on oral tradition, Perkins believes that Native Americans attended and participated in the drumming and dancing at Congo Square. Photo courtesy of Grayhawk Perkins.

Left: Turtle shell rattle leggings used for Choctaw stomp dance. Made by Margo Rosas, Bayou Lacombe Choctaw. Photo by R. Cataliotti.

Right: William "Dan" Isaac, rattle, and Simon Isaac, Choctaw drum, performing with Mystic Wind Choctaw Social Dancers at Bayou Lacombe Native American Month event, 2019. Photo by R. Cataliotti.

hickory and the head from deer rawhide. Ropes are laced through the head for tuning, and lead snares are strung along the bottom. William "Dan" Isaac, a "Knowledge Keeper" and leader of the Choctaw, Mississippi-based Mystic Wind Choctaw Social Dancers, explains that the Choctaw drum was acquired from the British militia bands as a kind of "spoils of war" during the War of 1812, and the beats that are played on it echo martial rhythms.[12] Artist and craftswoman Margo A. Rosas, who lives on Bayou Lacombe, is a native New Orleanian of Choctaw, Mexican, and French heritage. The traditional turtle shell rattles she made are used for the Choctaw stomp dance and illustrate how a tradition can be absorptive with her use of the leather from a pair of cowboy boots to shape the leggings to which the turtle shells are attached. That absorptive spirit is also evident in the hand drum and stick on display in the *Drumsville!* exhibit. Although these are not indigenous to Louisiana, Rosas, having spent time on the Cheyenne River Sioux Reservation in South Dakota, explored other Native American traditions and crafted the drum from an elk skin rawhide from an elk shot by Emanuel Red Bear, who signed the drum. Rosas skinned, scraped, and cleaned the hide to make the rawhide. She made the drumstick of willow from Bayou Lacombe, buckskin that she brain-tanned, and wool.

Clearly, Louisiana's indigenous people were constructing rhythm instruments and pounding out beats long before the Congo Square gatherings began. Based on oral tradition, Perkins believes that Native Americans attended and participated in the drumming and dancing at Congo Square:

> I wrote a song called "Chestnut Moon," and it's about the African and the Native American coming together in Congo Square, and it's our story; it's through our eyes, the stories that have been passed down to us about how that happened. Basically, we were pretty much forbidden at one point to even come near what we call the French Quarter or the ramparts. And the only way they could perform their traditional dances, their traditional songs, and things like that was to do them outside the ramparts, and I think after a while, how the story came about, our villages were not that far from here . . . When the Africans started playing, when they started chanting, Natives pretty much, they say we were curious because it sounded very similar, but different. We eventually got close enough to where, you know, you were watching, and the Africans noticed that. It took a little while before they, one or the other, pretty much invited each other to come, and that's when they, the Africans dancing, said, "Would you dance?" And they started doing some of their stomp dances and things. I think that's where that merge started. You started [having] the Africans watching some of the Native dances, and you started having the Natives watching the African dances, and the ideas and different rhythms and different things started merging.[13]

Native American hand drum and drumstick. Made by Margo A. Rosas, Bayou Lacombe Choctaw. Photo by Grace Patterson. Courtesy of the New Orleans Jazz Museum.

A possible drum interaction between the African-descended people and Native Americans in Louisiana during the time when drumming was happening in Congo Square can be found among the Choctaw who live on Bayou Lacombe. A study published by the Smithsonian Institution, *The Choctaw of Bayou Lacomb* (1909) by David I. Bushnell Jr., includes a photograph of a drum type that is only made by Bayou Lacombe Choctaw, as well as this description of the drum:

> This is 30 inches in height and 15 inches in diameter. It is made of a section of a black gum tree; the cylinder wall is less than 2 inches in thickness. The head consists of a piece of untanned goat skin. The skin is stretched over the open end, while wet and pliable, and is passed around a hoop made of hickory about half an inch thick. A similar hoop is placed above the first. To the second hoop are attached four narrow strips of rawhide, each of which is fastened to a peg passing diagonally through the wall of the drum. To tighten the head of the drum it is necessary merely to drive the peg farther in.

Although Bushnell suggests that the drum is quite similar to those made in West Africa, he cautions: "It is not possible to say whether this instrument is a purely an American form or whether it shows the influence of the negro."[14] It seems quite possible, however, that there were Choctaw who observed drums played in Congo Square or other locales in Louisiana and reproduced them with the materials to which they had access. Although there is no extant written documentation of Native Americans participating in the Congo Square gatherings, *Voyage aux États-Unis de l'Amérique en 1831,* a travelogue written by P. Forest, does describe Natives present at a gathering featuring African drumming and dancing at a place called "The Camp" near the edge of Bayou St. John:[15]

They are gathered in a large number of distinct groups; each has its own flag floating atop a very tall mast, used as the rallying point for the group. The negroes dance with extraordinary speed and agility. Actually their dance is rather a pantomime than a dance . . . They make their music by beating and rolling their sticks on their drums; a sharp sound is produced, repeated two or three times by the surrounding echoes. Several Indian families settled not far from the Lake also come to The Camp to share these ludicrous pleasures.[16]

Forest does not indicate if the sharing that took place was simply as spectators or if the Native Americans participated in the drumming and dancing, but it is not that hard to imagine them joining in, especially in light of the unique culture of the Black Masking Indian tradition or Mardi Gras Indians that emerged during the late nineteenth century.[17] The grooves they hammer out on tambourines and other improvised percussion instruments are integral to the evolution of the New Orleans beat. Percussionist Cyril Neville, one of the foremost exponents of the Black Indian grooves through his work with the Wild Tchoupitoulas, the Neville Brothers, and as a solo artist, describes the significance of that melding: "When African polyrhythms and a Native American four on the floor came together, that was the beginning of what became American music."[18]

AFRICAN DRUMMING: IMMEDIATE AND PERVASIVE

From the moment African people arrived in Louisiana, it is likely that the drumming commenced and that it was pervasive. Forest's account of the gathering at The Camp affirms that African-derived drumming and dancing were taking place throughout the region. Visitors to the city frequently encountered people of African descent dancing and drumming. The extant descriptions of these performances come largely from white European or American writers, and it is important to remember the ethnocentric, often racist perspective from which they viewed Africans.[19] In a travelogue called *Sketches of a Tour to the Western Country* (1810), Fortescue Cuming chronicles an 1807–9 journey that included a stop in New Orleans, where he observed, "On our way to the upper fort we saw vast numbers of negro slaves, men, women, and children, assembled on the levee, drumming, fifing and dancing in large rings."[20] In a letter from May 1808, Christian Schultz describes his encounter with African drumming and dancing:

In the afternoon, a walk in the rear of the town will still more astonish their bewildered imaginations with the sight of twenty different dancing groups of wretched Africans, collected together to perform their *worship* after the manner of their country. They have their own national music, consisting for the most part of a long kind of narrow drum of various sizes, from two to eight feet in length, three or four of which make a band. The principal dancers or leaders are dressed in a variety of wild and savage fashions, always ornamented with a number of the tails of smaller wild beasts, and those who appeared most horrible always attracted the largest circle of company. These amusements continue until sunset, when one or two of the city patrole show themselves with their cutlasses, and the crowds immediately disperse.[21] (italics in original)

Although he disparages the participants, Schultz correctly intuits that there is a spiritual dimension to the drumming and dancing and that the individual circles represent tribal groups. A January 1841 *Picayune* article describes a raid on a house "where a negro ball was in full tide" that included a reporter who described the scene: "In one part of the room a cotillion was going on, and in a corner a fellow was giving a regular old Virginia 'break-down'...A genteel looking darky, with Devonshire brown mustachios was acting as master of ceremonies, and the music consisted of a clarionet [*sic*], three fiddles, two tambourines, and a bass drum."[22] Drumming was not only to be found around the city but also in the surrounding region. During the 1811 German Coast uprising, a group of possibly five hundred enslaved people rose in an armed rebellion near LaPlace, about thirty miles upriver from New Orleans, and marched toward the city attacking plantations along the River Road. The uprising was brutally suppressed, and one of the participants who was captured was named Lindor. St. Charles Parish court documents reveal that "the negro Louis of M. Etienne Trépagnier denounces the negro Lindor of MM. Kenner and Henderson for be-

1811 Revolt, by Lorraine Gendron, 2000 (acrylic on canvas). The painting depicts the 1811 German Coast uprising of enslaved people of African descent. One of the participants who was captured was named Lindor and identified in court documents as the insurgents' drummer. Gift of Lorraine Gendron. The Historic New Orleans Collection. Accession number 2007.0396.

ing the insurgents' drummer."[23] We have no way of knowing what type of drum—a hand-made African-style drum or a militia drum—Lindor played as the insurgents marched toward New Orleans, but we do know from this testimony that drumming was taking place on these upriver sugarcane plantations, and it is likely that the rhythms Lindor beat out were a clear reminder of their African identity to these people who fought to be free.

SUNDAY AFTERNOONS IN CONGO SQUARE: "DE DRUM KEEP ON A BEATIN'"

Drumsville's exploration of the evolution of the New Orleans beat originates in Congo Square. The first extant use of the term "Congo" to describe the locale is found in a 1786 letter from a Catholic bishop complaining that the dancing in "Place Congo" was taking place prior to the end of Sunday mass. This governor responded by ruling that the gatherings could not begin until after religious services had concluded.[24] Restrictions on the public displays of African drumming and dancing continued to tighten, and by 1817 the gatherings were confined to Sunday afternoons in Congo Square. Today, it is possible to paint a fairly detailed portrait of the drumming, dancing, commerce, spiritual rituals, and socializing that took place, thanks to travelogues, newspaper accounts, and letters, along with the memories and family histories of African Americans recorded by the Works Progress Administration during the twentieth century. These were large gatherings; various reports estimate the number of participants from the hundreds to the thousands. Sunday afternoons at Congo Square attracted both the enslaved and free people of color, as well as Native Americans and Caucasian people—both locals and tourists—whose origins were in Europe and the United States. Perhaps the most revelatory account, despite his derogatory assessment, comes from the journal of Benjamin Henry Latrobe, an English architect who spent time in New Orleans from 1818 to 1820, thanks especially to the sketches he made of the instruments that were played. Latrobe relates stumbling upon "a croud [*sic*] of 5 or 600 persons assembled in an open space or public square," all of whom "seemed to be *blacks*," who were "formed into circular groups":

> In the first were two women dancing. They held each a coarse handkerchief, extended by the corners, in their hands, and *set* to each other in a miserably dull and slow figure, hardly moving their feet or bodies. The music consisted of two drums and a stringed instrument. An old man sat astride of a Cylindrical drum about a foot in diameter, and beat it with incredible quickness with the edge of his hand and fingers. The other drum was an open staved thing held between the knees and beaten in the same manner. They made an incredible noise. The most curious instrument however was a stringed instrument which was no doubt imported from Africa. On top of the finger board was the rude figure of a Man in a sitting posture, and two pegs behind him to which the strings were fastened. The body was a Calabash. It was played upon by a very little old man, apparently 80 or 90 Years old. The women squalled out a burthen to the playing, at intervals, consisting of two notes, as the Negroes working in our cities respond to the Song of the leader.[25] (italics in original)

The description testifies to the presence of two of the African-retention oral tradition building blocks. The singers are clearly engaged in a call-and-response pattern, and the dexterity he ascribes to the drummers is evidence of the rhythmic sophistication. It seems safe to assume, based on what generally takes place in drum circles and because of the extended nature of the gathering, that the third building block, improvisation, was also taking place. Latrobe clearly recognizes the process of cultural retention: "The allowed amusements of Sunday have, it seems, perpetuated here those of Africa among its former inhabitants."[26] Moving to another drum and dance circle, he describes "instruments of different construction":

> One, which from the color of the wood seemed new, consisted of a block cut into something of the form of a cricket bat, with a deep, long mortice down the Center. The thing made a considerable noise, being lustily beaten on the side by a short stick. In the same Orchestra was a square drum looking like a stool, which made an abominably loud noise: also a Calabash with a round hole in it, the hole studded with brass nails which was beaten by a woman with two short sticks.[27]

In his analysis of Latrobe's sketches, drummer and music scholar John Joyce asserts: "Latrobe, with his artist's eye for details, gives us precise descriptions of both the instruments and the manner in which they are played, accompanied by accurate drawings. They provide a small but concrete piece of evidence concerning the demographic status of the slave population in antebellum Louisiana." Joyce identifies the cylindrical drum and "cricket bat" (slit drum or gong) as corresponding to instruments found among the Yoruba; the "square drum looking like a stool" from Nigeria or Ghana; and the "open staved" drum from Dahomey. He asserts the calabash instrument is common in Angola, Zaire, Cameroon, Nigeria, and Ghana and identifies the stringed instrument as "a long-neck African lute" found in Zaire, Cameroon, Nigeria, Dahomey, and Ghana, a precursor to the banjo. Joyce concludes:

> The provenance of these various instruments ties perfectly into the early history of New Orleans, which was, successively, a French, Spanish, and Anglo-American city. The bulk of the slaves brought there by the French were from Dahomey. The great majority of Spanish-owned slaves were Yoruban from Nigeria, by way of Cuba and, after 1803, the Anglo-Americans brought, from the Southern plantations, Ashantis from Ghana. It would appear that, at a musical level, interaction of these separate tribal cultures had begun.[28]

The Congo Square section of the *Drumsville!* exhibit features traditional African instruments on loan from Southern University at New Orleans's Center for African and African American Studies, including a large drum, slit gong, metal bell, kalimba, and shakers—all

Sketches of instruments played in Congo Square. Benjamin Latrobe's journal, *Impressions Respecting New Orleans, Diary and Sketches, 1818–1820,* provides a firsthand account of the gatherings in Congo Square and sketches of the instruments that were played there. Courtesy of the Maryland Center for History and Culture, image number RS2243.

"Sinker cypress" log bamboula drums. *Front* (seated on drum), Luther Gray; *rear (left to right):* Kenneth "Afro" Williams, Millard Green, and Mario Tio performing in Congo Square, 2006. Photo by Mark J. Sindler. Courtesy of the New Orleans Jazz Museum.

originating from the Congo region, as well as a small kora from Senegal, which are examples of the instruments that would have been re-membered and constructed from the materials that were available in Louisiana. In addition, percussionist Luther Gray, along with Travis Ayers and Doug Redd, used a "sinker cypress" log to build the bamboula drum that is featured in *Drumsville!* Jazz Museum curatorial assistant Ilyanette M. Bernabel explains: "It is a reproduction of the large drums found at Congo Square. The carved figure of the antelope is the symbol of the Bambara ethnic group, from which many West Africans in Louisiana came in the French period. Bamboula drums are very large in order to create the low bass notes in a drumming orchestra."[29] Gray, who is the leader of the band Bamboula 2000, moved to New Orleans from Chicago in 1988 and was one of the founders of the Congo Square Preservation Society, reviving the Sunday drum circles at the Congo Square site in Armstrong Park. He explains: "You have to take into account, none of these folks were able to bring anything onto the boat with them, so everything had to be re-created or repurposed."[30] That repurposing is evident in the reminiscences of Francis Doby, a formerly enslaved woman who grew up on a plantation outside Opelousas. As she relates to a WPA interviewer:

> One day de old man dey call Antoine, he was so ole dat dey keep 'eem in de Camp to amuse de chilens. Well he says like dat one day, he says, "Watch you all. Wait till de Massa kill one old cow. I make you all a drum an beat on dat same drum like dat—Bou doum doum doum doum, boum doun doundoun." So one day, he come in de Camp wid de hide and says to us: "I got de hide, an watch me make dat drum." So he take a big barrel, empty barrel, an tack dat skin right tight, tight, tight. Den he don straddle dat drum an beat on it. And fist ting you know we was a dancing, a beatin de flooh wid de foots . . . Boum BoumbBoum Boumb and de drum keep on a beatin'. Chile we dance till midnight. To finish de ball we say: "Balancez Calinda" en den twist an turn an say agin: "Balancez Calinda" . . . and jist turn around den de ball was over.[31]

The re-membering of these instruments, like the drum created by old Antoine, reflects the impulse to improvise, to create something out of necessity from what was available to them. And, the Calinda dance Doby recalls was regularly performed in Congo Square. George Washington Cable's "The Dance in Place Congo" (1886) is another detailed account of the Congo Square gatherings. It is also notable because it was illustrated by E. W. Kemble, including the now iconic depiction of a dance circle, *The Bamboula*. Cable's description also testifies to the creative ingenuity of the musicians in constructing instruments:

> In the stolen hours of the night or the basking-hour of noon the black man contrived to fashion these rude instruments and others . . . One important instrument was a gourd partly filled with pebbles and grains of corn, flourished violently at the end of a stout staff with one hand and beaten upon the palm of the other. Other performers rang triangles, and others twanged from jew's-harps an astonishing amount of sound. Another instrument was the jawbone of some ox, horse, or mule, and a key rattled rhythmically along its

weather-beaten teeth. At times the drums were reenforced by one or more empty barrels or casks beaten on the head with the shank-bones of cattle.[32]

The gourd rattle in this passage is strikingly similar to the "chichicois" Le Page du Pratz observed the Chitimacha playing prior to their calumet ceremony with Bienville. The instruments crafted from a jawbone and a key, an improvised guiro, and the barrels and casks turned into drums are more evidence of improvisational ingenuity. In a travelogue recounting an 1834 visit to New Orleans, James Creecy recalls the instruments employed in Congo Square: "Groups of fifties and hundreds may be seen in different sections of the square with banjos, violins, tom-toms, jawbones, and various other instruments from which harsh or dulcet sounds may be extracted."[33] The inclusion of triangles, "Jew's harps," fifes, fiddles, tambourines, and actual banjos, along with reports of non-African-originated dances, like jigs, fandangos, and Virginia breakdowns and song titles like "Old Virginia Never Tire," "Hey Jim along Josey," and "Get along Home You Yellow Gals" illustrate the absorptive nature of the gatherings.[34] That absorptive, improvisational impulse would carry on long after the dances at Congo Square ended and led New Orleans drummers to play a vital role in the invention of the modern drum set.

THE RHYTHMIC FOUNDATION OF THE NEW ORLEANS BEAT: "SACRED GROUND"

The African-derived rhythms and the diasporic variations that filled Congo Square are the wellspring for the city's signature musical expressions—ragtime, brass bands, jazz, Black Masking Indian chants, rhythm and blues, and funk—and the foundation of the New Orleans beat. Many of the rhythms that were played in Congo Square are inextricably linked to re-membered African spiritual belief systems that evolved throughout the diaspora, such as Vodou (Saint-Domingue/Haiti), Santería (Cuba), and Voudou (New Orleans). Often during ceremonies, specific rhythms are played to summon spiritual entities (called loas in Vodou or orishas in Santería), investing these rhythms with powerful spirituality, which certainly manifested itself in Congo Square. Composer and drummer James Black, who was one of the city's most innovative and influential musicians, identifies the rhythms he played with the African-based spiritual presence in the city:

> There's this book called *Muntu* by Janhein Jahnz. Charles Neville gave it to me. It explained a lot to me about what I was doing. About where most of the rhythms and stuff that I was playing came from. They came from the voodoo rituals . . . It's almost a sort of ritualistic style of rhythms that came out of New Orleans. I really didn't know what it was until Charles gave me this book. I'd been playing it and noticing that after you played this kind of beat for a while—the people seemed like they changed. I was wondering *why*. It's because it embodies all these African rhythms and traditions.[35] (italics in original)

Percussionist Alfred "Uganda" Roberts, who was raised in the Treme neighborhood "a half a block from Congo Square coming up as a little boy," recalls a certain awareness of

Luther Gray (*left*) and Alfred "Uganda" Roberts performing at the opening of the *Drumsville!* exhibit, November 8, 2018. Photo by R. Cataliotti.

the history that took place there: "You know they worshipped out there and played the drums. People from the neighborhood considered it sacred ground . . . We realized it had something to do with slavery, and the Houma Indians used to be celebrating out there. We didn't have much of the Black history teaching in those days, but it was an open park for the people."[36] Although during his early years as a musician, Roberts didn't drum in the park, beginning in the late 1950s he played a crucial role in reviving the hand-drumming tradition and reinforcing African-based rhythms in New Orleans jazz, rhythm and blues, and funk. The sacred rhythms played in Congo Square provide a link between New Orleans and the Afro-Caribbean diaspora, particularly Saint-Domingue/Haiti and Cuba. Ned Sublette explains the pervasiveness and adaptability of one of those rhythmic patterns:

That four-note habanera/tango rhythm is the signature Antillean beat to this day. It's a simple figure that can generate a thousand dances all by itself, depending on what drums, registers, pitches, or tense rests you assign to which notes, what tempo you play it, and how much you polyrhythmicize it by laying other, compatible rhythmic figures on top of it. It's the rhythm of the aria Bizet wrote for the cigarette-rolling Carmen to sing . . . and it's the defining rhythm of *reggaetón*. You can hear it in the contemporary music of Haiti, the Dominican Republic, Jamaica, and Puerto Rico, to say nothing of the nineteenth century Cuban contradanza. It's Jelly Roll Morton's oft-cited "Spanish tinge," it's the accompaniment figure to W. C. Handy's "St. Louis Blues," and you hear it from brass bands at a second line in New Orleans today . . . You could write it as dotted eighth, sixteenth, and two eighths. If you don't know what I'm taking about yet, it's the rhythm of the first four notes of the *Dragnet* theme. DOMM, DA DOM DOM.[37]

The bamboula is a type of drum, a rhythm, and a dance that was performed regularly in Congo Square and derives from the four-note habanera/tango pattern. It has had the most profound impact on shaping the New Orleans beat. Luther Gray explains that when they reinstituted the Sunday drum circles, identifying how to play the bamboula rhythm was essential. They found the key when renowned percussionist and African folklorist Chief Bey [James Hawthorne] visited New Orleans:

We were trying to find out about the bamboula because we had read about it, but we were trying to figure out what the rhythm was. Nobody could really tell us. So, then Chief Bey came here for a residency. We asked him did he know the bamboula. He said, "Yeah, I know that." He started playing with us, and it was the second-line rhythm. So, in New Orleans we were already doing the bamboula; we just knew it as the second line.[38]

The bamboula rhythm gained worldwide exposure through the music of Louis Moreau Gottschalk (1829–1869), one of the first classical pianists and composers from the United States to gain global recognition. His parents, a Jewish British father and French mother, emigrated from Saint-Domingue and settled in the French Quarter. Gottschalk was nurtured by Sally, his family's enslaved nurse from Saint-Domingue, whom he referred to as "La Négresse Congo." It was probably from Sally that he learned the Creole melodies and rhythms that inform such compositions as "Bamboula," and "The Banjo."[39] Although he likely never attended the gatherings in Congo Square, Gottschalk clearly drew from the same wellspring of inspiration. He performed in Europe, South America, and the Caribbean and was highly regarded in Cuba, where he was associated with the pianist and composer Manuel Saumell Robredo (1818–1870), a master of the "contradanza," widely popular dance compositions based on the African-derived "habanera" rhythm, a first cousin to the bamboula. It is possible that contradanzas composed by both Gottschalk and Saumell provided inspiration for Scott Joplin and Jelly Roll Morton's ragtime compositions.[40]

The Sunday-afternoon gatherings carried on regularly through the late 1830s or early 1840s. In 1845, a petition was made to the New Orleans City Council to allow enslaved people of African descent to once again meet up in Congo Square on Sunday afternoons, but only in the summer months and with written permission from their enslavers. A few weeks later the *Daily Picayune* reported on participants performing on "rude instruments of their own contrivance." The gatherings were ceased when the Union army occupied the city in 1862.[41]

Sheet music to "The Bamboula" by Louis Moreau Gottschalk. The bamboula rhythm gained exposure through the music of Gottschalk (1829–1869), one of the first classical pianists and composers from the United States to gain global recognition. Courtesy of the New Orleans Jazz Museum. Accession number 1978.118(D).

A LIVING LEGACY:
"THAT PLACE WHERE AMERICAN MUSIC WAS BORN"

The legacy of Congo Square has had an enduring impact on the development of New Orleans music in the century and a half since the gatherings concluded. Those rhythms that percolated through Congo Square have had a definitive impact on the music. Many of the city's musicians have consistently viewed themselves as the progeny of those legendary drummers and dancers. In fact, one of the first major New Orleans jazz artists to establish himself as a world-class talent, the saxophonist, clarinetist, and composer Sidney Bechet (1897–1959), traces his ancestry to a Congo Square drummer in *Treat It Gentle: An Autobiography* (1960). Born in New Orleans to a musical Creole family, Bechet asserts that his grandfather Omar (who is conflated with the legendary maroon leader/outlaw hero Bras-Coupé), was central to the community of African-descended people who came to Congo Square. Bechet writes of Omar: "Sundays when the slaves would meet—that was their free day—he beat out rhythms on drums at the Square—Congo Square they called it--and they'd all be gathered there around him. Everyone loved him. They waited for him to start things: dances, shouts, moods even. Anything he wanted to do, he'd lead them." Omar con-

Cyril Neville performing at 2010 New Orleans Jazz and Heritage Festival. For Neville, Congo Square is "that place where American music was born." Photo by Jeffrey Dupuis. Courtesy of the New Orleans Jazz Museum. Accession number 2019.014.1.

structs his drums from the material at hand: "He made his own drums out of skins of a pig or a horse hide." And, his drums clearly connect him to Africa:

> That was how the Negro communicated when he was back in Africa. He had no house, he had no telegram, no newspaper. But he had a drum, and he had a rhythm he could speak into the drum, and he could send it out through all the air to the rest of his people, and he could bring them to him. And when he got to the South, when he was a slave, just before he was waking, before the sun rode out in the sky, when there was just that morning silence over the fields with maybe a few birds in it—then, at that time, he was back there again in Africa.[42]

Bechet's identification of his grandfather with Bras-Coupé may be more fanciful than factual; however, he seems to be attempting to link his own innovations in jazz to the African roots of New Orleans music.[43] Whether the connection Bechet makes is real or mythical, it ultimately testifies to the powerful significance of those roots to his identity as a New Orleans musician.[44]

For New Orleans musicians today, Congo Square is sacred ground. Live oaks surround a series of embedded stone circles that pay homage to the historical tribal circles that formed there on Sunday afternoons two centuries ago, and a series of sculptures honor the succession of artists who have carried on the spirit of those musical ancestors, including the original drummers and dancers; the brass bands; gospel singer Mahalia Jackson; Mardi Gras Indian Big Chief Tootie Montana; and jazz artists Buddy Bolden, Sidney Bechet, and Louis Armstrong. For Luther Gray, who can be found most Sundays leading a drum circle in Congo Square, the spiritual dimension of the drumming is crucial, and he sees the music as integral to everyday life: "Let's look at the sacred part of this place. Drumming is the second-oldest instrument in mankind, only next to the human voice. So, to have a city based on a rhythmic culture, drum culture, we carry on traditions that are hundreds of years old, but we don't really do it just because we know it's something from hundreds of years ago; we just do it because that's what we do."[45] Drummer and composer Herlin Riley, who comes from one of the city's prolific musical families, including three generations of drummers, recognizes Congo Square as the foundation of the New Orleans beat:

> A lot of this music is definitely connected to Congo Square and the fact that Black people during slavery were able to maintain their drumming and as a result of that most of the styles have evolved out of that . . . Even subliminally, I think that's still going on because here in New Orleans, we have a groove and a beat that's very unique to our own sprit and our own culture. Every region in the world has its own rhythm, and New Orleans definitely has its own rhythm that has been a part of the culture for a few hundred years now.[46]

When the Neville Brothers would perform the song "Congo Square," Cyril Neville often would proclaim, "We're gonna take you to New Orleans, to that place where American music was born, y'all, a place called Congo Square."[47] It is a declaration of the centrality of both the city's African heritage in shaping its musical legacy and the far-reaching impact of that legacy. Congo Square is the place where Drumsville was founded and where the evolution of the New Orleans beat began.

3

European Influence

"RATTLE-TE-BANGING AWAY"

Drumsville was also shaped by the Europeans who brought their musical traditions with them to Louisiana. Opera performances were continuous and pervasive in New Orleans, and classical concerts were a part of the city's musical scene. From its founding, the city was passionate about dance. Balls were held on a regular basis. The dance forms that were performed introduced distinctive rhythms into the repertoire of local musicians. The European musical tradition that had the most profound impact on the shaping of Drumsville was the militia bands. From its earliest days, militia bands and parades were part of the fabric of New Orleans culture. The music of European colonists and later settlers from the United States that took root in New Orleans melded with the music of the people of African descent and the indigenous people of Louisiana to establish the city as Drumsville and contributed to the evolution of its signature beat.

OPERA AND CLASSICAL MUSIC:
"I LEARNED QUITE A BIT FROM SUCH LISTENING"

During the eighteenth and nineteenth centuries, European music flourished in New Orleans. The city was home to a series of opera houses from the close of the eighteenth century through the early decades of the twentieth century. The first opera was staged in 1796, and Ann Ostendorf relates that the opera scene was soon thriving: "A decade later, in the span of four months, New Orleanians could witness twenty-one performances, which included sixteen different operas from nine composers. This town of only 12,000, one third of who were enslaved and who attended performances on discounted tickets, clearly valued and invested in public music performances."[1] The French established opera in the city, and the music continued to be performed under both Spanish and American rule. Other European immigrant groups added their musical preferences to the scene. As an 1856 *Daily Picayune* article asserts: "A very considerable portion of our population here is German, and we had a proof . . . that there is such a thing in New Orleans as a decided taste for German music; while English and Italian opera, oratorio, and con-

THE NEGRO GALLERY.

"The Negro Gallery" at the French Opera House. Both the free people of color and the enslaved often had access to the theaters that presented operas and concerts, where they were relegated to separate seating sections Courtesy of the New Orleans Jazz Museum. Accession number 1978.118(B).03228.

cert singing are received with a degree of favor, and an appreciativeness that show the existence of something besides a French musical taste in our midst."[2] Concerts were another significant outlet for European music. Henry Kmen explains that the concerts drew together musicians who performed in the house bands of different theaters and helped create a sense of community for local musicians. A source of supplemental income, the subscription concerts enabled local composers to showcase original works and local musicians to develop their instrumental prowess. They broadened the sonic palette of the city: "The concerts also provided opportunities for the playing of symphonies, concertos, quartets, and all the other kinds of music not ordinarily played in the theater."[3] Both the free people of color, the majority of whom were Creoles, and the enslaved had access to the theaters that presented operas and concerts, where they were relegated to separate seating sections. Even if Creoles or the enslaved were barred from entering the musical venues, they often could find alternative means of hearing the performances. This was still true for groundbreaking drummer Warren "Baby" Dodds when he was growing up in the early decades of the twentieth century: "In those early days I also used to hear classical music. Negroes were not allowed in the places it was played so I heard it by standing on the outside. Many times I heard symphonies that way. Sometimes we used to stand in the hallway of the Tulane Theatre in New Orleans. One side was the opera house and the other was the theatre and we'd stand in between to hear the music." Dodds makes it clear that listening to classical music had an influence on his drumming: "And I learned quite a bit from such listening. I used to carry any melody on the snare drums that a band played. I got that idea from listening to symphonic music and also from playing in street parades."[4] Dodds's comments reflect the melding process—the symphony meets the streets—that played a role in the evolution of the New Orleans beat.

Creoles often received formal training in music, and in response to the second-class status to which they were sometimes subjected, as well as the outright denial of access to some white musical venues, the Negro Philharmonic Society was formed in the 1830s. It featured more than one hundred members, including some white musicians.[5] Clearly musicians were very much in demand in antebellum New Orleans, and with both free and enslaved people of African descent performing—and some of them were surely drummers—in these European contexts, they were acquiring an alternative set of percussion skills and rhythms from what was going down on Sundays just blocks away in Congo Square.

THE BALLS: "I TRANSFORMED THESE STRAINS"

Dancing at the countless balls—both for whites and free people of color—that took place in the city throughout the year brought another European influence on the music of New Orleans, an influence that would profoundly impact the emergence of Drumsville. The dances that were performed introduced distinctive rhythms into the repertoire of local musicians. Henry Kmen explains that a tremendous variety of dances were incorporated into the balls: "The dancers must be ready for boleros and gavottes; for cotillions and gallops; and for waltzes, mazurkas, reels, and minuets, to say nothing of the ever-present French and English quadrilles. 'The eternal quadrille' seemed to one beholder to be 'given without cease,' but actually there were enough other dances to make the profession of dancing master common in New Orleans."[6] The bands that supplied the music for these dances included whites, free people or color, and the enslaved. Benjamin Latrobe attended a "*bal paré*," or full-dress ball, and observed one such musician—a percussionist. Latrobe lavishes praise on the whole affair with one exception, one that displays the same ethnocentrism that marks his descriptions of Congo Square: "The only nuisance was a tall ill-dressed black, in the music Gallery, who played the tambourin [*sic*] standing up, and in a forced and vile voice called the figures as they changed. But custom has drowned his voice."[7] The tambourine player was likely calling figures for an "eternal quadrille," similar to the caller in an American square dance, prompting the four couples to execute the steps for each part of the dance with its signature rhythm. Jazz pioneer composer, pianist, and band leader Jelly Roll Morton (Ferdinand Joseph La-Mothe 1890–1941) illuminates the significance of a musician of African descent providing the rhythmic accompaniment for this dance for the emergence of Drumsville.

> The *Tiger Rag,* for an instance, I happened to transform from an old quadrille, which was originally in many different tempos. First there was an introduction, "Everybody get your partners!" and the people would be rushing around the hall getting their partners. After a five minute lapse of time, the next strain would be the waltz strain . . . then another strain that comes right beside the waltz strain in mazooka time . . . We had two other strains in two-four time. Then I transformed these strains into the *Tiger Rag.*[8]

Like Baby Dodds adapting the symphonies he heard to his drum set, Morton used a European dance form that had been played for decades upon decades to provide the inspiration for one of the classic early jazz compositions. As Caroline Vézina points out, "The history of the quadrille in the Caribbean and New Orleans provides a good example of its appropriation (and creolization) by Creole musicians and its influence on early jazz musicians."[9] And, the quadrille was creolized as it was infused with the Afro-Caribbean rhythms that percolated through

Paul Barbarin plays a quadrille for dancers in antebellum costumes aboard the *President Riverboat,* February 1958. Photo by Al Rose. The William Russell Jazz Collection, The Historic New Orleans Collection. Acquisition made possible by the Clarisse Claiborne Grima Fund. Accession number 92-48-L.331.2780.

Congo Square. Additionally, the bands that provided the music for the balls also have a direct link to the single-most-important development in the founding of Drumsville and the New Orleans beat. Vézina asserts: "These balls certainly paved the way for orchestras like John Robichaux Orchestra (who carried the same kind of repertoire), that were in demand in post-bellum New Orleans when dances, lawn parties, picnics etc., were very popular. These are the bands that would eventually start to incorporate the 'hot' syncopated style of the Black musicians."[10] It was with Robichaux's orchestra at the close of the nineteenth century that Dee Dee Chandler, one of the stars of *Drumsville!*, rigged up a pedal to his bass drum and began playing both bass and snare drum simultaneously, creating the prototype for the drum set.

MILITIA BANDS: "A CORRESPONDING ADDITION OF SPIRIT"

The European musical form that was most influential in the founding of Drumsville was the martial band. Drum and wind instrument bands affiliated with the military can be traced back to the 1600s in Europe. William J. Schafer explains a development in the instrumentation of military bands that would provide the basis for the emergence of Drumsville: "In the late eighteenth century a fad for 'Turkish music' refined burgeoning military music patterns. The importation of Turkish (*i.e.* Middle-Eastern) percussion—snare drums, cymbals, large bass drums, triangles—and the formation of drum corps using these instruments established drumming centrally in military music."[11] The essential components that would be assembled to create the drum set had been introduced into the military bands, and Drumsville would play a fundamental role in the transforming of those components into the sole truly American instrument.

The many militias active in New Orleans had affiliated bands for funerals, elections, weddings, holidays, holy days, balls, and, of course, Mardi Gras.[12] Whites, free people of color, and the enslaved were recruited to perform in these marching bands. The sound of drums and wind instruments was pervasive in the city and, like Congo Square, drew the attention of travelers. One such visitor, James Creecy, was struck by the sound of a militia band intruding on the services taking place in St. Louis Cathedral, remarking that "while the organ in the venerable edifice is pealing anthems to Him on high, while the holy mass is being presented to the pious worshipers, the words of command, clash of arms, rolling of drums, the fife's shrill whistle, and the crack of rifles, are heard above all."[13] Henry Didimus recalls being awakened by a "drum and fife, which suddenly struck up the lively national air of 'Yankee Doodle.'" Looking out his window, he saw the band: "Two lusty blacks, in full regimentals, were playing a duet to a solo audience of their own colour, while a casual passer-by bestowed upon the group a grin of approbation."[14] Later in the day, while walking on the levee, Didimus encountered the band that had awakened him: "Drum and fife were now more fortunate in their audience, and consequently played with a corresponding addition of spirit. Bond and free were equally happy, and danced, and, shouted, poked each other under the ribs, and played shuttlecock with their neighbor's heads, in true equality of the Roman saturnalia. This is the Sabbath of the slave."[15]

Imperial Orchestra, ca. 1908. *Left to right:* John MacMurray, drums; George Filhe, trombone; James A. Palao, violin; "Big Eye" Louis Nelson, clarinet; Tene Baptiste, guitar; Manuel Perez, cornet; and Jimmy Brown, string bass. Courtesy of the New Orleans Jazz Museum. Accession number 1978.118(B).00550.

An 1839 article in the *Picayune* complains about the sound of militia drums "rattle-te-banging away . . . waking everybody up."[16] Over time, the martial bands evolved from employing fifes to brass and reed instruments and also found work beyond parading in the streets of the city. Kmen explains, "The popularity of bands for dancing was clearly evident in 1840 when the Neptune Band advertised its availability for quadrilles, adding almost as an afterthought that it could also be a military or brass band if required."[17]

Military marching bands were pervasive throughout the city during the colonial era, and under United States' rule they proliferated during the War of 1812. Perhaps the most renowned militia drummer was Jordan B. Noble, who, as an enslaved teenager, joined Andrew Jackson's Seventh Regiment of Infantry and played a crucial role in communicating orders through his drumbeats during the 1815 Battle of New Orleans. Noble was born in Georgia around 1800 and came to New Orleans with his mother in 1812, just in time to pick up a drum and serve in the military. His drumming earned Noble direct praise

Jordan Noble's drum. It is believed that Noble played this drum, which was manufactured by Klemm & Brother between 1828 and 1843. The Historic New Orleans Collection. Accession number 2019.0205.

from Jackson.[18] In addition to the War of 1812, he served as a drummer in militia bands in the Seminole Wars, the Mexican-American War, and the American Civil War.[19] Noble's drumming expertise and dedicated military service elevated him to celebrity status in the city. He was a participant in both the Emancipation Celebration in May 1864, the Abraham Lincoln Memorial Commemoration the following year, and the Cotton Centennial Exposition in 1884.[20] Until his death in 1890, he was renowned in the city as "Old Jordan" and was often seen at the head of parades beating his martial drum. When the celebrated drummer passed away, the *Picayune* headline for obituary read: "Answered the Last Roll: Death of the Drummer Boy of Chalmette."[21]

One cannot help but wonder if Jordan Noble or other drummers who performed in marching bands or in orchestras for balls or theaters made their way over to Congo Square to join in the Sunday gatherings. It seems likely that some did and that the rhythms they were performing moved back and forth between musical environments. One sure thing is that with African-derived drumming thundering away on Sunday afternoons, the percussionists propelling and accenting compositions in theaters and at balls, and the marching bands "rattle-te-banging away" all over town, New Orleans was well on its way to becoming Drumsville.

4

Improvised Percussion Instruments

"IT SOUNDED ALL RIGHT"

The tradition of improvising drums and other percussion instruments from natural materials and everyday objects reaches back to the musicians who performed in Congo Square. As the city's music scene evolved in the late nineteenth century, it is a phenomenon that continued and that, in many ways, can be credited to a cultural retention of the improvisational nature that is characteristic of African-derived creative expression. It also can be credited to the "can do" spirit of American invention. In the novel *Invisible Man* (1952), by African American author Ralph Ellison, the anonymous Black narrator talks about his ability to solve problems and invent gadgets: "I am in the great American tradition of tinkers. That makes me kin to Ford, Edison and Franklin. Call me, since I have a theory and concept, a 'thinker-tinker.'"[1] Often, individuals on the streets of New Orleans saw music making as an opportunity yet had no money to purchase an instrument. They decided to make one from what was available. Like the "invisible" narrator of Ellison's novel—and many of these people were invisible, that is, willfully overlooked by society—they had a "theory and concept" and can be considered "thinker-tinkers." For Ellison's narrator, the invisibility he experiences opens the door to possibility, which is why he also looks to New Orleans's native son Louis Armstrong as a role model: "Perhaps I like Louis Armstrong because he's made poetry out of being invisible."[2] The "thinker-tinkers" who crafted their own instruments from found and everyday materials likewise embody this notion of possibility.

During the late nineteenth century, "spasm" bands appeared on New Orleans streets performing on homemade instruments—a washboard scraped with thimbles or spoons, drums fashioned from boxes, bottles struck with sticks, or cans filled with pebbles. Evidence of this inventiveness in creating percussion instruments is seen in a Mardi Gras Indian beating out polyrhythmic grooves on an inverted plastic bucket or kids wrapping the tips of their shoes with metal to beat out a tap dance on a French Quarter sidewalk.

Spasm band, ca. 1920. During the late nineteenth century, spasm bands appeared on New Orleans streets performing on homemade instruments. The Hogan Jazz Archive Photography Collection, Tulane University Special Collections, Tulane University; New Orleans, LA. Accession number PH004025.

Across generations, many of New Orleans's greatest drummers talk about how they began playing on everyday or found objects like their mother's pots and pans or furniture. That improvisational spirit ultimately led to the invention of the drum set.

Although the Congo Square gatherings had ceased decades earlier, the writer Lafcadio Hearn observed people of African descent playing improvised percussion instruments in the late 1880s: "Every Sunday afternoon the bamboula dancers were summoned to a wood-yard on Dumaine street, by a sort of drum-roll made by rattling the ends of two great bones upon the head of an empty cask; and I remember that the male dancers fastened bits of tinkling metal or tin rattles about their ankles, like those strings of copper gris-gris worn by the Negroes of the Soudan."[3] Clearly as the nineteenth century was coming to a close, the process of re-membering African cultural retentions was still taking place among Black New Orleanians. The old saying about necessity being the mother of invention is certainly borne out by the thinker-tinkers who transformed mundane objects into musical instruments. Washboard Chaz Leary moved to New Orleans in 2000. His signature washboard is customized with a couple of coffee cans, a wood block, and hotel desk bell, and the sophisticated rhythmic wizardry he taps and scraps from the instrument excites audiences and enlivens bands in a wide array of musical contexts from blues to western swing, from traditional and modern jazz to roots rock. He explains the impetus to transform a washboard into a percussion instrument:

> A lot of instruments are made out of necessity or you use what you got, like the diddley bow. In all kinds of cultures, there's always been a scraping instrument. In most places, drums were obviously not allowed in the antebellum days because they were afraid of insurrection because drums could be used as a language. So, Blacks weren't allowed to have drums, but to have some kind of rhythm thing, you'd start using a washboard. They were used from right after the Civil War right up to when the drum set became popular.[4]

Unlike in other parts of the United States, people of African descent in New Orleans were able to hold on to their drums during the first half of the nineteenth century, but the racist repression of the post-Reconstruction era forced Black New Orleanians to look for other means to beat out a groove. As Leary explains, these instruments are found across many cultures, and the washboard became an ad hoc successor to the jawbones that had been played with keys as part of the polyrhythmic grooves in Congo Square; both are improvised versions of the guiro and similar instruments that create a scraping sound as something is dragged across a series of parallel grooves—like the corrugated metal on a washboard.[5]

SPASM BANDS: "ESPECIALLY THE RHYTHMS"

The washboard was a mainstay in spasm bands, a musical phenomenon that thrived on the city's streets at the turn of the nineteenth century. These bands usually consisted of groups of young boys who fashioned homemade instruments, playing and dancing, often comically, on street corners or by making their way into barrooms for tips. During the 1890s, the Razzy Dazzy Spasm Band was led by Emile "Stalebread" Lacoume, who became quite a phenomenon and—because he was white—was frequently mentioned in the daily newspapers. One of the band's percussionists was "Charley Stein, who manipulated an old kettle, a cow-bell, a gourd filled with pebbles, and other traps."[6] Likewise, Papa Jack Laine, a band leader and drummer who began working in the 1880s, started off with improvised instruments: "On the street we'd go around for blocks and bocks and blocks, you see, and parade. Some with tin flutes and so on, you know, and that's how we began to go along; mostly homemade instruments. The other kids had sort of a cane outfit, their daddies use to make 'em canes, cane flutes and stuff like that."[7] The trombonist Edward "Kid" Ory was one of the first New Orleans jazz musicians to make a national name for himself when he moved to Los Angeles in 1919. He launched his groundbreaking musical career by outfitting his band of young friends with homemade instruments. Ory cut a bucket in half to make a banjo and used variously sized boxes to construct a violin, a guitar, and a bass. He recalled: "Later I made a drum from a big tin tub, and put some cloth inside it to stop it ringing too much. Boom, Boom, you know. Then I made a foot pedal. They all sounded pretty good."[8] Another New Orleans music legend, the banjo player, guitarist, singer, band leader, and composer Danny Barker, got his start in the early decades of the twentieth century playing with a spasm band called the Boozan Kings:

> I got to thinking, and a bright idea was born. I would organize a spasm band. There were many spasm bands in the city. They played all sorts of gadgets that produced sound: musical saws, washboards, spoons, bells, pipes, sandpaper, xylophones, sets of bottles (each with a different amount of water), harmonicas, jews harps, one-string fiddles, tub basses, kazoos, ram horns, steer horns, bugles, tin flutes, trombones, and so many others I just can't recall.[9]

Barker says that the Boozan Kings imitated the jazz bands in the city and that "the music we created sounded fine, especially the rhythms."[10] He moved to New York in the 1930s and went on to perform alongside many jazz greats such as Cab Calloway, Billie Holiday, and Charlie Parker. When he and his wife, singer Blue Lu Barker, returned to New Orleans in the 1960s, he played a pivotal role in the revival of the brass band tradition. Barker also became the assistant to the curator of the New Orleans Jazz Museum and

Washboard Chaz Leary performing at the 2011 Crescent City Blues & BBQ Festival. For Leary, "a lot of instruments are made out of necessity, or you use what you got." Photo by R. Cataliotti.

can be seen in the *Drumsville!* exhibit in a photo playing a washboard, returning to the glory days of the Boozan Kings spasm band. Always the wry raconteur, Barker comments, "Even this one's going out of commission because they're using washing machines."[11]

Rhythm and blues pianist and singer Professor Longhair (Henry Roeland Byrd, 1918–1980) made an indelible mark on the New Orleans beat starting in the late 1940s with his propulsive "blues-rhumba" grooves. Longhair was also an accomplished drummer, and his first public performing experiences were with a spasm band on the streets of the city. In an interview conducted for the film *Piano Players Rarely Ever Play Together* (1982), Longhair recalls the instruments they crafted, including a washtub bass and a "kazooka," in which a kazoo was inserted into one end of a length of pipe with a funnel in the other end. He gives a detailed description of the drum set he made for himself:

> We just didn't have a drum then. So, we got a soap box, and we used to go down and get these big reels that the pictures, moving pictures come in. We'd get a couple of those and make a cymbal out of one and a snare drum outta the other. We'd get a tomato can or okry can and a potted ham can, and we'd make our little tum tums out of those, nail them on the box. We'd get a piece of shoe tongue or leather put it on stick at the bottom where it would make a flop sound and hit the bottom. Put the heel on another stick, then put a little rag or something, a piece of rubber on the top of the stick. It was a contraption was made where the drum would hit up against the box. Sometimes we'd put a pan or something behind that to make a bigger sound. We would change sounds with this pan. And, we could pick up maybe fifty or fifty-five or sixty dollars in a week's time or something like that. We'd divide up among who all was working in my group. That was the bass and the drums and the horn, harmonica, whatever they had, a Jew's harp, and we had three dancers. And, sometimes I'd get out and dance, and somebody else would play the drums. We had to make a living. We wasn't playing. We wasn't shucking. We were working.[12]

One of the most unique artifacts on display in the *Drumsville!* exhibit is the spasm band drum set that was built and played upon by the legendary street musician Joseph "Co-CoMo Joe" Barthelemy (1913?–1990). In addition, there is a photo of him on Royal Street in the French Quarter playing his contraption made of a packing crate, various sizes of tin cans, and toy instruments—his "one-man Buckie Band." It is strikingly similar in construction to Longhair's description of the homemade drum set that he built. CoCoMo Joe would begin his street performances by announcing into his "make-believe microphone made of a Christmas tree stand, a broomstick and a tin can punched through with holes": "We're broadcasting over radio station WGIN, the breath of New Orleans!" and deliver a set of traditional jazz classics, like "Ain't She Sweet," "Bill Bailey, and "Hello Dolly."[13] There are two films—one from 1928 and one from 1929—of spasm bands drumming and dancing on the streets of New Orleans. Based on the materials and construction of the drums in the films and their similarity to the "one-man Buckie Band," New Orleans Jazz Museum director Greg Lambousy has posited that these are films of CoCoMo Joe.[14] German trumpeter and drummer Norbert Susemihl, along with pianist Greta Milochi, performed with CoCoMo Joe during annual visits to the city. The trumpeter recalls: "He

Danny Barker playing a washboard, ca. 1965. Barker, former curator of the New Orleans Jazz Museum, demonstrated one of the oldest and handiest of spasm band instruments. "Even this one's going out of commission," Danny said, "because they're using washing machines." Courtesy of the New Orleans Jazz Museum. Accession number 1978.118(B).00396.

was such a good drummer, who also had the proper technique on the snare drum. His way of playing always reminded me of Zutty Singleton. With this 'Jackson Square Trio' we played for seven years in the spring, right there on the square. We were the first regular band he ever played with in his life. Joe's rhythm was a pure delight to play with." Susemihl took Barthelemy as a special guest on tour in Europe in 1989 and 1990.[15]

BLACK MASKING INDIANS: "THE ROOT OF MUCH OF THE MUSIC YOU HEAR IN THE WORLD"

Around the same time that the spasm bands emerged, another group of New Orleanians began hammering out rhythms on improvised instruments on the streets of the city. The connections between Native Americans and African Americans reach back to the earliest days of the Louisiana colony. Beyond the gatherings at Congo Square, interactions between the two groups can be traced to Indian tribes in the surrounding regions providing sanctuary to maroons, individuals who refused to remain enslaved, escaped bondage, and sought to live independently. African Americans seem to have first organized the Black Masking Indian or Mardi Gras Indians tradition in the early 1880s.[16] Since the founding of the Creole Wild West, numerous tribes have proliferated in the city. Mardi Gras Day and St. Joseph's Day are the two traditional holidays on which the tribes mask and take to the streets wearing their elaborate, technicolor suits, emblazoned with feathers, elaborate beadwork, sequins, and rhinestones and chanting their songs to polyrhythmic grooves pounded out on tambourines and improvised hand percussion instruments. The tribal structures, the lyrics, the rituals of Black Masking Indians have been transmitted through oral tradition, and, over the past fifty years, they have gained worldwide

Left: Joseph "CoCoMo Joe" Barthelemy performing with his "one-man Buckie Band" in the French Quarter, 1981. Photo by Sydney Byrd. Courtesy of the New Orleans Jazz Museum. Accession number 1994.03.33.100.

Right: Improvised drum sets. The drums of "CoCoMo Joe" Barthelmey's "one-man Buckie Band" (accession number 1993.103) and a re-creation of Baby Dodds's lard can, chair rungs, and antique nails drum set. Photo by Grace Patterson. Donated by R. Cataliotti. Courtesy of the New Orleans Jazz Museum.

Big Chief Juan Pardo's tambourine. Pardo is the leader of the Golden Comanche Mardi Indians. Photo by Grace Patterson. Courtesy of the New Orleans Jazz Museum.

exposure through recordings and concert and festival appearances. However, they have remained a largely insider culture. Some believe that African Americans began masking Indian as a way to subvert the ban on their participation in official Mardi Gras functions; as way to honor the sanctuary provided to the maroons; or as a response to the Plains Indians regalia featured in Buffalo Bill's *Wild West Show,* which performed in the city in the mid-1880s. In *Jockomo: The Native Roots of Mardi Gras Indians* (2019), Shane Lief and John McCusker argue that the impulse for Black men to mask Indian during Carnival—an already long-standing costume character for whites—may have been connected to African American Civil War veterans—identified by name and regiment—who witnessed the genocidal war waged by the U.S. Army against the valiant resistance of the Plains Indians at the close of the nineteenth century, just as their own hard-fought struggles for freedom and civil rights were usurped with the collapse of Reconstruction. They couldn't participate in Carnival as Black men, so they masked and recast themselves as Indian warriors.[17]

These and other factors may all be true, but because it is such a closed culture, the sources may always be cloaked. Saxophonist and composer Donald Harrison Jr. is one of most prolific and versatile contemporary New Orleans musicians. His father, Donald Harrison Sr., who had been a chief in both the Creole Wild West and the White Eagles tribes, founded the Guardians of the Flame in 1988.[18] Harrison, who first overtly explored his Black Masking Indian roots with his *Indian Blues* (1992) album, explains the private nature of the tradition: "Some of it you will never know about. That is just the way it is. Many say it is kept a secret purposely. My father knew the tradition of The Mardi Gras Indians backwards and forward. He passed insider information to me that has influenced my need to always make sure I know what I am doing from an insider's perspective."[19] While much of their tradition may remain hidden, the music they make has had a profound impact on the music of New Orleans. Harrison explains: "What is extremely important about this is that the group that keeps the sound of Congo Square alive is The Mardi Gras Indians. They continue to influence New Orleans music. In fact, they have influenced traditional jazz, rock and roll, R&B, funk, and hip-hop. The music they have influenced in New Orleans has in turn influenced the world. In that capacity they have become the root of much of the music you hear in the world."[20]

Certainly, the African cultural retentions that provided the building blocks for African American oral traditions that were present in Congo Square—call-and-response, improvisation, rhythmic sophistication—are key elements in Mardi Gras Indian music. Like the rhythms in Congo Square, the grooves they play and the dramatic suits they sew each year link the Black Masking Indians to the Pan-African diaspora. Because public gatherings dedicated to African drumming were suppressed by the late nineteenth century in the city, it has been suggested that the tambourine (which had been observed in Congo

Square) became the primary outlet for hand drumming in New Orleans.[21] In addition to tambourines, Mardi Gras Indians are highly creative in improvising percussion instruments to build their polyrhythmic grooves, including things as simple as cowbells, a stick and a glass bottle, a can filled with pebbles, or an inverted plastic bucket. In the documentary *Jazz Parades: Feet Don't Fail Me Now* (1990), folklorist Alan Lomax filmed the White Eagles during their practices playing these types of instruments, and in one scene the percussionist drives the groove by turning the side of a shotgun house into a drum as he beats it with a stick![22] Their call-and-response chants riding over hand percussion--driven, polyrhythmic grooves are integral to the evolution of the New Orleans beat.

IMPROVISING DRUMS: "MY TONE WOULD COME OUT, BIG"

The development of the drum set is directly linked to the tradition of improvising percussion instruments from found or everyday objects and materials because that was how many of the pioneering, first-generation jazz drummers in New Orleans got started. They were definitely "thinker-tinkers," and their inventive spirit played a central role in shaping this new American instrument. Even the self-proclaimed inventor of jazz, Jelly Roll Morton, recalled that his first attempts at making music came from an ad hoc drum set: "My first instrument was made up of two chair rounds and a tin pan. The combination sounded like a symphony to me, because in those days all I heard was classical selections."[23] The legendary brass band and jazz drummer Paul Barbarin, the man who composed "Paul Barbarin's Second Line" and "Bourbon Street Parade," iconic articulations of the city's second-line groove, also played his first beats with improvised percussion instruments: "I used to take two forks, you know, and I'd whistle and sing, just playing forks. Beating away while my mother and my sisters were all dancing in the kitchen. I broke up one of the chairs, probably from beating on it, and since it was broke, I took two rungs out and made points and from then on used them for sticks."[24]

Drumming is so pervasive in New Orleans culture that many youngsters tried to emulate what they heard in the streets on what was available to them when they got home. A video in the exhibit from the Allison Miner Music Heritage Stage from the 2011 New Orleans Jazz and Heritage Festival features reminiscences of improvised instruments from two iconic brass band drummers, Benny Jones and "Uncle" Lionel Batiste. Jones, one of the original members of the Dirty Dozen Brass Band and the founder of the Treme Brass Band, followed that very process as a kid:

> I always paid attention to what all the guys were doing in the brass bands. And, I watched
> the snare drum players. I watched the bass drum players. And, I'd steal one or two of his
> licks. When I go home in the evening, I got a whole pocket full of music. At my house, my
> mother had a bunch of kids. I started off playing pots and pans around my house. Some
> people don't understand about music, when you have a mother with a bunch of kids around
> the house, there's always rhythm around the house with your mother cooking, cooking red
> beans, hitting on the side of the pot, stirring up something, doing all kinds of rhythm.[25]

Joseph Boudreaux Jr. of Cha Wa. Boudreaux is the son of Big Chief Monk Boudreaux and Second Chief of the Golden Eagles. He is also the front man for the band Cha Wa. Photo by Eliot Kamenitz. Courtesy of the New Orleans Jazz Museum.

Jones's mimicking the sounds of his mother cooking red beans and rice has to be the ultimate homemade New Orleans beat. Batiste, Jones's longtime drumming partner in the Treme Brass Band, also fashioned his first bass drum from everyday objects: "My first drum that I made was from a number five washtub. And I made my mallet from a rubber ball. My cymbal was off the slop jar. I put a hole in it, and that was my cymbal."[26] Batiste's use of a washtub, rubber ball, and the cover of slop jar is about as everyday as anyone could get. Rebirth Brass Band drummer and musical director for the Roots of Music program Derrick Tabb grew up in Treme listening to drummers like Jones and Batiste. He also recalls building his own drum to get started: "We used lard cans, old CDM coffee cans, put some pennies in it, and it make a real snare drum sound with the pennies hitting the bottom. We had some times in the backyard with those makeshift instruments."[27]

Benny Jones (*center*), an original member of the Dirty Dozen and founder of the Treme Brass Band who played his mother's pots and pans as a child, leads a second-line parade with bass drummer Mike Duffy during the 2103 Satchmo Summerfest. Photo by R. Cataliotti.

Warren "Baby" Dodds is perhaps the most significant New Orleans drummer in the transition from brass band drumming to the drum set. He was inspired to play music by his older brother Johnny, the renowned clarinetist. Dodds's first drum was completely improvised and handmade:

> I picked up that I wanted to drum. I got me some tin cans and cut rounds out of my mother's chair. I shaped them up like drum sticks. I commenced to beating with my heel on anything that was solid and would give a tone. Then I got a lard can and put a lot of holes in it. I put some ten-a-penny nails in it. Not the large ten-a-penny nails—the small ten-a-penny nails. It sounded all right, so I beat on that lard can for a long time. I was still beating on that lard can when we moved across Lake Ponchartrain to Waveland, Mississippi . . . We had a "back house" there and the baseboard had a deep hollow sound. I would take my lard can out there and beat it and kick my heel on that baseboard. The tin can was the snare drum, baseboard was the bass drum. Sometimes Johnny would stand outside the door, playing clarinet. I'd be inside and my tone would come out, big.[28]

Dodds shapes an absolutely stunning image. This young musician was truly a "thinker-tinker" whose capacity for invention when applied to putting together an actual drum set would profoundly shape the course of modern music.

Subsequent generations of New Orleans drummers would follow in Dodds's footsteps in building on his contributions to how the drum set was approached and the rhythms that he played. They also carried on the practice of improvising the actual instruments on which they were performing. Modern jazz master Ed Blackwell, who made his mark in Ornette Coleman's groundbreaking quartet, improvised in putting together the first drum set he used professionally:

> Well, I didn't build them. I converted some drums. I took a 16-inch military snare that I used to play in high school, bought some hoops for it and converted it into a bass drum. I had a tenor drum that a girl in school gave me. I put some legs on that and made a floor tom-tom out of it, and I had the regular mounted tom-tom. Then my brother painted it for me and put some glistening sparkles on it and made a real nice set out of it. I had a lot of fun with that set. In fact, Billy Higgins really loved that set. It was nice sounding, but it looked like a set of toy drums. The tenor drum was a 9 × 13 I think. The snare drum was regular. There was an album recently published by Harold Battiste called *New Orleans Heritage: 1956–1966*. I'm playing that set of drums on the record.[29]

Similarly, James Black, who was equally adept at jazz and funk drumming *and* a brilliant composer and trumpet player, constructed his own drum set: "I owned a snare drum and we had a pasteboard box filled with paper and we had a little makeshift foot pedal we put on. This is when I was somewhere around eight or ten years old. I played snare drum and the box! I didn't own a set of drums until I was about seventeen or eighteen."[30] Black went from playing a paper box to being given complete drum sets through endorsements from major instrument manufacturers.

Today things have come full circle. Washboard Chaz Leary played many different kinds of music before moving to New Orleans, but he took his washboard back to its origins and learned the local grooves by playing on the street. He explores new directions and expands the rhythmic vocabulary on his simple everyday object–turned-instrument by absorbing what modern-day New Orleans drum masters are laying down: "Coming down and playing in Jackson Square with Tuba Fats [Lacen], that solidified it because then I was able to play with the brass bands, the second-line stuff, get some of the rhythms. I go and check out guys like Herlin Riley all the time and try to do what he's doing on the washboard."[31] The innovative spirit of the "thinker-tinkers" who improvised percussion instruments found in spasm bands, in Mardi Gras Indian tribes, and in brass bands pioneered the way for emergence the drum set.

Eureka Brass Band, ca. 1965. The brass band parade is emblematic of the way that the city's African Americans come together to celebrate a sense of community and express an African-rooted identity. Courtesy of the New Orleans Jazz Museum. Accession number 1978.118(B).00881.

5

Brass Band Drumming
— and the —
Emergence of the Drum Kit

"A DRUM REVOLUTION"

A popular phenomenon throughout the United States during the closing decades of the nineteenth century, brass bands developed particularly deep roots in the New Orleans African American community and continued to thrive there when their popularity waned elsewhere. They may be called "brass bands," but an essential part of the lineup is two (originally three) percussionists performing on bass drum, snare drum, and cymbals. And, it is from those drummers that the stage was set for the emergence of the drum set and the New Orleans beat—that enlivening, syncopated parade rhythm that is called the second line.

"WELL SUPPLIED WITH THE BEST OF MARTIAL MUSIC"

At the turn of the nineteenth century, brass band music was the popular music that reigned supreme across the United States. Bands could be heard and seen marching in communities all over the country, and it was a form of music that was embraced by people of diverse ethnic backgrounds. Massive marching bands led by John Philip Sousa and Patrick Gilmore were the musical superstars of the day.[1] With a tradition of militia bands "rattle-te-banging away" reaching back to the city's earliest settlement, along with the proliferation of military bands during both the War of 1812 and the American Civil War, New Orleanians literally jumped on the bandwagon. Almost all of the musicians, who were largely either white or Creoles of color, had formal training and could read the musical scores for the marches they played.[2] Although the wind instruments in the colonial era bands were mostly fifes, a succession of technical advances over the years brought brass and eventually woodwind instruments into the bands.[3] Initially, brass bands featured three percussionists: a snare drummer, a bass drummer, and a cymbal player, but in

Christon's Brass Band in Southern Park, ca. 1890s.
Photo by Nat Rvengo. Courtesy of the New Orleans
Jazz Museum. Accession number 1978.118(B).00526.

a step toward the development of the drum set, the cymbal was attached to the bass drum, eliminating one of the percussionists.

Brass bands held sway in American popular culture through the first decade of the twentieth century. As other forms of entertainment moved into the spotlight, the phenomenon faded, and this was true for many white brass bands in New Orleans. However, for the city's African American community, brass band music had developed deep roots and continued to thrive.[4] James M. Trotter became a teacher, soldier, historian, and government official after his manumission from enslavement. In his *Music and Some Highly Musical People* (1878), a historical overview of African American musicians, he recognizes the sophistication of the African American brass band tradition in city:

New Orleans has several fine brass bands among its colored population. "Kelly's Band" and the "St. Bernard Brass Band" deserve particular mention here. The "St. Bernard" is composed of a very intelligent class of young men, studious, and of excellent moral character; in fact, they form a splendid corps of musicians, equalled [*sic*] by but few others, and excelled by none. With these two bands and some others, the names of which I have not now at hand, the people of New Orleans are always well supplied with the best of martial music.[5]

One of the central factors in the proliferation and maintenance of African American brass bands was (and in many ways still is) the establishment of benevolent associations and social aid and pleasure clubs, which were organized to provide a support system for African Americans. As Danny Barker explains, "members banded together in these societies as protection and precaution in times of sickness, trouble, death."[6] One of the primary benefits they provided was a funeral parade and burial that included brass band accompaniment. The brass band parade became emblematic of the way that the city's African Americans come together, like the gatherings in Congo Square, to celebrate a sense of community and express an African-rooted identity. Clarinetist, band leader, and scholar Dr. Michael White points out that although these are freewheeling, improvisational events, they have an established structure:

> Very different from New Orleans' better known Eurocentric Mardi Gras parades, the black social club events consisted of three main parts: divisions of colorfully dressed social club members, one or more brass bands (attired in standard band uniforms or black suits and a white cap), and the second line—a crowd of up to several thousand people who follow and dance alongside the parade throughout its several-hour duration. The free-form second line dance performed by club members and the crowd, both of whom dance with umbrellas and handkerchiefs, is derived from West African processions.[7]

Today the term "second line" signifies not only the crowd of participatory dancers following a brass band parade but the actual event itself, as in "There's a second line in Treme on Sunday." "Second line" is also the name of the signature rhythm that defines the New Orleans beat. White explains:

> Separate snare and bass drums established the tempo and strengthened the rhythmic pulse. The snare drum played off of military-style press roles and cadences. The bass drum gave the New Orleans brass band its most characteristic sound—the exciting syncopated pattern derived from the type of African drumming heard at Congo Square. This "second line beat" is the foundation of not only jazz but all locally interpreted musical styles.[8]

Arthur "Zutty" Singleton, a Baby Dodds contemporary, describes the iconic New Orleans brass band funeral format. On the way to the cemetery, the band played "Funeral marches. Dead march time." But at the conclusion of the services, the snare drummer would kick off the up-tempo second-line revelry: "Right after that, out of the graveyard, the drummer would throw the snares on quick, roll the drums, get the cats together, light out. The cornet would give a few notes, Then, about three blocks from the graveyard, they would cut loose."[9] Two drummers along with a tuba or sousaphone player form the engine that drives the brass band's groove. In second-line parades, the role of each member of the band is clearly defined. For Dodds, the snare drummer was pivotal in making sure the parade moved at the right pace at the right time:

> In the funeral marches, the snare drummer carries the whole responsibility. The simple reason is, he beats time for them to walk when the band isn't playing and he's got to break the time, because you don't walk as slow after you get through playing as when you're playing. Then, after you've walked at a certain little brisk pace, you break that time down to a very slow walk, and the bass drum comes in with a last, slow beat. And the band comes in and keeps that beat on through the funeral number that they are playing. After that very slow march, the snare drum picks up the marching time again—not too fast, but just fast enough for a guy not to burn himself out.[10]

Knowledge of how the band is supposed to work has been passed down through generations; however, one of the hindrances that arises when examining the emergence of the New Orleans brass band tradition is that the first recordings were not made until the mid-twentieth century.[11] So, the primary source of information is found in writings and oral histories provided by the musicians who followed in the footsteps of the pioneers. Nevertheless, these types of sources paint a vivid picture of outstanding musicians and their contributions to the New Orleans beat.

LOUIS COTTRELL SR.: "HE COULD HOLD THAT ROLL ALL NIGHT"

One of the early drummers who is consistently singled out is Louis Cottrell Sr. (1878–1927). He was highly regarded by Abbie "Chinee" Foster (1900–1962): "Cottrell, I think he was the best rolling drummer we had. He could make more different rolls than any man I heard in my life. He was very good in the street like in the action between the band numbers, when the band would stop playing and march to the snare drum alone. Cottrell was good on that, and also when they'd send a band off, roll off. He'd get the real natural tone out of a drum."[12] Banjo player and guitarist Johnny St. Cyr (1890–1966) lauded Cottrell's musicianship: "Old man Cottrell had a beat called the 'Steady Roll.' And it was a steady roll. He had the accent on the second and fourth beats and he could hold that roll all night. You couldn't detect a flutter."[13] Cottrell's drumming also left an impression on Paul Barbarin: "Louis Cottrell was the best snare drummer they ever had. No one like him. When he hit that snare drum you heard a snare drum. Boy, I'm the only guy trying to imitate him."[14] "Old Man" Cottrell's influence reaches from giving lessons on how to read music to a young Baby Dodds up to his great-grandson Louis Cottrell III (Louis Chevalier), who traced back his great-grandfather's impact on the tradition and carried on his drumming legacy:

> Major influences would have to be Louis Barbarin, Paul Barbarin, Cie Frazier, and Freddie Kohlman, who all, of course, I remember except Paul Barbarin, who passed before I was

born. Also, I took an interest in them because they were all drummers who were taught by my great-grandfather, and this was documented on all the records. Whenever I'd pull a record and see a drummer I felt I could connect to my great-grandfather, it was always of interest.[15]

Because the tradition is viable, a drummer like Cottrell could piece together an understanding of what his great-grandfather was laying down a century earlier.

A. J. Piron and his Novelty Orchestra, ca. 1920s. The band features drummer Louis Cottrell Sr. (*third from left*), a highly influential teacher and performer, whom Paul Barbarin declared "the best snare drummer they ever had." Courtesy of the New Orleans Jazz Museum. Accession number 1978.118(B).07443.

"OUR RELATIONSHIP TO THE BASS DRUM"

The same building blocks that shaped the musical expressions in Congo Square—call-and-response, improvisation, and rhythmic sophistication—were fundamental to the development of the city's African American brass band tradition. Clearly all three of these

Paul Barbarin with his Onward Brass Band at Tulane Derby Day, 1962. Barbarin was a masterful artist in brass bands and on drum set. Loaned by the Hogan Jazz Archive Photography Collection, Tulane University Special Collections, Tulane University; New Orleans, LA. Accession number OPH000091.

components are evident in the drumming. For many New Orleans musicians, it is the pulse of the bass drum that is the heartbeat of the music. Danny Barker recalls as a youngster the power of hearing that booming bass drum: "The bass beat on the bass drum, beautifully executed by Black Benny Williams, Ernest Trappanier, or Albert Jiles[,] would suddenly silence a crowd of seven or eight thousand loud and boisterous pleasure seekers."[16] James Black also sees the bass drum as the foundation of New Orleans drumming: "The bass drum is very important in the style of drumming that we play here in New Orleans, because the first thing you hear in the parades is the bass drum. You know when you hear that beat from far away, 'Man, it's a parade!' Our bass drum was the main thing. In Dixieland[17] jazz, the bass drum was the thing. The bass drum and the snare drum—they were both important, but the bass drum most of all."[18] Shannon Powell, who was mentored by both Barker and Black, also testifies to the seductive power of the bass drum as a second-line moves through the streets: "Growing up in the Treme, I remember listening to the traditional brass bands either with a funeral or a social and pleasure parade. That's pretty much what started my career. When I heard that bass drum as a child, I said, 'Oh, oh, I want to play that bass drum like that one did.'"[19] Herlin Riley emphasizes the primacy of the bass drum in New Orleans drumming: "But the central part of all New Orleans drummers is our relationship to the bass drum. That's a central concept, I would say, to all New Orleans drummers. We have a relationship to the bass drum, and there's always a dialogue with the snare drum. I think it comes from the whole concept of street playing, second lining, the whole concept of the brass bands."[20] Riley's cousin drummer Joseph Lastie Jr. concurs: "I'm gonna be totally honest with ya, bruh. It's got to be that bass drum. It's got to be the bass drum. There's a song that was written—I think it's the 'Second Line': 'When you hear that beat, New Orleans you'll greet.' When you hit that bass drum, when people feel that bass drum, that distinguishes the New Orleans drummer from any other drummer to me. 'When you hear that beat,' and that beat is what? The bass drum."[21] The innovation that African American drummers brought to the bass drum's role in a brass band is called the "big four." The bass drummer sets up a call-and-response between the bass drum and cymbal on the first three beats of a measure, and on the fourth beat the two are hit simultaneously, creating a kind of lilt to the groove that seductively and irresistibly generates a spontaneous, freeform, rolling dance party. In his autobiography *Satchmo: My Life in New Orleans,* Louis Armstrong describes the effect of the music's uplifting, life-affirming spirit: "Once the band starts, everybody starts swaying from one side of the street to the other, especially those who drop in and follow as the 'second line' and they may be anyone passing along the street who wants to the hear the music. The spirit hits them and they follow along to see what's happening."[22]

"FREE TO EXPRESS YOURSELF FROM DEEP INSIDE"

Brass band musicians traditionally had musical training and could read music. This written music, often referred to as "heavy music," could be fairly complex, and band members were expected to perform it as it was written.[23] Yet, the dominance of formally trained

musicians would be challenged. At the close of the nineteenth century, the established Creole musicians found that there was a new group of musicians ready to step up and fulfill the growing demand for brass bands in the African American community. After the Civil War, newly emancipated African Americans were on the move and looking to leave rural life behind, and New Orleans was a prime destination. This societal transformation would have a significant impact on the music that was played as these émigrés brought along forms like spirituals, work songs, field hollers, and possibly a rural approach to the blues. With a freewheeling improvisational spirit, both the newcomers and formerly enslaved New Orleanians picked up brass band instruments, incorporated their own musical roots into the mix, and began expanding the boundaries of the brass band tradition.[24] Barker's grandfather Isidore Barbarin, a cornet and alto horn player, looked down upon these upstarts who eschewed reading music for improvisation. Barker recalls: "Isidore referred to musicians who played jazz music in the many six-piece jazz bands about the city as 'routine' musicians. It was a slur. To him, 'routine' meant playing by ear, with no music, in the now 'classic' jazz pattern: melody, then variations on the theme." But as Barker goes to explain, this new approach caught on: "Who cared if you read music? You were free: free to take liberties, free to express yourself from deep inside. The public was clamoring for it."[25] While turn-of-the-nineteenth-century brass bands, which were incorporating both Creoles and the African American "routine" musicians, locked into a symbiotic relation with the improvising second-line dancers in the streets, they also were moving from the streets into venues like dance halls and theaters, much like the martial

Left: Emile Knox, ca. 1974, parading with Dejan's Olympia Brass Band. Courtesy of the New Orleans Jazz Museum.

Right: Emile Knox's bass drum. Herlin Riley: "The central part of all New Orleans drummers is our relationship to the bass drum." Photo by Grace Patterson. Courtesy of the New Orleans Jazz Museum.

A New Orleans jazz funeral, 1971. Brass bands were integrally linked to performing in the funeral parades provided to members of social aid and pleasure clubs. Photo by Luke Fontana. Courtesy of the New Orleans Jazz Museum. Accession number 2016.033.10.

bands that had played for the dancers at balls in antebellum New Orleans. Baby Dodds recalls playing many of the same types of dances that had been en vogue for the antebellum balls: "When I first began playing, in certain halls in New Orleans, the bands all had to play waltzes, quadrilles, 'mazookas,' polkas, and schottisches."[26] A major shift in dance tastes had a profound impact on the music, as group dancing moved toward "closed couple styles."[27] The dances that Dodds recalled were replaced by "a simple walking and sliding dance—the two-step—ideally suited for ragtime."[28] This transition from the streets to performing in more compact spaces had a direct impact on drummers. The invention of the drum set would make it possible for one drummer to lay down the beats for the band.

"A SENSATION WIDELY IMITATED"

The heart of the *Drumsville!* exhibit is an 1896 photo of the John Robichaux Orchestra, a eight-piece band that includes three brass players, a clarinetist, two violinists, a bassist, and *one* drummer.[29] That drummer is Edward "Dee Dee" Chandler, and he sits at the far left in the front row. On the ground in front of him slightly to his left is a snare drum; directly in front of him is a bass drum. Attached to right side of the bass drum is a crude overhanging or swing bass drum pedal. It is the first extant picture of a working drummer with the device that would make the drum set possible. One man could now simultaneously play the snare drum, bass drum, and cymbal, roles in marching bands that had once required three percussionists. Early on, a cymbal was attached to the bass drum, eliminating the need for one percussionist in a band. Once again, the impulse toward innovation with percussion instruments is evident, and the improvisational "thinker-tinker"

The John Robichaux Orchestra of New Orleans, 1896. Featuring Dee Dee Chandler on drums, this is the first extant photo of a working musician with a bass drum pedal. Loaned by the Hogan Jazz Archive Photography Collection, Tulane University Special Collections, Tulane University; New Orleans, LA.

spirit can be seen as it became standard practice for many bass drummers to use a cymbal beater, sometimes made from a bent wire clothes hanger attached to a piece of broomstick.[30] The next stage in the movement toward a drum set eliminated the need for a second percussionist. As the music was shifting in terms of its performance context, drummers were making the dramatic adjustment.

While there are records of numerous patents for bass drum pedals prior to the photo of Chandler with the Robichaux Orchestra, there is no extant evidence of another drummer actually performing with one.[31] Chandler deserves the credit for blazing the trail. In his *Jazz: New Orleans 1885–1963,* Samuel Charters details how Chandler constructed his pedal:

Chandler took a standard brass band bass drum and bolted a piece of spring steel on the top of it, bent so that the loose end of the spring was over the center of the drumhead and

Reliance Band with Papa Jack Laine, 1910. The band members include Manuel Mello, Alcide Nunez, Leonce Mello, Alfred Laine, Chink Martin, and Mike Stevens (standing, *left to right*), with Laine (seated). Loaned by the Hogan Jazz Archive Photography Collection, Tulane University Special Collections, Tulane University; New Orleans, LA. Accession number PH00365.

a few inches away from it. He put a covered block of wood on the loose end so that the block would hit the drumhead, if the spring was bent. On the floor he put a hinged wooden pedal, cut out of a Magnolia Milk Company carton he'd gotten from the King Grocery where he worked, with a chain stretched from the raised end of the pedal to the end of the spring. When he stepped on the pedal, the chain pulled the block against the drumhead, and when he released the pedal, the spring pulled the block back. He tied a trap drum onto the side of the bass drum with rope. The sound was probably erratic, but Chandler was a sensation widely imitated. Some of the drummers improved on his design by using a steel rod and baseball instead of the spring and wooden block.[32]

Just like the drummers who had preceded him in Congo Square and in the spasm bands on street corners, Chandler constructed his pedal from everyday objects and found materials and literally drummed up a drum revolution!

With Chandler paving the way, other drummers starting to craft their own versions of bass drum pedals. Papa Jack Laine was one of those innovators. In *Sonic Boom: Drums, Drummers & Drumming in Early Jazz*, Dr. Karl Koenig discusses Laine's contribution to the development of the drum set: "Laine's interest in the bass foot pedal was nearly unavoidable. In addition to being a drummer, Laine was a blacksmith. He claimed to have been the designer of the first baseball-on-a-stick version of the bass drum foot pedal. The ball and stick were attached to a rocker arm that the drummer operated with his foot." The *Drumsville!* exhibit features one of Laine's bass drums, along with an overhanging pedal that likely he made, although it has a cloth-covered mallet head rather than a baseball as a striker. Koenig states that two alternative pedal designs emerged, a heel pedal that was patented by E. M. Anderson and a toe pedal patented by the Ludwig Company, both in 1909.[33] Ludwig's toe pedal became the version that was embraced by most drummers, and the exhibit features one of these that was loaned by Stanton Moore. The bass pedal opened the door to making the drum set ubiquitous across genres of popular music, and as Herlin Riley explains, it continued to be technically refined:

When the bass drum pedal was first invented, there was only one tension on it. There was probably only one action, one speed that it was able to play at. That evolved, so now you can set more or less tension on the bass drum pedal. You can adjust the attack; you can adjust the beater to be as far back from the bass drum as you like. It also allows you to play faster strikes because you can adjust the tension to an individual's ability to strike the bass drum. Some people have real, real fast feet, so they can adjust the bass drum pedal to accommodate that.[34]

Eventually, a small cymbal was attached to the bass drum so that the foot pedal beater would strike the cymbal and drum head simultaneously. Indianapolis-based drummer Ulysses G. Leedy invented the folding snare drum stand, and the company he founded began manufacturing them in 1898.[35] With a bass pedal attached to the bass drum, a snare mounted in a stand, and a cymbal attached to the bass and/or suspended from a T-shaped stand, the drum set enabled a single drummer to simultaneously perform on multiple drums and cymbals with greater facility and complexity.

"A LOT OF CONTRAPTIONS"

The innovative spirit that had been applied to percussion instruments really kicked in, and drummers started adding components that would expand their rhythmic and sonic palette. Many drummers, including Baby Dodds, added tom-toms, adopting traditional Chinese tack drums made of wood with pigskin heads attached with large brass tacks. Freddie Kohlman, who started out in Red Allen's Brass Band of Algiers, moved to Chicago, where he built his reputation, and returned home in the 1950s to work regularly on Bourbon Street and later at Preservation Hall, recalls one of these Chinese drums: "Before tom-toms came out, I used to have a set of drums that had a little Chinese tom-tom that used to hook to the side of the bass drum."[36]

Bands provided a live soundtrack for a variety of theatrical and entertainment performances, from minstrel shows to musicals, and the drummer was indispensable in providing sound effects to accompany the action onstage (or on film). Drummers added all sorts of accessories to their sets, including cowbells, wood blocks, temple blocks, ratchets, slapsticks, whistles, chimes, gongs, and other devices that were labeled "contraptions," one possible source of the term "trap drums." During the vaudeville era, African American acts like Bessie Smith and Butterbeans and Susie performed at the Lyric Theatre, where Louis Cottrell Sr. was the drummer in the pit band. Kohlman, who was Cottrell's student, remembers his traps from attending Sunday-afternoon shows: "That was the first drummer I saw in my life sitting up there with everything around him—chimes, vibraphone, xylophone, marimbas and everything. Back in those days, if drummers had to play a show, they had to have the different effects—boat whistles and everything. They were percussionists."[37] Paul Barbarin recalls one contraption used by the influential New Orleans drum pioneer John MacMurray (1875–1919), who clearly was in the "thinker-tinker" tradition as he had converted a banjo head into a snare drum: "MacMurray always carried a lot of contraptions with him. Whistles and ratchets and all that for breaks. In one particular tune he used a chain, like on a horse and wagon. Well, he would take that chain and lift it . . . and drop it. It would come out perfect in time."[38] Another "thinker-tinker" innovation came when drummers were required to bring the vol-

Papa Jack Laine bass drum with bass drum pedal, and 1909 Ludwig bass drum pedal. Laine purportedly made an overhanging bass drum pedal (which would normally be on the back of the drum). Laine's pedal was loaned by Hogan Archive of New Orleans Music and New Orleans Jazz. The 1909 Ludwig bass drum pedal was loaned by Stanton Moore. Photo by Grace Patterson. Courtesy of the New Orleans Jazz Museum.

Zutty Singleton's wood block and ratchet. Drummers added all sorts of accessories to their sets, including cowbells, wood blocks, temple blocks, ratchets, slapsticks, whistles, chimes, gongs, and other devices that were labeled "contraptions," one possible source of the term "trap drums." Photo by Grace Patterson. Courtesy of the New Orleans Jazz Museum.

ume level down; they employed fly swatters or whisk brooms in place of sticks, eventually leading to the invention of wire brushes.

A central component of the modern drum set, the hi-hat or sock cymbal—two cymbals that clapped together from working a foot pedal—also has a distinct New Orleans connection. It was designed with Baby Dodds in mind, and he was the first drummer to try out the low boy, a precursor to the hi-hat. In 1919, drum manufacturer William Ludwig approached him on the riverboat in St. Louis:

> I used to always stomp my left foot, long before other drummers did, and Ludwig asked me if I could stomp my toe instead of my heel. I told him, "I think so." For a fact, I thought nothing of it. So he said, "Well, we'll try that." And he measured my foot on a piece of paper and measured the space where I would have it and where it would sit and he made a sock cymbal. Two cymbals were set up and a foot pedal with them. One day he brought one along for me to try. It wasn't any good, so he brought one on the boat, raised up about nine inches higher. Well, I had just taken the cymbal off my bass drum because I didn't want to hear that tinny sound any more and I didn't like the sock cymbal either.[39]

Despite Dodds's rejection, the hi-hat went on to be a crucial component of the drum set, especially thanks to the stunning timekeeping wizardry of Papa Jo Jones with the Count Basie band in the 1930s and 1940s. New Orleans drummer Ray Bauduc also contributed to the evolution of the drum set through his consultation with the Zildjian company in developing a splash cymbal.[40]

Over the years, the drum set continues to evolve, incorporating new designs and materials—even electronics—for drums, cymbals, sticks, and other contraptions, but when drummers like Baby Dodds first sat down behind the set, the core components were in place. As Herlin Riley explains: "I can play anything on the drum set with just the snare, the cymbal, and the bass drum. I could play any style because that's the core of the drum set itself, the bass drum, the snare drum, and the cymbal, which come from the marching band."[41] The drum set revolutionized drumming, launched perfectly in sync with the blossoming of jazz, and New Orleans drummers were at the forefront in defining what it means to play both this new, distinctively American instrument and music.

Traditional Jazz

"FROM THE BOTTOM UP"

At the close of the nineteenth century, the drum set and how it was played developed hand in hand with the emergence of traditional New Orleans jazz. Rooted in the brass band tradition, this new music that came to be called "jazz" incorporated a wide range of source material. New Orleans drummers played a crucial role in shaping both the drum set itself and the basic "language" of the drums—the beats, grooves, sounds, and techniques that would become stock-in-trade for this new instrument. For drummer Ricky Sebastian, that call-and-response between the bass and snare drums in brass bands was crucial to how the drum set was approached: "I think it is important to be clear on the way that the two drummers in a brass band play together with constant improvisation in their beats and rhythms, constantly playing off of each other in the process. I've always believed that the improvisatory nature of the way the drummers play together has had a huge impact on the development and evolution of jazz."[1] According to Herlin Riley, the bass drum orientation of these early New Orleans set drummers was essential to the evolution of the city's distinctive beat: "It just so happened that once the drum set itself was in place, then people were trying to find different ways to create different grooves. In New Orleans drumming, the grooves are pretty much created from the bottom up, the bass drum up, and you deal with straight ahead or bebop playing, modern jazz playing, it's pretty much from the top down."[2] Pioneering drummers established Drumsville's reputation and had a profound impact on the broader jazz world as they migrated to places like Chicago and New York, expanding the influence of the New Orleans beat.

"WHERE JAZZ MUSIC REALLY STARTED TO GET ITS LILT"

This new music was not initially referred to as jazz. Some, like Isidore Barbarin, disparagingly called it "routine." Other terms that described what increasingly had become in demand in dance halls around the city included "ragtime," "ratty," "barrelhouse," "head music," "faking," or "in the alley."[3] The makeup of the bands playing this new music was generally cornet (later trumpet), clarinet (later saxophone), trombones, upright bass (or

Kid Ory's Original Creole Jazz Band, 1919. Trombonist Edward "Kid" Ory was one of the first New Orleans jazz musicians to make a national name for himself when he moved to Los Angeles in 1919. *Left to right:* Warren "Baby" Dodds, Edward "Kid" Ory, Mutt Carey, Ed "Montudie" Garland, and Wade Whaley. Loaned by the Hogan Jazz Archive Photography Collection, Tulane University Special Collections, Tulane University; New Orleans, LA. Accession number OPH001120.

tuba/sousaphone), guitar or banjo, and a drum set. Gradually, piano was added to the format. The repertoire encompassed blues, popular dance tunes, marches, folk tunes, spirituals, and hymns. The music that they played featured an infectious syncopation that prompted dancers to hit the floor for new dances like the slow drag, the two-step, and the foxtrot. According to Dr. Bruce Raeburn, drummer and curator emeritus of the Hogan Jazz Archive at Tulane University, the front-line musicians collectively improvised arrangements and engaged in a call-and-response that interwove polyphonic lines based on the melody. They sparingly took individual solos and developed instrumental effects like smears, growls, and slurs to evoke the tonality and feeling of blues or gospel singers.[4] At the forefront of this new "hot" music was the cornetist Charles "Buddy" Bolden. Wynton Marsalis believes that Bolden played a central role in shaping the New Orleans beat: "Buddy Bolden invented that beat we call the 'big four,' that skip on the fourth beat, or so legend has it . . . So, on the fourth beat the drum and the cymbal hit together, and that point is where jazz music really started to get its lilt."[5] That loosening up of the strict martial cadence by New Orleans drummers possibly can be attributed to a cultural legacy passed down through generations of the city's musicians that reaches back to the polyrhythms of antebellum Congo Square. As Raeburn explains:

> If you go to the streets, to the second lines, and you hear brass band drummers, they're going to be playing clave-based, cinquillo, tresillo. You go to the Mardi Gras Indians, you're gonna be hearing similar rhythmic patterns. In the recorded work of New Orleans jazz artists from the 1920s on, you're gonna hear habanera clave, some similar patterns, although prior to 1926 they tend to be kind of subtle because you're not getting the full benefit of the drum set being recorded because of acoustical recording technology having some limits. But this has been ever-present in New Orleans music.[6]

As this new music emerged, the relationship with Afro-Caribbean rhythms was likely reinforced by a number of factors, including the popularity of Cuban dance tunes. John Doheny declares: "The presence of Afro-Cuban rhythms in New Orleans dance music of the early 1900s, though, is a documented fact. The ingress of these rhythms would seem to be both a matter of popularization of songs that employed them (like 'La Paloma') and musicians with obvious affinities toward these styles."[7] The related rhythmic patterns, the habanera, the tresillo, and the cinquillo, that accompanied many of these tunes are cousins to the bamboula, and the syncopated "big four" bass drum pattern upon which the second-line groove is built is a descendant of those patterns. It is this family of rhythms that pianist and composer Jelly Roll Morton famously described as essential to authentic jazz. In his iconic interviews with Alan Lomax, Morton explains how he transformed "La Paloma" into New Orleans style by syncopating what he was playing with his right hand. He explains: "Now in one of my earliest tunes, *New Orleans Blues,* you can notice a Spanish tinge. In fact, if you can't manage to put tinges of Spanish in your tunes, you will never be able to get the right seasoning, I call it, for jazz."[8] Doheny asserts that New Orleans musicians were not trying to re-create Cuban music, but the incorporation of these rhythmic patterns into the evolving jazz style was a "means of generating rhythmic interest which would be attractive to dancing couples attending the social and ceremonial functions at which they performed."[9] Additionally, the Afro-Caribbean influence was likely impacted by the many musicians on the scene who were of Latin American ancestry. Another possible Latin influence was the repeated visits to the city by the Eighth Calvary Mexican Band in the 1890s.[10]

"TIME IS HIS JOB"

For almost two decades beginning in 1900, the Storyville district, with its brothels, saloons, and dance halls, provided an outlet for the musical development of these small groups playing "routine" music. The drum set and how it is played are integrally linked to the evolution of this new music that was eventually dubbed jazz. Traditional jazz is a democratic form that emphasizes individuals interacting in a communal context, and New Orleans drummers saw their role as timekeepers who locked in a groove, brought dynamics to the band, set up and supported soloists, and stepped out when it was time

The Evolving New Orleans Beat

Three iconic variations on the New Orleans beat—Paul Barbarin's "Second Line," Smokey Johnson's "It Ain't My Fault," and Zigaboo Modeliste's (with The Meters) "Hey Pocky A-Way"—are illustrated in drummer Ricky Sebastian's transcriptions that appear here. He recognizes the Afro-Diasporic roots of the city's signature beat and points to what makes it distinctive. "In my opinion," he says, "the biggest difference between the second-line rhythm and the rhythms from Brazil and Cuba is in the feel. I mean the second line has a swing feel to it, like a jazz-type swing feel. I think that's the roots of where jazz comes from, swing. I'd have to say the swing aspect is the one really unique thing about New Orleans second line in regard to those other styles."

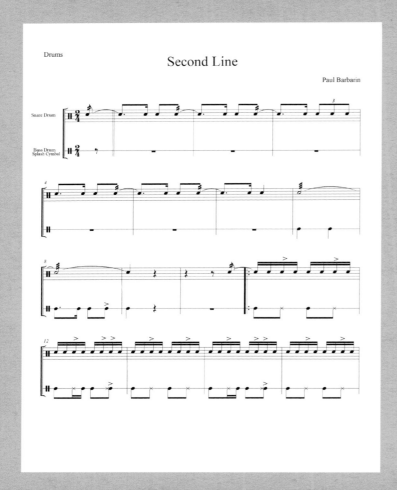

The transcription of Paul Barbarin's "Second Line" is based on a Liberty Brass Band recording from the album Through the Streets of the City (2014) and features Paul Barbarin, the composer's great-great nephew and son of the late trombonist Lucien Barbarin, on snare drum and Cayetano Hingle on bass drum.

Sebastian sees "Second Line" as a definitive version of the city's signature beat. "The Paul Barbarin song is indicative of a typical second-line groove that's unique to this city," he attests. "I've never heard that style of drumming in any other kind of music."

It Ain't My Fault

Smokey Johnson

Hey Pocky A-Way

Zigaboo Modeliste & The Meters

The transcription of Smokey Johnson's "It Ain't My Fault" comes from the iconic single on Nola Records (1964). It testifies to how creative variations contribute to the evolution of the beat. "It's obvious to me," says Sebastian, "that he took rhythms that he played in brass bands when he was a kid or whatever [Johnson credited a cadence he wrote in high school], and he applied them to the drum set in a unique way, playing them on the hi-hat instead of on the snare drum. He just broke it up around the drum set instead of keeping it on one sound source. The part he's playing on the hi-hat, just the accents, I've heard so many drummers play that exact rhythm in second-line bands."

The transcription of The Meters' "Hey Pocky A-Way" is based on the recording from their album *Rejuvenation* (1974). For Sebastian, Zigaboo Modeliste's playing shows how the city's beat continues to reflect connections to Pan-African rhythms: "'Hey Pocky A-Way' sounds like a Mardi Gras Indians–influenced song to me. He played basically one groove through the whole song. And then they break it down. It has this tambourine part that was so out front that I said, 'Let me put that in here too.' And that tambourine rhythm is very similar to an Afro-Cuban rhythm, which is called 'cascara.'"

Abbie "Chinee" Foster, 1961. Foster: "You never stop that bass drum because that's your time." Photo by Carey Tate. Courtesy of the New Orleans Jazz Museum. Accession number 1978.118(B).03122

to take their solos. Timekeeping was a central responsibility for these fledgling drum set players, and Baby Dodds asserts that it is the drummer's first and foremost task: "Time is his job. You don't rush time. You don't pull time. You've got to keep it solid."[11] Abbie "Chinee" Foster echoes Dodd's emphasis on timekeeping: "Your feet is time; your hands are what you make your foolishness with. See, in other words, I can play a 3/4 waltz time or a two beat 2/4 time on the bass drum with my foot, yet I'm playing in groups of four with my hands, that's what you make your monkey shines with, but I keep time with the bass drum. You never stop that bass drum because that's your time."[12] Drum solos were not central to the new music, as evidenced by Foster's references to "foolishness" and "monkey shines." However, the traditional jazz drummer was expected to support the improvising front-line musicians. "Play for the benefit of the band" was the cardinal rule for Dodds, a lesson imparted to him by an early teacher, the legendary Walter Brundy: "It was my job to study each musician and give a different background for each instrument. When a man is playing it's up to the drummer to give him something to make him feel the music and make him work. That's the drummer's job . . . The drummer should give the music expression, shading, and the right accompaniment. It's not just to beat and make noise."[13] Steeped in the city's drumming tradition, today Derrick Tabb carries on that emphasis on the drummer's role to support and inspire the other band members. He calls it playing "in the pocket":

When you get it, it's like, "Hold up, I'm in the pocket." It's a different feel; you understand how to hold a groove and at the same time jump in and out, bringing people in, bringing the trumpet section in, bringing the solo line in, taking the background . . . The drummer's supposed to be keeping time, bringing dynamics to the band. Then, when it's time for him to shine, you shine, but until then you're a supporting act.[14]

New Orleans drummers point to bass drum beats as first and foremost in the characteristics of the traditional New Orleans drumming style. Press rolls on the snare drum are also seen as crucial to the sound and style. In *New Orleans Jazz and Second Line Drumming,* Riley describes how to play a press roll and how it is fit into the groove: "Well, a lot of guys used rolls on the snare drum, and if you're counting 1, 2, 3, 4, 1, 2, 3, 4, they'd play the rolls on the "and"—1 and 2 and 3 and 4 and . . . It is produced by dropping the stick [left hand], then before the stick stops vibrating or rebounding, you drop the other hand [right hand], and then the stick can freely bounce and rebound."[15]

The improvisational spirit of innovation that was exhibited by drummers from Congo Square to spasm bands and the construction of rigged bass pedals helped to define how the drum set was approached. The musicians sitting behind newly rigged-up drum sets were truly pioneers entering unexplored territory. Many of the musicians playing in the "ratty" small dance bands simultaneously worked in brass bands, so the snare and bass drumming beats and techniques could be transferred over, but in this new context, drummers were on their own, required to use both their hands and their feet, and had to figure out the possibilities of this newfangled contraption.

Baby Dodds: "I Knew I Had to Make Good"

Dodd's ad hoc lard-can snare drum and backhouse-baseboard bass drum proved that he was a first-rate "thinker-tinker," and he applied that same ingenuity to the drum set. Although many set drummers laid down a foundation before him, Dodds is genuinely the father of drum set musicians. He was a central architect of the traditional jazz approach to drums and the foremost exponent of this new instrument who went out into the broader world of American music and showed just how it was done. It is clear that he explored every aspect of his set, and every surface had a sound possibility. Dodds was all about creating the right sounds and grooves to enhance the overall performance of the band:

> It was on the riverboat that I began using rims instead of the woodblocks. I don't remember the number but on one that called for woodblocks I used the rims of the bass drum instead. And it sounded so pretty. The woodblock gave a loud sound, and I substituted the shell of the drums, and it sounded so soothing and soft. Sometimes I used faster beats on the rims. Then again, when it was a slow number, I'd do it in triplets. It was pretty and soft, and still it would make the number lively. I worked out these things by myself on the boat because I knew I had to make good.[16]

In 1921, Dodds and Louis Armstrong left the riverboat gig with Fate Marable and moved to Chicago to join Joe "King" Oliver's band. Just like Armstrong, the absolute mastery Dodds displayed on his instrument completely captivated his new audience, especially the young musicians on the scene. In "A Tribute to Baby Dodds," a 1962 *Down Beat* article, drummer George Wettling testifies to the transformative influence that Dodds had on the development of jazz drumming: "I'll never forget the first time I heard Baby with the great Oliver band. The band had a beat that guys are still trying to get. I can still feel and hear it. From that time on, I became a Baby Dodds fan." He details the drum set that enabled Dodds to create all the magic: "You take a 28-inch bass drum; a 6 1/2-inch, all metal snare drum; an overhead pedal; four tuned cowbells; a woodblock; a slapstick; a 16-inch Chinese crash cymbal; a 16-inch Zildjian cymbal; and a 10-inch Chinese tom-tom. You've got the drum setup that Baby Dodds used at the Lincoln Garden (formerly Royal Garden Cafe) in Chicago when he played there with Joe Oliver in the middle 1920s." The profound impact that Dodds had on many up-and-coming jazz drummers is made clear: "When it came to playing on rims and woodblock, Baby was a master. He had a triplet beat that was really something, and Dave Tough, George Stafford, Chick Webb, and I all did our versions of it." Although cymbals had not been central to Dodds's approach in New Orleans, he clearly adapted and grew. Wettling continues: "As I remember, Baby was that first drummer I ever heard play the basic cymbal beat that we all use today on our ride cymbal, that is, in

Warren "Baby" Dodds, 1945. Dodds is genuinely the father of drum set musicians. Courtesy of the New Orleans Jazz Museum. Accession number 1978.118(B).00573.

Baby Dodds's drum set, ca. 1930. Dodds was a central architect of the traditional jazz approach to drums and the foremost exponent of this new instrument who went out into the broader world of American music and showed just how it was done. Photo by Grace Patterson. Courtesy of the New Orleans Jazz Museum. Accession number 2011.141.1a.

4/4 time, a quarter and two-eighths and a quarter and two-eighths, or one, two, *an,* three, four, *an,* etc."[17] Just considering the statement that Dodds shaped "the basic cymbal beat that we all use today" speaks volumes about the foundational role he played in establishing what it means to play the drum set.

During the early years of jazz recordings, acoustic recording technology could not handle the volume of a snare and bass drums, so drummers emulated their Congo Square and spasm band forebears and employed inventiveness and improvisation with the instruments they used in the studio. As Dodds explains: "When I first began to record, I was with the Oliver band. That was a crew that was really together. It was then I began to use wood blocks, the shell of the bass drum and cymbals more in recording than I usually did, because they would come through. Bass drum and snare drum wouldn't record very well in those days and it was my part to be heard."[18] Unfortunately, the technical limitations deny future generations the opportunity to actually hear what Dodds was playing on the full drum set during these crucial formative years; however, he can be heard applying his rhythmic wizardry on these alterative percussion devices on many classic early jazz re-

Warren "Baby" Dodds, ca. 1949. Dodds on the drummer's role: "Time is his job. You don't rush time. You don't pull time. You've got to keep it solid." Courtesy of the New Orleans Jazz Museum. Accession number 1978.118(B).02675.

cordings, including sides with Louis Armstrong's Hot Seven, Jelly Roll Morton's Red Hot Peppers, and his brother Johnny Dodds's Chicago Footwarmers.

Dodds continued to perform and was lauded once again during the traditional jazz revival that took off in the 1940s. He clearly knew his significance in the history of the drum set and worked to preserve his contributions. He collaborated with Larry Gara on an autobiography, *The Baby Dodds Story* (1959), and recorded instructional albums for both the Circle and Folkways record labels, talking about the history of his drumming, explaining and demonstrating his innovative techniques and beats, and improvising solo performances.

"Zutty" Singleton: "Whip Them Cymbals, Pops"

Born in Bunkie, Louisiana, Arthur James "Zutty" Singleton (1898–1975) was raised in New Orleans. His uncle Willie Bontemps, a guitarist and bassist, introduced him to music making and brought Singleton to see the band featuring Baby Dodds that was playing on the steamer *Sidney* on the wharf in New Orleans. Dodds recalls: "He was still a kid in school but he used to love my drumming. He once asked his uncle, 'I wonder, will I ever drum like that fellow?' I never taught Zutty a thing but I was his inspiration."[19] Singleton found a role model whom he would follow and, in some ways, surpass. Like so many other musicians in the city, the brass band–led second-line parades made a powerful im-

Zutty Singleton, ca. 1930s/1940s. Singleton's set incorporates Chinese drums/tom-toms. He is often considered a bridge between traditional New Orleans drummers and the swing era. Courtesy of the New Orleans Jazz Museum. Accession number 1978.118B.06406.

pact on Singleton. He performed in brass bands and dance bands, and by 1923, he was performing in the pit band at the Lyric Theatre with the John Robichaux Orchestra, the drum chair that Dee Dee Chandler had literally created three decades earlier. The young drummer was already attracting attention as evidenced by a mention in a *Chicago Defender* review: "Arthur Singleton is the drummer and oh boy! He has the spotlight on him so often the performers threaten to give notice. Our boy beats a wicked drum!"[20]

The path that Singleton traveled to becoming one of the most renowned jazz drummers was similar to the one Dodds had taken a few years earlier. He performed on the riverboat with Marable and eventually brought his New Orleans beat to Chicago and attracted the attention of many of the young drummers on the scene. He worked regularly with Louis Armstrong, both live and in the studio. In a posthumously published reminiscence, "The Satchmo Story, 2nd Edition" (1959), the trumpeter's esteem for Singleton is apparent as he recalls him joining the Carroll Dickerson band in Chicago at the Sunset Café: "Later on— Zutty Singleton (one of the greatest pioneer drummers—Humorist good natured guy—my idol, and a many many things, good, that is) . . . Joined the band . . . Then it *did* jump."[21] Like Dodds, the "big four" on the bass drum and press rolls on the snare were Singleton's stock-in-trade; he also had an array of contraptions and placed a premium on his role as timekeeper: "When we soloed we had all kinds of gimmicks—skillets, ratchets, bells, Chinese toms, Chinese cymbals—everything. But there was very little rhythmic syncopation. All you had to do was keep good time."[22] Unable to play his drums because of the sonic limitations of the acoustic recording equipment when he was in the studio for the landmark second Armstrong Hot Five sessions in 1928, Singleton adopted a new contraption called a "Bock-a-da-bock" hand cymbal, two bell-shaped cymbals on spring-action tongs that make a metallic clapping sound. At the conclusion of a comic spoken-word intro between Armstrong and pianist Earl Hines on "A Monday Date," the trumpeter intones, "Say, c'mon Zutty: whip them cymbals, Pops," prompting Singleton to kick off the tune with this trap. Singleton employs the "Bock-a-da-bock" on additional classic tracks like "West End Blues," "Sugar Foot Strut," and "Fireworks," punctuating musical lines, providing texture behind soloists, and delivering short solo breaks with the suppleness of a tap dancer.

Singleton embraced other new innovations in drum equipment and was one of the first drummers to excel at the use of wire brushes: "The first pair of brushes I ever had were given to me by Louis Cottrell. I studied Cottrell's work a lot during the early days. But Louis didn't care about brushes, so he gave them to me. They were the first pair of brushes I ever saw in my life. Before that, you had to get your soft effects by controlling your touch with the sticks."[23] In addition, Singleton was an early master of the hi-hat cymbal and was one of the trailblazers in performing drum solos. In Martin Williams's

Jazz Masters of New Orleans, when asked if the solo was his invention, Singleton coyly responded, "I can't remember getting it from anybody." Williams describes Singleton's innovative approach to the drum solo: "He offered an orderly drum solo, fitting it exactly to the form of the piece they were playing. He would hum the melody over mentally as he improvised, and not only finish at the end of twelve or sixteen or thirty-two bars, but also mark off the internal four- and eight-bar phrases as they came along."[24] Singleton is often considered a bridge between traditional New Orleans drummers and the swing era, influencing drummers like Wettling, Dave Tough, Gene Krupa, and Big Sid Catlett. Like Armstrong, many New Orleans band leaders looked to Singleton to provide the hometown beat for their recordings, including Jelly Roll Morton, Henry "Red" Allen, and Sidney Bechet, who in the 1950s wrote that the drummer was "still beating it out as good as they come."[25] He also did outstanding work with Roy Eldridge, Earl Hines, Victoria Spivey, and Fats Waller. And Singleton was able to change with the times, advancing his playing to the point where he drummed on recordings with bebop innovators Charlie Parker and Dizzy Gillespie in 1945. He was featured in a number of Hollywood films, among them *Stormy Weather, New Orleans,* and *Young Man with a Horn,* and was in demand during the traditional jazz revival working throughout the 1950s and 1960s at Jimmy Ryan's in New York City.

Paul Barbarin: "A Good Beat"

The Barbarins are an iconic New Orleans musical family. The patriarch, Isidore, was an alto horn player and stalwart of the brass band tradition, having played with the Onward, Excelsior, and Tuxedo brass bands. All four of his sons became musicians; three of them were drummers. Adolphe Paul Barbarin (1899–1969) gained the most widespread renown as his drumming took him on a career trajectory similar to that of Dodds and Singleton; however, in contrast, Barbarin maintained deep roots in New Orleans, returning to his hometown on a regular basis and, ultimately, became a fixture on the scene during the last three decades of his life. He worked around the city in both brass bands and dance bands. In 1917, he headed to Chicago, initially to work in the stockyards, but soon landed a gig in a band with some fellow New Orleanians, including clarinetist Jimmy Noone and cornetists Freddie Keppard and King Oliver. One of the musicians that Barbarin connected with on a sojourn back home was the Panamanian pianist Luis Russell, and they worked together on and off for many years to come. In 1924, they both joined Oliver's band, and Barbarin is featured on many of the groundbreaking recordings that Oliver made as leader. Barbarin went to New York in 1934 and joined Russell's big band, which became Louis Armstrong's backing band the next year.[26] It is with Armstrong that Barbarin made his reputation as a hard-swinging drummer. He may have been steeped in traditional jazz drumming, but he was able to adapt to what current trends demanded. In "The Satchmo Story, 2nd Edition," Armstrong writes that "Ole Paul Barbarin could 'get down there and really get,'" describing him as "a swing modern drummer" who "has always had a good band . . . Right til this day in N.O."[27] Barbarin's ferocious sense of swing

Paul Barbarin, ca. 1950s. Louis Armstrong: "Ole Paul Barbarin could 'get down there and really get.'" Courtesy of the New Orleans Jazz Museum. Accession number 118(B).07797.

is captured on the 1933 track "Mahogany Hall Stomp," recorded with the Armstrong-led Russell big band. Barbarin, bassist George "Pops" Foster, and guitarist Lonnie Johnson essentially lay down *the* rhythm section template for modern American music. Despite his ability to master the four-beat swing-style groove, Barbarin preferred the two-beat approach of traditional New Orleans jazz: "The two beats is good for dancing. A good beat. If you've got a bass man working with you and can play that two beats, you can really push a band and especially the dancing people."[28] His infectious grooves were in demand, and he recorded with many of the all-time greats, including Jelly Roll Morton, Sidney Bechet, and Henry "Red" Allen. His affinity for his New Orleans roots led Barbarin to return home permanently in the mid-1940s.

Over the next quarter century, Barbarin stood tall among drummers in New Orleans. He led his own dance bands and founded the second incarnation of the Onward Brass Band in 1960, keeping the flame of traditional New Orleans brass bands burning. Barbarin also was a talented composer who contributed two of the most iconic numbers to the brass band/traditional jazz repertoire, "Bourbon Street Parade" and "The Second Line," songs that spontaneously conjure the signature beat of his hometown. Barbarin played a central role in the development of the New Orleans beat, and he extended that tradition through his influence on future generations. Ed Blackwell, who opened up new frontiers in drumming through his "free jazz" innovations with Ornette Coleman, counted Barbarin as a direct influence:

> We played beside each other in a club in New Orleans. He played with the Dixieland band in the big part of the club, and I played in the smaller part. Our group played the after-hours session, so when the Dixieland band would get off we would start. So maybe I would go down early and I'd sit around and listen to him play. He used to sit down and talk to me a lot about the drums and drum rolls; how he played and how he *learned* to play. He was very interesting.[29] (italics in original)

Paul Barbarin certainly gave his all to the New Orleans beat. In 1969, he passed away while playing snare drum marching with the Onward Brass Band in a Carnival parade.

Louis Barbarin and Cie Frazier: "All of the Right Ingredients"

Both Louis "Bob" Barbarin (1902–1997) and Josiah "Cie" Frazier (1904–1985) exemplify New Orleans traditional jazz drumming, and both men, unlike Dodds, Singleton, and Paul Barbarin, largely built their reputations through years of performing on the local scene. They both were steeped in the city's musical heritage, beginning their studies in drumming with the venerable Louis Cottrell Sr. and concluding their careers performing at Preservation Hall.

Louis Barbarin joined the original edition of the Onward Brass Band at age sixteen, and over seven decades of drumming the New Orleans beat, he performed with many of the iconic bands, including Celestin's Original Tuxedo Jazz Orchestra, Sidney Desvigne, Albert French, and George Lewis. Dr. Michael White considers Barbarin the quintessential traditional drummer: "He had all of the right ingredients in his playing and style that typified great New Orleans drumming." For White, the smoothness of Barbarin's signature press rolls "sounded like tearing paper."[30] Historian and New Orleans Jazz Museum emeritus curator Don Marquis observed Barbarin's tremendous skills: "He was a fast drummer. All you could see was his wrists barely moving. He used to say, 'It's all in the wrist.'" Marquis also recognized the simpatico relationship that existed between the two Barbarin brothers when they played together in the reconstituted Onward Brass Band: "The two brothers often would play their drums simultaneously as they marched, making it sound as if one person were making the music."[31] In the 1960s, Barbarin gained more widespread renown through his regular appearances at Preservation Hall and toured Europe with the New Orleans All-Star Jazz Band and with Lars Edegran's New Orleans Joymakers.[32] As a youngster in the early 1970s, Shannon Powell heard Barbarin regularly at the Hall: "Mr. Barbarin was a studious drummer. He knew how to read. He knew how to play rudiments and things like that. He knew how to play very precise. His drum playing and rhythms was very precise. He had a hell of a way of rolling on the snare drum with the groove, with the New Orleans groove."[33] Barbarin's sophistication and technical mastery also helped extend the tradition of the New Orleans beat through his expertise as a teacher, mentoring important drummers like Earl Palmer and Bob French.

Louis Barbarin, 1993. Shannon Powell: "He had a hell of a way of rolling on the snare drum with . . . the New Orleans groove." Photo by John McCusker. Courtesy of the New Orleans Jazz Museum. Accession number 1994.119.01.

Cie Frazier certainly had deep roots in the city's jazz drumming tradition and drew upon many of the giants who opened the doors for him to make his own mark on Drumsville:

> I didn't work with John Robichaux at the Lyric Theatre. Happy was the drummer at that time, fellow called Red Happy [Bolton]. I used to look at him all the time. That would have been around 1918 . . . Red Happy was one of the fastest drummers that I think you had in the city of New Orleans. Next to him was Zutty Singleton for jazz bands, Zutty Singleton. We had another drummer that gave me ideas in a jazz band with Chris Kelly and them was "Face-o" [Eddie Woods]. I never knowed Face-o's right name. Everybody knew him as Face-o. The man helped me with how to handle the snare drum. He used an old bass drum, a snare drum, an old crash cymbal, no sock cymbal, and four cow bells, very seldom he had a little tom-tom with him. My idea he was one of the best jazz drummers I've known. Good timekeeper. That's one I used to follow.[34]

Frazier was another drummer whom Powell heard on his visits to Preservation Hall: "Cie played from the heart, a lot of press rolls on the snare drum, a lot of bass drum and snare drum, not too much cymbal work."[35] Like Louis Barbarin, Frazier did not travel extensively early in his career; however, his drumming was indispensable in Drumsville, and his resume reads like a who's who of the city's traditional bands, both brass and dance,

Left: Josiah "Cie" Frazier at home, 1982. Frazier: "Now a lot of drummers don't listen to the melody when they play but I'm always following it, and sometimes hum along." Courtesy of the New Orleans Jazz Museum. Accession number 1983.043.02.

Right: Josiah "Cie" Frazier's bass drum. Frazier added some flair to his bass drumhead, which is embellished with painted stars and musical notes in black, "CIE" in black at the top, and "JF" in black inside silver rectangle at left, and a light installed inside. New Orleans Jazz Museum Collection, Accession Number: 2012.079.01 Photo by Grace Patterson. Courtesy of the New Orleans Jazz Museum.

including the Young Tuxedo Band, Emile Barnes's Louisiana Joymakers, Kid Howard's La Vida Band, the Eureka Brass Band, Percy Humphrey, Billie and DeDe Pierce, Oscar "Papa" Celestin, and Sweet Emma Barrett. During World War II, he served in the U.S. Navy dance band.

Many traditional jazz drummers emphasize the importance of knowing the melody of a tune in order to support and enhance the band's performance. This was true for Frazier: "Now a lot of drummers don't listen to the melody when they play but I'm always following it, and sometimes hum along."[36] When British drummer Trevor Richards took lessons from Frazier during his tenure at Preservation Hall, he found that the veteran often would sing the tune and play the drum part. When it came time for Richards to execute what he learned, Frazier was a stern taskmaster:

> And then in the evening when he was playing with Billie and DeDe Pierce, for example, in the Hall, he'd say, "Come and sit in," and he'd be sitting beside you, watching you, and as soon as you did something he didn't like, he'd reach around you and start to hold your hands with the sticks and say, "No, like this." He'd make it like a lesson with a hall full of tourists watching and wondering what the hell's going on! It was really embarrassing if you did something wrong, and he'd step in and start telling you how to do it.[37]

Frazier may have stuck close to home during most of his career, but when he began playing with Preservation Hall, he traveled far and wide—including an opening set with Billie and DeDe Pierce for the Grateful Dead at the Fillmore West in 1968—and was responsible for turning on countless listeners to the New Orleans beat.

Deacon Frank Lastie: "It's the Same Beat"

Like the Barbarins, the Lasties are a New Orleans musical dynasty. Their patriarch is Deacon Frank Lastie, who received his first musical training in the Colored Waif's Home band with Louis Armstrong around 1915. Although he was a grand marshal in second-line parades, ultimately Lastie's focus was not on brass bands or dance bands; it was on church. That should not be surprising because many African American musicians' first experiences making music took place in their families' churches. Paul Barbarin felt that rhythms abounded throughout everyday life in New Orleans, but he singled out the rhythms emanating from churches as the most compelling: "You heard the pastors in the Baptist churches. They were singing rhythm. More so than a jazz band. And some churches, when you passed by, they were swinging like crazy."[38] Frank Lastie is recognized as the musician who introduced drums into the services of the Spiritual Church. In the late 1920s, he was encouraged to play the drums in church by his mentor, Mother Catherine Seals. As he explains in a sermon that is quoted in Jason Berry, Jonathan Foose, and Tad Jones's *Up from the Cradle of Jazz* (1986): "I endured the rebukes and scorns. Now, they're very few churches that don't have drums."[39] He eventually became the pastor of Guiding Star Spiritual Church, which was located in the Lower Ninth Ward. Mac "Dr. John" Rebennack recognized the spiritual essence and groove implications of Lastie's sanctified drums and their significance to the New Orleans beat:

> I knew the spiritual church music was solid. If you ever heard Deacon Frank Lastie or Reverend Hill play drums, you was hearing some of the beats of New Orleans in their original forms—styles related to African ritual drumming as it came down to New Orleans—just like if you ever heard Paul Barbarin play drums you'd be hearing the original second-line drumming. This drumming really turned me out, and led me to check out not just spiritual-church music but a lot of other things connected with the hoodoo church.[40]

While Lastie integrated his version of the New Orleans beat into the church, he also raised a family who initially learned to play gospel music but branched out into the realms of jazz and rhythm and blues. His daughter Betty Lastie was a singer and pianist and led a family gospel group. His sons, saxophonist David Lastie Sr., trumpeter Melvin Lastie, and drummer Walter "Popee" Lastie, were renowned jazz and R&B musicians. "Popee" brought the New Orleans beat to countless audience members through his work with Fats Domino's band.

Frank Lastie's drumming legacy is still central to the New Orleans beat through the work of his grandsons Herlin Riley and Joe Lastie Jr., both of whom learned directly from their grandfather. Riley has achieved widespread renown playing everything from traditional to cutting-edge modern jazz with artists like Danny Barker, Wynton Marsalis, Ahmad Jamal, and Marcus Roberts. And, Lastie Jr., a regular at Preservation Hall, has

Deacon Frank Lastie, Guiding Star Spiritual Church, 1973. Mac Rebennack: "If you ever heard Deacon Frank Lastie . . . you was hearing some of the beats of New Orleans in their original forms." Photo by Michael P. Smith. Copyright © The Historic New Orleans Collection. Accession number 2007.0103.4.25.

concentrated on traditional jazz and gospel. So, it's not surprising that he can move effortlessly between those styles because of his experiences in his grandfather's church: "My grandfather and them used to march around the church with "When the Saints Go Marching In" and "The Sweet By-and-By" and "Down by the Riverside" and stuff like that. Then when you get to a song called "The Royal Garden Blues" or a secular trad song, and I found it's the same beat."[41]

Ray Bauduc: "All I Want to Do Is Play Jazz"

Raymond Bauduc (1909–1988) also came from a musical family. His father, Jules, was a professional horn player and musicians' union organizer; his older brother Jules Jr. played drums and banjo; and his sister Marguerite was a pianist. Bauduc's initial experience came through his brother: "When I was a kid, still going to grade school, I started to fool around with my brother Jules' drums at home. He had a couple sets of drums and was always switching parts from one set to the other, according to the job he had to play. That gave me a chance after school to fool around with his drums."[42] His brother tutored him, and although they were white, he guided him toward the drumming of such African American innovators as Baby Dodds and Zutty Singleton: "And he showed me how to play the right way. I mean, he'd say, 'Play this way, don't do that and don't do this. Go listen to Zutty and go listen to this guy. Don't go over there.' He told me the right kicks."[43] Jules would arrange for his underage brother to hear Singleton, taking him to a club where the drummer was performing and leave him in the alley outside the back door. Then, he would ask Singleton to open the door and let Bauduc in so he could check out the band. Eventually, Bauduc befriended Singleton and would regularly attend his performances on a local riverboat excursion:

> But Zutty, Zutty, we had a ball. We just loved each other. I used to go on the boat on Sundays and go up on the roof. I'd get a chick that had a basket, see and they use to go to St. Rose, we'd go out to St. Rose and everybody'd ride on into St. Rose with a basket lunch with 'em. But I used to go upstairs on the roof, so I'd find a chick that's got the right kind of chicken and stuff, so we'd go up on the roof and have Zutty share it with us (laughs). We used to have a ball though. Wonderful.[44]

Bauduc's father was a "legitimate," as opposed to ratty or jazz, musician, and he wanted his son to learn to read music. Bauduc attended enough lessons to pick up the basics but rejected formal training: "After that I went back home and said that's enough music for me. I said I want to learn to play my way and not the way somebody else is gonna write. You see what I mean? That's how I started to play my way." He conceived of himself as a jazz musician: "But all I want to do is play jazz, make people happy. Jazz music is a happiness music, and that's the way it works out with me."[45]

As a teenager, Bauduc played all over New Orleans—in theaters accompanying motion pictures, in pavilions out at Spanish Fort and the Lakefront, and in downtown clubs and restaurants. He left the city to tour with Johnny Bayersdorffer in 1924 and never looked back. He was on the road bringing the New Orleans beat to national audiences throughout the swing era. Bauduc moved to the forefront of big band drummers in Ben Pollak's orchestra when he took over the drum chair from Pollack, who gave up drumming to front the band. Bauduc's use of traps, press rolls, and that big bass drum beat—he preferred to play in 2/4, rather than 4/4 time—made his New Orleans roots easily distinguishable.[46] Like a number of New Orleans drummers, he was very conscious of playing the song rather than just beating out a pulse: "I play a melody. A lot of guys say he plays a melody drum [*laughs*]. Just like trumpet player's playing the chords, I'm singing the chords all the time in my head what I would want to play on the trumpet."[47] In 1935, he was propelled to stardom when he joined the Bob Crosby Orchestra (and Bob Cats small group), which delivered an exuberant blend of big band swing and traditional New Orleans jazz that some began referring to as "Dixieland" jazz. According to Dr. Michael White, one of today's foremost artists and scholars of the traditional jazz, that term is a disrespectful usurpation of the music created by New Orleans Black musical artists: "The post–Civil Rights climate of the mid 70s was a time when some older musicians and younger ones, like myself, openly expressed resentment at the term 'Dixieland' in reference to black traditional jazz. In addition to its negative historical racial implications, 'Dixieland' implied a white imitation of jazz. It was commonly understood and

Ray Bauduc, autographed photo. In 1935, Bauduc was propelled to stardom when he joined the Bob Crosby Orchestra (and Bob Cats small group), which delivered an exuberant blend of big band swing and traditional New Orleans jazz. Courtesy of the New Orleans Jazz Museum. Accession number 1978.118(B).00483.

defined as such in early jazz history." The term is used by some of the drummers in quotations that appear in this book, and White recognizes that Black musicians used it but clearly believes that it is an unacceptable representation of the music: "Over the years I heard older musicians debate among themselves about using the term. Some accepted the label and others did not. Some saw it as an insulting attempt to steal or cover up original black jazz and others used the term as did many modern jazz musicians, writers, music publishers, and record companies, as a catch-all phrase for any jazz style before swing and bebop."[48]

During this time, drummers were often a draw for the bands, and Bauduc was one of those stars, along with Gene Krupa, Buddy Rich, Louis Bellson, Jo Jones, Sonny Greer, and others. His experiences in New Orleans shaped him not only as a drummer but also as a composer. One of his tunes that the Crosby band recorded was called "Smoky Mary." The title refers to a passenger train that ran out to the Milneburg camps near Lake Ponchartrain where social clubs hired bands. Bauduc describes the impact of the train ride in a series of handwritten memoirs bound with cardboard and labeled with magic marker as "The Bible":

> I would always go to the last car or coach, then to the observation platform—on the back of the train, then when "Smoky Mary" would get going, the sound of the wheels gave out with a "rhythm pattern" "a tempo," then I would pull out my drum sticks and start beating it out. It was a funny thing about that sound, it would increase its speed or slow down—so I was always free to play anything I wanted to. 4 beats, 2 beats, syncopation, waltz time. boogie woogie, shuffle rhythm, or anything that came to mind. Even at that stage of my drumming I really worked out quite a few patterns that I still use now & then. As I went along in years getting to play better on drums, I started to play with different bands, then my playing got to be pretty good and have more of a definite or more solid beat. I always added some of those rhythm figures or patterns to my style.[49]

What a great image! Another New Orleans experience that inspired Bauduc to write a song was his attendance at a parade by an African American social club called the Bulls: "And I said, one of these days I'm gonna write a tune to represent this. It's gotta be a parade, it's gotta be a parade march, and the whole story it was there when I got together with [bassist Bob] Haggart and wrote the thing out, see. It got be a pretty famous flag waver for the Bob Crosby Band, and now all bands play it, once in a while, you know."[50] The song is "South Rampart Street Parade," and it still shows up at second lines. The innovative spirit of Drumsville was definitely at work on "Big Noise from Winnetka" (co-composed with Haggart), a one-of-a-kind performance where Haggart whistles while Bauduc plays a "drum" solo on the G string of Haggart's bass. In "The Bible," Bauduc narrates the evolution of the improvised performance:

> Finally I started beating on the big floor tomtom [*sic*] and I started vamping with one stick on the "G" string and one stick on the floor tomtom—then I looked up at Hag & he got the "cue." I kept vamping and he got the microphone & started whistling through his teeth. He

whistled a few tunes then he went into the theme, we had been fooling around with backstage. The he started arpeggioing up & down the G minor scale, & I started playing with him on my Greeko cyms, woodblock, cowbell & rims of the drums, tomtoms, cyms & etc. Finally I got back to the big floor tomton vamping. Then I started playing with both sticks on the "G" string. Then Hag started to finger up and down on the "G" string as I was playing on it with my sticks.[51]

The crowd went wild, and the following week the band re-created it in the studio, named it for a group of high school fans who attended the initial performance, and it became one of the Bob Cats' biggest hits.

Bauduc was totally engaged with the drums. He consulted with drum and cymbal manufacturers to design instruments that would be particularly appealing to jazz drummers. And he wrote two of the earliest jazz drumming instructional books, *Dixieland Drumming* (1936) and *150 Progressive Drum Rhythms* (1940). During the late 1950s and 1960s, he worked with banjoist and guitarist Nappy Lamare. Even though Bauduc was on the road, he consistently viewed himself as a New Orleans drummer and always acknowledged his debt to his three major influences, his brother Jules, Baby Dodds, and Zutty Singleton.

NEW ORLEANS DRUMMERS:
"INNOVATING THE INSTRUMENTS AND THE SOUND"

With a beat that reached back to its founding, New Orleans drumming finally made its mark as traditional jazz artists took the country and world by storm. Adonis Rose, drummer and artistic director of the New Orleans Jazz Orchestra, explains that New Orleans traditional jazz drummers were the source point that opened the door for jazz drummers everywhere:

> If you wanted to play the drums, you were listening to Baby Dodds. That's where you had to go. If you were listening to music at the time when he was playing, that was the source. There's just no way around it. If you're playing jazz, which was the most popular music in America at the time when they were creating it, there's no way around dealing with New Orleans drummers. They were the people that were innovating the instruments and the sound.[52]

New ideas, beats, and techniques would meld with and transform the foundational approach as jazz innovation took place in cities like Chicago and New York. New Orleans drummers would continue to contribute to that evolution, and their signature beat would also continue to evolve at home and generate new forms of music that would once again transform American music.

7

Modern Jazz, Rhythm & Blues, and Funk

"THE BEAT, THE BEAT, THE BEAT"

During the second half of the twentieth century, New Orleans drummers continued to make their mark—often playing a defining role—in modern jazz, rhythm and blues, and funk. In New Orleans music, the categorization of genres is often irrelevant. The New Orleans beat is adaptable to any musical context, and drummers have prided themselves on playing "whatever the gig calls for." This chapter is divided into two sections, one that focuses on modern jazz and another that looks at rhythm and blues and funk, not because those categories are mutually exclusive but rather to look at these drummers in the context of the styles in which they attained their greatest recognition. The drummers who are included here are recognized for technical innovations that influenced and extended the development of the New Orleans beat, as well as the renowned contributions they made to iconic bands and landmark recordings. Once again, *Drumsville!* is intended to be representative rather than comprehensive, and there are many other drummers who merit inclusion.

MODERN JAZZ

As the jazz tradition advanced—from swing to bebop to cool and hard bop to modal and free to fusion—drummers from outside New Orleans had major impacts on approaches to the instrument. Ricky Sebastian explains how the rhythmic foundation of jazz evolved as innovations emerged outside New Orleans:

> It is important to understand how drumming evolved in places like Chicago and New York, from a 2-beat feel to a 4/4 pulse on every beat going from traditional jazz to the swing era and on to the bebop era. You might describe a 2-beat feel as beats 1 and 3 being the strong beats on bass drum and bass. A very New Orleans groove. With the 4/4 feel, the bass and ride cymbal/bass drum are playing all four beats in the measure, but with the emphasis on

2 and 4 where the hi-hat is playing. This gives the music a forward motion. This was a major change in the evolution of the music.[1]

New Orleans drummers both absorbed those advancements *and* continued to contribute to the evolution of jazz drumming, driving innovation with the rhythmic sensibilities and techniques derived from the ever-evolving New Orleans beat.

Freddie Kohlman: "A Guy You Could Set Your Watch By"

On a May night in 1953, drummer Freddie Kohlman and his band, the Mardi Gras Loungers, were joined by tenor saxophonist Sam Butera for a benefit concert at the Municipal Auditorium in New Orleans. It was recorded by MGM Records, and four tracks were released on a ten-inch LP, *Jazz Solos in New Orleans.* The band, named for the club at 333 Bourbon Street where they worked regularly, included trumpeter Thomas Jefferson, trombonist Waldron "Frog" Joseph, clarinetist Willie Humphrey, pianist Quentin Batiste, and bassist Clement Tervalon. Mardi Gras Lounge owner and clarinetist Sid Davilla, who regularly sat in with the band, also joined them that night. The music they are playing is similar to what might have been heard at the era's Jazz at the Philharmonic all-star shows—a blend of swing, bebop, and blues styles that includes the band riffing behind individual soloists on "Stomping at the Savoy" and "Mardi Gras Lounge Blues," a honking saxophone showcase for Butera on "Christopher Columbus," and a ballad feature for Jefferson's trumpet and poignant vocal by Kohlman on "I Can't Get Started." That same approach is apparent on *Blowout at Mardi Gras,* another album from this period that was recorded at the French Quarter club. Kohlman is certainly the leader of the band, as he drives the grooves, inspires the soloists, and delivers his own solos with stunning speed, power, and invention. His playing is clearly rooted in traditional New Orleans jazz; this is evident in a rare 1953 film of Kohlman and the band at the Mardi Gras Lounge on two takes of the traditional jazz warhorse "When the Saints Go Marching In." His solo soars to such heights that even he stands up with the band as they ride out the final chorus. While that traditional approach—the bass-drum emphasis, the press rolls, the syncopated cowbell fills—is exhibited on the two albums, at the same time it is clear that his extensive work touring and as a house drummer in Chicago clubs led him to incorporate a modern, hard-swinging sensibility—often keeping time on the ride cymbal and using the bass drum for accents.

Louis Freddie Kohlman (1918–1990) was born in Algiers, directly across the Mississippi River from the French Quarter, a neighborhood that is home to many of the city's traditional jazz greats. Kohlman studied with the multi-instrumentalist Manuel "Fess" Manetta, who was a pianist in Storyville during its heyday and subsequently established himself as a music teacher in his West Bank home. Kohlman's inspiration to play the drums was sparked by the brass band parades he followed, and one of his earliest drumming gigs came through another neighborhood legend, cornetist Henry Allen Sr.: "I got the opportunity to play in a parade when Red Allen's daddy had a brass band, old man Henry Allen. He hired me one day to play a parade and that was the greatest thing

Freddie Kohlman (*left*) and Clement Tervalon at the Mardi Gras Lounge, 1953. Kohlman learned from the pioneers who established what it meant to be a traditional New Orleans drummer, and he was a role model for the modern jazz and R&B drummers in the generation that followed him. Photo by Ralston Crawford. Loaned by Ralston Crawford Photography Collection, Tulane University Special Collections, Tulane University; New Orleans, LA.

in my life. I was about 13, 14 years old."[2] And like so many New Orleans drummers from earlier generations, Kohlman was drawn to the drumming of Louis Cottrell Sr.: "It's like I was crazy about drums; during my time as a kid, I used to follow [clarinetist] Louis Cottrell's daddy. He used to play the snare drum in the parade and I always wanted to be the snare drum player in the parade band because the way he played was so beautiful."[3] He eventually came under the tutelage of the venerable master. On Sundays, Kohlman's mother would give him the money to attend the Black vaudeville shows at the Lyric Theatre in the French Quarter, where the pit band included Cottrell applying his percussion skills to a vast array of traps in support of the featured variety acts. Cottrell was responsible for giving Kohlman his first opportunity to play a drum set.[4] He gained experience working behind such traditional jazz maestros as A. J. Piron, Joseph Robichaux, Papa Celestin, and Sam Morgan.

In the 1930s, Kohlman followed the same Great Migration north that a generation earlier had brought the revolutionary drumming techniques and beats of Baby Dodds, Paul Barbarin, and Zutty Singleton to Chicago. Influenced by swing-era drumming, he adapted his traditional approach, performing in Chicago with pianists Albert Ammons and Earl Hines, violinist Stuff Smith, and fellow New Orleanian trumpeter Lee Collins. Like Barbarin, Kohlman returned home to work on the local scene. After a stint with Louis Armstrong's All Stars in the mid-1950s, Kohlman took up residence as the house drummer at Chicago's Jazz Ltd. club, supporting acts like Art Hodes and Billie Holiday. His reputation as a primary exponent of the New Orleans beat is testified to in a story he tells about being called to a Barbara Lewis/Impressions recording session in Chicago because the drummer could not play the groove the producer wanted: "I sat down there and I played a parade beat and the man jumped up and he said, 'That's it! That's what I want—exactly.' And he gave me 150 dollars just for showing the other drummer the beat."[5]

Kohlman moved back to New Orleans in the early 1960s and worked with brass bands, including Paul Barbarin's Onward Brass Band, performed at Preservation Hall, and frequently toured Europe. His modern approach to traditional material is in evidence on the album *Cookin'!* (1982) that he recorded with the Heritage Hall All Stars, which also featured trumpeter Teddy Riley, clarinetist Manuel Crusto, trombonist Fred Lonzo, pianist Ellis Marsalis, and bassist Walter Payton Jr. Kohlman's roots in traditional brass band drumming, as well as his skills as a soulful vocalist, earned him a guest artist slot, along with Mac "Dr. John" Rebennack, on British trombonist Chris Barber's homage to the Crescent City, *Take Me Back to New Orleans* (1988). He provides the crucial bass drum groove to Dr. John's Mardi Gras classic "The Big Bass Drum" and a warm, soulful vocal on "Do You Know What It Means (to Miss New Orleans)?" Kohlman brought his traditional jazz mastery literally to a new generation on Harry Connick Jr.'s first two albums, *Dixie-*

land Plus (1977) and *Pure Dixieland* (1979), recorded when the pianist was respectively ten and eleven years old.

A crucial bridge between generations of New Orleans drummers, Kohlman learned from the pioneers who established what it meant to be a traditional New Orleans drummer. And he was a role model for the modern jazz and R&B drummers in the generation that followed him. As Earl Palmer recalls: "He was kind of an inspiration to all of the young drummers. For Vernel Fournier, we used to always say that Freddie Kohlman was a guy you could set your watch by. His time was so impeccable. He had the personality of a drummer. He had a perpetual smile on his face, and another thing I copied from him, I like to cook as a hobby . . . Freddie was a great cook and a great drummer."[6] Joseph "Smokey" Johnson, who came into his own on the R&B scene when Palmer left New Orleans for California in the late 1950s, credits Kohlman with teaching him the proper technique for using the Chinese cymbal in traditional jazz drumming: "Freddie Kohlman showed me how to use that cymbal . . . Freddie Kohlman was great at it."[7] And, near the end of his career, Kohlman influenced a whole new generation of drummers, including Shannon Powell and Herlin Riley. Schooled by the original masters who put traditional jazz on the map, Kohlman took the New Orleans beat out into the broader jazz world, incorporated new ideas and techniques, and became a Drumsville master.

Vernel Fournier: "If It's Good, Everybody Partakes"

During the early 1940s, a newly formed band comprised of teenagers started performing around New Orleans in neighborhood halls like Economy Hall, the San Jacinto, and the Gypsy Tea Room. Vernel Fournier (1928–2000) gained his first professional experience with that band and went on to develop a reputation as an innovator and stylist who epitomized the concept of a drummer's drummer. With dedicated practice and a helping hand from some elder musicians, the band carved out a place for themselves on the local scene. Dooky Chase Jr. played trumpet in the band and became the leader; his father, the famed restauranteur, bought their uniforms. Fournier recalled:

> By the time we were twelve or thirteen, we had formed a group called the Young Swingsters. The older musicians wrote simple arrangements for us, for a quarter, fifteen cents, whatever. We would rehearse two times a week, and our mothers got together and promoted us. The next thing you knew—maybe my mother had a club, so they'd have us play. The band grew to sixteen pieces, and we actually started competing with professional bands, taking their jobs.[8]

They began playing swing band charts but soon fell under the sway of the emerging modern sounds of bebop. Fournier played hooky from school once a week to hear good white dance bands, along the lines of Glenn Miller, at a theater on St. Charles. They heard Black bands at weekend dances: "We were able to hear the two sides of it. Finally, we heard Dizzy's [Gillespie] big band, and that did it. Dizzy came down with the Hepsations of 1945. That just wiped out everything. We didn't bother with the rest of the stuff."[9] Fournier and

Vernel Fournier (*left*) and trombonist Benny Powell in New York, 1985. They began their careers in Dooky Chase's Young Swingsters in the 1940s and were drawn to the sounds of bebop. Photo by R. Cataliotti.

his colleagues fully embraced the bebop ethos: "We were wearing tams, bebop glasses, dark glasses, zoot suits, long chains. They could pick us out anywhere, and we insisted on being that way. Come hell or high water, that's the way we were gonna be."[10] Many of the established musicians in New Orleans, as was the case all over the United States, were alienated by bebop, but Fournier recognized the new music as an extension of the music he had come up playing: "We got a lot of help, but we got a lot of flak too, from the older musicians. There was a lot of turmoil because many of your great musicians at the time said, 'Bop is crazy music.' But, I realized that a lot of tunes Charlie Parker played, like 'Rosetta,' 'Idaho,' and 'Back Home Again in Indiana,' these were tunes we were playing traditionally."[11]

Fournier's musical training began at Joseph A. Craig Grammar School: "Miss Duvernay was the band instructor, and she demanded excellence. We had rehearsal three times a week *before* school. We had to get there at eight o'clock in the morning. Marches, all marches, but they were all from the book, everything was in the book. We were all reading, from fifth to seventh grade. I started in fifth grade."[12] His first professional drum instructor was Sydney Montegue, who taught him rudiments and that cornerstone of New Orleans drumming, a press roll. Fournier found his first major influence in Paul Barbarin. Just as he recognized that both traditional jazz and bebop applied their distinct approaches to the same standard tunes, Fournier found that Art Blakey's drumming with Billy Eckstine's big band was a modernized version of the "big wide beat and an aggressive sound" he heard in Barbarin.[13] When he graduated from high school, Fournier attended Alabama State Teachers' College. In 1946, after a year of touring with the school's big band, the opportunity arose to go on the road with the King Kolax R&B band during summer vacation. He took it and never looked back. He went on to work with tenor saxophonist Paul Bascomb and spent three years in pianist Teddy Wilson's trio.

Like New Orleans drummers from previous generations, including Singleton, Dodds, and Kohlman, Fournier took a gig as a house drummer in a Chicago club. At the Bee Hive from 1953 to 1955, he got the chance to play behind such modern jazz giants as Lester Young, J. J. Johnson, Sonny Stitt, Ben Webster, and Stan Getz. In 1956, Fournier joined the pianist Ahmad Jamal's quartet, and his work with this group, which included bassist Israel Crosby, has ensured him legendary status in jazz history. His syncopated, second line–influenced drumming anchors the highly influential album *At the Pershing: But Not for Me* (1958), which stayed on the *Billboard* jazz charts for more than two years and is one of the all-time best-selling jazz albums. It features their landmark seven-minute-plus rendition of "Poinciana," which as an edited version became a jukebox hit. Jamal comments that "if you listen to his work on 'Poinciana,' you'd think it was two drummers! [*laughs*]. He was so multidimensional: a master of brushes, master of content, master of metronomic time, and feeling."[14] Jamal's piano dances across the seductive groove that Fournier lays down, employing a mallet on the snare and floor tom and the back end of a drumstick on a cymbal, drawing on traditional bass drum parade beats.[15] As Fournier explains: "I think 'Poinciana' is worthwhile because that type of coordination originated in New Orleans with the bass drum and cymbal. I never created it; I discovered it. It was there already."[16] The album had a significant impact on the modern jazz world. One of its most enthusiastic fans was trumpeter Miles Davis, who acknowledged its effect on the evolution of his conception of modal playing: "I loved his lyricism on piano, the way he played and the spacing he used in the ensemble voicings of his groups."[17] Fournier began playing with brushes with this group, cementing his reputation as an empathetic drummer who could play with taste and restraint but still bring the fire to a performance. For drummer and pianist Jack DeJohnette, Fournier's playing on the album was a touchstone: "When I heard *Live at the Pershing*, I wanted to go out and get brushes, before I even had a drum set. Vernel had that balance of precision and looseness, and just always knew what to play, the right thing to play within the music. He was a master of the understatement."[18]

Fournier worked with the Jamal Trio from 1956 to 1961 and again from 1965 to 1966. They recorded ten albums, including *Extensions* (1965), which features the track "This Terrible Planet." Fournier says that Jamal and bassist Jamil Nasser shaped the sound they wanted and looked to him provide the appropriate underpinning:

> And from the rhythmic pattern that was set with the total melody, then the drum pattern was developed. Not to talk about the drum pattern on this thing, but for the drummers out there, it's interesting . . . If you can understand, it was a 6/8 time, but 1, 3 and 5 was on the bass drum, and 2, 4 and 6 was on the snare drum, so it was like a 4/4 fighting the 6/8, which seems almost impossible, but your right foot will always fall out on 1—so it starts the sequence over and over again. And once you get used to that, then the rest of it is easy. And the tambourine was used on the side. I didn't know what to do with that tune, and I played the tambourine, and I guess Ahmad smiled, and so I kept it there. That's what you look for really—what pleases the guy that you're working for.[19]

Once again, Fournier constructs a groove that is both rhythmically complex and, drawing upon his New Orleans roots, incredibly funky, thanks partially to the jangling tambourine he includes. Like Baby Dodds, his focus is on playing what is best for the band performance.

Fournier went on to work with jazz greats such as pianist George Shearing, singer Nancy Wilson, and saxophonist Clifford Jordan, among many others. In 1975, he converted to Islam, taking the name Amir Rushdan. He moved to New York in 1980 and established himself on that most demanding of jazz scenes as a performer and teacher. Like so many New Orleans drummers, Fournier placed a premium on musicality: "When I play as a percussionist, I always play tunes. In fact, I had a hell of a compliment. I worked a gig with Joe Wilder and Eddie Barefield and some other cats, and I took a solo. Joe Wilder turned around and said, 'Hey you didn't miss a change, did ya?' And that's coming from a great trumpet player. In other words, he could follow what I was doing just like a horn player. That's what I've been working for, and it's coming."[20] He may have scaled the heights of the jazz world, but Vernel Fournier always remained true to the ultimate goal of Drumsville's New Orleans beat: "One of my greatest rewards in playing music is if I've got such a groove going that I get someone in the audience to start second linin'. That's just like a doctor's degree or a medal of honor. That's what I was raised on. You hear the music; if it's good, everybody partakes."[21]

Ed Blackwell: "Everything He Played Was Danceable"

In April 1967, Ed Blackwell (1929–1992) was performing with pianist Randy Weston's sextet at the Cinema Agdal in Rabat, Morocco, the final stop of a three-month, fourteen-country, State Department–sponsored tour of West and North Africa. He played a solo that years later still resonated for Weston, who recalls in his autobiography: "Ed Blackwell took a tremendous drum solo during the concert and the audience went nuts. Blackwell being from New Orleans, everything he played was danceable, no matter how complicated the rhythms were."[22] Blackwell is one of the great jazz drumming innovators from the second half of the twentieth century. Deeply rooted in the New Orleans drumming tradition, he was one of the pioneers of the 1960s cutting-edge "free," or "avant-garde," jazz and was in the forefront of exploring African heritage in the new Black consciousness movement.

The street beats of New Orleans parades were the initial inspiration for Blackwell: "My biggest influence in jazz was being able to follow the street parades in New Orleans. The rhythms that they had going with these parades were so beautiful that even now I still feel the rhythmic inspiration that I got just from being able to run along behind the parades coming from the funerals and things. It was such a gas, man!"[23] He also absorbed the polyrhythmic, call-and-response grooves of the city's Black Masking Indian tradition: "The rhythms they played with their tambourines, that was something else. Most of the Indians were congregated down below Canal, and down in that section is where Professor Longhair lived. And they were very heavy on that rhythmic thing. In fact, we used to go down to their practices where they would have their rehearsals."[24] Blackwell's journey toward drum mastery began in the drum and bugle corps at Booker T. Washington High School in Uptown New Orleans, where he was tutored in beats and rudiments by his friend Wilbur Hogan: "That's when it really started. That's when I got serious about the drums, marching around and playing press rolls at the football games."[25] Like his contemporary Vernel Fournier, Blackwell was drawn to the new sounds of bebop. He immersed himself in the music and had a drum store order him the latest Charlie Parker recordings.[26] His role model was drummer Max Roach: "Every interview I've ever had, I've always mentioned how much influence I got from Max. He *still* knocks me out. He's still *the* man to me" (italics in original).[27] Key aspects of Roach's playing that helped shape Blackwell's innovations were the emphasis on melodic drumming and the application of a song's harmonic structure to his solos.

Bebop gigs were in short supply in New Orleans in the late 1940s, so Blackwell joined an R&B band led by the Johnson brothers, tenor saxophonist Plas (of "The Pink Panther Theme" fame), and pianist Ronald. He continued to play bebop with a coterie of musicians in New Orleans, and it was at this time that he met saxophonist Ornette Coleman, who was stranded in between gigs. Coleman was already developing his free jazz improvisational approach, and Blackwell began to jam with him, laying the foundation for crucial advancement in the development of the jazz tradition. In his liner notes to Coleman's complete recordings on the Atlantic label, Robert Palmer explains: "According to Coleman and Blackwell, the kind of playing that would be labeled 'free jazz' really began here. A recording of some of these sessions would be like a Rosetta Stone for deciphering the subsequent course of jazz."[28] Eventually, Coleman moved to Los Angeles, and Blackwell spent almost a year on the road with Ray Charles, who bought him a set of drums.[29]

In 1956, Blackwell's enthusiasm for modern jazz drew him back to New Orleans to join with his like-minded colleagues—pianist Ellis Marsalis, clarinetist Alvin Batiste, saxophonist Harold Battiste, and bassist Richard Payne—to form the American Jazz Quintet. Coleman sent for Blackwell to come to Los Angeles, so he, Marsalis, and Harold Battiste jumped in Battiste's Chevrolet and headed west.[30] Blackwell and Coleman worked day jobs but continued to develop the saxophonist's innovative approach to improvisation, which was transformative for the drummer: "He was really showing me a new way for the drums to be played, the way I hadn't heard because I was one of the devotees of Max Roach. He showed me a different thing about the drums, about the sound and how they could be made to speak so you could play with more freedom."[31] The American Jazz Quintet recorded its first album in New Orleans later that year, although it remained unreleased for two decades. Nevertheless, it laid the groundwork for an independent, artist-owned record label, A.F.O. (All For One). Blackwell and his associates played in clubs and recorded a live album (which also remained unreleased for decades). In 1960, Blackwell headed to New York and immediately made his mark as one of the architects of the free jazz.

Ornette Coleman had created a tumult in the jazz world with the release of his first album, *Something Else!!!!* (1958), and through performances in New York by his group with trumpeter Don Cherry, bassist Charlie Haden, and drummer Billy Higgins. When Higgins was prohibited from performing in clubs due to a cabaret card issue, Coleman contacted his old associate in New Orleans. Most jazz histories that survey Coleman's career assert that Blackwell came to New York to take Higgins's place in the quartet, but actually Blackwell was simply returning to *his* gig and the music he had helped Coleman forge during the previous decade. Blackwell took jazz drumming into uncharted territory. As Palmer

Ed Blackwell, ca. 1968. Deeply rooted in the New Orleans drumming tradition, Blackwell was one of the pioneers of the 1960s cutting-edge "free," or "avant-garde," jazz and was in the forefront of exploring African heritage in the new Black consciousness movement. Photo by Francis Wolff from the box set *The Complete Clifford Jordan Strata-East Sessions*, copyright © Mosaic Images, 1986. Loaned by Mosaic Records.

explains: "With his highly evolved command of multiple rhythm patterns, Blackwell was able to depart from the regular meter at will, springing the rhythm's pivot-points free of the standard, unvarying 1-2-3-4. He always knew where he was and where he was going with the rhythms, and no matter what he played, he was always going to swing."[32] Blackwell's innovations also enabled him to further extend the drummer's melodic possibilities. In his groundbreaking essay "The Jazz Avant-Garde" (1961), LeRoi Jones (Amiri Baraka) discusses the implications of freeing the drummer from timekeeping:

> Because rhythm and melody complement each other so closely in the "new" music, both bass player and drummer also can play "melodically." They need no longer be strictly concerned with thumping along, merely carrying the beat. The melody itself contains enough rhythmic accent to propel and stabilize the horizontal movement of the music, giving both direction and impetus. The rhythm instruments can then serve to elaborate on the melody itself. Wilber Ware's [bass] playing is a perfect example of this. And so it is that drummers like Blackwell, Higgins, and Charles [Moffet] can roam around the melody, giving accent here, inferring actual melody elsewhere.[33]

Blackwell toured and recorded with Coleman through 1965 and appears on such seminal recordings as *Ornette!* (1961), *This Is Our Music* (1960), and *Free Jazz: A Collective Improvisation* (1960), which features two quartets improvising simultaneously, including Blackwell *and* Higgins. Musicians in New York were quick to recognize Blackwell's incredible drumming skills, and he was recruited to play on landmark albums such as John Coltrane and Don Cherry's *The Avant-Garde* (recorded 1960, released 1966) and *At the Five Spot* (1961), a live recording by Eric Dolphy with Booker Little.

Blackwell joined Randy Weston's band in 1965, making three trips to Africa with the master pianist, who called his music African Rhythms. In 1969, the drummer moved his family to Tangier to live with Weston. The exposure to traditional drumming had an impact on Blackwell's drumming: "I had been woodshedding for quite some time on getting my hands and feet involved on the kit. But when I heard these African drummers and heard the way they were dealing with 12/8 and 6/8 and 6/4 rhythms, then I really got serious with it and started really trying to concentrate on coordinated independence."[34] He also connected his experiences in Africa to his New Orleans roots that reached back to the Sunday-afternoon gatherings in Congo Square:

> I learned that the African drummers play a rhythm in such a way that it's continuous. Individually they were very simple rhythms that would become complex when they would merge. But if you had the chance to walk around the group while they were playing, you could see each cat playing a different rhythm. It was a very simple rhythm that they played, but when you hear the overall thing . . . man! It remined me so much of the way the guys used to play in New Orleans.[35]

When he returned from Africa, Blackwell rejoined Coleman's band, and in 1972 was named Artist in Residence at Wesleyan University in Middletown, Connecticut. Although he was dealing with a serious kidney condition, he continued to collaborate with a wide array of artists, including the Coleman-inspired band Old and New Dreams with Haden, Cherry, and saxophonist Dewey Redman; Karl Berger; Joe Lovano; David Murray; Mal Waldron; and many others. In 1986, he joined forces with a younger generation of New Orleans musicians, trumpeter Terence Blanchard and saxophonist Donald Harrison, to record a two-volume live album in remembrance of the historic Dolphy/Little Five Spot recordings. His sound is so distinctive; he is immediately recognizable after a beat or two on his snare. And when he solos, it is like listening to a musical composition that is *both* structured and freewheeling. His career came full circle in 1987, when he was honored at the Edward Blackwell Festival at the High Museum in Atlanta, uniting with the original American Jazz Quintet—Ellis Marsalis, Alvin Batiste, Harold Battiste, and Richard Payne, along with special guest alto saxophonist Earl Turbinton. New Orleans poet Kalamu ya Salaam bears witness to their performance in a *Wavelength* magazine review: "Friday and Saturday night in Atlanta witnessed the second burning of that city as Blackwell press-rolled, cow-belled, cross-rhythmed, foot-stomped, Chinese-gonged, and cymbal-stroked both fellow musicians and attentive audience into so happy a delirium that, had the pope been there, he would have instantly canonized Edward Blackwell."[36] When the saints go marching in, Ed Blackwell surely will be in that number.

Leo Morris/Idris Muhammad: "Tuned at the Key of Idris"

On the stage of the Biltmore Theater on April 28, 1968, drummer Leo Morris/Idris Muhammad (1939–2014) was sitting on an upturned apple crate in front of a pared-down drum set, along with seven other musicians, on the back of a flatbed truck for the Broadway opening of *Hair: The American Tribal Love-Rock Musical.* Muhammad reached back to his Uptown New Orleans origins to kick off the first number, "Aquarius": "I start playing with my hands on the tom-tom. The same street beat I heard as a kid in New Orleans, I start playing it with my hands to establish a real tribal sound."[37] Muhammad stayed with the show for four and a half years, and the grooves he improvised were considered crucial to the success of the show.

Raised in New Orleans's Thirteenth Ward, Morris took the name Idris Muhammad when he converted to Islam in the 1960s. He was from a musical family; his father played banjo, and all his brothers played drums, including Weedy Morris, a renowned jazz artist in his own right. Morris drew his primary inspiration from two sources he encountered in the streets of the city: the bass drums in brass bands and the Mardi Gras Indians' tambourines:

> My bass drum patterns are from the bass drum player marching in the Second Line. I play from the bottom up. A lot of drummers play from the top down so they very rarely understand what's happening down there . . . The second part of my rhythms is the tambourine patterns that the Indians play while they're dancing to Mardi Gras. I capture those rhythms between the hi-hat cymbals and the snare drum.[38]

His first gig came on Mardi Gras Day when he was nine years old and was drafted by a brass band to play bass drum on the back of a truck in a parade—a scene that would be

Left: Idris Muhammad in performance at the Telluride Jazz Festival, 1980. Photo by R. Cataliotti.

Right: Idris Muhammad's cymbal. Muhammad: "If you take something I create, and you do something with it, then someone else will take it and move it to another stage." Photo by Grace Patterson. Courtesy of the New Orleans Jazz Museum.

echoed decades later when he performed in *Hair:* "They had a big bass drum and one snare drum and a cymbal. They built up some beer cases for a seat for me and I played with these old guys, man. And these guys were saying, 'This kid can play.'"[39] His earliest musical associations were with his neighbors, the Neville family, and one of his first professional gigs was with Art Neville's Hawketts. Cyril Neville recalls hanging out with Joseph "Zigaboo" Modeliste and listening to Morris practice: "Leo had the funkiest beats. Studying his style, I'd lean my head so intensely on the screen door in front of his house that I'd have marks on my skin."[40] Morris played in school bands but largely learned his craft from the musicians and the culture of his neighborhood. The one formal drum lesson he ever had was with the legendary Paul Barbarin, who told him not to be impressed when people told him he was great.[41]

That greatness was undoubtedly apparent to a lot of people because for more than fifty years his drumming opened door after door for him. Morris played on the classic New Orleans R&B hit "You Talk Too Much" by Joe Jones. And Jones introduced the young drummer to Sam Cooke, who hired him after he beat out a groove on the table in the Dooky Chase restaurant. In addition to touring with Cooke, Morris appears on the singer's hit records such as "Chain Gang," "Wonderful World," and "Cupid." Singer Maxine Brown bought him a set of drums for an appearance at Harlem's Apollo Theater; Morris met singer Jerry Butler there and began working with him. Dee Clark was next, and he played on her hit "Teardrops." Butler then hired Morris to serve as his musical director. Curtis Mayfield was in that band, and when he left to form the Impressions, Morris went with him to Chicago, drumming on nine Impressions albums, as well as the hits "Gypsy Woman," "Keep on Pushing," "Amen," and "People Get Ready." Morris's drum work provided a spark that lit a fire under these singers because he was not just beating out a rhythm; he was *playing* the song: "One unique thing about my playing was how I would play with the vocalist and help him sing the song better. Behind the soloist or behind the guy singing the song, I would play the chord changes and play the rhythm at the same time."[42]

The next door opened when he moved to New York and was hired as the house drummer at the Apollo. This gig gave him wide exposure and shifted the trajectory of his career. Even though Muhammad consistently insists that he is a funk and not a jazz drummer, he assumed a commanding position in the world of jazz drumming. He garnered the admiration of two of his drummer heroes, Art Blakey and Elvin Jones, giving him the confidence that he could play jazz. After the Apollo shows, he was hanging out in the city's jazz clubs. This was how he landed a gig with saxophonist Lou Donaldson, and Muhammad brought the funk from his New Orleans R&B session work into groove jazz, immediately scoring a hit with the album *Alligator Boogaloo* (1967). From that point on, the jazz gigs took off, including Betty Carter, Nat Adderley, Grant Green, George Benson, Sonny Stitt, George Coleman, Gene Ammons, and Shirley Scott, among many others. Like the R&B singers he supported so effectively, the jazz musicians who hired him were drawn to his distinct grooves, which reach back to his bass drum orientation: "I was able to play the bass drum on the offbeat, where it grooved and it locked in—but it *swang*. The bass drum beat: it's skippin', it's skippin', it's skippin'. That's one of things I was known for when I came to New York . . . That's what all the jazz cats liked."[43] Muhammad's influence moved to another level through the wide audience he reached and the innovations he developed while performing in *Hair*. Because the band was set up on the back of a truck, Muhammad played on a stripped-down drum set:

> I could only have one ride cymbal and the hi-hat. So I played all of this music off of the hi-hat, and I accented off the ride cymbal. After a year and a half I became sick, so they sent in a sub to play for me, and it was a disaster! After I came back, [composer] Galt [MacDermot] made me get a book written up. Eventually, I had nine drummers subbing for me. This started with Bernard Purdie, Billy Cobham, Alphonse Mouzon. All these guys were subbing for me, 'cause this was the hottest musical on Broadway. So I'd created this thing off the hi-hat; Bernard comes by and looks at the book and says, "I can't play this shit, Idris!" And he leaves. Next time I heard that thing was on Aretha Franklin's "Spanish Harlem." I saw Bernard, he said, "Did you hear what I stole from you? This hi-hat lick." So guys were taking things from my drum playing and incorporating it into their style of drum playing.[44]

In 1973, Muhammad followed his tenure in *Hair* by keeping a promise to join Roberta Flack's band, and he appears on her *Killing Me Softly* (1973) and *Feel Like Makin' Love* (1975) albums. Like Blackwell, Muhammad's approach to the drums was transformed by his travel to Africa: "When I returned to New York from Sudan I changed my drum sound.

I brought in all this bottom end. This is when I added the second floor tom and second ride tom. And when I changed my set up it provoked me to try something different in my playing. I started playing different rhythms."[45]

After extended associations with both the Blue Note and Prestige record labels, Muhammad established a relationship with Creed Taylor's CTI label, contributing his grooves to numerous hit albums and becoming a recording star in his own right, mining the funk/fusion genre on a series of albums. Stardom did not sit well with Muhammad, and he gladly returned to the role of sideman, working with jazz giants such as Pharoah Sanders, Ahmad Jamal, Randy Weston, and John Hicks. Deeply engaged with the art of drumming, he took pride in his distinctive sound: "My drum playing is very personal to me. You can hear my drum playing because my special tuning process—both drums and cymbals—is unique to me . . . I start tuning with the deepest floor tom and work back to the snare drum with the snares turned off. You can hear the intervals, but it's not to specific notes. A piano player might say, this is A or this is F. But it's really tuned at the key of Idris."[46]

In 2011, he moved back to New Orleans and reconnected with one of his earliest rhythmic inspirations—the Black Masking Indian tradition. Big Chief Donald Harrison Jr., whose father had been the big chief in the drummer's Uptown neighborhood when he was growing up, named Muhammad "Big Chief Red, the First Chief of the Congo Nation," and he masked with them on Mardi Gras Day. While Muhammad's beats and grooves were highly influential on R&B, funk, and jazz, the hip-hop generation also has mined his work for samples. He sees it as part of a continuum: "It don't really belong to me, man; I'm only the creator. If you take something I create, and you do something with it, then someone else will take it and move it to another stage. And this is what happened with hip-hop. This is in my aura."[47]

James Black: "The *Mission Impossible* Drummer"

During the winter of 1963, drummer James Black (1940–1988) was performing regularly in a quartet with pianist Ellis Marsalis, tenor saxophonist Nat Perilliat, and bassist Marshall Smith at the Music Haven club. In an effort to pick up where he had left off a decade earlier with the American Jazz Quartet, Harold Battiste decided to make another modern jazz recording. Problems with the sound quality of engineer Cosimo Matassa's live tapes from the club sent the group into his iconic J&M Recording Studio to rerecord the material, and the result was a landmark New Orleans album, *Monkey Puzzle* by the Ellis Marsalis Quartet. It remains a stunning testimony to the breadth of Black's musical talents through both his commanding drumming and the four original compositions he contributed to the seven-track program.

Black was born in the French Quarter and was drawn to the drums by the second-line parades he heard as a child. His music teachers from Joseph A. Craig Elementary to Southern University at Baton Rouge, however, insisted that he play trumpet, and he was good at it. In his freshman year at college, he played a Hayden trumpet concerto with a symphony orchestra. But he continued to follow his passion: "I knew I was a drummer so I went on and played the drums anyhow."[48] It was during his last semester at Southern that he got the call from Marsalis to form the band that would take up residence at the Playboy Club and ultimately move to the Music Haven. A gig with R&B star Joe Jones took Black to New York, where his percussive skills were immediately recognized. He performed with pianist Horace Silver at Birdland and joined Lionel Hampton's big band for an extended stay. His rhythmic sophistication and fierce independence got him fired. As he told WWOZ radio host Pat Jolly: "I wouldn't play four beats on the bass drum. I was into jazz and bebop, and I didn't want to be tied down to playing 'doom, doom, doom, doom' on the bass drum, so I rebelled and got my two weeks' notice."[49] Reed player Yusef Lateef hired

James Black

© Rick Olivier

James Black, 1984. Johnny Vidacovich: "He was using different timbres of the set and approaching it like a small orchestra." Photo by Rick Olivier. Courtesy of the New Orleans Jazz Museum. Accession number 2009.032.16.

Black and featured his composition "Magnolia Triangle" on the album *Live at Peps* (1964). He returned to New Orleans in the late 1960s and began working R&B and funk studio gigs with artists like Irma Thomas, Lee Dorsey, and Allen Toussaint. A session with pianist Eddie Bo produced "Hook & Sling," one of the low-down, greasiest funk grooves of all time. Bo recalls: "Not many folks could play that many rhythms at one time . . . Now James, I never had to tell James what a pocket was. He'd go out of the pocket and play in the pocket at the same time. Now how he got there, I don't know, but all those rhythms he was playing, I didn't need extra drummers or to hit on something extra to get that second beat, he did it himself."[50] Black recorded several R&B/funk sessions under his own name from 1969 to 1976 released posthumously on the album *(I Need) Altitude* (2002). During this period, he also reunited with Marsalis to keep the modern jazz flame burning, regularly performing at the club Lu & Charlie's. The drummer prided himself on his versatility: "Now I get a chance to play a little R&B, a little rock, a little jazz, a little Afro-Cuban and a little of this and that. A little Martian music! Play some music from Pluto for a while; some of the avant-garde kind of stuff and just space out! Just get all your stuff out of you. Then after you play your little avant-garde for a while, go back and play some funk. If you can do that, you're well rounded."[51] And, he knew he was good. As he told Jolly: "I'm sort of like the *Mission Impossible* drummer. When nobody else can play it, they'll call me."[52]

Black is perhaps the most consistently admired of all modern New Orleans drummers, and his mastery of the set and his compositional skills have made him a legend in Drumsville. In 1963, Harold Battiste already knew Black was a genuine visionary: "He is constantly bored with the present because the future is unexplored, and his mind is in the unexplored future . . . the present is always past."[53] Ernie Elly, who was a contempo-

James Black's drum set. Black: "I owned a snare drum and we had a pasteboard box filled with paper and we had a little makeshift foot pedal we put on . . . I didn't own a set of drums until I was about seventeen or eighteen." Photo by Grace Patterson. Courtesy of the New Orleans Jazz Museum.

rary of Black, recalls, "He had the New Orleans feeling, plus different polyrhythms, cross-rhythms, everything, he was phenomenal."[54] For conga player and percussionist Alfred "Uganda" Roberts, "James Black was like Jimi Hendrix on drums."[55] Johnny Vidacovich drew inspiration from Black's compositional approach to drumming: "He was real good at playing a tune as a composition, and I found the parts he would play to be quite meaningful. He was using different timbres of the set and approaching it like a small orchestra."[56] As a young drummer, Ricky Sebastian often saw Black perform with Ellis Marsalis at Lu & Charlie's: "I started bugging James to sit in once in a while, and he was hard on me man. I later found out that the reason he was hard on me was because I was young, and he saw that I had a lot of talent. He gave me a lot of shit, which made me work harder, and his approach to polyrhythms has stayed with me my entire life."[57] Vernon Severin studied with and befriended Black, who taught him two arcane beats, "Papa Legbe" and the "Nigerian Six," that shape captivating grooves: "So, now the whole thing opened up. To me, it wasn't like just playing drums no more, it was like a musical experience . . . and I want to tell you something, even now, it's still some of those things he taught me that I'm working on."[58] Black was one of Jason Marsalis's first drum teachers, but it was not until years later when he discovered his father's vinyl copy of the *Monkey Puzzle* album that he recognized the magnitude of Black's innovations. He was particularly taken by Black's composition "Whistle Stop":

At this point, I'm starting to get a little bit of a better understanding about form and structure, and I'm hearing these odd phrases. *Whistle Stop* is this tune that has a 3/4 bar in the middle, which, at the time in the '60s, was unheard of. You either played in 4/4 or you played in 3/4 or you played in 5/4. At that time, there was no such thing as you're playing in 4/4, you're going to have one bar of 3 and then go in 4. I said, man, you did this in the '60s![59]

During the 1980s, Black was featured on recordings by singer Germaine Bazzle, Ellis Marsalis, and with Marsalis, along with his sons, trumpeter Wynton and saxophonist Branford on the album *Fathers and Sons* (1982). Ironically, with all his talent as a musician and composer, Black never recorded an album as leader. Yet, his legacy lives on, particularly through his still-challenging compositions, and is passed along from one generation to the next in Drumsville. Poet Kalamu ya Salaam wrote an elegy to Black that appeared in *Wavelength* magazine in October 1988. In one section, the poet declares:

> Although he started out on trumpet and, I'm told, was good at it, James Black was truly a drummer born. When Black was on the stand keeping time, the potency of old gods was resurrected. / James Black time keeper, could within seconds, give us the gift of eternity in music—no one who really heard him will ever forget him.[60]

David Lee Jr.: "Extending, Extending, Extending"

Trumpeter Dizzy Gillespie was making his way along Bourbon Street in 1969, and he was looking for a drummer. He found David Lee Jr. (1941–2021) playing with George French's Funk Incorporated at the Horse Stable club, and by the end of the night, Gillespie offered Lee a job. Lee turned him down, but Gillespie was persistent and returned the following night. Lee finally agreed, if the trumpeter would get him a new set of drums. He set out on a road that would make him one of the most in-demand jazz drummers during the 1970s.[61]

Lee's story is a classic New Orleans drum story. As a child, he was completely taken by the sound of the bass drum on Mardi Gras. Inspired by the parade music, he improvised by drumming on telephone books and got his first drums as a teenager. He learned from his three brothers, who were drummers, and played in high school. He developed by playing with other up-and-coming drummers. He would get together with Mickey Conway and John Boudreaux and set up three drum sets: "Just trading fills, trading eighths, playing sixteenths, whatever. You know, play up, play slow, play ballads, trading ideas, getting ideas from each other." One of his earliest professional gigs was with R&B pianist and singer Eddie Bo. Lee joined the U.S. Army after high school and played in the Fourth Army Band in Texas and the Eighth Army Band in Korea.[62]

Back in New Orleans, Lee connected with the brothers pianist Willie Tee (Wilson Turbinton) and saxophonist Earl Turbinton, drumming in their R&B/funk band Willie Tee and the Souls, which also included guitarist George Davis and bassist George French. This gave Lee an outlet to play funk; however, they also formed the New Orleans Jazz Collective, which enabled Lee to experiment and develop his jazz chops. Lee recalls: "I used to play timpani and other percussion instruments in the concert band, and so when I listened to music I would hear [that] the drums shouldn't be playing in this spot, or this should be a timpani roll here, and I started to play like that. And Willy and [the others]

David Lee, ca. 1975. Lee was one of the most in-demand jazz drummers in the 1970s, working with the likes of Dizzy Gillespie, Sonny Rollins, and Roy Ayers. Photo by Bob Cummins from the India Navigation LP. Courtesy of Beth Cummins. AI-enhanced image courtesy of JS Makkos/Intelligent Archives for the New Orleans Jazz Museum.

went with me to the point where we didn't sound like nobody down here."[63] A young Johnny Vidacovich witnessed many of those performances: "David was always taking a chance, moving forward, even at the risk of being criticized or not sounding good, but at least he was trying something new, extending, extending, extending."[64] Fred Staehle also attended the Sunday sessions and was knocked out by Lee's drumming: "Bad. He surpassed James Black, and all he did was add another tom-tom. He was using four tom-toms instead of three and making up melodic figures the way he played. He was outstanding."[65]

That ability to move between funk and jazz seemed to be what Gillespie was searching for that night on Bourbon Street. Lee recognized that the veteran bebop innovator was looking to update his sound: "Dizzy was bridging the gap between boogaloo, swing and bebop."[66] That boogaloo beat gained prominence in jazz thanks to Idris Muhammad's "Alligator Boogaloo" with Lou Donaldson, and Lee's variation on that second line–derived groove is evident on tracks like "Alligator," "Matrix," and "Soul Kiss" that he recorded with Gillespie on the album *The Real Thing* (1970). He remained with the trumpeter for about a year, and his reputation was established. Lee moved to New York, and the status he attained is indicated by his work on pianist Joe Zawinul's album *Zawinul* (1971), playing percussion alongside the likes of Billy Hart, Joe Chambers, and Jack DeJohnette. After working with vibraphonist Roy Ayers, Lee joined saxophonist Sonny Rollins for a three-year stint starting in 1972, including recording two studio albums, *Next Album* (1972) and *Horn Culture* (1973), and a live album, *The Cutting Edge* (1974). During his time in New York, he also drummed for a wide array of jazz artists, including Chet Baker, Leon Thomas, Charlie Rouse, and Larry Coryell.

In 1974, Lee released his independently recorded *Evolution* album, one of the most innovative—if underrecognized—Drumsville recordings. Only about four hundred copies were released on his own Supernal label. Conceived as a "suite for drums," on the three tracks it features his longtime bandmate George Davis on guitar (who also joined Gillespie's band that fateful night on Bourbon Street) and bassist Bob Cranshaw, a veteran Rollins sideman. The trio tracks reflect Lee's R&B background, as well as the then current jazz fusion approach of bands like Tony Williams's Lifetime and Chick Corea's Return to Forever. The remaining twelve pieces are multitracked solo performances by Lee—a modern-day extension of the solo recordings Baby Dodds made three decades earlier—on a vast array of percussion instruments, including drum set, cow bell, hand bells, orchestral bells, beads, chimes, shaker plunk, vibes, tympani, tambourine, and gong. He also adds bass, guitar, piano, organ, and vocals. The technique and chops are absolutely dazzling, regardless of what percussion instrument Lee picks up, whether it's the cosmic swirl of cymbals on "Spirit Voice" or the tom-tom, hi-hat African-derived groove on "Wymbo-Ngoma," the fluid jangling of bells on "Freedom Bells," or the rolling Gamelan-like "Acknowledgement." Coming up in New Orleans, Lee found a role model in Ed Blackwell, whose influence on his drum set playing is evident in the seven-part *Evolution* suite. His approach to percussion is compositional; the performances are structured, evoke moods, and tell a story. *Evolution* is absolutely a visionary work, and, thankfully, it was reissued on CD by Soul Jazz Records in 2010. Lee returned to New Orleans in the 1980s, working with an array of local leaders, including Earl Turbinton, singer Germaine Bazzle, and Ellis Marsalis and keeping the beat alive through teaching such Drumsville stars as Brian Blade, Jason Marsalis, and Adonis Rose.

RHYTHM & BLUES AND FUNK

During the late 1940s and early 1950s, the rhythm and blues genre emerged and came to the forefront of African American popular music. New Orleans drummers led the way in establishing grooves for this new sound, particularly at the legendary J&M Recording Studio, which produced a parade of genre-defining hit records. By the late 1960s, the New Orleans beat played a central role in the advent of funk music, shaping seductive, enduring grooves that eventually provided beats that were frequently sampled by hip-hop artists.

Earl Palmer: "A Professor of the Drums"

On November 10, 1945, following his service in Europe during World War II, Earl Palmer (1924–2008) was discharged from the U.S. Army in Newport News, Virginia. After a stop in Camp Shelby, Mississippi, he arrived back in New Orleans and shortly thereafter attended a double-bill, big band concert featuring Dooky Chase's Young Swingsters opening for the Billy Eckstine Orchestra. Palmer recalls: "Vernel Fournier played with Dookie [sic] Chase's band and he was boiling. I heard Vernel and Art Blakey the same night just after I come out of the service and right then and there's what got me playing drums."[67] Palmer's decision to become a drummer was a major step forward in the evolution of the New Orleans beat; his signature backbeat—the emphasis on the second and fourth beat of a 4/4 or 12/8 bar—would transform the next half century of American popular music and make Drumsville's impact felt throughout the music, film, and television industries.

Rhythm was ubiquitous in Palmer's life. Born in Treme, his father was most likely the pianist and band leader Walter "Fats" Pichon, with whom Palmer had very little contact. His mother and aunt, Thelma and Nita Theophile, were dancers in a number of vaudeville troupes. By age four or five, Palmer was tap dancing on Bourbon Street for tips, and like "Stalebread" Lacoume and Danny Barker before him, he and his friends improvised their first instruments: "We used to make our drums out of crates, lard cans, can covers, inner tubes for springs and take 'em out there and dance. We'd put Coca-Cola tops under our

Earl Palmer, in 2002, when he donated his Rodgers drum set to the New Orleans Jazz Museum. During the 1950s, Palmer's signature backbeat transformed the next half century of American popular music and made Drumsville's impact felt throughout the music, film, and television industries. Photo by Greg Lambousy. Courtesy of the New Orleans Jazz Museum.

shoes and then the more you'd dance on 'em, the deeper they dug in there, so we even made our own taps for our shoes."[68] He and his friends also performed for tips at Louis Prima's club at Beverly Gardens. But, Palmer's days on the streets of New Orleans were limited, and he was soon on the road with his mother and aunt, including an extended stay with Ida Cox's *Darktown Scandals*. He became a featured tap dancer and picked up some basics on the drums during his eleven years on the vaudeville circuit.

Following through on his resolution to become a drummer after hearing Fournier and Blakey, Palmer purchased his first set of drums from band leader Harold Dejan. Palmer recalls that those drums "had a beautiful waterfall and a nude woman on the other side and a 25 watt light bulb and when you hit the bass drum, the vibration of that bass drum on the opposite head, the vibration [would] come right from the center and go outward, so the nude woman was moving right under the waterfall."[69] Encouraged by tenor saxophonist Alvin "Red" Tyler to use his GI benefits to get formal musical training, Palmer enrolled in the Grunewald School of Music: "My drum teacher was [Louis] Bob Barbarin, Paul's brother. Bob was the formal drummer—see Paul didn't read or anything like that, he was just a great player. Bob was the one who was able to teach."[70] While he was already considered a top drummer in New Orleans, Palmer studied music theory and learned to read music and write arrangements—skills that would serve him well as his career evolved. Even though Gruenwald's was segregated, Palmer found that the jam sessions held with both groups of musicians helped to break down some of the racial barriers that African American musicians faced:

But, the important thing to us was when we got an opportunity to mix with the guys downstairs because there were many wonderful musicians and nice guys down there. You know, everybody isn't a Klansman. But we were able to mix with them and exchange musical ideas, and that was good for us 'cause it also gave an opportunity to let them hear our musical expertise, except listening to it on Bourbon Street or in a funeral setting. And playing with them, we were able to exchange ideas and get to know each other.[71]

By 1947, Palmer had joined trumpeter Dave Bartholomew's band, and when Palmer made his recording debut with the leader, Drumsville was at the forefront of the emergence of R&B and, soon after, rock and roll, once again generating a rhythmic revolution in American popular music. Drummer John Boudreaux, a member of the next generation of New Orleans drummers, describes Palmer's innovation: "Earl Palmer is credited with playing a six-eight blues beat, six-eight with a backbeat. He's supposed to be the one guy that started that. And they made a million records with that beat on it."[72]

Palmer played a central role in initiating the rise to stardom of pianist and singer Antoine "Fats" Domino, boosting his early career and laying down an infectious beat on a series of hits, including "The Fat Man," "I'm in Love Again," "Poor Me," and "I'm Walkin'."

For a decade, Palmer was the go-to drummer at Cosimo Matassa's J&M Recording Studio, where the Bartholomew band provided the backup for a succession of artists looking for the New Orleans beat to propel them to the top of the charts, including, to name just a few, Lloyd Price, Little Richard, Shirley and Lee, Big Joe Turner, and Larry Williams. Palmer was a tremendous asset for Bartholomew, who produced and wrote many of these hits: "He was instrumental in doing everything on a session; he was never lost for ideas. Most people say Earl Palmer was a rock 'n' roll drummer. He's not a rock 'n' roll drummer, . . . Earl Palmer's a professor of the drums. He could play any kind of rhythm, and on top of that he'd write music and read music, so all that made it good. He was a finished drummer and he could adopt any style."[73] Likewise, Matassa, who engineered the sessions, viewed Palmer's drumming as crucial to the live, largely no-overdub recordings: "First of all, he was an absolute master at controlling tempo . . . He had an amazing sense of time, and his beat was like the Rock of Gibraltar; it was just as steady and solid. You could build on anything he did, 'cause it was not gonna waver. And also, he drove a group; he could play without raising the tempo or speeding up as they went along. You knew it was more impulsive and driving and demanding, you know."[74]

Left to right: Cosimo Matassa, Antoine "Fats" Domino, and Earl Palmer, ca. 2000. Record producer Matassa: "[Palmer] had an amazing sense of time, and his beat was like the Rock of Gibraltar; it was just as steady and solid. You could build on anything he did, 'cause it was not gonna waver." Photo copyright © David Lind. Courtesy of the New Orleans Jazz Museum. Accession number 201.025.8.

Even though Palmer was essentially defining what it meant to play drums in R&B and rock 'n' roll, he viewed himself as a jazz drummer in the tradition that Baby Dodds had established. Palmer describes one of his innovations:

> I started playing jazz and New Orleans style blues, which later became rhythm & blues, when you start putting more of a beat to it from the drum aspect. The rhythm played on the hi-hat changed too. It used to be: *Tish—ship-ta tish—ship-ta.* I don't care what kind of old jazz you were playing, that was it, until they started playing: *Tick—ta tick—ta tick—ta tick—ta.* Which was the shuffle on the hi-hat, still keeping the afterbeat on the snare. After the shuffle on the hi-hat came straight eighths and then triplets for the ballads. The blues and rhythm & blues was a more exuberant music, so you played a little harder and you played on the hi-hat so it wasn't ringing through everything, as it would if you were on the ride cymbal. You were behind singers most of the time. You couldn't cover them up with a swimming cymbal.[75]

This new rhythmic conception was grounded in traditional jazz and ultimately in the interaction between the bass drum and the snare drum in New Orleans brass bands. As Palmer explains:

> In my case I combined what the snare drum players were playing with what the bass drum players were playing with a little more up-to-date funky thing. Take one old drummer like Bill Phillips. He was doing that already, playing what two snare drum players and a bass

Earl Palmer's floor tom. Palmer: "Dr. John and Earl King tell me I was the first one to use the word funky in relation to music. I had forgotten all about it." Photo by Grace Patterson. Courtesy of the New Orleans Jazz Museum. Accession number 2005.014 a.

drum player in a parade band, a funeral band, would play—he'd be playing that on a set of drums. The same thing with New Orleans traditional jazz drummers.[76]

Like Buddy Bolden introducing the "big four" lilt into the emerging jazz form six decades earlier, Palmer's backbeat, with its the emphasis on the second and fourth beat, was similarly transformative, and his description of the approach he introduced as a "more up-to-date funky thing" illustrates how his drumming embodies a continuum of the rhythmic conceptions that stretch from turn-of-the-nineteenth-century New Orleans brass bands and traditional jazz to modern jazz, rhythm and blues, rock and roll, and the rise of funk. In fact, Palmer may have introduced the term "funky" to describe a musical approach: "Speaking of funky, Dr. John and Earl King tell me I was the first one to use the word funky in relation to music. I had forgotten all about it."[77] Biographer Tony Scherman sums up his impact on modern drumming:

> In Earl Palmer you also got an innovator who rewrote the book on rhythm in popular music. Earl may or may not have been literally the first, but he was easily the first widely heard drummer to streamline the shuffle beat of rhythm and blues into the proto-typical rock-and-roll beat . . . [H]is achievement was to overhaul pop music's rhythmic foundation, discarding an "old-fashioned" jazz-based sound for something new: the headlong thrust of rock and roll.[78]

In 1957, Palmer headed west to the burgeoning recording studio scene in Los Angeles, expanding the horizons of the influence of the New Orleans beat. Palmer's extensive work in New Orleans with Bartholomew gave him the confidence to explore new turf: "Well, when I first went out there I went out there knowing that I was going to do some work right away because most of the guys, the record companies that I worked for out there before I started doing the film work, were guys who were bringing the bands here to make records with our group."[79] He became a member of the legendary group of top-flight session players known as the "Wrecking Crew." Testimony to Bartholomew's assessment that Palmer was a "finished drummer" who "could adopt any style" is certainly found in the volume and range of records on which he performed in Los Angeles, including such singles as Bobby Day's "Rockin' Robin," Little Richard's "Good Golly Miss Molly," Richie Valens's "La Bamba," Ray Charles's "I Can't Stop Loving You," Jan and Dean's "Surf City," Sam Cooke's "A Change Is Gonna Come," and Ike and Tina Turner's "River Deep—Mountain High." Palmer's drum mastery was featured on albums by artists that ranged from Frank Sinatra to Ricky Nelson; from the Beach Boys to Dizzy Gillespie; from the Monkees, to James Brown; and from Barbara Streisand to Tom Waits. He also took his drum mastery into the realm of soundtracks for film, including *Judgement at Nuremberg, Cool Hand Luke, In the Heat of the Night, Lady Sings the Blues,* and *The Rose,* and for television with *77 Sunset Strip, I Dream of Jeanie, The Odd Couple,* and *M*A*S*H.*[80] Considering his pervasive presence in music, film, and television, it would be hard for an individual who had any contact with popular culture for almost three decades to not be exposed to his drumming rooted in the New Orleans beat.

Palmer boasted that "New Orleans was a town that was known for drummers,"[81] and his awareness of the transformative influence his rhythmic talents on the evolution of the New Orleans beat is evident in *Drumsville,* the title of his 1961 album of instrumental remakes of classic hits he propelled. The stature that Palmer achieved is also evident in his election to serve as the treasurer for Local 47 of the American Federation of Musicians in Los Angeles. He used his position to help many older recording artists and/or their families, particularly from New Orleans, to access royalties that had accrued over the years. In 2000, he was inducted into the Rock & Roll Hall of Fame in the "Award for Musical Excellence" category. From the rhythms that he learned as a kid on the streets of New Orleans to his professional work first as a dancer and then as a drummer, Earl Palmer spread the New Orleans beat far and wide and made an indelible impact on the development of American popular music.

EARL KING: "THEY CAME HERE MOSTLY FOR DRUMMERS"— CHARLES "HUNGRY" WILLIAMS, JOSEPH "SMOKEY" JOHNSON, AND ALBERT JUNE GARDNER

Earl Palmer's departure for Los Angeles in 1957 opened the door for a new wave of New Orleans drummers to contribute to the evolution of Drumsville. As singer, guitarist, and songwriter Earl King explains:

> Here in New Orleans, everybody used to come to record. They came here mostly for drummers, late '40s, early '50s. Drumming was the most significant thing. Everybody would come down here and say, "The beat, the beat, the beat." Over the years drummers have contributed a lot to the R&B scene that emanated out of New Orleans. We had Earl Palmer here, who was a very versatile drummer. He pioneered a lot of things. I think when the R&B scene really got stiff here that's when Charlie Williams—we call him "Hungry" . . . began doing things with this Latin connotation added to the Dixieland music. So people began coming down here to get, they would get "Hungry" and fly him different places to make sessions. Then we had Smokey Johnson, who came up and formulated some things off of Charlie Williams and kept the ball going. We had numerous drummers back in the '50s who evolved the R&B scene down here.[82]

Charles "Hungry" Williams: "I Started Double Clutchin'"

In his early teens, Charles "Hungry" Williams (1935–1986) began hanging out at a club called the Pepper Pot in Gretna. The house band was a trio led by pianist and singer Professor Longhair and included Walter "Papoose" Nelson on guitar and Milton Stevens on drums. Williams recalls those days at the West Bank club in an interview with Tad Jones and Mac Rebennack: "I used to go up there to dance and things, and Fess was playing up there. I'd worry Fess to death to sit in with him. At the time, he had a guy named Milton Stevens on drums. He was one of the best brush men to ever come out of New Orleans . . . I finally convinced him to let me sit in. My timing and things was bad, but I did the best I

Charles "Hungry" Williams, ca. 1983. Alvin "Red" Tyler: "[Williams] would do things on the drums most drummers would say, 'How does he do that?' And it was only because he didn't know you weren't supposed to do this." From *Wavelength Magazine*. Gift of Dr. Connie Atkinson. Courtesy of the New Orleans Jazz Museum. AI-enhanced image courtesy of JS Makkos/ Intelligent Archives for the New Orleans Jazz Museum.

could do."[83] Things may have started out "bad" at the Pepper Pot, but within a few years, Williams advanced the evolution of the New Orleans beat with the "Latin connotation" described by King and became one of Drumsville's premier session men.

Like both Louis Armstrong and Deacon Frank Lastie before him, Williams's initial musical training came when he was sent to the Municipal Boys Home (Colored Waif's Home for Boys), where he was taught by Peter Davis, the same teacher who had introduced Armstrong to the cornet. Davis insisted that Williams learn to play the trumpet, despite the youngster's desire to play drums. And, like so many New Orleans drummers who preceded him, Williams improvised a way to beat out the rhythms he was hearing:

> So even after Mr. Dave used to try and drive this into my head, I used to go sit in the gym in the evening when I got out of school, and I'd take my knee and sit on the bench next to a door. I used to beat my knee for a bass drum on the door, and I had me two wooden sticks and I'd beat on the bench. I had everybody in the gym crowded around me. I was doing it then. I sounded good even with that.[84]

Davis made Williams a drum major and eventually put him on snare drum in the parade band. But Williams was determined to get behind the drum set, and Davis finally let him practice with a drummer named "Crazy Harold," who every weekend had a set of drums in the gym: "One evening Mr. Dave said, 'Look, Charlie, while Harold is in the gym practicing, you can practice with him.' So that's how I got introduced to a set."[85] Returning to his mother's West Bank home in McDonoghville, Williams revived his improvised drumming by playing on tin cans on a bench outside a sweet shop and eventually got behind Stevens's drum set with Longhair at the Pepper Pot. When his mother moved across the river to the Lower Ninth Ward, Williams came into contact with local hero pianist and singer Fats Domino, who was performing in neighborhood clubs. He became Domino's valet and often would set up Cornelius "Tenoo" Coleman's drums. Williams found his "idol," who was another left-handed drummer: "The cat, man, the fastness. This cat had hands, man, out of sight. And he was so unorthodox, you know, because Tenoo would be sitting way down here, and the drums would be way up here; he had to reach up . . . He was about 5′8″, 5′9″, or something like that. And the things that he'd do. I couldn't understand how he got around those drums sitting like that. And he was so fast, man, and the cat used to *play*" (italics in original).[86]

Williams began sitting in at a downtown club, the Tijuana, and wound up taking over the drum chair in the house band. Earl Palmer recalls hearing him there: "Hungry came up around a place called The Tijuana a blues club where they used to have female impersonator shows and that kinda stuff. That's where Hungry played most of the time. He sure could play. He didn't know how good he was because he wasn't no formal drummer. Man, he was awesome."[87] It was a transformative gig for Williams. His wife, Sarah, who was a bartender at the Tijuana, used her savings to buy him his first set of drums, and the exposure brought him recognition as an innovator on the instrument:

Paul [Gayten] and Earl Palmer and all of 'em used to come up there just to listen to me play, because they couldn't understand what I was doing. I used to, I still do it, I played thirty-second notes with my left hand, and no drummers could do that. Plus I had a mixture. My music, my drumming, is between calypso and rock, you know, blues. I had something different going. Like I say, it's a mixture. I had calypso going and funk at the same time. I started the "double clutchin'" with my bass drum, with my foot. I started "double clutchin'." Didn't no other drummer do that.

Williams describes "double clutchin'" as "a double beat on the bass drum that makes it funky."[88] It was also at the Tijuana that Williams began jamming with a Cuban drummer and adapting Latin rhythms to his playing on a drum set: "We had a cat named Ricardo Lopez; he was Cuban. We'd have like a battle between the congas and the bongos and the drums. So maybe that's why my drummin' is a mixture of Latin American."[89] Earl King witnessed those jams:

I've seen him do things with his left hand; I'm still waiting for another drummer to do it. It would go off like a machinegun, man—brrrr—real fast, and you look at it and you don't believe it. You'd say, "Wow, man!" Charles' playing emanated out of the calypso-type stuff, that Latin-type stuff. When I first heard him he really sounded Latin; he used to play with a Cuban guy. Every Latin rhythm he could play, Charles would duplicate it on the set—they used to have battles at the Club Tijuana.[90]

He also worked regularly with band leader Paul Gayten, who recognized Williams's rhythmic genius: "For a while I had one of the greatest drummers in the world—that was Hungry Williams."[91] Mac Rebennack explains that Williams stepped up and filled the void in the Drumsville studio scene left by Palmer's departure: "There was search high and low; every session practically had a different drummer for a time. And finally Charlie Williams, who was the funkiest of them all, he just took it."[92] And like Palmer before him, Williams was featured on a parade of hits by a who's who of New Orleans R&B, including Fats Domino's "Whole Lotta Loving"; Huey "Piano" Smith's "Don't You Just Know It"; Chris Kenner's "Sick and Tired"; Earl King's "Well'o Well'o Well'o, Baby"; Bobby Mitchell's "I'm Gonna Be a Wheel Someday"; Frankie Ford's "Sea Cruise"; and Tommy Ridgely's "The Girl Across the Street." For a leader like Ridgley, Williams was indispensable to the records' grooves: "Hungry was on drums; this particular beat was his style—nobody could duplicate what he was doing."[93] Williams also reconnected with Gayten, who had moved from performing to producing for Chess Records. He brought Williams into the studio to make a number of sides as a leader, including the single "So Glad She's Mine" with its captivating syncopated groove. Williams describes the impact of the innovations that he brought to the New Orleans beat:

When I went into the studio, and started playing all these different things, they were surprised, because I started a whole new thing in rock. And people started eating it up. I have had drummers come and ask me what I was doing. Even when I came to New York in '57 when I was working with Mickey and Sylvia . . . the guy asked me did I need any help, 'cause at the time they were using a drummer to play the high hat and another one to play the backbeat, because the drummer couldn't play the 6/8 on the cymbal at the same time. They were using two drummers to do that. I said, "I don't need that, man."[94]

He was a natural who reinforced the Afro-Caribbean polyrhythms that had laid the foundation for the New Orleans beat in antebellum Congo Square. For saxophonist Alvin "Red" Tyler, Williams was a one-of-a-kind musician:

> This guy had more natural ability than all of them put together. He was another musician who couldn't read a note, but as far as feeling, he would do things on the drums most drummers would say, "How does he do that?" And it was only because he didn't know you weren't supposed to do this. He did a lot of things and [would] go into passages that better drummers would say, "He's not going to come out on time," but he did. The whole feeling had something to do with the popularity of the records as well.[95]

From beating out rhythms on a gymnasium bleacher and tin cans on the street, Charles "Hungry" Williams went on to provide the compelling grooves for countless classic R&B recordings and extend the development of the New Orleans beat.

Joseph "Smokey" Johnson: "You've Gotta Be on Fire"

By 1964, "Smokey" Johnson was a mainstay on sessions at J&M Recording Studios. He was the perfect drummer to deliver the second-line funk for a session produced by Earl King and Wardell Quezergue, which was aimed at reviving Professor Longhair's career with a recording of King's composition "Big Chief." Johnson arrived early at J&M to meet with Longhair and work out the groove. And what a groove he came up with! Johnson drew upon that improvisatory spirit that reaches back to Congo Square in a studio that stood directly across the street from the locale of those antebellum drum circles: "I was looking for something [unique] to play on a record. I turned the floor tom over on its side and played on the side of the floor tom [right hand] and I was playing rim shots on the snare drum, I also took two sticks full of Coke caps that I had nailed on. I had two big ones that I overdubbed on that track."[96] Johnson recalled that it was a marathon studio session. As he told interviewer Bunny Matthews: "We must've did about 35 takes. My hand was bleeding from playing the drums."[97] The effort (and blood) was worth it, and the two-part single released on Watch Records is a New Orleans R&B classic.

Joseph "Smokey" Johnson (1936–2015) earned his nickname purportedly when Palmer said his drumming was so intense that he saw smoke coming out of the bass drum. Like Palmer, Johnson was born and raised in the Treme neighborhood:

> I started playing drums when I was about 12 years old. Before I started on the drums, I was on the trombone. I played in the school band at Craig School and I played at Clark High. My music teacher used to live next door to me—her name was Yvonne Bush. She taught all the cats that can play—John Boudreaux, James Black, Arthur Reed, Nat Perrilliat, George

Davis. She was a trombone player. Her sister was a drummer—Dolores Bush. I used to always be banging on her drums so I just moved over to the drums.[98]

Johnson's drumming skills advanced so rapidly that when he was a freshman Miss Bush placed him in the senior band at Joseph S. Clark High School. It is likely that the milieu of Treme was equally important in shaping Johnson as a musician. He recalls working together with drummers like John Boudreaux: "We used to practice for eight hours a day, every day!"[99] He began working professionally before he graduated: "Back in those days, we had to get permission to play in the clubs—the principal had to sign. I started playing in clubs when I was about 17. The most popular joint was the Dew Drop. I played at the Tiajuana [*sic*] and I would go on the road with different cats during my summer vacation. I was playing with Sugar Boy [Crawford]—the band was called the Cane Cutters or the Chapaka Shaweez."[100] Other early experiences included playing R&B with singer Roy ("Good Rockin' Tonight") Brown and jazz with saxophonist Alvin "Red" Tyler. Longtime friend saxophonist Edward Kidd Jordan told Geraldine Wycoff: "He was a very creative musician and he could play in all genres of music. And he could do it at a very young age."[101]

Johnson came into his own when he became *the* drummer for producer and bandleader Dave Bartholomew, appearing on countless sessions for the Imperial label, including classic recordings with artists like Earl King and Snooks Eaglin. Johnson's versatility on the drums is evident on Bartholomew's big band jazz album *New Orleans House Party* (1963) featuring the hard-swinging instrumental showcase "Portrait of a Drummer." Johnson recalls: "I did a big band album with Dave. After I did that album, I was recording with everybody."[102] Johnson was a busy man, and his street beat–inspired drumming also was essential to many of the recordings produced by Quezergue.

Thanks to Johnson, the New Orleans beat played a profound role in shaping the soul music that began dominating the national charts in the early 1960s. In 1963, led by producer/promoter Joe Jones, a contingent of New Orleans musicians, including Johnson, King, Jordan, Quezergue, George French, Johnny Adams, and Esquerita (Eskew Reeder) traveled to Detroit to meet with Motown label founder Berry Gordy. Johnson describes the venture: "We thought we were going up there to record but when we got there we actually found that we were going up there to audition. Well, we weren't gonna go up there and do no auditions. But after Berry Gordy heard what we had—we went up there with a lot of original tunes, especially Earl—after he heard that band, he was ready to start recording then and there."[103] King feels that it actually was Johnson's drumming that most impressed the Motown honchos: "In fact, if Clarence Paul and Berry Gordy hadn't been so knocked out by Smokey's drumming, we might have been on our way home the day after we got there. But they heard Smokey and said be there by 7 a.m. tomorrow and be ready to cut."[104] For Esquerita, it is their bottom-up rhythms that captivated the Detroit musicians: "We just started jammin', payin' no mind, carryin' on and Berry taped us right there in Hitsville USA. I saw 'em all there, Diana Ross, Smokey Robinson, all of 'em. They were nowhere near our sound, that funky bottom stuff we brought up from New

Joseph "Smokey" Johnson. Joseph "Zigaboo" Modeliste: "Smokey, that was the drum god for me . . . [He had] so much attitude to drumming, so much spirit." Photo by Eric Waters.

Orleans." Johnson also feels it was the bass drum emphasis that knocked out the Motown folks: "The difference is the bass drum. The cats don't play the bass drum nowhere else. New Orleans drummers—they're laying it down. That comes from hearing them street parades, them marching bands and all that—you hear that bass drum. When they start to play, they learn how to play the bass drum."[105] Jones bears witness to the impact of Johnson's drumming: "They had Stevie Wonder study Smokey; they made Motown drummers into a school and studied just what he was doing."[106] Johnson recalls the impact that his grooves had:

> And I'll tell you another thing, this ain't no brag. Gordy used to use two drummers on a recording session because them cats didn't play no bass drum. But after he heard the New Orleans stuff I was laying down, he didn't need but one. I'd be sitting behind the drums messin' around and they'd be recording that stuff. I tell you what we were doing. I was recording from like nine o'clock in the morning every day 'til five o'clock in the evening. I can't remember all the stuff I was playing on 'cause they were recording 24 hours a day.[107]

Contractual issues torpedoed the New Orleans/Detroit alliance, and although Johnson stayed with Motown for a few months, he headed south when he got homesick.

Continuing to work sessions in New Orleans, Johnson stepped out on his own on a collaboration with Quezergue on the iconic second-line funk of "It Ain't My Fault," based on a cadence called "Ratty #9" that he had written years earlier as an exercise for Miss Bush. The tune was developed during a rehearsal held in the back of the One-Stop Record Shop on Rampart Street. As Johnson explains: "So Wardell's sitting by the piano. And I was playing this beat. I said, 'Check this beat out, Wardell.' So we got it together right there, by the piano. It took us about ten minutes to put the tune together. 'It Ain't My Fault'—that's where it was born at. Cos [Matassa] told me, he say, 'Wotcha gonna name that, Smokey?' I said, 'I don't know—it ain't my fault!'"[108] Herlin Riley describes the innovative lessons he learned from Johnson's performance on the tune:

> When I heard Smokey play "It Ain't My Fault," it's a tune that's based on the New Orleans street beat drum groove. It's four-bar drum sequence. It starts with a tom-tom roll on the "and" of the four that leads into a bass drum hit on beat one, which starts the sequence. And, then the hi-hat pattern starts on beat two. The bass drum hits again on the beat of the third measure. Then the hit-hat plays the same pattern again. It culminates with a hit of the "big four" in the fourth measure. And, then the sequence starts again. Smokey was able to take a traditional street beat and make it into a signature original composition.[109]

"It Ain't My Fault" stands with Paul Barbarin's "Bourbon Street Parade" and "The Second Line" as ultimate expressions of the second-line groove for brass and marching bands. Johnson recorded a number of tracks as a leader, and with his stripped-down, broken-up syncopated rhythms on songs like "Tippin' Lightly" and "Funkie Moon," he lays down the template for the genre-defining funk instrumentals recorded a few years later by drummer Joseph "Zigaboo" Modeliste with the Meters.[110]

Like the pioneering traditional jazz drummers in New Orleans at the turn of the twentieth century, Johnson's conception of his role was to be at the service of the band. When he backed up leaders like Eddie Bo or Fats Domino, he knew exactly what they were looking for: "You gotta play behind Eddie. You can't be back there, like he'd say, 'shuckin' and jivin'.' You've gotta be on fire behind him because he works hard. You've gotta push. I used to do that behind Fats. I'd put it on him. That's what he likes. But I never was a showoff. I'd just do what I know how to do."[111] In 1973, Johnson joined Domino's touring band and stayed for over two decades. When he had time off, he stretched out playing jazz in clubs around New Orleans with longtime associates like pianist Edward Frank; saxophonists Kidd Jordan, Red Tyler, David Lastie, and Fred Kemp; percussionist Alfred "Uganda" Roberts; and bassist Erving Charles. He brought the syncopated rhythms that can be traced back through traditional jazz, brass bands, and Congo Square to his modern jazz playing:

Al "Carnival Time" Johnson, Smokey Johnson, and Alfred "Uganda" Roberts. Thanks to Smokey Johnson, particularly because of his session work at Motown, the New Orleans beat played a profound role in shaping the grooves for the soul music that began dominating the national charts in the early 1960s. Photo by Eric Waters.

> Well, New Orleans swing music—or Dixieland, as the old men call it—New Orleans swing music has a beat. And you don't hear that beat being played anywhere else. And it kind of rubs off on drummers when they're young. I can be playing a tune like "Cherokee," or "Giant Steps" at a fast tempo, and I can break it down in the chorus by changing rhythms. I can play some second line for eight bars. So you can hear that type of New Orleans swing music in a lot of jazz drummers around here.[112]

Riley explains: "When he plays straight ahead, he knows how to slide the bass drum inside the rhythm to create syncopation."[113]

In 1993, debilitating health issues kept Johnson from getting behind the drum set, but he certainly did not stop keeping the beat. Saxophonist Red Morgan improvised an instrument that Johnson could play by attaching a tambourine and cowbell to a cymbal stand. His final public performance came in a percussion section with drummers Herlin Riley and Alfred "Uganda" Roberts supporting Dr. John at the 2013 Voodoo Fest.[114] The old saying goes, "Where there's smoke, there's fire," and in carrying on the Drumsville tradition, Smokey Johnson was always on fire.

Albert "Gentleman" June Gardner: "People Thought There Were Three Drummers on It"

On January 12, 1963, Sam Cooke took the stage at Harlem Square Club in Miami. The recording from that night, *Live at the Harlem Square Club, 1963* (released in 1985), captured the raw, gritty, incendiary side of the soul music superstar engaged in a dynamic call-and-response with the audience in a predominantly African American nightclub. Drummer Albert "Gentleman" June Gardner (1930–2010) drives the music with his propulsive,

"Gentleman" June Gardner performing in Economy Hall at the 2009 Jazz and Heritage Festival. Photo by Stewart Harvey. Courtesy of the New Orleans Jazz & Heritage Archive.

in-the-pocket rhythms as he works alongside Cooke's regular guitarist Clifton White in a band led by saxophonist King Curtis. That Cooke insisted Gardner remain behind the drums with the saxophonist's renowned outfit, the Kingpins, speaks volumes about the singer's confidence in Gardner to bring the funk to the bandstand. Gardner's Drumsville roots are clearly on display on tracks like "Feel It (Don't Fight It)," with its dynamic snare and bass drum interplay, the way he works the rims of his set on "Cupid," and the unrelenting backbeat on "Bring It on Home to Me." With its release two decades after that night in Miami, *Live at the Harlem Square Club, 1963* is considered one of the greatest live albums of all time.

A testament to why Cooke placed so much faith in Gardner is found on another strikingly different live album, *Sam Cooke at the Copa* (1964), recorded on July 8, 1964, during a two-week engagement at the Copacabana nightclub in New York City. In an interview with Almost Slim, Gardner recalls: "He was great on stage, man! He never went on cold; he'd study the audience from the wings. Sam could dance and sing, but knew just what the pulse of the audience was like. He had little signals he'd give us to change tempos or do a turn-around. Sometimes just before we'd go on he's say, 'Okay guys let's really tear 'em up!'"[115] Clearly Gardner was ready to provide the soul man with whatever groove he wanted, and in New York he was working in a very different setting for a very different crowd. The drummer and the members of Cooke's regular band are joined by Joe Mele's 16-piece Copacabana Band with a program that barely resembles the Miami performance from the previous year. Gardner, who considered himself primarily a jazz drummer, is right at home driving the Copa's horn section. He swings hard on numbers like "The Best Things in Life Are Free" and "Bill Bailey," works in tandem with percussionist Sticks Evans to shape a jaunty Latinesque groove on "Blowin' in the Wind," delivers some handclap-inducing brush work on Cooke's "hootenanny" singalong "If I Had a Hammer," and lays down a funky, second line–inspired, boogaloo beat on "Tennessee Waltz." Gardner's conception of the New Orleans beat placed him at the forefront of shaping the era-defining soul music sound.

Gardner grew up on St. Andrew Street in the neighborhood then known as the Melpomene (Central City), where he convinced his mother to buy him his first set of drums, and, like so many other Drumsville players, he learned his craft in a communal context: "I got lessons from Professor [Valmont] Victor at the Tom Lefont [Thomy Lafon] School. Lessons were 25 cents a week, which was a lot of money then because times were tough. There were a lot of good drummers studying with Professor Victor at the time: Edward Blackwell, Tom Moore and Wilbert [Wilbur] Hogan. We'd get together and exchange ideas and practice."[116] By 1945, he joined guitarist Edgar Blanchard's Gondoliers and found himself at the center of the city's R&B scene working as the house band in the Dew Drop Inn. Gardner's earliest experiences on the road included stints with blues and jazz vocalist Lil Green and R&B pioneer Roy Brown, with whom he recorded such tracks as "This Is My Last Goodbye," "Bootleggin' Baby," and "Up Jumped the Devil": "We cut a lot of those things for the Deluxe label up in Cincinnati! We had a hell of a band then. We had guys like Teddy Riley on trumpet, [Leroy] 'Batman' Rankin on sax and Edward Santino on piano. It was a real learning experience working with Roy; we had some good times and some bad times, but man, we played every place in the country twice!"[117]

Back in New Orleans in the late 1950s, Gardner worked in the studio and on jazz gigs in clubs around town. In 1957, Gardner's jazz chops earned him a call to tour the Middle East with Lionel Hampton's big band. His facility at melding jazz and R&B is featured on the album *Rockin' and Rollin'* (1959) by saxophonist Alvin "Red" Tyler and the Gyros, a band that featured Allen Toussaint on piano, Frank Fields on bass, Justin Adams on guitar, and James Booker on organ. Their version of "The Peanut Vendor," originally the classic Cuban "son-pregón" (street vendor's song), highlights Gardner's mastery of syncopated polyrhythms as he works cowbells, shakers, and his tom-tom and steps out on a percussion/saxophone duet section. And on the track "Snake Eyes," Gardner, like Earl Palmer, flashes his ability to adapt Drumsville's second-line cadences to a rock-and-roll groove.

In 1960, Gardner connected with Cooke through Joe Jones. He essentially switched gigs with Leo Morris, apparently at the instigation of Cooke's band leader, Clifton White. Gardner recalls Cooke's invitation to join the band: "One day he just called me and said he had a job in Richmond, Virginia, and needed a drummer. I said, 'Just wire me the money I'll be there!' It was beautiful right from the beginning."[118] It was quite the auspicious beginning; when he arrived in Richmond, he took the stage with Cooke as part of Irving Fields Biggest Show of Stars that also featured Bobby Rydell, Duane Eddy, Dion, and Bo Diddley.[119] For the next four years, Gardner was on the road with one of soul music's top stars. Although Cooke tended to record in Los Angeles using Earl Palmer, who had played on his initial R&B hits recorded at J&M, Gardner can be heard on the traditional jazz flavored "He's a Cousin of Mine" and the folky adapted children's song "The Piper."[120]

After Cooke's tragic death at the close of 1964, Gardner returned to New Orleans, performing jazz and R&B at clubs and recording sessions. He was one of the pioneers of funk grooves, and his work in the studio with Toussaint resulted in one of the genres early classics: "One of these sessions I'm most proud of is Lee Dorsey's 'Workin' in a Coal Mine.' After the record came out Allen Toussaint told me he'd been in New York and the people thought there were three drummers on it. I did a lot of session with Allen back then."[121] Like Smokey Johnson, Gardner also went into the studio as a leader under the aegis of Wardell Quezergue. The material was right in Gardner's wheelhouse, combining funk grooves with big band horn section arrangements. Highlights include "Mustard Greens," evoking the Afro-Caribbean polyrhythmic percussion of Tyler's "Peanut Vendor," and the King Curtis–style, funky southern soul of "99 Plus One."

Gardner passed the baton to his son Albert "Lil' June" Gardner Jr. (1951–1999), who played drums with the Neville Brothers, Professor Longhair, and Irma Thomas. In his later years, Gardner freelanced around town, working with younger musicians like David Torkanowsky and Irving Mayfield and leading his own traditional jazz outfit, June Gardner and the Fellas. Ultimately, it is his years in the national spotlight with Sam Cooke that made Gentleman June Gardner into a Drumsville legend: "It's pretty gratifying! Playing with Sam was a beautiful period of my life. Nobody's sending me any money but it makes me feel appreciated!"[122]

DR. JOHN: "THE ROOTS OF NEW ORLEANS IS DRUMS"— JOHN BOUDREAUX, FRED STAEHLE, HERMAN "ROSCOE" ERNEST III

Drummers are usually sidemen, and over the years band leaders in New Orleans have had the luxury of choosing from an array of Drumsville musicians who can propel a band with their individual, inventive variations on the signature New Orleans beat. Mac "Dr. John" Rebennack was one of those leaders, and he consistently pointed out the crucial innovations and creative contributions drummers had on bringing the funk to New Orleans music *and beyond.* Throughout a career that spanned seven decades, Rebennack worked with many of the city's finest percussionists. His liner notes to the album *N'Awlinz Dis Dat or D'Udda* (2004) open with the declaration, "The roots of New Orleans is drums."[123] A celebration of the second-line groove, the album features tracks that bring together various combinations of such homegrown drummers and percussionists as Earl Palmer, Smokey Johnson, John Boudreaux, Herman Ernest, Alfred "Uganda" Roberts, and Kenyatta Simon. In his autobiography, *Under a Hoodoo Moon* (1994), Rebennack sings the praises of drummers who have crafted their own take on the second-line groove:

> There are many different styles of second-line drumming, and they are as extreme and different as "Zigaboo" Modeliste drumming on the Meters' records, Vernell Fournier's samba-type groove on Ahmad Jamal's "Poinciana," Earl Palmer's fonky feel on Little Richard's "Slippin' and Slidin,'" or Charles "Hungry" William's fonk on Huey Smith's "High Blood Pressure," or Junie Boy's second-line feel on Lee Dorsey's "Working in a Coal Mine." Of course, the source for this rhythm goes much further back than that. All the old marching bands (and most of the current ones, such as the Dirty Dozen Brass Band) have it. So do spiritual-church cats, like Melvin and David Lastie's father [Deacon Frank Lastie], who was spiritual-church drummer. This style was developed in the fifties by Earl Palmer and Charlie Williams. Later, in the late fifties and early sixties Smokey Joe Johnson and John Boudreaux took it even further.[124]

Rebennack certainly believes that New Orleans drummers were not given their due for the influence they exerted on shaping the grooves that provided the foundation for rock, soul, and funk through the session work of artists like Palmer, Williams, Boudreaux, and James Black. He particularly is aware of the impact of Smokey Johnson's visit to Motown: "They bled a lot of stuff from New Orleans and became the trend setter of a record city when it really bothered me that a lot of their trick drum things and all was Smokey Johnson, John Boudreaux, James Black—New Orleans people." Rebennack asserts that Motown borrowed bits and pieces from New Orleans funk drummers, obscuring the true origin of the grooves and beats: "That's what the American public heard as what funk was. Later when they heard the real shit from New Orleans, it didn't have the impact on them that it should. This is to me a crime.[125] For Rebennack, New Orleans is the source point for funk. As he explains in the liner notes to his *Gumbo* album: "The origin of Funk is in New Orleans, coming out of Mardi Gras music: your basic 2-4 beat with compounded rhythms and syncopation added on."[126] So, it's no surprise that New Orleans drummers were a seminal influence on the drummers who played crucial roles in shaping James Brown's rhythmic funk revolution—John "Jabo" Starks, Clayton Fillyau, and Clyde Stubblefield.[127] Brown may be the man who exhorted his listeners to "give the drummer some!,"[128] but for Rebennack, New Orleans drummers are the ones who deserve wider recognition: "How many musicians do you know who start their musical genesis at the Beatles, or James Brown? Well what do they know about the guy James Brown got his shit from? You got to look at the whole picture if you're going to study music and your instrument."[129]

Rebennack worked with a who's who of New Orleans drummers over the years, from Palmer and Modeliste to Black and Herlin Riley. But the three drummers who most consistently brought the New Orleans beat to his bands both in the studio and on the road were John Boudreaux, Fred Staehle, and Herman "Roscoe" Ernest III.

John Boudreaux: "You Play the Funk Real Tight"

In October 1967, a motley crew of New Orleans musicians came together in Gold Star Studios in Los Angeles to conjure up the music that would become the album *Gris-Gris* (1968), the musical calling card for Dr. John the Night Tripper, the funky, psychedelicized, Mardi Gras, hoodoo, guru persona that Rebennack constructed. Members of his hometown supporting cast included producer and multi-instrumentalist Harold Battiste; pianist Ronnie Barron; singers Tami Lynn, Jessie Hill, and Shirley Goodman; guitarist Ernest McLean; saxophonist Plas Johnson; and drummer John Boudreaux (1936–2017). Billed in the album credits as Dr. Boudreaux of Funky Knuckle Skins, the drummer had been a longtime Rebennack collaborator reaching back to session work at J&M studio in the late 1950s. For *Gris-Gris,* Boudreaux, along with Richard "Didimus" Washington on percussion and Hill on tambourine, broke new rhythmic ground, churning out steamy, swamp funk polyrhythmic grooves.

Boudreaux was born in New Roads, Louisiana, and, at around the age of ten or twelve, moved to New Orleans with his mother to live with his grandmother on St. Philip Street. His grandfather had played bass drum and been Grand Marshall in Mardi Gras parades back in New Roads, but drums were not Boudreaux's first choice: "I wanted to play saxophone but the drum and the saxophone were two different prices. The drum—we're talking snare drum—was a lot cheaper, so my mother bought the drum. That's how I started playing drums. I must have been 14 then."[130] His first musical experiences were in the band at Joseph T. Craig Elementary School, and he played in the marching and

Dr. John Playing congas, performing with Jessie Smith (*right*) and Robbie Montgomery (*above right*), Mardi Gras 1973, St. Bernard Civic Auditorium. Photo by Tad Jones. Loaned by the Hogan Jazz Archive Photography Collection, Tulane University Special Collections, Tulane University; New Orleans, LA. Accession number OPH000790.

AFO executives, early 1960s. Standing, *left to right:* Alvin "Red" Tyler, John Boudreaux, Roy Montrell, and Peter "Chuck" Badie; (sitting, *left to right*): Melvin Lastie and Harold Battiste. From the Harold R. Batiste Papers. Courtesy of Amistad Research Center.

concert bands, first at Booker T. Washington and later at Clark High Schools.[131] Boudreaux bought his first drum set for seventy-five dollars by saving up his three-dollar weekly pay from an after-school job at the laundry where his mother worked.[132]

The communal spirit among New Orleans drummers, aimed at both advancing their skills and maintaining and extending the tradition, played a role in Boudreaux's development. He often practiced alongside other drummers like Leo Morris (Idris Muhammad), David Lee Jr., Mickey Conway, James Black, and Smokey Johnson. Muhammad recalls those practice sessions: "It was a natural thing—John Boudreaux and Smokey (Johnson) and I used to practice in my house and they were the better drummers. Smokey could play all of Art Blakey's stuff, John could play all of Max Roach's things, and I was just listening . . . I thought it was unusual that three drummers could play and be such close friends, you know, we were just trying to play the instrument."[133] The willingness to encourage and share knowledge between drummers was also evident when Muhammad's older brother, drummer Weedy Morris, heard Boudreaux and Johnson drumming in the street on the way home from a football game:

> So [Leo's brother] came up to us and he said, "Man, you all know anything about rudiments?" 'Cause we didn't know. [LAUGHS] I mean we wasn't great at the time, but we had a knack, you know, we was getting there. So he looked at us, and he knew we didn't know shit, you know. [LAUGHS] So he said, "I'm going to show you fellows how to play a single paradiddle." And he showed us that one rudiment. From then on, me and Smokey was looking up rudiments to play, 'cause I never knew that a drummer was supposed to play rudiments.[134]

By 1954, Boudreaux was a member of the Hawketts and made his first mark in New Orleans funk history with the recording of "Mardi Gras Mambo," a song that clearly illustrates the relation of the New Orleans beat to the Afro-Caribbean diaspora. He explains: "The band used to do calypso/rumba types of stuff because that came off of Professor Longhair 's music, so it was easy to go in that direction . . . He had a rumba rhythm with another kind of New Orleans–type drum sound. *Mardi Gras Mambo* wasn't exactly like that, but we were trying to play a calypso-type style."[135] Boudreaux went on the road with a phony Shirley and Lee act, worked with pianist Eddie Bo, and was the house drummer at the Dew Drop Inn, supporting such artists as Charles Brown, Big Maybelle, and Joe Tex. He also took over the drum chair in the House Rockers so Jessie Hill could become the front man.

By the late 1950s, Rebennack had begun to oversee sessions for record labels like Ric, Ron, and Ace; Boudreaux was often the drummer he called, playing on the Ron label's biggest hit, Irma Thomas's first recording, "Don't Mess with My Man." Rebennack tapped

Boudreaux for the 1959 Professor Longhair session on Ric, which resulted in the iconic Carnival recording, "Go to the Mardi Gras." Longhair, who had drummed in spasm bands as a kid, possessed an ingenious rhythmic sensibility that had a defining impact on the New Orleans beat. Boudreaux describes the complexity of that sensibility: "Basically he would play two or three, maybe four different rhythms just by himself. He would kick the piano with one foot, play a bass line sort of in a half-time, play his right hand in double-time motion. And sometimes a triple or quadruple motion. It was sort of like a very hip rhumba. That's the only way I can explain it."[136] In the studio, the pianist and singer knew exactly what he wanted from his drummer. Rebennack recalls: "We began recording his song 'Hey Now Baby, Hey Now Honey Child.' For starters, Fess sat down on John's drums and played what he wanted John to play. Fess was very specific about what he was looking for in the drums; John played it to death."[137] For Boudreaux, Longhair's rhythmic influence was profound: "He made everybody start thinking a little different."[138]

With a track record of working under Rebennack's aegis, Boudreaux soon found himself in the studio with producer Allen Toussaint. His distinctive take on the New Orleans beat propels such R&B classics as Ernie K-Doe's "Mother-in-Law," Chris Kenner's "Land of a Thousand Dances," and Lee Dorsey's "Ya Ya." Toussaint had definite ideas on what he wanted his session musicians to play, but Boudreaux had the chops and creative impulses to give the producer what he was looking for:

> I guess I had a certain simplicity . . . I didn't play so complicated as the other drummers played and then too . . . I could be dictated to . . . Toussaint was a really hard fellow to please. He used to give me things that seemed almost impossible to do at first until I'd play with it awhile. I remembered on this session, LAND OF A 1000 DANCES, I was sittin' by, while Saint was rehearsing the band, without drums. So when it came time for me to play the drums, I had thought of a little beat that I was scared to try 'cause I thought they'd all laugh. So I played it, and Nat [Perrilliat] and Toussaint looked up and said, "Whaat?"[139]

Responding to Toussaint's demands helped shape Boudreaux's conception of funk drumming: "He'd say, 'Play something other than cymbals. Find something else to play on.' So what I started doing was playing on the rim of the floor tom." His focus turned to the roots of the New Orleans beat: "Because the cymbals resonates all over the music. I mean, in jazz, that's the thing. That's what they want. But this funky music, you can't really play that tight if you're playing it on the cymbal, you know? You play the funk real tight. Most New Orleans drummers had a knack of playing on the snare drum because it came from the parade thing, the second line. It just had a funkier sound."[140] His captivating grooves and masterful ability to provide just the right accents and feel for songs made him one of the city's most in-demand sidemen. As studio engineer Cosimo Matassa told John Broven: "Yeah, John was an accomplished drummer, probably one of the two or three best drummers. He never got the recognition for drumming that he deserved and part of that was his personality, which was kind of introverted and shy—a quiet type. His command . . . he could do whatever needed to be done, and I don't think that there was anything that was foreign to him"[141]

Boudreaux's stature as a top-flight Drumsville session man led to his becoming one of the founders of the African American musicians' collective record label All For One (A.F.O.); he was a member of the house band, the A.F.O. Executives, which also included Battiste on alto saxophone and piano, Melvin Lastie on cornet, Chuck Badie on bass, Alvin "Red" Tyler on tenor saxophone, and Tami Lynn on vocals. The music they made covered a wide range of styles, from the cutting-edge modern jazz on the album *Compendium* (1961) that features the drum showcase "Le John," which illustrates the influence of Ed Blackwell's "correctness and precision" on Boudreaux,[142] to proto-funk R&B on tunes like Barbara George's "I Know" and Prince La La's "She Put the Hurt on Me." Rebennack, who produced and performed on many R&B tracks for A.F.O., is keenly aware of the drummer's far-reaching impact on the conception of funk beats: "What John Boudreaux was doing with the drums on a record like 'She Put the Hurt on Me' deserves a special look. Instead of playing a backbeat on the snare drum, he played all four beats on the snare, a little New Orleans funk cha-cha. Suddenly, the Supremes' 'Baby Love' and other Motown hits had John's groove stamped on them. They didn't know how to play as funky as Boudreaux, but you could hear it all the same."[143] The A.F.O. Executives migrated to Los Angeles in 1963, but contractual issues and the music business's refusal to accept a group that played diverse genres led to their breakup. Some went back to New Orleans. Others, including Boudreaux, stayed, picking up session work and sideman gigs.

He reunited with Rebennack through the session work, leading to his groundbreaking grooves on *Gris-Gris*. The Night Tripper extravaganza was embraced by the psychedelic rock/counterculture audience, which inspired the album *Babylon* (1969). Boudreaux's rhythmic sophistication was central to the project. While it was rooted in New Orleans traditions, it pushed the music into new realms. As Rebennack explains in *Under a Hoodoo Moon:* "The album was based around New Orleans chants, tilted sideways by the odd meters we set them in." Boudreaux's versatility and exceptional skills were perfectly suited to execute those "odd meters" and help Rebennack bring to fruition his sonic vision of a tumultuous, politically charged society. He recalls in his autobiography:

> At times hard-driving, at other times following a deliberately spacy groove, *Babylon* was the band's attempt to say something about the times—and do it with a few unusual time signatures ("Barefoot Lady," for instance, was cut in 11/4, 5/4 and 4/4). The lead song, "Babylon," sets the tone. To a 3/4 and 10/4 groove, it lays out my own sick-ass view of the world then—namely, that I felt our number was about up.[144]

Boudreaux's mastery of complex rhythms and adaptability are apparent on the album as he goes back to New Orleans brass band roots with his martial snare work on "The Patriotic Flag-Waver," lays down some propulsive second-line funk on "Black Widow Spider," and delivers explosive free jazz-like polyrhythms of "The Lonesome Guitar Strangler." When the band was booked for a European tour, Boudreaux decided to step aside; however, the swamp funk sound that he shaped for the first two Dr. John albums extended the rhythmic and sonic possibilities of the New Orleans beat.

Boudreaux remained in Los Angeles doing session work and sideman gigs with a number of New Orleans artists, including Alvin "Shine" Robinson, Jessie Hill, Shirley Goodman, and David Lastie, as well as jazz and blues giants like Eddie "Lockjaw" Davis, Dexter Gordon, Big Mama Thornton, and Eddie "Cleanhead" Vinson.[145] One of the outstanding projects he worked on was *The Lost Paramount Tapes* (1973) sessions with James Booker. Finally released in 1995, Boudreaux's drumming is outstanding, particularly the stunningly funky 12/8 groove on "Feel So Bad," the rollicking second line of "Junko Partner," and the churning polyrhythms of "African Gumbo" and "Tico Tico." He reunited with Rebennack for the live-in-the-studio recording *Hollywood Be Thy Name* (1975). In 2001, Boudreaux released his first album as a leader, *Past, Present and Future,* focusing on the modern jazz he had so masterfully played with the A.F.O. Executives. In the later years of his life, he went back and pursued his initial musical impulses and learned to play saxophone and concentrated on that instrument after suffering some physical setbacks that kept him off the drums. Boudreaux explained to Jeff Hannusch the essence of the New Orleans beat:

> Well first of all, there's so many different styles of music here and the drummers have to be able to handle them all. Secondly, the parades. In any other city in the world when you say parade, people there think military parade. Of course in New Orleans it's not military, it's a funky, second line parade. New Orleans drummers have to learn that second line beat. Any gig you play in New Orleans, at some point you're going to have to play that second line beat. That's what makes the New Orleans drum style so unique.[146]

Rooted in the New Orleans tradition, John Boudreaux played a crucial role in the development of Dr. John's musical vision and will be remembered as a versatile artist who took funk drumming to realms where no drummer had gone before.

Fred Staehle: "The Feeling That Came from My Heart"

During the summer of 1970, Fred Staehle (b. 1944), who replaced Boudreaux for Rebennack's European tour, found himself behind the drum set at London's Trident Studios surrounded by a mob of rock musicians, including Mick Jagger, Eric Clapton, future Derek and the Dominoes members Bobby Whitlock, Carl Radle, and Jim Gordon, saxophonist Graham Bond, and singers Doris Troy, Tami Lynn, and Shirley Goodman, recording material for a proposed Dr. John triple album. Ultimately, the sessions led to the single disc *The Sun, Moon & Herbs* (1971). Schooled in the old-school approach, Staehle had firsthand interactions with many of the legends of the New Orleans beat, and, for almost twenty-five years, was often Rebennack's drummer of choice both on tour and on a number of recording projects, most notably the benchmark homages to his hometown grooves, *Dr. John's Gumbo* (1972) and *Goin' Back to New Orleans* (1992).

Staehle's engagement with the music was passed along through the family. His brother Paul, who was almost a decade older and had gone to New York to study with Gene Krupa and Cozy Cole, introduced Staehle to the basics: "He started out teaching me rudiments on a barrel that he put a piece of rubber tube over it, and he was showing me the differ-

Dr. John, Paris, 1970. *Left to right:* Wayne Brooks, Leo O'Neill, Dr. John (with skull), Joenie Jones, Shirley Goodman, Freddy Staehle, and Michael Gilman. Photo courtesy of Fred Staehle.

ent rudiments, the mama papa roll, the single stroke roll, the triplet, and the paradiddle, things like that."[147] When Staehle started playing drums at Sophie B. Wright Junior High School, he was immediately promoted to the twelfth-grade band thanks to his mastery of the samba beat: "My brother, he taught me a Latin beat, a swing beat, and a samba beat." One of the first Drumsville legends that Staehle encountered was Ray Bauduc: "I got on the Tony Americo talent show on Friday nights, the Famous Theater on Claiborne, and I won, so they put me on Sundays with the Tony Americo Dance Band. Ray Bauduc was the drummer . . . I had to set up my drums with the calf-skin heads on the stage and play along with the band."

Staehle's schooling in the New Orleans beat came primarily through listening—to Poppa Stoppa spinning hit records on the radio, to his brother Paul, and to the musicians he met through Paul, one of Rebennack's first drummers. Rebennack recalls: "Paul Staehle was bad. I remember him having drum battles with Edward Blackwell and all the top drummers."[148] Staehle would go on the gigs with the band that featured Paul, Rebennack, Earl Stanley, and Henry Guerineau. One night when the band was about to take a break, they sent Staehle out to play drums in front of the big crowd: "God, I had to be twelve years old, and whenever I finished playing whatever I played, there was a lot of clapping and people, at first they just stood there and looked. I had everybody's attention, and then they started clapping, and I became shy about going on the stage, which is why I never learned to sing properly. I was overwhelmed, that's all." Paul also brought Staehle to sessions the band was playing at J&M Recording Studios: "I got to watch John Boudreaux, Smokey Johnson, Eugene Jones, James Black, Earl Palmer, yeah, those were cats that I would sit and watch how they play. More than anything, what I got from watching them play is how they felt, you know." Staehle tried his hand at enhancing the beat in the legendary studio: "There was a time in the summer when I was out of school. They were in the studio two or three times a week, and I was sitting in there, even one time I played a cowbell on one song, but Dave Bartholomew didn't like it. I did a paradiddle right in time with the groove, but he said no."

As a teenager, Staehle drummed in a series of bands, including the Emperors, who played at the Metairie Lodge on Saturday nights. He gained valuable experience backing up guest New Orleans R&B stars: "Ernie K-Doe, Danny White, Benny Spellman, those beats were pretty easy to play for them, you know, because I had heard them on the radio." The gig, however, brought Staehle two priceless lessons in the New Orleans beat. One Saturday, Professor Longhair was on the bill. As in the studio session with Boudreaux, the pianist made sure the drummer knew how to lay down the beat he was looking for: "I was like fourteen years old, and I go over to the piano, and he said, 'Listen, when I play this style, I want you to play this beat.' And, he showed me on the piano, and he said, 'That's what my drummer

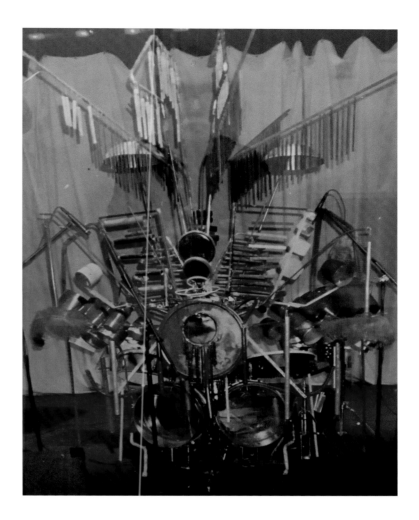

Fred Staehle's winger tree. The winger tree is built on a frame around a drum set and fashioned from pots, pans, funnels, wind chimes, and other found materials that create fifty distinct tones; it has two feathered wings that are operated by foot pedals. Photo courtesy of Fred Staehle.

plays.' So, that's where I learned to play some of the Professor Longhair styles of grooves. And then when I got with Mac . . . it just locked in on those kinds of songs." When singer Irma Thomas appeared at the Lodge a second time, she brought her own drummer along: "She said, 'Now look, Freddie, I want you to listen to how he plays the shuffle.' And, that was the kind of shuffle, 2/4, Smiley Lewis style of shuffle." Learning that beat also came in handy when Staehle was working with Rebennack: "You know, like 'Goodnight Irene' on the *Goin' Back to New Orleans* album, that's the beat; it's a 2/4 shuffle, second line."

In 1964, Staehle's first big break came at age twenty during a gig at the El Maraca club on Bourbon Street. Trumpeter Al Hirt and his clarinetist Joseph "Peewee" Spitelera walked in while the drummer was soloing on "Take Five." Hirt offered him a gig as soon as came off the bandstand:

I really didn't realize who he was or how good he played. And then he asked me to go to his club and just catch the show. And, I went down there, and I heard the show and I thought "This drummer's fantastic, a jazz drummer. I couldn't sit in his chair." So, I told Al later that I didn't think that I could cut it. He said, "I want you to come to a rehearsal and play with me and see how it goes." So, I went to a rehearsal. I asked him, I said, "How do you want me to play this?" He says, "Just play it like you feel." So, he did like some Dixieland tunes which I was familiar with that beat, and then he did "Java" and "Cotton Candy," and I did an almost kind of Latin beat with a little Afro-Cuban on the bell, like the record, and I could play all those, and he says, "You got the gig."

Staehle toured the world and recorded with Hirt. One of the musical benefits from being in the band was that on the road he was roommates with pianist Ellis Marsalis: "Ellis was very refined. He spoke high English, and he liked to talk, and I always listened. So, in that year and half that he was a roommate, when we traveled on the road I learned a lot about the concepts in music and different ways to, if I was gonna think about it, develop a concept. Realizing that once I play, I had to stop thinking. But, it helped me form my music knowledgeability."

Staehle left Hirt in 1970 and went to Las Vegas, where he worked briefly as the house drummer at Caesar's Palace and played in some top-forty bands. Then he got the call to replace Boudreaux in the Dr. John the Night Tripper band for the European tour: "We played all of the music from the *Gris-Gris* album, which I was able to learn, duplicate the beats, and play it." A live album of the band, *Great American Radio Volume 5* (2020), recorded at Syracuse University in 1972, features Staehle driving the band and interacting with conga player Jai Johanny "Jaimoe" Johanson of the Allman Brothers, who were on the bill that night. When the band went on hiatus back in Los Angeles, Staehle decided to attend the Scientology Celebrity School, where he studied a range of subjects, including communications, sociology, psychology, psychiatry, and philosophy. Rebennack reformed the band with the focus shifting from Night Tripper revelry to classic funky New Orleans R&B, and Staehle was the drummer that he wanted to lay down those old-school grooves on *Gumbo*. As Rebennack explains in *Under a Hoodoo Moon:*

> Freddie has his own idiosyncratic thing, of course, but he follows a New Orleans style that leans heavily on the bass drum playing double-clutch rhythms (like two eighth notes rather that one quarter note as the basic pulse). Rather than play the one-bar patterns typical of most rock and even R&B drummers, the New Orleans–schooled drummer will break up the beat into two- and four-bar patterns (and sometimes even an eight-bar pattern). Two and four on the back beat is sometimes only implied; sometimes the groove is felt in cut time, which is one half the tempo, or double time, doubling up the groove.[149]

During the 1970s, Staehle's work on *Gumbo* probably exposed more people to second-line drumming than any other New Orleans drummer. In the album's liner notes, Rebennack recognizes Staehle's contribution to the recording: "The great thing on this record is our drummer Freddie Staehle's laidback, second-line drumming. This is classic New Orleans second line style where the drummer plays relaxed licks all around the beat, but with perfect time. You could call it 'melody drums.'"[150] Staehle is aware of the high profile he had in the arena of rock music playing in Rebennack's band: "There were drummers in New

Orleans that were still alive doing it, but they weren't traveling around. John Boudreaux and Earl Palmer, those were the only two drummers out in California, but those guys were in the studio with other people."

The two Dr. John follow-up albums to *Gumbo* were produced by Allen Toussaint, who wanted to pair Rebennack with his Sea-Saint Studio house band the Meters, which included Joseph "Zigaboo" Modeliste on drums. Before he went back to California, Staehle did contribute to the biggest success that came out of the sessions. Rebennack asked him for some input on a song he was working on: "I said, 'I'm not much of a poet or one with words. But, there was a motto we had at some of these junior high schools, McMain. 'If you go McMain, you come out insane.' But, I went to Sophie B. Wright, and the motto I made up was, 'You go in Wright, you come out wrong.' You can figure out what Mac did with that, 'Right Place, Wrong Time.'" The next touring band that Rebennack put together included James Black on drums and James Booker on keyboards. A conflict between the two musicians sent Black back to New Orleans, and Staehle got a phone call to come to Texas and join the band. Rebennack knew Staehle could handle the drums and hoped his studies in psychology would help him deal with Booker's idiosyncrasies. Staehle wound up with another great pianist roommate—albeit one quite different from Marsalis: "I went to Texas, and he was one of the funniest people I've ever met . . . He was a character."

It speaks volumes that when Rebennack decided to record his second major homage to New Orleans, *Goin Back to New Orleans,* he once again had Staehle behind drums laying down the funk. The project was initiated when Staehle was in New York staying at Rebennack's apartment. The duo made a demo tape of all the New Orleans tunes that appeared on that album and sent it to producer Stewart Levine, who immediately greenlighted the project and insisted that Rebennack use the same drummer and play the same grooves that were on the tape. Staehle's exposure as a kid to so many Drumsville legends came in handy:

> I did about four, five different grooves that I just picked up playing while I was in Mac's apartment with just him and I playing. "Milneburg Joy," he says, "'Hungry Man' Williams had this groove that he did that was sanctified, second line.'" That's where that beat comes from. And, there was another one that was like Smokey Johnson and one like John Boudreaux. A few of the other ones, I made up myself, like the actual song "Goin' Back to New Orleans." I created that beat, and "Litanie des Saints," Mac and I always talked about doing a tango funk tune. Because nobody ever used a tango beat in the music, so I came up with that beat, a little simple beat, "Litanie des Saints," and that is my all-time favorite song that Mac ever recorded. Then he got the Nevilles to sing on it; Cyril Neville did the lead vocal. I mean it was just excellent, just excellent. [*laughs*]

Staehle returned to the studio with Rebennack for the follow-up album, *Television* (1994): "That's the last album I did with Mac, which is actually a very cool album. The beats on that, all of them I made up from my imagination, and I was using two hi-hats, one on the right side of the snare and the regular hi-hat on the left side to get some of those grooves. And that was it. I got out of the band after that.

Staehle is in the tradition of the "thinker-tinkers" who improvised drums with available everyday materials, from Congo Square to spasm bands to the first drum sets. Fittingly for a musician who played in the phantasmagoria of the Night Tripper bands, he built the totally unique "winger tree," a "melodic percussion instrument" that is both aurally and visually stunning. Like his initiation into New Orleans drumming, this impulse possibly can be traced back to his brother Paul, who Rebennack recalls had painted and built a flashing light system for his drum set: "When he played his solos, he hit a button and that shit all came on. He'd be playing the drums, they'd light up, and it was something to behold."[151] Standing over ten feet tall, the winger tree is built on a frame around a drum set and fashioned from pots, pans, funnels, wind chimes, and other found materials that create fifty distinct tones and has two feathered wings that are operated by foot pedals. The conception of the winger tree reaches back to Staehle's days playing on Bourbon Street when he met drummer David Lee Jr., who, along with Earl Turbinton, George Davis, and Harold Battiste, was involved with the Rosicrucian religion; they shared their beliefs with the young drummer:

> It was based on the concept that when the Lord created human beings, he created around a scale of notes, music notes, starting with the feet, B flat, going through the body, different notes . . . They also taught about a soul note that vibrates through the medulla oblongata, the bottom of the brain, top of the spine, and when you become clairaudient, you can actually hear the tone, and each person born under a zodiac sign has a soul note.

Staehle connected the idea that "human beings are created on a scale of notes" to the Tree of Life in the Bible: "Then I called it the winger tree, the flying tree, the tree of life that's in the Garden of Eden, which I believe was sound. What the tree of life dealt with is intangible, and no one ever explained to me well what is the life part, a tree with life in it. So, I just put both of these ideas together and made the winger tree." Rebennack had Staehle play the winger tree on a number of his albums and found sessions for him to play it on, including drummer Levon Helm's version of "Havana Moon." Staehle and his creation are also featured in Toto's "Push Back the Walls" video. The winger tree is most prominently featured on *Fonk Horn* (1999), trumpeter/flautist, longtime friend, and musical associate Charlie Miller's duet album with Staehle. Staehle's playing extends from in-the-pocket second-line grooves to atmospheric textures to a swirling street parade of percolating percussion.

For Staehle, the bass drum is the key to the New Orleans beat: "I think playing off of your bass drum groove, more than the left hand is what I used to do. It's kind of a dominant way of playing a groove." Ultimately, he believes that feeling is the essential aspect that distinguishes the city's approach to drumming:

> Well, I think old school, the drummers that played those types of rhythm, it came from their heart. It's not something that they studied and learned. They didn't try to apply the technique. It's something that was created just from feeling . . . Like when I did "Iko," it turns out to be a clave, but when I was recording it, I didn't know it was a clave. It's like the feeling that came from my heart playing with Mac.

In recent years, Staehle has brought that distinctive feeling to a series of local gigs, including with the Royal Rounders at Buffa's Back Room and with Steamboat Willie at Legends Park, back on Bourbon Street. And, his winger tree (and a smaller "winger bush") continue to evolve.

Herman "Roscoe" Ernest III: "A Lot of Cats Call Me the Back-Up Drummer"

Over the course of a week in January 1996, Dr. John and his band, which featured drummer Herman "Roscoe" Ernest III (1951–2011), bassist David Barard, guitarist Bobby Broom, percussionist Chief "Smiley" Ricks, saxophonists Alvin "Red" Tyler and Ronnie Cuber, and trumpeter Charlie Miller, performed a series of shows at the renowned Ronnie Scott's club in London that were recorded for Rebennack's first official live album, *Trippin' Live* (1997). The band, which was eventually dubbed the Lower 911, delivered the freewheeling funk that was essential for Rebennack: "The more tight a band is, it's a basic consideration for a New Orleans band, the more tight a band could play, the looser we can play. That's what I wanted to get captured on a live recording of it."[152] The tight/loose duality that the band displays on the recording also perfectly captures the essence of Ernest's inventive approach to funk drumming with its deep roots in the New Orleans beat. His playing featured a stunning technical facility and rock-solid timekeeping that allowed him to provide whatever a band leader demanded, *and* he laid down seductively funky grooves that drove a band with a spontaneous energy and intuitive interplay. Ernest was Rebennack's right-hand man over the course of three decades for countless live performances and contributions to ten studio and three live albums. In an interview by Keith Spera from when the drummer passed away, Rebennack acknowledges their special relationship: "He did a lot of stuff for me when I was messed up, and when I got clean. He was like a podna that you know is good in-your-corner people. Some guys are in your corner to a point, but they ain't goin' beyond that point. He wasn't like that. Wherever it went, that's where he was. That's a special thing in my heart. He was a loyal cat, right to the bitter end."[153]

Familiarly called "Roscoe" and, at times, dubbed "Herman the German" by Rebennack, Ernest was known as a humorous, free-spirited individual. He was raised in the Seventh Ward, and inspiration to play the drums came when he was seven or eight years old. His mother took him to a Fourth of July party at Pontchartrain Beach, and he was fascinated by the drummer he saw performing: "It amazed me. And from then on I wanted to play drums. I had to play!"[154] His role models included Hungry Williams, John Boudreaux, Robert "Bulldog" Bonney, Earl Palmer, and Smokey Johnson: "Dixieland was always around, but those cats took Dixieland, along with some syncopated strokes and movements and beats, and incorporated all those sounds into New Orleans ratty drumming. That's why it was so difficult for drummers all over the world to duplicate the sound—because it was laid-back funky. Lots of people felt New Orleans players were off the beat. They were missing it, didn't get it." He further explains: "If you play it laid back, then it's behind the beat just a hair. It's still on the one, bro, got to be. Everything got to be on the

one!"[155] Ernest first began drumming with neighborhood bands, and by the mid-1960s was working with R&B artists like Oliver Morgan and Ernie K-Doe.

He may have been recognized worldwide for his work with Rebennack and as one of New Orleans's most in-demand session drummers, but Ernest also served as a deputy sheriff for NOPD, drummed for his mother's Greater Liberty Baptist Church, and taught young musicians at the Louis Armstrong Summer Jazz Camp. Like so many Drumsville greats, Ernest's foundation was in the city's traditional music. He described his conception of second-line drumming to Debra Devi:

> The Dixieland I came up on was more or less a raw groove. People used to play on metal or a box with this kind of shuffle rhythm. It was done so manually back then that people looked at it as a Dixieland jazz thing, but it's not just that. If you listen to it real hard, you can hear shuffles—single shuffles, double shuffles—you can hear swing. It's all coming off the snare drum. And, if you accent real hard on the four, that is considered a New Orleans groove.[156]

Ernest was deeply impacted by the rhythms of Mardi Gras Indian tribes playing drums and hand percussion and call-and-response chanting as they moved through the neighborhood. In an interview with Dan Thress on the DVD *New Orleans Drumming: From R&B to Funk* (2004), he describes the experience of witnessing Black Masking Indians and the influence they had on his drumming:

> It was mostly one tom tom from some kid's set in the background, and the rest was cowbells, tambourines, shakers. That's all you heard. You'd hear it in the background, and you'd know they were coming. You'd say, "Alright." You can feel the excitement in the air. The people in the neighborhood start rousing, "Here comes so and so tribe. Here they come.

They're getting ready." They may be two blocks down, and you can still hear that [*plays tom*] with the tambourines and stuff on top of that. You can hear it in the neighborhood. You can feel the excitement. So those rhythms was happening back then [*plays tom*]. See, that's where I get most of my rhythms from, the street rhythms of the Mardi Gras tribes and the street grooves, and I just polish it up and add a little slick bass drum part to it because you didn't have bass drums playing, except for Dixieland bands then.[157]

Ernest absorbed traditional elements of the New Orleans beat and recast them to create the seductive, propulsive grooves that were the signature of his personal approach. As he explained to Thress: "I just took it and enhanced it my way and laid my version of, my interpretation of it on that part of the groove, which keeps me in that era, and it also keeps me over here too." Keeping that tradition vital, he also passed along his knowledge to younger drummers like Shannon Powell, who was a teenager when he met Ernest: "Herman brought a different sound with his backbeat. You got to remember I was 13 years old. I was trying to learn how to play New Orleans funk, New Orleans trad, gospel. And Herman was a big part of my education because he showed me how to play a pocket beat."[158]

One of earliest gigs that drew attention to Ernest's skills was touring as a member of the Rhythm Masters backing New Orleans R&B singer King Floyd in the wake of his success with the single "Groove Me" (1970). But Ernest would truly make a name for himself through the session work he did with producer Allen Toussaint at his new Sea-Saint Studios. It's not surprising that he would flourish as a session player because of his ability to excel at so many genres of music. As Powell observed: "Herman was one of the most underrated drummers in New Orleans. He could swing, he could play funk, he could play blues, he could play gospel, Latin, whatever."[159] In the early 1970s, Ernest essentially was in the right place at the right time, as he stepped in and became one of the primary drummers for Toussaint's productions. The grooves that he laid down for the two albums Labelle recorded at Sea-Saint—*Night Birds* (1974), with its smash-hit single "Lady Marmalade," and *Phoenix* (1975)—ensured his legendary status in Drumsville. Labelle brought a demo of the song with a disco beat, hoping to inject some New Orleans funk into the recording. The studio rhythm section featured three of the Meters—Art Neville on keyboards, George Porter on bass, and Leo Nocentelli on guitar, plus Ernest on drums and Toussaint on piano and percussion. In his interview with Thress, Ernest relates the evolution of the iconic groove for "Lady Marmalade." He says that after many takes, Toussaint grew frustrated, left the studio, and called Ernest upstairs to get his ideas on how to approach the track: "He talked to me, asked me, 'Well, how can we make this song dance?' I said, 'I don't know, Allen. I'm hearing all kinds of things. I don't know what you want.' I played this little lick right upstairs there on my leg (scats). And Allen kind of like, you can tell when he's on, you know, he knows when the magic is getting ready to happen. 'Let's go try it again. Let's go downstairs and try it again.'" As they started to play, Toussaint began refining the groove Ernest had created, instructing him to add "an extra bass drum lick" and "answer your snare drums." The drummer recalls the emergence of the iconic funk groove:

Then he orchestrated everyone's parts, and LaBelle, they kind of looked because they knew something was going down. They didn't know what was happening. They didn't even think it was "Lady Marmalade." They thought it was a new song we was getting ready to work on. It jelled so good, it got to be magic, and it was like a first take for the first time that day. Everybody got this new energy in 'em. And then, as we were growing with the song. The song is cooking. Allen say, "One more thing Herman," his thing was, "Okay, just play drums, no, wait, put a hi-hat thing in there between those licks before you answer your snare drum." I said, "Okay," and I went [*plays lick with hi-hat added*] And, the session took off, that was it. History man, a hit.[160]

Ernest's narration of the groove's evolution illustrates what made him so effective as a studio drummer. He possessed the chops that were needed to execute, the ingenuity to rework core elements into something new, the ability to interact with and respond to the conceptions of the producer, and the creative fire to bring it all alive. Ernest's versatility is evident in the many Toussaint productions on which he drummed, including with such artists as John Mayall, Richie Havens, Lee Dorsey, Ramsey Lewis, and Etta James.[161]

Another studio project that exemplifies Ernest's pivotal position in the Drumsville lineage is his work on the Neville Brothers' *Fiyo on the Bayou* (1981). Two of the songs on the album, the title track and "Hey Pocky Way," were already certified New Orleans classics that had been recorded by the Meters and featured drummer Zigaboo Modeliste's essential funk grooves. The challenge for Ernest was to come up with something original and still maintain the essence of Modeliste's approach. He delineates to Thress the evolution of the groove he developed for "Hey Pocky Way":

So I said, "How can I do anything to 'Hey Pocky Way' without destroying it?" So, I started to thinking about what Zig was doing. I said, "Okay by me being, having a certain technique about my playing and my studio experience," I said, "Well, I think I can incorporate some kind of hi-hat part or some cymbals or drum fills." I said, "Okay, the song didn't have any drum fills." I thought of that. I said, "Okay, that's one down." I said, "How can I keep what Zig did and incorporate some rhythm off the hi-hat?" So, right in that booth back there [*plays*]. They say pick it up, faster. I said alright (plays adding hi-hat). Keep the same bass drum pattern that Zig did [*plays*] and not as much cadence on the snare, more singles [notes] but still have the cadence feel, instead of doing what Zig was doing [*plays*] you know, he kept that marching thing going. I just broke it up [*plays*]. That was enough. I did not need to do anything else to it because it was gonna just totally mess it up. And then as we was doing that song, I added fills. That's all I did, and it took off.[162]

Similarly, on "Fiyo on the Bayou," Ernest wanted to acknowledge Modeliste's classic groove and add something new for the Nevilles' version: "There again, we kept the Zigaboo thing going. All we did was just pick it up. I broke the lick up and added some little fills, some cymbal crashes, and that was it."[163]

His first recording with Dr. John was on the album *Tango Palace* (1979), which also featured drummers Steve Gadd and Andre Fisher, percussionists Neil Larsen, Paulinho da Costa, and Ronnie Barron; and Fred Staehle on winger tree. But Rebennack had something very specific in mind for Ernest, who drums on four tracks—"Renegade," "Bon Temps Rouler," "Something You Got," and "I Thought I Heard New Orleans Say": "He brought me in to just play the New Orleans stuff, grooves, more or less, not Mardi Gras beats, just the feeling, because he had stuff with a lope in it, you know you have that lope, you need a drummer that understands the lope part of the New Orleans groove."[164] In addition to *Trippin' Live,* Ernest appears on two other live Dr. John recordings, *Right Place, Right Time* (2009) from a Mardi Gras at Tipitina's in 1989 and *Live at Montreux 1995* (2005). Beginning with *Anutha Zone* (1998), Ernest was Rebennack's main drummer on nine consecutive studio albums, including *Duke Elegant* (2000); *Creole Moon* (2001); *N'Awlinz Dis Dat or D'Udda* (2004); *Sippiana Hericane* (2005); *Mercernary* (2006); *City That Care Forgot* (2008); and *Tribal* (2010). Ernest became the leader of Rebennack's band the Lower 911 and was credited as coproducer on *Tribal.* Rebennack often presented the band with demos of his compositions when preparing for a new recording. He could count on Ernest to enhance the groove. As Rebennack explains to Keith Spera: "I can guarantee you one thing whatever I put as a drum thing, Herman shifted all of that immediately. And he always came up with something that was better." Ernest's ability to enhance what the band leader was trying to accomplish, while staying grounded in the tradition *and* innovating fresh grooves, is evident in the syncopated drum break he plays at the close of "Perdido" from the Duke Ellington homage *Duke Elegant.* Rebennack continues: "Whatever I was thinking for 'Perdido' would have been more dated sounding. Herman turned it into a tribute to all the New Orleans drummers, like Smokey (Johnson) and Zig (Modeliste) and James Black and John Boudreaux, that era of New Orleans drummers. It was such a cool idea."[165] Ernest's creative rhythmic impulses epitomized that tight/loose duality that Rebennack felt was so crucial for a New Orleans band. It's embodied in his signature technique:

> Back-up funk. All it is is just stopping the tempo whenever I'm playing a funky lick and, uh, maybe leave out a backbeat or put the backbeat *anywhere* just for one measure or so or one beat. For instance [*plays*], then I would say I'm gonna back it up, you know just throw the backbeat anywhere but remember where you got to come back. So, you know, that's my trademark. In town, a lot of cats call me the back-up drummer.[166]

Working full-time with the Dr. John and the Lower 911, his studio sessions with a who's who of New Orleans R&B and funk artists including Earl King, Snooks Eaglin, Irma Thomas, Johnny Adams, Al "Carnival Time" Johnson, as well as drumming and vocal contributions to Paul Sanchez and Colman deKay's musical adaption of *Nine Lives,* are a testimony to the creativity and energy of Herman Ernest III's backup funk.

Joseph "Zigaboo" Modeliste: One of the Best Ever

During 1968, drummer Joseph "Zigaboo" Modeliste (b. 1948) was on the bandstand six nights a week, five sets a night at the Ivanhoe club on Bourbon Street as a member of the

Zigaboo Modeliste, performing at the 2007 Jazz and Heritage Festival. Photo by Leslie Parr. Courtesy of the New Orleans Jazz & Heritage Archive.

Neville Sounds, along with organist Art Neville, bassist George Porter, and guitarist Leo Nocentelli. It was an experience that helped shape four uniquely talented musicians into one of the tightest and most influential funk bands of all time. As Modeliste explains: "Six nights a week, that will make any band, whether they're marginal players or great players. The cohesion that it would provide, you study, going over your text, going over your data, by it being so repetitive . . . you try to exhaust every little ambiance about a song to make it sound good, and if you're doing that with people on a regular basis, six nights a week, you get tight." From time to time, producers Allen Toussaint and Marshall Sehorn stopped by the Ivanhoe, and eventually Toussaint offered the band an opportunity to work with him in the studio: "He said he wanted to use us as a recording backup band for some projects that he had, local projects. We agreed to it, and then we started doing that for a while and that got interesting."[167] Things certainly did get "interesting" as the collaboration between the band, renamed the Meters, and Toussaint would have a seismic impact on the evolution of the New Orleans beat. The stripped-down, broken-up beats of Modeliste's funk drumming place him in the ranks of Drumsville's most significant, genre-defining drummers, alongside Warren "Baby" Dodds in traditional jazz; Earl Palmer in R&B and rock and roll; and Ed Blackwell in free jazz.

Modeliste's initial inspiration to be a drummer came when he went with his parents to a Masonic dance, and he heard a band featuring veteran brass band and traditional jazz drummer Andrew Jefferson (1912–1985): "The cat was just really slick. He had it going on . . . They played like New Orleans standards, stuff like that. They didn't have no heavy-duty thing going on, but they did have that New Orleans traditional sound, and he was a drummer and singer, so that's where I really believe that I got the original idea that something like that could occur." During Modeliste's formative years, there was no mass media through which he could gain exposure to drummers, but, of course, his hometown is Drumsville, so there was a wealth of talented players around for him to observe:

> My thing came from a lot of local artists and the cultural aspects of New Orleans, what musicians really did. You know, a lot of them were blue-collar musicians. It wasn't nothing outstanding, but they knew their craft, and they probably didn't get enough attention back then because there was a focus on something else, I suppose, but I really met some really fantastic drummers in New Orleans for the most part until I kind of got with the Meters. That's when I started really, for some reason or another, getting introduced to a lot of elder drummers that I never thought I would ever get the opportunity to meet.

Some of the drummers he admired included Clarence "Junie Boy" Brown, who was a member of the Hawketts and toured with Fats Domino; Eugene Jones, who worked regularly with Clarence "Frogman" Henry; and, above all, Smokey Johnson: "Smokey, that was

The Meters at Jazz Fest

© Michael P. Smith

the drum god for me. Smokey Johnson, because [he had] so much attitude to drumming, so much spirit." Modeliste points out that his education on drums came through observing and listening, rather than formal lessons:

> I never sat down with any drummer that would tell me about how to play drums, what to do, any advice, how to read, how to do anything like that, not one of 'em. But I had a lot of heroes, but my experience was I had to put in the time to go see them wherever they was playing, keep my mouth shut and just watch, and see what I could retain just from looking at it, listen to how it sound when they did certain things. So, it was an interesting process, a bit slow, but interesting.

And perhaps it was that self-education process that makes his conception of funk drumming so original and unique.

The Meters at Jazz Fest, 1974. Art Neville: "Because I'm a percussive keyboardist, and because Zig and Leo and George are so inventive rhythmically, the groove became king." Photo by Michael P. Smith. Copyright © The Historic New Orleans Collection. Accession number 2007.0103.2.229.

The "cultural aspects" of life in New Orleans were the wellspring that fed Modeliste's creative impulses. His earliest musical explorations took place Uptown in the Thirteenth Ward, where his neighbors were the Neville family. He was close friends with Cyril Neville, who recalls those formative years hanging out with Modeliste in the autobiography *The Brothers* (2000): "We became brothers, bonded in our love of the drum."[168] Like generations of drummers before them, they were drawn to the second-line parades. Modeliste also remembers that they regularly followed behind the Rebels, a drum and bugle corps from Texas that marched each year at Mardi Gras:

> It's like it happened yesterday. I mean the cats were so clean and shooooooo, man, they had it going on, really. You had your marching bands, but the drum and bugle corps, I thought was the stuff. I thought that had a lot of energy, and it was focused, very focused. And, these guys was just tremendous in the execution. And, I saw 'em a couple of times, so I was kind of familiar with their beats and what they had to offer. I thought it was really unique. I took a part of that and tried to incorporate it into my way of thinking.

Of course, the grooves that were hammered out by the Mardi Gras Indians also were a seminal influence that Modeliste describes as "the premier well to go to if you wanted to be introduced to rhythms in the city":

> The Mardi Gras Indians was something I saw every Mardi Gras. And, once you see that twenty or thirty times, you kinda get the idea of where it's all coming from, the epicenter of it all. And, I had friends that was Indians, masked and stuff like that, and I've been to a few Indian practices, and I used to love to join in, play tambourine, but it was never something that I was just gonna stop right there. I would just keep on going and exploring. That's the nature of the music that was surrounding me, the cultural aspects of that vicinity that I was living in.

He certainly did "keep on going and exploring," and years later, Modeliste's absorption of those "rhythms of the city" would help shape the first commercial funk recording of Mardi Gras Indian music through his drumming on the initial Wild Magnolias single "Handa Wanda" (1970). His groundbreaking work with these distinctive rhythms would continue when the Meters and Toussaint joined forces with the Neville Brothers to support their uncle Big Chief Jolly (George Landry) in the recording of the landmark Mardi Gras Indian album *Wild Tchoupitoulas* (1976).

Modeliste's parents purchased him a drum when he joined the band in junior high school, but that drum would take on a different and, in the long run, more significant role as Modeliste and future Meters band members Cyril Neville and George Porter pursued their aspirations to become professional musicians:

> Cyril, George, and myself, we used to sit, my parents bought me a marching drum, a mahogany marching drum for me to be in the band. That's all I had, but I would put that up, put a little towel over the top of it, stomp my feet on the floor for my bass drum, man we'd go to town, and George always had a little box guitar he played . . . He knew a few cowboy chords,

and we just had fun just being ourselves back then. Then, when he moved in my neighborhood, that's what we did all the time.

Those ad hoc, teenage jam sessions laid the foundation for Modeliste, Porter, and Neville to make earthshaking funk grooves with the Meters. Early on, Modeliste had the opportunity to work with R&B legends such as Professor Longhair and Snooks Eaglin, but his first big break came when Art Neville needed a drummer to fill in with the Hawketts and hired *both* Modeliste and younger brother Cyril:

> Yeah, Art Neville and the Hawketts, and I made a few gigs with him, and I had my first taste of playing professionally with seasoned musicians. My parents bought my first parade marching drum when I was in seventh grade in junior high school. Cyril and I used to practice all the time, but Cyril didn't know as much as I did, and I didn't know that much. We was just great admirers of the art form. So, we was teaching each other different things, you know, in the back room of my house. The craziest thing, he would get me to play the gig and Cyril too. So, Cyril would play a few songs; I'd play a few songs. It was like that. So, I mean it was a great experience because nobody else at the time that had that kind of recognition had ever hired me.

Zigaboo Modeliste, ca. 1980. Modeliste: "I was trying to improvise while I was playing. I didn't want to wait to get to a solo." From *Wavelength Magazine.* Gift of Dr. Connie Atkinson. Courtesy of the New Orleans Jazz Museum.

When Art went out on the road to back brother Aaron, who was touring in support of his hit "Tell It Like It Is" (1966), Modeliste joined guitarist and singer Deacon John Moore's band, an experience that helped shape the young drummer's sense of what it meant to be a professional musician: "He taught me a whole lot about the business, the decorum, how you should dress, you know, how you should act, what you should do, what's the protocol, for that time. I picked up a lot from Deacon John." He rejoined Art Neville, who had formed the Neville Sounds, along with George Porter on bass, Leo Nocentelli on guitar, Aaron Neville and Cyril Neville on vocals, and Gary Brown on saxophone. The band worked a regular gig at the Nite Cap Lounge. Modeliste's drumming attracted a young drummer to the club, Jonathan "Sugarfoot" Moffett, who recalls: "All of this rhythm and all of this sound was coming out of that building and your spirit just lit ablaze."[169] Moffett absorbed Modeliste's innovations and went on to drum for a star-studded roster of pop artists, including Michael Jackson, Madonna, and Elton John.

The move to the Ivanhoe club required Neville to pare down the lineup, and the stage was set for the Meters' funk revolution. They were a rhythm machine, and the interplay between the four musicians generated irresistible grooves. As Art Neville explains: "Because I'm a percussive keyboardist, and because Zig and Leo and George are so inventive rhythmically, the groove became king. As opposed to playing songs, we were flat-out grooving, vamping on beats that could go on for hours."[170] Toussaint employed their seductive funk grooves behind a wide array of singers, including Lee Dorsey, Earl King, Chris Kenner, and Ernie K-Doe. Modeliste is particularly proud of his drumming on

Zigaboo Modeliste (*left*) and George Porter performing in the Foundation of Funk at the 2019 Jazz and Heritage Festival. Photo by Brenda Ladd. Courtesy of the New Orleans Jazz & Heritage Archive.

King's "Street Parade" and Betty Harris's "There's a Break in the Road." With Toussaint producing, the Meters brought the funk to Dr. John's albums *In the Right Place* (1973) and *Desitively Bonaroo* (1974): "We helped to reconstitute his recording career. 'Right Place, Wrong Time' and 'Such a Night' was two of his biggest records he ever recorded, and I thought *Desitively Bonaroo* was an even better record."

The band started to record instrumental tracks on their own, and in 1969, Sehorn licensed some of that material to an independent label, Josie, that released the album, *The Meters,* and much to everyone's surprise scored hit singles with "Sophisticated Cissy," "Cissy Strut," and "Ease Back." Smokey Johnson recognized the influence of his drumming on "It Ain't My Fault" in Modeliste's hi-hat rhythms and accents played on the side of the bass drum on a track like "Cissy Strut." In *Zigaboo: The Originator of the New Orleans Funky Drumming,* Johnson notes: "I think Zig heard that and a little bit of that is in his playing, but ain't nothing wrong with that because I got a little Earl Palmer, Ed Blackwell, Charlie Williams, I can name the drummers, and I put a little Smokey in with it."[171] Johnson's comment illustrates how individual drummers drew upon what came before them and added their own innovations to the development of the New Orleans beat *and* clearly adds Modeliste to that lineage. The Meters grabbed the baton from Booker T and the MGs to become the 1970s foremost instrumental group in the realm of R&B, releasing three albums and a dozen singles on Josie. Modeliste, Porter, and Art Neville began contributing vocals as the band broadened its approach, and Cyril Neville eventually joined on vocals and congas. The Meters signed with a major label, Reprise/Warner, and released a series of albums that featured some of the most quintessential funk tracks to come out of New Orleans, including "People Say," "Jungle Man," "Hey Pocky Way,"

"Africa," "Fire on the Bayou," "They All Ask'd for You," "Be My Lady," and "Funkify Your Life." Modeliste is particularly proud of the band's later efforts: "Most of the people that I've ever talked to about the Meters point out 'Hey Pocky Way' or 'Cissy Strut' or something like that, but I really like the work that we did when we started stretching, like on 'Ain't No Use.'"

Modeliste's drumming was a revelation—the taut snare sound, the syncopated dialogue between the snare and bass, the scintillating hi-hat work, the broken-up beats—that immediately marked him as another Drumsville innovator advancing that tradition that reached back to Congo Square. He is conscious of the source point for his drumming: "It's an African thing, man. I've never been to Africa in my life, but I understand now how it migrated and how African influences went everywhere, all over the Caribbean, all over the Americas. They went everywhere, and they mixed cultures with the destinations, but they kept that African art form. They made that strong enough where they didn't deviate enough where you couldn't recognize it." For critic Robert Christgau, Modeliste's drumming is the key to the Meters' irresistible funk: "The secret: listen to Ziggy Modeliste. He plays more off-beats and eccentric patterns than any soul drummer you ever heard, yet never breaks up the band's spare clever riff structures; it's almost as if he's the lead."[172] Modeliste expresses an awareness of how he extended the tradition of New Orleans funk drumming that developed from Earl Palmer's 1950s innovation with the backbeat:

I do think that I brought something to the table. Some people say syncopation. Some people say swamp funk or whatever they want to describe it as, but I was just being a little bit more busy than a backbeat, two and four or that kind of thing. I was trying to do a lot more in there. I was trying to improvise while I was playing. I didn't want to wait to get to a solo. This was my way of thinking. I wanted to solo while I was playing in the linear part of it. So, it never was the same all the time. It was just what my recall would do instantly.[173]

His conception of how he approaches a drum set is also rooted in New Orleans tradition, that the essential components—the bass drum with a mounted cymbal and the snare drum—existed in brass band drumming:

Well, basically I always looked at drums like you're looking at a plate of food. I always felt like the snare drum and the bass drum were your main entrees. Those are the main groove essential components that make everything else happen with set drumming. You're never gonna go hear a drummer play a set of drums, set up the whole set of drums and don't play nothing but the tom-toms or the cymbals. You're not gonna see that nowhere. The premise is always gonna be, the epicenter is always gonna be the snare and the bass and the relationship they have with one another through motion, especially repetitive motion. That's what I discovered, so I basically thought that I could say everything that could be said about music with a hi-hat, a snare drum, and a bass drum.[174]

He said a lot with those three basic components, and people listened. The Meters toured as an opening act for the Rolling Stones in the mid-1970s, and guitarist Keith Richards decided to join guitarist Ronnie Wood's 1979 solo tour when he heard that Modeliste had been recruited on the recommendation of Charlie Watts. Richards explains in his autobiography *Life* (2010): "Ronnie was going on the road, and he put together the New Barbarians, which was an incredible band—Joseph "Zigaboo" Modeliste on drums, one of the best ever. And that's why I immediately jumped in. Drummers from New Orleans, of which Ziggy is one of the giants, are great readers of the song and how it goes; they feel it, tell the way it's going even before you do."[175] *Rolling Stone* ranked Modeliste as number 18 in "100 Greatest Drummers of All Time," proclaiming: "On Meters' songs like 'Cissy Strut' and 'Just Kissed My Baby,' Modeliste's stick work practically makes the trap set sing."[176] And *Drum!* magazine ranked him among the "50 Most Important Drummers of All Time," declaring: "Modeliste's work with the legendary New Orleans funk band the Meters inspired scores of drummers to try to 'turn the beat around.' By combining the steady pulse of r&b with the reckless street beats of second-line brass bands, Modeliste devised a loose, linear drum-set style that used every rhythmic permutation he could possibly fit into a bar of 4/4 without repeating himself."[177]

Although he has recorded with everyone from Robert Palmer, John Fogerty, Allen Toussaint, and Robbie Roberston to Erykah Badu and Mark Ronson, today Modeliste, who lives in the Bay Area, focuses on his own band, the New Aahkesstra: "Well, currently, I've been playing a few gigs but with my own bands because in my old age I'm just kind of selfish right now. I don't want to go learn nobody else's music. I mean I could do it; I could cherry-pick that. There's just some people I just love and admire, and I'd play with them under any circumstances, but most of the time, I try to write music. I'm still working on my craft of writing songs." He and his wife, Kathy Webster-Modeliste, run the publishing company Jomod Music Publishing and record label JZM Records, which has released four solo CDs. His drum instruction DVD *Zigaboo Modeliste: The Originator of New Orleans Funky Drumming* (2012) provides insight into his pioneering funk techniques. Of course, that type of resource was unavailable when he was coming up, and he does see a difference in the approach of today's drummers: "Most drummers today though they just play a groove, and then they wait for the time for them to have a seven-minute solo, three-minute solo, and then they do all these rudiments and exercises, which I think that's beautiful, and I love it. I love to hear other cats do that. It's mathematics. It has its place, though, but I do think it's like, it's not something that everybody wants to hear. People are more in tune to continuity." Modeliste's drumming has exerted a powerful influence on the hip-hop generation. His beats have been sampled by such hip-hop artists as Queen Latifah, Run DMC, NWA, Ice Cube, Salt N' Pepa, Cypress Hill, EPMD, Public Enemy, A Tribe Called Quest, Beastie Boys, Naughty by Nature, and Eminem. He also has reunited with George Porter in the Foundation of Funk to revisit the music of the Meters with assistance from a revolving cast of all-star friends, old and new, including Cyril Neville, Ian Neville, Ivan Neville, Tony Hall, Eric Krasno, Anders Osborne, John Medeski, Jimmy Herring, Jojo Hermann, Jon Cleary, Neal Evans, and Eddie Roberts. In 2018, the enduring legacy of the Meters was recognized when they were awarded a Grammy Lifetime Achievement Award for their "trademark sound of syncopated layered percussion intertwined with gritty grooves on guitar, bass, and organ, blends funk, blues, and dance grooves with a New Orleans vibe that is regarded as one of the most influential in music history."[178] Joseph "Zigaboo" Modeliste is one of the giants of Drumsville; his funky drumming absolutely revolutionized the New Orleans beat. Looking back on a remarkable career, he reflects, "I like to think that I used the tools that I had the best way I knew how to do it."

Alfred "Uganda" Roberts: "I'm the Old-Timer from the Gang"

Professor Longhair played his first and only performance in Great Britain at the New London Theatre on Drury Lane in London on March 28, 1978. His sole accompanist on stage was his right-hand man, conga player Alfred "Uganda" Roberts (1943–2020). The recording of the show, *The Complete London Concert,* which features a fourteen-song set, including such classics as "Mess Around," "Hey Now Baby," "Tipitina," "Big Chief," and "Go to The Mardi Gras," provides a unique opportunity to hear the interplay of these two masters of the New Orleans beat laying down funk-fueled grooves in a stripped-down setting. Longhair and Roberts had been performing together regularly over the previous six years after New Orleans Jazz and Heritage Festival producer Quint Davis suggested that they would sound good together. Roberts recalls, "So, he took me to a house party, which was at Davell Crawford's grandmother's house on Louisiana Parkway and Broad, and Professor Longhair was the piano player, and I brought my drum, and I sat in with him, and that was the beginning of a beautiful friendship."[179] Roberts may be best known for his years drumming with Longhair, but he is a significant figure in his own right thanks to the compelling Afro-diasporic grooves he created with a wide array of New Orleans bands and the central role he played in reinvigorating the hand drumming tradition that flourished during the nineteenth-century Sunday-afternoon Congo Square gatherings.

Raised by his godparents, his "marraine" and "parrain," in Treme a few blocks from Congo Square, Roberts first encountered Afro-Caribbean rhythms as a teenager at a club called La Havana on St. Bernard Avenue:

> All the merchant marines when they would get off from work, they'd come to this club and have a shang-dang-doodle, you know. A woman by the name of Georgina owned the club, and they was all friends, and they would also bring her records from Havana, Cuba, like Celia Cruz and Mongo [Santamaria], Tito Puente, all them kind of cats. And, she put 'em on the juke box, and the juke box would go all night . . . They had these bar stools; the top was metal, and you'd hit 'em, and they sound almost like steel drums [*taps table*], and we used that for bongos and stuff like that, dance all night.

Like the ancestors who drummed in Congo Square, Roberts and his friends improvised their percussion instruments from everyday objects. He eventually acquired a set of bongo drums, and, while still going to school, landed his first professional gig. Roberts assumed the persona of "Jamaica Joe," playing bongos to mambo and cha-cha-cha records behind burlesque dancer Chris Owens in her French Quarter club: "She had a little stage that came to a point, and I would sit at the end of the stage, and the records would play

Alfred "Uganda" Roberts. Roberts played a central role in reintroducing hand drumming to New Orleans. Photo by Curtis Knapp. Courtesy of the New Orleans Jazz Museum.

and her and the maraca girls would come out with the maracas, and she was doing the cha-cha-cha. And, I had a calypso shirt on, big straw hat." Fellow Treme resident Smokey Johnson encouraged Roberts to switch to conga drums, which would fit in better on the jazz jam sessions that took place in neighborhood clubs like Holly's: "Smokey Johnson. Him and I used to really hook up, play different rhythms. He used to have a thing he did on the sock cymbal that would go like this [*scats*], and I'd answer him with my conga [*plays congas*]." Roberts taught himself how to play congas, modeling his approach on master Cuban congueros: "So, I came up with a sound looking at Mongo Santamaria, Armando Peraza, cats like that." Conga drums and their accessories were not readily available in New Orleans when he first began playing, so Roberts exhibited that "thinker-tinker" improvisational spirit. He often had to refurbish damaged drums that he found in pawnshops; he would "see people working on boats in the neighborhood" who taught him how to repair drums using fiberglass: "Some of 'em would be egg-shaped because they had so much fiberglass on them. We had one we used to call Egghead." He would also design his own equipment and have it custom made. His wife, Linda, recalls:

I tell you a story about Alfred. When Alfred was fourteen, fifteen years old, my dad had an antique repair shop in the French Quarter, and he used to do some of his work in the little backyard we had, and Alfred heard him and came back there at fourte, fifteen, and asked him could he make him some drum stands for his congas, and my dad told him—I was a little girl, maybe six or seven years old—my dad said, "No, I don't deal with metal. I only deal with wood," but that's how long he's been playing those drums.

Roberts ultimately went to a blacksmith and used flowerpot holders as the template to have metal stands made for his congas. His setup includes three conga drums which, along with his nickname, was inspired by a conga drummer in a Ugandan dance company that he and a friend saw perform at Southern University.

Roberts played a central role in reintroducing hand drumming to the local scene: "The guys always came by my house, and we'd have a big jam session, and I taught 'em. I gave each guy a pattern to play, and the man on the bottom would play [*plays congas*]. And, he'd keep that going, and we had another guy play [*plays congas*], that kind of stuff. And, another guy would play cowbell, and somebody else might be playing the shakers. And then, another rhythm would be [*plays congas*]." He says they consciously did not drum in Congo Square: "I don't know, there was something we didn't want to be involved with tourism, you know, people coming from the French Quarter out there to see us and asking us if we were performing any particular kind of religion and stuff like that, which we did encounter sometimes." But he did help revive drum circles in the city: "On the weekends after I grew to become a young man, there were guys from different parts of the city that liked to play those conga drums like I did, and we would go on the Lakefront and get together, like on Sundays, and play the conga drums and have a ball." One of the young drummers who showed up at the Lakefront was Cyril Neville, who recalls those gatherings in an interview with Jake Feinberg: "Alfred Roberts. That's another great percussionist. Basically, that's who I learned from. We used to do the thing on the Lakefront every Sunday, a bunch of drums and stuff out there every Sunday, and that's another street school that I got a chance to get my chops together."[180] Roberts clearly appreciated the recognition: "He used to come out to the Lakefront with us when he was young. He used to enjoy sitting out there, playing with us. As a matter of fact, he said that on one of his interviews on the internet, that he learned a lot going out to the Lakefront playing with me on Sundays, which was nice to hear him say it because he used to be out there as a little boy. I'm the old-timer from the gang." Roberts also extended the African-based drumming tradition in the city at the Jazz and Heritage Festival through the drum circles he organized and the onstage performances with his own Afro/Calypso Band in the Koindu area (today called the Congo Square Stage). Shannon Powell is another drummer who discovered African drumming through Roberts: "Shannon Powell was a little boy then. When I started doing the Jazz Festival, he would pop up on the stage as a little kid."

It was through the Jazz Fest appearances that Quint Davis decided to connect Roberts and Professor Longhair, leading to the eight years that the drummer and pianist teamed up playing those rhumba-driven blues grooves that Roberts calls "Afro-Caribbean Rhythm and Blues." In addition to the London concert, their work together is documented on numerous recordings, including live sets, like *Live on the Queen Mary* (1978) and *Big Chief* and *Rum and Coke* (recorded in 1978 at Tipitina's), and studio albums, like *Rock 'n' Roll Gumbo* (1978) and *Crawfish Fiesta* (1980). The title track is one of the highlights of that last studio session featuring just Longhair's piano, Roberts's conga, and Walter Payton's tuba, a showcase for the percolating, polyrhythmic syncopation of the New Orleans beat. The drummer's relationship with the pianist was fulfilling, both musically and personally:

> He was a drummer and rhythm maker. He used to kick the piano with his foot, and when I came along, he said, "I ain't gonna kick my piano no more." Lots of times just him and I would play, traveling, and the people would like to hear just the congas and the piano 'cause they could hear him tickle them keys . . . I always sat close to him, looking at what he was doing and listening to what he was doing, and we never did rehearse. We'd always just go somewhere and start playing, any part of the world, and we got along like brothers.

For Shannon Powell, Roberts's partnership with Longhair delivered the essence of the New Orleans beat: "All that stuff he did with Fess, I mean incredible. He made Fess sound like a really good New Orleans groove with an African feeling too. You can hear the African rhythms in the music with the old New Orleans rock-and-roll sense of swing."[181]

In addition to his work with Longhair, Roberts was in demand for recording session work and was a regular sideman at Sea-Saint Studios. His congas can be heard on classic Meters' tracks like "Africa" and "Hey Pocky Way," and he appears on Allen Toussaint's albums *Southern Nights* (1972) and *Love, Life & Faith* (1975). Dr. John also included Roberts in the incredible parade of drummers he worked with over the years on such albums

Professor Longhair (*center*) and Alfred "Uganda" Roberts (*left*) performing at the 1978 Jazz and Heritage Festival with Earl Gordon on drums and unidentified bassist. Photo by Michael P. Smith. Copyright © The Historic New Orleans Collection. Accession number 2007.0103.4.693.

as *Goin' Back to New Orleans* (1992) and *N'Awlinz Dis Dat or D'Udda* (2004): "I had the ability to change my rhythms to fit the kind of music that they wanted me to play, with the Meters and Dr. John. Dr. John used to call it, 'Hey Uganda, give me that swamp sound, baby.' And, I would come up with swamp style . . . The same thing with Allen. He would play something and say, 'See what you can do with this, Uganda.'" Roberts's talent at constructing intricate, propulsive grooves with a distinct New Orleans feel led to recordings with such artists as John Mooney, Donald Harrison, the Hot 8 Brass Band, Coco Robicheaux, and Maria Muldaur.

One of Roberts's most significant contributions to the evolution of the New Orleans beat is his conga playing on the first two Wild Magnolias albums, *The Wild Magnolias* (1974) and *They Call Us Wild* (1975). These recordings that meld the deepest funk grooves with the polyrhythmic percussion and call-and-response chants of the Black Masking Indian tribes opened the doors for new creative possibilities for New Orleans music while maintaining roots in the city's traditional culture. Roberts brought a familiarity with the rhythms to the sessions, having played tambourine or cowbell with Indians in his neighborhood: "I went to Indian practices. They got a guy in the Treme called Chief Jake. He always liked for me to come around, and I could beat on some kind of percussion instrument, mix with what they was doing at Indian practices." His brand of "Afro-Caribbean Rhythm and Blues" was a perfect fit in the New Orleans Project, the band pianist Willie Tee assembled for the recordings, because Roberts recognized that the rhythms of the Indian music were cousins of the Afro-Cuban rhythms that had initially inspired him: "Yeah, because they had the tambourine, the cowbell, and what I was doing was kind of on the Caribbean side. And it was a good mix because the way Bo Dollis sound, the tone of his voice, we could put some dance music to that and come up with some hits." With Chiefs Bo Dollis and Monk Boudreaux up front and Roberts and a gang of Indians beating out polyrhythms on hand percussion instruments over a funk band foundation, they created some of the most distinctive tracks in modern New Orleans music, including "Handa Wanda," "Smoke My Peace Pipe (Smoke It Right)," "Two Way Pak E Way," "Injuns Here We Come," and "Fire Water." For Roberts, looking back over forty years to the recording sessions, the standout track is "New Suit." Sitting at his dining room table, he sings, "Every year at Carnival Time we make a new suit." As he sings, he plays a rhythm on the tabletop; it's the conga drum part that he played on the original recording: "I would over-emphasize a cha-cha-cha, mambo rhythm to open it up, like [*sings the lyrics and beats rhythm on table*]." It's instantaneously recognizable from the recording and absolutely obvious that the whole song rides on that conga line he created; it *is* the song. And, it's a testimony to Robert's creativity and the power of the drum.

Roberts may have considered himself the "old-timer," but he certainly did not rest on his laurels. In 2007, he joined the band Groovesect, weaving his beats into their mix of funk, jazz, rock, and soul. He also collaborated with pianist JoJo Herman from Widespread Panic, performing and conducting seminars that honored the legacy of Professor Longhair's music, and he toured Brazil with guitarist John Mooney. Roberts had a long history of mentoring young drummers, and he taught formally at New Orleans Center for Creative Arts (NOCCA) and Crescent City Drum Camp. Some of his notable students include Michael Ward, Kenyatta Simon, and Jonathan Bloom. Fittingly, Roberts toured *Drumsville!* on the opening night of the exhibit and drummed alongside Luther Gray in tribute to the drummers who started it all in Congo Square. In January 2020, he reunited with drummer Johnny Vidacovich from Longhair's band for his final recording session, backing up Irma Thomas on her LP *Love Is the Foundation,* and sadly passed away a few months later. Alfred "Uganda" Roberts was a culture bearer, a groove master, and an integral influence on the evolution of the New Orleans beat.

"Mean" Willie Green: "He Felt the Soul of It"

The Oakland Coliseum was filled to capacity on December 28, 1989, when drummer "Mean" Willie Green (b. 1956) joined Grateful Dead drummers Bill Kreutzmann and Mickey Hart onstage for the improvisational interlude "Drum" that had been a ritual in the band's performances since the late 1970s. The three drummers jammed on an incredible array of percussion instruments, including "The Beast," which is built from variously sized bass drums hanging from a metal frame. Also joining in were band members Jerry Garcia, Bob Weir, Phil Lesh, and Brent Mydland, and the music they created during the set, which was eventually dubbed "Post-Modern High Rise Table Top Stomp," appears on the album *Infrared Roses* (1991). "Drum" performances were often freeform, spacy journeys into the sonic stratosphere, but with Green on board that night, primarily on bass drum, snare drum, and hi-hat, there's a decidedly, funky propulsive groove that owes a lot to his signature take on the New Orleans beat. Green connected with Kreutzmann and

Hart through his three-decade-spanning tenure anchoring the drum chair with the Neville Brothers, who were an opening act for the Dead on numerous occasions. Green says that the first time he joined in on "Drum" was scary because there were with just three drummers onstage in front of a massive audience, but following the initial experience, he was ready to jam:

> After that, the second one was like, "Okay, I got this." And the third one, Mickey [was] like, "Willie, come play my set. Come on, play my set." I said, "I'm gonna play this set, then I'll go to that set." Then, I say, "Got to play The Beast tonight, got to play The Beast." So, I played every drum up there . . . I played every f—ing drum on that stage. Both of the drum sets, all of the drums, and The Beast. That was a wonderful feeling.[182]

It's unlikely that, growing up just outside New Orleans, Green ever could have anticipated drumming with the Grateful Dead. Expressing himself through rhythm was just something that seemed to come to him naturally:

> I grew up in Shrewsbury, beating in school on the desk and getting suspended for making noise. I used to beat on cars just for sound. It would be like [*beats rhythm out on table*] I don't know, just all these grooves going through my mind, and I didn't know where they should be going, and there was really no, I hate saying it, there was really no school teaching for what I was doing, and I didn't realize I was creating shit by doing all this [*pounds out rhythm*] I'm just thinking I'm having fun, but I'm inventing stuff.

He bought his first drum set in a Western Auto store; it didn't last long: "Broke the head. That's because no training [*scats on unorganized rhythm, then laughs, making tearing sound*]. Oh, man." He pieced together a second set that had a Rogers bass drum, and the rest was made by Sears. And perhaps the Grateful Dead connection was not so farfetched. His early tastes in music might be a surprise to those familiar with the ferocious second-line funk grooves he generated with the Neville Brothers. Green was a classic rock fan: "Listening to the radio station at my house, I was the only Black guy I knew listening to white music . . . I wasn't too much of an R&B man. I used to only like Zeppelin or Deep Purple, Rare Earth or Yes, Journey, Grand Funk. I used to like people like that. I didn't sit on the radio and listen to Aretha Franklin and James Brown all day." He worked with some local bands and moved to New Orleans, where his first major gig was with organist Sammy Berfect.

The break that would bring him worldwide renown came one night when he was subbing for the drummer in keyboardist Ivan Neville's band: "Aaron [Neville] and his wife came to see me, and I'll never forget when Aaron said, 'I want that drummer in our band.'" When Green talks about drumming, he often scats a rhythm or beats out a groove on his leg or on the table to make his point. What's going on technique-wise is not nearly as important to him as the feeling that he generates, and he thinks that's what Neville heard that night at his son's gig:

> He heard feeling. He didn't hear somebody trying to play, somebody playing. He heard something coming out of somebody while they're playing. He felt the soul of it. I can't say

it any other way, say it the wrong way, but Black people got touch in them, you know, sometime they pray to God and hope for this happy day to come, and it don't really come, but they got that belief in 'em. After that I got with the Neville Brothers. That's '81, and that came to end, and then I went with Dr. John in '81 and '82 and went back to the Neville Brothers and never left.

It's rather amazing that for someone who is considered a Drumsville master, Green came to learn the intricacies of the New Orleans beat only later in his life: "When I played with the Nevilles, I didn't know how to play 'Pocky Way.' I didn't have one album by the Meters; I didn't have one album by Dr. John. I had to learn the songs . . . I had to kind of find out what Herman Ernest was doing with Dr. John, what Zig was doing, so I had to listen. I didn't have nobody sit down and say, 'No, this is how it go, brother.' I didn't have a tutor." Like so many New Orleans drummers, Green's approach to the drum set was shaped by brass band drumming: "The brass band, the Dirty Dozen made me learn how to play snare and bass drum." And when he considers the distinctive grooves he played on so many Neville tracks that have become classics, he locates their genesis in his intuitive approach: "They came out of my feelings, how I felt the bass line, how I felt about how Aaron was singing it, how I felt about how Cyril was singing it, how I felt that this is our music, so it goes like this. That's the way I felt. 'Yellow Moon,' I had another beat, but Aaron didn't want it, so we put the funky beat on it. All the stuff from Cyril, it was pretty much natural. It was a family."

The Neville Brothers were among the foremost ambassadors of the New Orleans beat. In performance, they were a polyrhythmic percussion extravaganza, as testified to by the recording of a 1982 Tipitina's show captured on the album *Nevillization* (1984). Green flashes his versatility as the band moves from a ballad like "Tell It Like It Is" to reggae on "Why You Wanna Break My Heart" or the Latin feel of "Caravan." But the most captivating moments come on the driving funk numbers, including "Big Chief," Africa," and "Fear, Hate, Envy & Jealousy." These recordings finally enabled listeners to bring home the intensity of the band's shows that for the most part, at that time, could only be experienced in New Orleans. Green drives the grooves with his thundering bass drum and syncopated snare drum and hi-hat work locked in with bassist Daryl Jones. And, he spars with Cyril's explosive drumming on congas and timbales: "He follows me, unless he do some crazy shit and I like it, I'll add on to him. He follows me. He'll let me know, 'Pick it up, pick it up, pick it up.' 'Okay' [*scats rhythm*]." The grooves were further ramped up as Art and Ivan Neville added to the mix with percussive attacks on keyboards, and Aaron and Charles joined in, hammering out cross rhythms on cowbells or tambourines. In addition to the band's legendary live shows, Green's drumming provided the foundation for an expansive range of music over the course of five studio albums: *Yellow Moon* (1989); *Brother's Keeper* (1990); *Family Groove* (1992); *Mitakuye Oyasin Oyasin/All My Relations* (1995); and *Family Groove* (1999). His intuitive approach certainly came in handy be-

"Mean" Willie Green. For Green, what's going on technique-wise is not nearly as important to him as the feeling that he generates. Photo by R. Cataliotti.

cause he was essentially providing the grooves for four distinct leaders: "See, one person could tell you one thing; you got four brothers . . . I had to deal with all four of their personalities, totally different." Looking back, he had no idea where the gig would take him, but he embraced his role as drummer for the Neville Brothers, and he took his job seriously:

> I didn't predict being on Johnny Carson, Jay Leno, David Letterman, *Saturday Night Live, Good Morning America,* all of those things. I didn't look at that. I didn't look at opening up for Santana, Ziggy Marley, playing at the Woodstock. I wasn't dreaming that. I was just going, "This is a nice f—ing ride." It's a ride. I wasn't sitting down saying, "Hey bro, I think you oughta do this next. Or y'all should go there . . ." I didn't get in it that deep like that. I just went with the flow for what it was and made sure my head was good every night on the set.

Green believes that his approach was a culmination of New Orleans funk drumming: "I left the last tattoo that they gonna get." He finds on the city's contemporary scene that the essence of the New Orleans beat is in the music with the deepest roots: "The closest thing you got to that is listen to the brass bands [*scats rhythm*]. That's the closest thing to New Orleans to me, is listening to a second-line band outside or going to see the Indians with a second-line band. That's the closest you got to New Orleans to me." And, while he's proud of what he achieved in exposing audiences around the world to New Orleans drumming, he also believes that the grooves and beats developed by him and others have been co-opted:

> We still have a special sound that nobody has . . . All this shit is here. They stealing our shit. Or they coming down here from another state trying to get our gigs because they learned our shit . . . Sometimes I go around the city and say, "Man, this mother sounds like me." You ever hear that, when you go around the city? You hear, "Man, this guy sounds like Zig." Say, "No, that guy sounds like Green. That's my groove."

Over the years, his grooves and versatility have been in demand. He's recorded with such artists as the Wild Magnolias, Chief Smiley Ricks and the Indians of the Nation, Bob Dylan, Willie Nelson, Daniel Lanois, Paul Simon, and Elvis Costello. After the breakup of the Neville Brothers, Green laid down the grooves alongside former Radiators bassist Reggie Scanlan in the funky roots rock outfit the New Orleans Suspects. For "Mean" Willie Green, it has been a remarkable journey from banging on cars in Shrewsbury to recognition as a Drumsville legend. And, when he's asked about the position he's taken in the lineage of drummers that includes Ed Blackwell, Idris Muhammad, Smokey Johnson, James Black, John Boudreaux, and Zigaboo Modeliste, Green replies:

> Listen to the names you just named. That's a hard, you got to be a kicking mother—er to be with [them] . . . So, I feel good being up there with all them people. I feel good having my name mentioned with all them people, not just listed with them. They can just throw you in there to throw you in there, but I have history behind my name. I don't just have a name . . . That make me feel good. That make me feel good to be part of the family. It's a hard family to get with.

8

Extensions and Variations

PASSING IT ON

THE REACH OF NEW ORLEANS DRUMMING: "HE TAUGHT ME A LESSON"

Looking back over the evolution of the New Orleans beat reveals the remarkable reach of the drumming that has emanated from the city. The influence of Drumsville has been felt by countless musicians across many approaches to music making. One encounter with a New Orleans drummer stands out for its contribution to one of the most significant musical phenomena of twentieth-century popular music. In 1959, the traditional jazz revival brought clarinetist George Lewis and his band to Great Britain. The drummer on the tour was Joe Watkins (1900–1969),[1] and there's a picture of him and bassist Alcide "Slow Drag" Pavageau looking out from the compartment window as their train is pulling out of a station en route to Liverpool for the next concert. A young drummer named Richard Starkey (b. 1940) attended that show, and within five years, he—known as Ringo Starr—would become one of the most famous drummers in the world. Starr was asked by *Goldmine* magazine about the rock-and-roll concerts he saw in Liverpool before the rise of the Beatles, and he said there really weren't any. He did say that two performances he attended stood out in his memory. The first was by guitarist and singer Sister Rosetta Tharpe. The second was the show by Lewis: "I saw the George Lewis Band of New Orleans and the drummer was so great. He taught me a lesson. I was 18. He only had a bass drum and a snare drum and when it came to tom-tom stuff he just leaned down and played the bass drum with a stick. It was like, 'Oh my God!' You don't see Ringo playing a huge 15-piece drum kit. I stick to three at the most. And I learned that from that guy."[2] "That guy" was Watkins, and Starr credits him with shaping his conception of a drum set. And, the drum set he would use when the Beatles appeared on *The Ed Sullivan Show* on February 9, 1964, probably inspired the purchase of more drum sets than any other single performance in history. Drummer Stanton Moore believes the image of Starr behind that drum set sparked widespread interest in drumming: "In the drummer world, the guys that are just a little older than me, guys that were born between 1955 and 1960,

Left: Joe Watkins (*right*) and Alcide "Slow Drag" Pavageau on a train to Liverpool, 1959. Ringo Starr on the influence of seeing and hearing Watkins perform in Liverpool: "You don't see Ringo playing a huge 15-piece drum kit. I stick to three at the most. And I learned that from that guy." Loaned by the Hogan Jazz Archive Photography Collection, Tulane University Special Collections, Tulane University; New Orleans, LA. Accession number OPH001180.

Right: Barry Martyn (*left*) and Cie Frazier, early 1960s. In addition to playing with and learning from many New Orleans jazz greats, Martyn has done invaluable work in documenting the tradition through articles, books, recordings, and films. Courtesy of the New Orleans Jazz Museum. Accession number 1994.120.029.

almost universally, those guys are like, 'I saw Ringo Starr on *Ed Sullivan,* and that's what I wanted to do.'"[3] That was certainly the case with Ricky Sebastian, growing up in southwest Louisiana: "I mean I remember just being totally transfixed by the Beatles, like so many kids back then in the early 1960s watching. I think that probably got me interested in just watching drummers in bands that I'd see on TV."[4] The impact on a whole generation of fledgling drummers of Starr sitting atop a band riser playing his iconic Ludwig set with its drop-T Beatle logo on the bass drum head is powerful testimony to the reach of New Orleans drumming. A few years after the British tour, Watkins would travel to Japan as part of Lewis's band, and his work as a drummer and vocalist—exemplifying what gave Starr that "Oh my God!" moment—is featured on the live albums *George Lewis in Japan, Volume One* and *Volume Two.* It is unlikely that when Watkins got back on the train in Liverpool he was aware of how far he had extended the reach of the New Orleans beat.

During that 1959 tour, British drummer Barry Martyn (b. 1941) and a group of traditional jazz enthusiasts actually met the Lewis band as their train arrived at Euston Station in London. And by 1961, Martyn was making his way by bus from Montreal to New Orleans. Almost immediately upon his arrival in New York, Martyn was sitting with Zutty Singleton in his apartment in the Alvin Hotel across the street from the renowned jazz club Birdland. It was an auspicious start to a deep involvement in traditional jazz that stretches over six decades. Immersing himself in the New Orleans scene, he was associated with many Drumsville greats, including Watkins, Alfred Williams, and Cie Frazier. His first invitation to sit in with a band on Bourbon Street came from Paul Barbarin.

Talk about getting to the heart of the matter! The band, however, was not happy with his four-beats-to-the bar approach. As Martyn recalls: "What they wanted was the first and third beats on the bass drum. It took me a long while to learn to do it correctly, but it got a lot easier when I took lessons from Cie Frazier; I could make syncopations with it."[5] As the title of his memoir indicates, Martyn was *Walking with Legends* (2007). Over the years, in addition to playing with and learning from many New Orleans jazz greats, Martyn has done invaluable work in documenting the tradition through articles, books, recordings, and films. After many years as a New Orleans resident, he truly understands just how deeply the beat is immersed in city's culture. As he explains to Dr. Bruce Raeburn during an interview at Allison Miner Music Heritage Stage during the 1999 Jazz and Heritage Festival: "It's kind of like if you're from New Orleans, and you can't cook. It's unusual. And, if you come from New Orleans and can't get a beat going on the drums, that's unusual."[6] Another British drummer in early 1960s London who moved in the same circles as Martyn and was drawn to the New Orleans beat was Charlie Watts (1941–2021). In July 2019, as Hurricane Barry moved toward New Orleans, the Rolling Stones were hunkered down in the city waiting to perform a delayed concert at the Superdome. Watts and his drum tech Don MacAulay made their way through the deserted French Quarter to the Jazz Museum for a tour of the *Drumsville!* exhibit. Watts knows his New Orleans jazz—from traditional to modern; R&B; and funk drumming. He was totally absorbed in the exhibit in terms of both the historical narrative and the drum equipment on display. Standing in front of Baby Dodds's iconic drum set, he recalled that the first record he ever bought was by the drummer's older brother clarinetist Johnny Dodds. Watts, Starr, and Martyn are just a few of the musicians from around the world who were touched by the reach of the New Orleans beat.

Charlie Watts visits the *Drumsville!* exhibit. The late drummer from the Rolling Stones was steeped in the New Orleans drumming tradition from Baby Dodds to Zigaboo Modeliste. Photo by Bailey Badawy. Photo by R. Cataliotti.

TAKING THE BEAT BEYOND DRUMSVILLE

New Orleans drummers have extended the reach of the beat beyond Drumsville through their influence on drummers around the world—from Baby Dodds and Zutty Singleton establishing what it means to play jazz drums to Earl Palmer's backbeat providing the driving energy for rock and roll, from Ed Blackwell pioneering the possibilities of free jazz improvisation to Zigaboo Modeliste laying down the foundations of funk. But New Orleans drummers, such as Juno Lewis, Ernie Elly, Jonathan Moffett, and Brian Blade, among many others, have also extended the reach of the New Orleans beat through their work behind major artists in American music.

Western Recorders Studio on Sunset Boulevard in Hollywood is the locale where popular artists such as Sam Cooke, Phil Spector, the Beach Boys, and the Mamas & the Papas recorded countless hits. But, on October 14, 1965, the drummer/percussionist, singer, and instrument maker Juno Lewis was in the studio collaborating with saxophonist John Coltrane, who had assembled a band that included his classic quartet of drummer Elvin Jones, pianist McCoy Tyner, and bassist Jimmy Garrison, as well as saxophonist Pharoah Sanders, bassist/bass clarinetist Donald Garrett, and drummer Frank Butler. The session was focused on recording Lewis's "Kulu Sé Mama (Juno Se Mama)," an eighteen-minute-plus performance that comprises the first side of Coltrane's *Kulu Sé Mama* (1967) album. Lewis's composition is a percussion-driven, chanted ancestor prayer that connects Lewis to his family and the African diaspora from New Orleans with its Congo Square drumming heritage to the Motherland, which, according to liner-note writer Nat Hentoff, is performed "in an Afro-Creole dialect he cites as Entobes."[7]

Julian Bertrand Lewis (1931–2002) was born in New Orleans and grew up in the Thirteenth Ward. At an early age he learned to play trumpet and fashion his own drums. The inside jacket of the *Kulu Sé Mama* album features a version of the poem in English, part of which traces the lineage of drummers in his family history:

I JUNO
a drummer born. American.
My father
a tuxedo drummer,
"once a tuxedo drummer, always a
tuxedo drummer."
My mother's father was a captain's
drummer,
F Company, 84th Regiment, Union Army
during the Civil war, 1863–6.
For the past 12 years I have been a
maker, designer,
a Son . . . . . of drums.[8]

He identifies his maternal grandfather, Jules Narcisse, as a nineteenth-century drummer in a militia band. His "tuxedo drummer" father could have played in a dance band and/or a jazz band and/or a classical ensemble—all were possible in New Orleans, but his tuxedo certainly indicates he was a professional. As a teenager, Lewis worked in nightclubs in New Orleans. He moved to Los Angeles in the mid-1950s, where he formed an Afro-Caribbean–type band, performing in clubs and hotels around Los Angeles, Las Vegas, and Palm Springs.[9]

Lewis's real passion was making drums and other instruments, and he largely gave up performing to open Juno's Conga Villa, where he sold his instruments and taught classes.

Coltrane's quartet came to Los Angeles in 1965 to perform at the It Club, and during this engagement mutual friends introduced Lewis to the saxophonist. Remarkably, within days, Lewis was making his recording debut with the band assembled by Coltrane. It is a haunting, hypnotic piece with Lewis's vocals weaving through the droning polyrhythmic pulse and dramatic instrumental solos. A unique entry in Coltrane's discography, *Kulu Sé Mama* was the last album released before the saxophonist's death in 1967.

The Afro-centric consciousness that Lewis and Coltrane explored with *Kulu Sé Mama* flourished in the late 1960s and early 1970s with the Black Arts Movement. It had an impact on Ed Blackwell's early collaborator Harold Battiste, who had become musical director, producer, and arranger for Sonny Bono of Sonny and Cher. In 1971, when Bono asked Battiste where he thought music was heading, the reply was "all the music was going back to Africa." Shortly thereafter, Bono approached Battiste "with an idea to do something African."[10] Influenced by a book he had been reading called *African Genesis* by Robert Ardrey, Battiste began planning an Africa-related project: "I did some research on languages and musical instruments at UCLA, and I also found a homeboy in Los Angeles, Juno Lewis, who was deep into making and playing African percussion instruments."[11] Lewis created a number of instruments for the project, which was called *African Genesis Suite,* including the Daka d'Belah—"a six-tone combination of wood drum and xylophone that makes an echoing, waterfall-type sound."[12] A band was assembled, and a number of tracks were recorded, but artistic differences between Battiste and Bono caused the project to be shelved. Lewis performed from time to time with artists like Billy Higgins and Freddie Hubbard and remained an artistic leader in his Leimert Park community, including the establishment of the Children's Music Center Inc., which provided musical resources and instruction. His creativity as an inventor of instruments certainly links him to his Drumsville "thinker-tinker" forebears—from the shapers of early drum sets to the spasm bands to the drummers in Congo Square.

Ernie Elly: "He Knew New Orleans Musicians"

Ernie Elly (b. 1942) was born in the Sixth Ward, learned rudiments and how to read from Ms. Yvonne Bush at Joseph S. Clark High School, and as a teenager played in R&B bands. Drawn to the sounds of modern jazz drumming, Elly listened on the radio to Art Blakey, Max Roach, and Art Taylor. One performance that confirmed his dedication to the approach was hearing Vernel Fournier at a high school sock hop. Elly continued to develop his drumming in the 539th Air Force Band at Lackland Air Force Base in San Antonio and after his discharge at Grambling University.[13] In 1970, he received a call to audition for Ray Charles's band. He prepared by listening to recordings by Charles, and Elly also had an advantage in his early Drumsville training: "He had some charts that you'd read, go back to high school, Ms. Bush, you know. She gave us that foundation. The reading wasn't a problem."[14] Elly was aware that Charles had a connection to New Orleans: "Ray had spent a lot of time around New Orleans. He knew New Orleans musicians. He liked New Orleans musicians."[15] Elly got the gig and toured with Charles for

Ernie Elly (*right*), 1994. After touring and recording with Ray Charles, Elly returned home to play traditional jazz. Pictured here at Palm Court with Percy Humphrey, trumpet; Brian O'Connell, clarinet; and Chuck Badi, bass. Courtesy of the New Orleans Jazz Museum. Accession number 1994.122.

three years. He appears on two albums of big band jazz, *My Kind of Jazz* (1970) and *Jazz Number II* (1973). Highlights of Elly's work and testimony to his masterful versatility on the albums include: the cracking rim shots that punctuate the funky Charles original "Boody-Butt"; the pulsing boogaloo beat he lays down on Lee Morgan's "Sidewinder"; the textured Brazilian rhythms on Luiz Bonfá's "Morning of Carnival (Manhã de Carnival)"; and the percolating polyrhythms on Jimmy Heath's "Togetherness." In the years after he left Charles, Elly immersed himself in the nuances of traditional jazz drumming. Today, he is one of the mainstays at Preservation Hall, and his tenure with Ray Charles proves that he is a versatile drumming master who extended the reach of the New Orleans beat to one of the most distinctive and renowned artists in American music.

Jonathan "Sugarfoot" Moffett: "Whole New Door of Possibilities"

Perhaps no drummer since Earl Palmer has taken New Orleans–based drumming as far into American pop music as Jonathan "Sugarfoot" Moffett (b. 1954). His high-profile gigs include recording and touring with the Jacksons, Michael Jackson, Madonna, Elton John, Stevie Wonder, and many others. For Joe Lastie Jr., Moffett deserves recognition as a Drumsville legend: "You know Sugarfoot was from New Orleans. He was Michael Jackson's drummer. You got to give this cat his respect."[16] One of the distinguishing characteristics of Moffett's drumming that links him to the New Orleans beat is his stunning bass drum pedal technique. Herlin Riley recalls: "In the '70s, coming out of high school, he had one of the very fastest pumps around, and that's how he developed his name. He could play the bass drum really fast, you know, strokes."[17] When Moffett was coming up in New Orleans, folks often called him "Little Zig" because he was so deeply influenced by Joseph "Zigaboo" Modeliste's groundbreaking work with the Meters: "It opened up a whole new door of possibilities of pattern sequences because he was imagining things that no one had imagined before."[18] Moffett extended the reach of New Orleans drumming through his work with megapop stars on countless world tours. He also took the "thinker-tinker" role of drummers innovating percussion instruments into the space age with his self-designed drum sets that thematically complement the elaborate stage designs for tours. Drumsville has certainly come a long way from Dee Dee Chandler's homemade bass drum pedal and Professor Longhair's spasm band drum set of rigged-up boxes and tin cans.

Brian Blade: "It's Always There, That Pulse and Memory of That Place"

Brian Blade (b. 1970) grew up in Shreveport, steeped in the sounds of the Black church. His father, Brady Blade Sr., has been the pastor of Zion Baptist Church since 1961. The youngster's first instrument was the violin, but at age thirteen, he took over the drumming duties in the church when his older brother, Brady Jr., headed off for college. Blade was exposed to a variety of music in northwest Louisiana—R&B, blues, country, rock, and jazz—and at age eighteen the reach of the New Orleans beat drew him to study at Loyola University and the University of New Orleans. The experience of studying drumming in New Orleans brought him in contact with two instructors who guided him with very different approaches to the instrument. As he explains to Ted Panken: "John Vidacovich was very important. There's a deep sense of groove, but also a deep concern with creating melodic motion from the drums, with moving and shaping the music. He's more of a philosophical teacher than one that taught in a methodical way. David Lee had me play out of books, and placed names on certain beats—one is a calypso, another is a Merengue."[19] He immersed himself in the Drumsville milieu—visiting Congo Square to drum, picking up on the street beats and marching in Mardi Gras parades, listening to vintage recordings of legends like Paul Barbarin, absorbing the feeling and technique of drummers ranging from Ernie Elly to Herlin Riley, and performing with the likes of Ellis Marsalis, Germaine Bazzle, Alvin "Red" Tyler, Tony Dagradi, Harold Battiste, and others.[20] After five years of studying and performing in Drumsville, he left New Orleans for New York and in the ensuing years established himself as one of the most prolific, versatile, and accomplished drummers in contemporary music. Given his talent, along with the training and experiences he had in Drumsville, it's not surprising that Blade would find success in the broader jazz world, and that success was formidable—with his own band, the Brian Blade Fellowship; as a regular member of saxophonist Wayne Shorter's quartet; performing in a trio with pianist Chick Corea and bassist Christian McBride; and working as a sideman with a who's who of the contemporary scene, including saxophonist Joshua Redman, pianist Kenny Werner, bassist John Patitucci—the list goes on and on. But what is quite remarkable is that Blade's drumming has been in demand with a whole other side of contemporary music. He met and began working with producer Daniel Lanois in New

Orleans, leading to Blade playing on a series of albums with both Joni Mitchell and Norah Jones. And he has appeared on recordings with Bob Dylan, Marianne Faithful, Shawn Colvin, and Sarah McLachlan. He not only supplied his percussion skills for these singer/songwriters, but he explored the genre on his own albums, like *Mama Rosa* (2009), singing and accompanying himself on guitar! His sojourn in New Orleans left an indelible mark on Blade. He describes the city's impact to Ted Panken: "Sometimes when I listen back to things and hear myself, I think, 'Wow, there's New Orleans!' It's always there, that pulse and memory of that place, my teachers and heroes there. It all has formed my way of playing music and seeing the world to a certain degree as well."[21] Brian Blade felt the reach of the New Orleans beat, and it drew him to the city. He left with that beat as a part of him, and his music extends that reach through his associations with a broad range of contemporary jazz and popular artists.

CONTEMPORARY MASTERS

Today, Drumsville and the New Orleans beat are flourishing. Drummers Johnny Vidacovich, Herlin Riley, Ricky Sebastian, Joe Lastie Jr., and Shannon Powell are contemporary masters who extend the tradition. Once again, it is important to note that the exhibit and this book are intended to be representative and not comprehensive. There are numerous other contemporary masters on the scene. One of the things that makes these five artists unique is that they are rooted in the history of New Orleans drumming and are fluent in the styles that evolved over the past century, *and* they continue to experiment and invent, bringing new rhythmic patterns and techniques to the music.

Johnny Vidacovich: "An Unconscious Dance"

One of the quotations emblazoned across a wall of the *Drumsville!* exhibit comes from Johnny Vidacovich (b. 1949): "What makes a New Orleans drummer is an unconscious dance. And it's primitive, and it's pelvic. I look at drumming as a lower energy and an upper energy. I like to fuse these combinations."[22] The duality he describes is evident in his drumming, which has brought an enlivening beat to a myriad of bands from the streetwise "blues rhumba" of Professor Longhair to the probing jazz improvisations of Astral Project. That dualism also characterizes his conversations about music; he is a unique character, a droll, down-to-earth guy who speaks in a classic N'Awlins drawl and, at the same time, a philosopher of the drums expressing a broad awareness and sophisticated conception of the creative process. He makes the primal aspect of drumming very clear in an interview with Michael Vosbein: "Playing drums is from the neck down, wood, tree trunks, skin stretched over it, you beat it with a stick. It hasn't changed in thousands of years."[23] The straightforward aspect of his conception also is apparent in one of the factors that he believes makes New Orleans drumming unique. As he explained during an "Improv Conference: A Festival of Ideas" panel discussion at the Jazz Museum: "The air is thicker. The resistance in the air, that also makes the music a little thicker. It's gonna be looser and, to me, more melodic because it floats. It's thick; it's below sea level here. So, the drummers here automatically are gonna play different because of the density of the air. I know 'cause when I go to places that are higher altitude, I can play faster, and it's easier to play."[24] The abstract side, the "upper energy" of drumming, is exemplified in an insight he reveals to interviewer Geraldine Wycoff: "I was always very impressed about how you could feel the music although it looked invisible. Now, I'm finally realizing that the music is not invisible at all. It's actually sound waves and molecules and specific structures. It's just unfortunate that our species isn't refined enough to be able to see music, we can only hear it."[25]

The drum set has been central to Vidacovich's life. He improvised his first "set" by applying his percussive skills to the pots and pans in the kitchen of his family's Mid-City home. Vidacovich recognizes the significance of the instrument's development, a narrative that is central to the *Drumsville!* exhibit:

> People should know how universal the drum set is and how it came to being in the United States because the drum set is not from any one particular country, other than the United States, which is pretty late in the development of an instrument. Like the bass drum and snare drum represent western Europe; the tom-toms represent Africa and the Native American Indians; the cymbals represent the Orient. So, you see the drum set is a very worldly thing that was never in any other country prior to the United States, coming together in the late 1800s, early 1900s. The drum set became what it is in the United States . . . The sound of the drum set is the sound of the world.[26]

He is steeped in the history of drumming in New Orleans and how important a sense of tradition is in distinguishing, maintaining, and extending the city's trademark beat. He also acknowledges another key aspect of the *Drumsville!* narrative, the innovative role New Orleans drummers played in the drum set's development:

> New Orleans played a big role because a lot of prototypes developed here in New Orleans, especially the two main prototypes, the bass drum pedal and the sock cymbal or the hi-hat. And also New Orleans drumming historically, we still maintain in our contemporary playing, we still maintain some of its early beginning roots of rhythm . . . So the music of the drums is still growing based on its historical roots. We still have a lot of root characteristics in our music.[27]

At age eight, Vidacovich got his first drum set, and by age thirteen, he began taking drum lessons at Campo's Music Store, an experience that profoundly shaped his musical development: "I was taught all of the traditional tunes as a kid. That's a lifesaver, man. Charlie Suhor was my teacher . . . He taught me how to play music, not only just drums but how to play music, how to play drums in the music with a band. It was not just all about just playing drums."[28] That distinction between playing music and simply playing drums is one that still defines Vidacovich's conception of himself as an artist. In his book *Jazz in New Orleans: The Postwar Years through 1970,* Suhor, a drummer, teacher, and music journalist, recalls the first time he sat Vidacovich at the pieced-together, rag-

Johnny Vidacovich. Kevin O'Day on Vidacovich: "I just loved the looseness and the interplay he would have with the bass, and then when soloists would improvise, he would be interactive with them too, still keeping that incredible second line greasy feel that he had." From *Wavelength Magazine.* Gift of Dr. Connie Atkinson. Courtesy of the New Orleans Jazz Museum. Accession number 2009.030.0850.02a.

gedy, old drum set that the music store used for lessons: "Johnny, about thirteen years old at the time, leaned tentatively into the ride cymbal, adjusting his wrist and his stroke instinctively until it got a resonance and a consistency of sound I had not heard before. He approached the snare, bass, sock, and other drums with the same relaxed inquiry into their sonic potential. His ear and his reflexes made it clear that he was a natural, and I never looked scornfully at the old set again."[29] Looking back on that first lesson with his star pupil, Suhor explains to Jake Feinberg: "When I heard him over the years, he always had a tonal approach to the drums and the cymbals, everything. He looked at the drums as an ensemble of sounds, and that was exactly what happened when I first put him on the set."[30] Vidacovich continued to study with Suhor until he was eighteen, and he excelled in music education programs at St. Aloysius High School and Loyola University. Meanwhile, he was pursuing an independent study in Drumsville. One of his regular "classes" took place every Friday night at a teen function at the Germania Hall, a white establishment that featured mostly Black R&B stars like Eddie Bo and Ernie K-Doe. The drummer usually was Smokey Johnson: "I'd spend a quarter and not move for three hours. I'd buy a couple cokes and end up getting a three-hour music lesson for less than a dollar."[31] Both James Black and David Lee were also important influences on the developing drummer:

> They both had the ability to play funk as well as jazz, and I used to go to different places as a teenager and listen to them play. They were also able to incorporate a "street" approach to playing the drums, because they're from here. I think when I was young, I really realized the relationship between marching street-type snare drumming and applying that to jazz or rock, funk or whatever. I could hear those elements in their playing.[32]

Other New Orleans drummers that he admired included Ernie Elly, Fred Staehle, Zig Modeliste, and Jack Sperling. Of course, he was aware of innovative drummers from outside New Orleans, such as Shadow Wilson, Max Roach, Tony Williams, and particularly Paul Motian: "There's something about his time, he's so unaffected by excitement and things, he's just so focused. He plays a lot of little phrases and contour melody-type ideas on the drums."[33]

Vidacovich, who rejects the notion of musical genres, has been drumming in bands of all shapes and sizes in New Orleans for parts of seven decades, ranging from Dunc's Honky Tonks, a youth trad band that entertained at hospitals, to strip clubs in the French Quarter, from the Real Dukes of Dixieland to the modern jazz of saxophonist Al Belletto's quartet and big band. He followed in the footsteps of so many Drumsville legends when he took over the drum chair in Professor Longhair's band. He tells Bunny Matthews: "He was a great guy to me, taught me a lot of stuff, spent time with me. He would play rhythms on my leg in the van when we were traveling. He was a tap dancer and a drummer, and he could play really fast stuff with his hands."[34] His buoyant take on the second-line groove is featured on the pianist's final studio album *Crawfish Fiesta* (1980). In an interview with Yorke Corbin, Vidacovich recalls that in the studio Longhair, who inexplicably referred to him as "Jawaski," was not interested in laid-back grooves: "Like he told me in the studio, 'just keep kicking. Keep agoing right on me. Keep agoing right on me. Just keep pushing.'

Professor Longhair's road band, 1978. *Left to right:* Ronald Johnson, Andy Kaslow, Johnny Vidacovich, Longhair, Tony Dagradi, and Dave Watson (Jim Moore and "Uganda" Roberts not pictured). Photo by Michael P. Smith. Copyright © The Historic New Orleans Collection. Accession number HNOC 2007.0103.4.840.

I'd say, 'Okay, Fess. Let's go babe.'"[35] His versatility and intuitive approach to enhancing the complete performance rather than showing off his skills also garnered him work with two other very different pianists, James Booker and Mose Allison.

In 1978, Vidacovich, a master improvisor, found an outlet for his contemporary jazz explorations with Astral Project, along with saxophonist Tony Dagradi, bassist James Singleton, guitarist Steve Masakowski, and, until 2001, pianist David Torkanowsky. More than four decades later, the band continues to enable him to stretch out and explore his compositional approach to drumming, which he variously calls "melodic rhythm, linear rhythm, lyrical rhythm, horizontal rhythm," a conception that was influenced by listening to David Lee. As he explained to Bruce Raeburn at the 2019 Allison Miner Music Heritage Stage: "David, to me, was one of the first drummers that I understood and heard, and what made a mark on me was his linear, horizontal approach, his melodic approach to playing the drums, as opposed to vertical, a lot more horizontal . . . I learned a lot of stuff from David Lee, phrasing, not to be afraid of space."[36] That melodic approach, which also can be found in the playing of New Orleans drummers from Dodds to Vernel Fournier to Ed Blackwell to Black, invests his drumming with a fluidity and compositional structure that enables him to *play the song* rather than just keep the beat. Astral Project is a band that allows Vidacovich to employ his formidable technical skills, but, like so many New Orleans drummers reaching back to Baby Dodds, he always plays at the service of the band. The "unconscious dance" takes over when he's improvising, but he's always aware

Stanton Moore (*left*) and Shannon Powell (*center*) listen to Johnny Vidacovich at the Jazz Museum's 2019 "Improv Conference: A Festival of Ideas." Vidacovich: "You've gotta get your head out of the game. It's from the neck down, and you've gotta feel that other player." Photo by R. Cataliotti.

of the drummer's role in making sure the band is working together. As he explained at the "Improv Conference: A Festival of Ideas" panel:

> You've gotta get your head out of the game. It's from the neck down, and you've gotta feel that other player. Am I making him feel comfortable? Is he playing on his game tonight? What can I do to make his game sound better? What can I do to make him feel comfortable? So, you have to learn how to read and hear body language and music language, what you're doing as part of the accompaniment to make the music comfortable, not only the guys playing it, but then, everybody has to make the audience feel comfortable too, you know, to a certain degree. You don't have to play down to the audience, but you sure as hell have to play for 'em. You don't have to play down to the audience like they don't know anything about music. You go ahead and try to take 'em on a trip. You have to be aware and careful and be paying attention to see what effect you're having.[37]

His bandmates are certainly aware of the incredible sensitivity he brings to the bandstand. As Dagradi explains: "If you talk to John Vidacovich, he'll tell you he just watches people's body language. He knows when somebody is going to take the next chorus or not. That's the way he plays. He watches people and looks to help shape the individual solos by his support."[38] Likewise, Singleton recognizes that having such empathetic support can be a lifesaver when improvising: "He can erase clams [mistakes] like no one I've ever heard. That's what makes him one of the most brilliant accompanists that I've encountered in my entire life. I'm pretty much convinced it's almost a hundred percent unconscious. He's just being so subservient to the good of the music that if something comes by that needs to be erased, he will do it."[39]

Vidacovich has become one of the Drumsville's elder statesman. Since the early 1980s, he has taught percussion at Loyola University, and his former students include such standout drummers as Stanton Moore, Kevin O'Day, and Brian Blade. Over the years, when a jazz soloist comes to town, frequently it is Vidacovich who fills the drum chair in the rhythm section, affording him the opportunity to support countless renowned artists. Astral Project carries on and has released six albums. He plays a long-standing trio gig on Thursday nights at the Maple Leaf with a revolving cast of players organized by his wife, Deborah. He's recorded four albums as a leader that feature a number of his own compositions: *Mystery Street* (1995); *Banks Street* (1996); *Vidacovich* (2002); and *'Bout Time* (2020), as well as *We Came to Play* (2003), a live trio recording with June Yamagishi on guitar and George Porter Jr. on bass. In addition to albums with former band leaders Belletto, Longhair, Booker, and Allison, Vidacovich drums on recordings by a broad range of artists that clearly reflects his refusal to be constrained by genres. The main reason Johnny V. has been around so long and made so much great music with so many different artists is because he knows exactly what a drummer is supposed to do: "You're basically hired to accompany people, to basically make people sound good. That's your job."[40]

Herlin Riley: "We Have Our Own Culture and Our Own Groove Here"

The Guiding Star Spiritual Church located in the Lower Ninth Ward neighborhood is the starting point for the journey that has taken Herlin Riley (b. 1957) to the status of one of the most highly regarded drummers in the world of jazz. An ambassador of the New Orleans beat known for his versatility, technical mastery, and captivating grooves, Riley was the first jazz drummer on a Pulitzer Prize–winning recording for his percussion work on the oratorio *Blood on the Fields* (1997) with Wynton Marsalis and the Lincoln Center Jazz Orchestra. Looking back on his roots, he explains: "It started in church. That's where I got it; everything comes out of the church for me."[41] Riley received his first lessons as a child in the family home as his grandfather Deacon Frank Lastie used butter knives to tap out a pattern at the breakfast table and then challenged the youngster to repeat it. He had drumsticks in his hands by age three, and he was playing his grandfather's drum set in the church by age five. The lessons he learned provided the fundamentals that still distinguish his playing. As he told Dan Thress:

> So, in checking him out, I began to realize the significance of how the music was supposed to feel. Early on, he always stressed to me, "Man, when you learn how to play, learn how to play time." Because when I first started to play the drums, I wanted to play all kind of wild stuff all over the drums. I'd get in church and I'd go into all this wild stuff and he'd look at me and give me the eye: "Hey man, what are you doing back there?" And I knew right away to go back into playing time.[42]

Music was a family affair in the Lastie home. Riley's mother, Betty Lastie, was a gospel singer and pianist, his three uncles—Melvin Lastie on trumpet and cornet, David Lastie

Left: Herlin Riley performing at the 1989 New Orleans Jazz and Heritage Festival. Photo by Michael P. Smith. Copyright © The Historic New Orleans Collection. Accession number HNOC 2007.0103.8.1302.

Right: Herlin Riley's tom-tom drum. Riley: "I use whatever is around me, but the most important thing is understanding what the timbre is and how to use it and how to incorporate it inside of what you're playing." Photo by Grace Patterson. Courtesy of the New Orleans Jazz Museum.

on saxophone, and Walter "Popee" Lastie on drums—were in-demand R&B and jazz players, and his cousin Joe Lastie Jr. was also learning to play drums. In addition to church, they performed together in the band A Taste of New Orleans. Rehearsals were a part of everyday life, and musicians like Professor Longhair were regular guests: "He came to my grandparents' house when I was a kid, and when he would play the piano and kick the front of it, and actually before Katrina, my grandmother had a piano that he had worn out the wood in that spot."[43] Riley looks at the experience of growing up in a musical household as "part of the walk of life of being a family member of older musicians who already played." He continues: "Growing up in a family of musicians, you hear the music, you absorb it, and then you get an opportunity to play it on an instrument."[44] Popee Lastie, who is included in that great cadre of drummers who played behind Fats Domino, introduced his nephew to the concepts of drumming in more modern forms like R&B and bebop, as well as another lesson that is essential to New Orleans drumming: "Whenever he would sit down and tell me anything about playing the drums he would say, 'Whenever you play a solo, think of the melody and try to play the form of the tune so that people can relate to it.' As opposed to just playing a beat or playing a lot of wild licks. Whatever I play, I always try to make it musically coherent."[45]

Despite his early initiation to the drums, Riley's formal studies in music came on the trumpet. Two of the people he learned from were pillars of New Orleans music education: band director Ms. Yvonne Bush and clarinetist Alvin Batiste, who was an artist in residence at George Washington Carver High School. He continued his education on trumpet at Southern University, where he played in the band under the direction of Kidd Jordan. Although he did not graduate, those formal studies were carried over to his approach on the drums, providing him with music reading skills and an understanding of composition and song forms. Outside of school, he found one of the city's great musical mentors, guitarist, banjo player, and singer Danny Barker, who recruited the young trumpeter into the Fairview Baptist Church Brass Band. Riley credits Barker with introducing him to traditional New Orleans music: "Danny took us kids, about 14 or 15 years old, myself and people like Tuba Fats [Lacen] and Leroy Jones, and put together his Fairview Band. That's when I really began to be exposed to the old style of music, like the '20s sound, playing choke cymbals and press roll–type snare drums. I got that from Danny. He's a great man. He took time with us kids and shared things that today we use and appreciate."[46]

The transition to full-time drummer was gradual. During a tour with the family band featuring Riley on trumpet and his uncle on drums, a 1950s rock-and-roll band offered Popee a gig; he declined but suggested Riley for the job. It provided valuable experience and boosted his confidence that he could hold down the drum chair in a band. His uncle David, who was playing on Bourbon Street behind Clarence "Frogman" Henry, also played a role in the transition when he suggested his nephew for a gig playing for strippers at the 500 Club.[47] He was hired as a trumpeter and occasionally filled in on drums, and when the regular drummer quit, Riley wound up as the house drummer because he was familiar with the act and how and when to accentuate the dancers' bumps and grinds with various percussive effects.[48] He was a long way from the Guiding Star Spiritual Church, but all those years of drumming paid off: "I was very fortunate and blessed to have the natural ability to just kind of put together the rhythms that I heard, coordinate myself to play whatever I heard. Of course, it took time to develop myself to be steady without speeding up or slowing down."[49] His drumming reached a new level when he began an extended run in pianist and singer Johnny Bachemin's trio:

> When I worked with Johnny Bachemin I really came into my own as a drummer because in a trio situation every tub stands on its own bottom. You don't have horns to lean on. You don't have a whole lot of synthesizers or guitars and stuff. It's not very loud where you can just kind of hide behind the noise. In a trio situation, playing in a small club, I learned to play with brushes. I learned to use my mallets. I learned to play, I would say, with a little taste, how to play dynamically, soft and loud. Besides that, this guy was a great showman and I watched him, and he taught me a lot about how to sell yourself from the stage.[50]

A measure of Riley's growth as a drummer and his stature in Drumsville can be found as he built his resume. He worked with trumpeter Al Hirt, and he took over the drum chair from Freddie Kohlman in the Heritage Hall Jazz Band, providing his first opportunity to play with pianist Ellis Marsalis. In 1981, he joined the company of the musical *One Mo' Time* for a six-month run in London, further expanding his percussive skills by immersing him in the nuances of 1920s-era drumming and learning the specific demands of theater work. In 1982, Riley solidified his reputation as a world-class drummer when he joined the Ahmad Jamal Quartet—a gig that will always be associated with Vernel Fournier: "Emory [Thompson] called about 8 a.m. and said, 'Hey, Herlin, Ahmad Jamal needs you.' I said, 'What, this is eight in the morning, come on, man, this is not the time

Herlin Riley. Tambourine *(top)*, washboard *(right)*, and cymbal *(bottom)*. Riley: "I was very fortunate and blessed to have the natural ability to just kind of put together the rhythms that I heard, coordinate myself to play whatever I heard." Photos by Eliot Kamenitz. Courtesy of the New Orleans Jazz Museum.

for fooling around.' Can you imagine somebody waking you up out of your sleep telling you that one of the world's greatest piano players would like you to work in his band? Emory said, 'No, I'm serious, he really would like you to work with him.'"[51] That same night Riley was on the bandstand with Jamal in Phoenix, Arizona; he stayed for five years and returned in 2009 for an additional five years.

In 1988, Riley began a seventeen-year collaboration with trumpeter Wynton Marsalis in his quintet/septet and as a member of the Lincoln Center Jazz Orchestra. One of the things he brought is an emphasis on playing for the benefit of the band: "What I think of is making music. I don't think of just playing the drums. I'm sensitive to the people who are around me, who are playing music with me because I want to contribute to the cause, and the cause is to make good music."[52] His approach had a transformative impact on the other musicians:

When I came into the band, I didn't play a lot of drums inside of the swing. Tain [Jeff Watts] played a lot of polyrhythms and stuff, and I didn't play that way. I tried to play that way at first, and it was okay, but it wasn't me. Then I started to play in a way that the soloists were able to just speak out, and I would be more of a supportive . . . like a cushion under the soloist—with some interaction as well. But I think they were able to hear more. Then the fact that I was from New Orleans and I played second line stuff, he could hear . . . It was a different feeling. I think I brought a different feeling to the band, a feeling of more groove and dance-oriented kind of rhythms.[53]

The years of working with Marsalis opened up opportunities for Riley to apply and develop his percussive skills and expand his rhythmic conception over an incredible range of creative contexts. He immersed himself in the repertoires of icons like Louis Armstrong, Duke Ellington, and Thelonious Monk and played their music with many of the veterans who had performed with them. He drummed alongside artists from Africa, Cuba, and Brazil and with symphony orchestras and gospel choirs. He appears on more than two dozen albums with Marsalis, always pushing the soloists to greater heights and enhancing the complete performance. On *Blood on the Fields* alone, he displays remarkable diversity in his approaches. He goes back to his grandfather's church and drives "Plantation Coffle March" with his tambourine. On "Forty Lashes," his explosive attack is absolutely devastating, especially the evocative, gut-wrenching hits to his snare. And, on "Juba and a O'Brown Squaw," singer Jon Hendricks rides on Riley's funky second-line groove. In the completely different setting of *Standard Time Vol. 3: The Resolution of Romance* (1990) that features him in a quartet with Marsalis, bassist Reginald Veal, and pianist Ellis Marsalis, he delivers an understated, restrained swing, as exemplified by his use of brushes on the trio outing "A Sleeping Bee" and his dancing stick work on "Flamingo." For *The Majesty of the Blues* (1989), Riley and Marsalis reunite with their mentor Danny Barker on banjo, along with hometown traditional jazz specialists Dr. Michael White on clarinet, Teddy Riley (no relation) on trumpet, and Freddie Lonzo on trombone. He takes things down to the roots of Drumsville with his snare and bass drum dialogue on the funeral dirge "The Death of Jazz" and enlivens "Oh, But on the Third Day (Happy Feet Blues)" with a buoyant second-line rhythm.

Today, based in New Orleans, Riley plays in a variety of contexts, teaches, and leads his own band. He is totally dedicated to the maintaining, extending, and passing along the tradition of the New Orleans beat and proudly declares: "We have our own culture and our own groove here in this city." And, when asked about its distinctiveness, his mantra is always: "In New Orleans drumming, the grooves are pretty much created from the bottom up." He takes great pride in the integral role his hometown played in the development of the drum set—a central theme in the *Drumsville!* narrative: "It's African Americans who kind of invented the drum set as we know it because of the invention of the bass drum pedal . . . That was a major part of the drum kit when the bass drum pedal was developed by Dee Dee Chandler and John Robichaux during that time. When they came up with it, it revolutionized the whole concept of drums."[54] Riley is also aware of how the advancement of the equipment impacted the music: "So with the evolution of the equipment and things getting more sophisticated with the equipment, it allowed drummers to execute at a much faster rate, so as a result of doing that, we started hearing rhythms differently and started playing rhythms differently, and that obviously affects the music.[55] An incredibly resourceful, cutting-edge improvisor, Riley also harks back to the tradition of "thinker-tinkers" who created percussion instruments from everyday objects. His sensitivity and awareness are on display when playing at clubs like Snug Harbor. In the heat of improvisation both he and his compadre Shannon Powell frequently expand the sonic palette of their drum sets by beating on the pipe that runs up the wall next to the stage:

> Drummers like myself and Shannon, we have this freedom, you know, we're free to play; we're constantly looking for ways to be creative and ways to use other elements or other things around us. Everything that you hit has a tone or has a timbre, everything that you hit. Whether or not you can incorporate that timbre into the drum set or into your expression while you're playing, it depends on the individual drummer and if he has that kind of freedom or he has that kind of openness and awareness to use those different elements that are around you. I use the pipe on the wall at Snug Harbor. Sometimes I'll hit a music stand. I'll play the side shell of the drums. I use whatever is around me, but the most important thing is understanding what the timbre is and how to use it and how to incorporate it inside of what you're playing.[56]

For Riley, jazz improvisation is about freedom but also about staying within the parameters of a form. His versatility is evident in the roster of artists with whom he has recorded, including Harry Connick Jr., Marcus Roberts, Cassandra Wilson, Wycliffe Gordon, Dr. John, Maria Muldaur, Mark Whitfield, Diane Reeves, McCoy Tyner, Ron Carter, George Benson, Dr. Lonnie Smith, Johnny Adams, Delfeayo Marsalis, Kermit Ruffins, and many more. He has released four albums as a leader, which increasingly focus on his original compositions, *Watch What You're Doing* (2000); *Cream of the Crescent* (2005); *New Direction* (2016); and *Perpetual Optimism* (2019). Riley's deep commitment to the legacy of New Orleans drumming perhaps is exemplified best by his original composition "Connection to Congo Square" from *New Direction,* a complex, polyrhythmic salute to the original Sunday gatherings that, just like those drum circles, features rhythmic masters from New Orleans and Havana, Cuba, Riley on drum set and Pedrito Martinez conga. The music remains as vital today as when he first picked up the drumsticks in the Guiding Star Spiritual Church: "This music is a living, breathing art form. It's always in the moment."[57] And, after his more than fifty years behind a drum set, Riley's creative impulses are still very much alive: "Take the chance, step out, step out of yourself sometimes, just be expressive, you know, art comes out of the bowels of who we are, and so, if we don't ever take chances and do stuff that's unconventional, stuff stays sterile and it stays stagnant."[58]

Ricky Sebastian: "The Science of Rhythm"

Ricky Sebastian (b. 1956) may have been born in Cajun Country, but he found a home in New Orleans through his devotion to the drums. His mastery of the New Orleans beat is evident in a story that he tells about performing with jazz flutist Herbie Mann at a festival at the Great Lakes. Singer Germaine Bazzle was on the bill, and although she couldn't see the band from backstage, she distinctly recognized the New Orleans beat as Sebastian went into a second-line groove for the drum intro to a Louis Armstrong tune: "She saw me a little later and said, 'I heard y'all earlier, and I told myself when that song started, "That's a New Orleans drummer."' She said, 'I got up from my chair and I started dancing.' So, if I made Germaine Bazzle dance, I knew I was doing the right thing."[59] Sebastian is a highly versatile musician who over the years has mastered many different styles of world music, but it was in Drumsville that he first established himself. He points to two fundamental elements when asked what makes New Orleans drumming distinctive:

> The first thing that comes to my mind is the way drummers here play the bass drum, and that's a direct result of knowing how to play second line and the street beats that exist here. There's a certain feel and certain accents that a drummer from New Orleans plays that you won't hear drummers from other places play, not even other countries like in Africa, so even though this style has roots from Africa, it's completely unique . . . The other thing is buzz rolls, press rolls. New Orleans drummers have the ability to play those like nobody else because it's also an integral part of second line drumming.

His first exposure to the city's rhythms came through the brass bands marching during his family's trips to the Mardi Gras and the soul music he heard on the radio that featured hits by New Orleans artists that were built on "that kind of second line beat, Mardi Gras Indian rhythms," which, of course, were played by drummers like Earl Palmer, Smokey Johnson, Hungry Williams, and John Boudreaux. As he matured as a drummer, Sebastian tuned in to that distinctive beat sixty miles downriver from his home: "So, I would say about sixteen, seventeen, I was starting to become aware that there was a special thing going on here as far as drumming styles."

Born in Opelousas and raised in Gonzales, Sebastian was constantly beating out rhythms as a child, annoying his parents and prompting one teacher to swat him in the back of the head with a rolled-up newspaper. His grandparents took notice of the precocious percussionist and bought him a toy drum set from TG&Y department store: "They had paper heads, and it lasted about a week. I just beat the hell out of it. But, if anything, it kind of sunk the desire in me. It was that first little drum set. And, after I trashed that one, I started, like a lot of kids do playing drums, making sets out of old pots and pans and boxes." The fledgling drummer clearly exhibited that innovative "thinker-tinker" spirit, and when he was around age eight his father finally bought him a snare drum. In the Catholic elementary school he attended, there was no money to buy drums for the band, so when the auditions for drummers were held, the students beat on folding metal chairs: "You talk about a racket. I mean, fifteen kids trying to play drums on metal chairs, but when most of the kids found out that they'd have to learn how to read music, I think five returned the next day, so that was a lot more manageable. So, that was my introduction to drumming and rhythm from a formal perspective." Sebastian says that around age nine or ten he began to focus on drummers when he listened to records or watched bands on television. He doesn't recall any specific instance when he decided drumming was his life's work: "There wasn't really an 'Ah ha!' moment from my childhood where it was like

Ricky Sebastian, ca. 1985. Sebastian: "There's a certain feel and certain accents that a drummer from New Orleans plays that you won't hear drummers from other places play." From *Wavelength Magazine.* Gift of Dr. Connie Atkinson. Courtesy of the New Orleans Jazz Museum. Accession number 2009.030.0717.02.

'I wanna do that,' you know, 'I wanna be a drummer.' Just as far back as I can remember, I was always fascinated with what I call the 'science of rhythm.'" Attending junior high and high school in Ascension Parish, Sebastian, who played in the marching bands and was a drum line section leader, benefited from the expertise of two band directors, Carl DeLeo and Carl Schexnayder. He augmented his percussive skills by learning to play xylophone, vibes, and marimba. His drumming was so advanced that by age seventeen, he got permission to go out on tour with Emmett Kelly Jr.'s All Star Circus.

As a teenager, his musical tastes leaned toward progressive rock bands like Emerson, Lake and Palmer and Yes, but he was soon drawn to the sounds of the emerging style of jazz rock fusion coming from such artists as Chick Corea and Return to Forever and Herbie Hancock and the Headhunters: "I've talked to a lot of the musicians over the years that have a similar story as me about gravitating toward fusion, basically bands that are younger and more in your generation, so to speak, and learning that style of music." Fusion opened the door to the jazz world, and Sebastian was soon exploring the lineage of the master drummers and their innovations:

> And then you start backtracking and going through the generations of drummers in jazz, in particular, and you start to realize there's a whole vocabulary that's developed in this music over the decades, and you start to hear where one person got certain licks and ideas, this guy that he listened to. One of my all-time favorite drummers is Tony Williams. When I started listening to, for example, Philly Joe Jones, I could hear the direct connection there. But Tony had studied a lot of the great drummers before him, you know, like Max Roach, Art Blakey, Philly Joe Jones, so he knew every one of those guy's style and could imitate it like incredibly well.

He worked his way back through the jazz tradition until he arrived at the source: "All the way back to New Orleans. It took me until age 17 to backtrack to where I was without even leaving."[60] Exploring the New Orleans music scene, Sebastian discovered the history of drumming there *and* a thriving music scene that revealed drummers with stunningly original approaches to the instrument. He was particularly impressed with James Black and Johnny Vidacovich:

> Their styles were just so very different, but I remember the first time I saw each of them thinking, "I didn't know you could play the drum set like that." So, it was really an eye opener for me . . . Well, with Johnny's style, he was just so fluid and more melodic than rhythmic, and I had never seen or heard a drummer play like that before. James had this ability to take rhythm out of the time it was in and play what they call polyrhythms. He was very advanced with that, his ability to superimpose a different time feel over the original one and always maintain where he was originally. That floored me; I wanted to know how to do that.[61]

He continued his musical studies at the University of Southwestern Louisiana in Lafayette for a year and then headed to Boston to study at Berklee College of Music for a semester.

At age nineteen, Sebastian moved to New Orleans, and like so many drummers before him during that era, he was able to develop his art and craft working regularly on bandstands in the French Quarter: "Berklee, for me, was great technically. I came back to New Orleans and started working on the Street—Bourbon Street. This club, that club, that's where I learned how to play, but I had all this technical knowledge to apply, to adapt."[62] Over the next six years, he performed in a variety of contexts, refining his approach to the New Orleans beat and incorporating additional stylistic influences playing behind such artists as Dr. John, George Porter, Exuma, Sam Rivers, Bobby McFerrin, and Clarence "Gatemouth" Brown. In 1983, Sebastian moved to New York in the hope of finding the opportunity to perform with some of his jazz heroes; he was not disappointed. Leaders who recognized the versatility and proficiency that enabled him to light a fire under a band include Herbie Mann, Jaco Pastorius, John Scofield, Harry Belafonte, Emily Remler, Michael Brecker, and JoAnne Brackeen.

On the Big Apple scene, Sebastian's mastery of the New Orleans beat along with Cajun and zydeco grooves distinguished him: "It was definitely a feather in my cap to have been from here. That definitely helped, the fact that I knew these rhythms, knew how to play that feel, you know, 'cause that's the hardest thing to acquire; anytime you want to learn a different style of music, it's one thing to learn it technically with the correct beats and all, how to put things together, but the most difficult aspect is to get the feel." His experiences in New Orleans led to a whole new aspect of his career as a drummer. The owner of the Drummers Collective, who was a big New Orleans music fan, heard Sebastian playing with Dr. John and urged him to come teach a master class:

> I had never done anything like that before and just threw some ideas together. Went in and did the first one, and it was a huge success. Then I did another one, and he said, "We'd really like you to be on the faculty here." So, that's how I started teaching for the most part, but when I was young and coming up in New Orleans, there were so many elder musicians that just kind of took me under their wing and would teach me stuff. You know we didn't have jazz programs in universities back then. So, the only way you could really learn was to hang out with these guys on the gig. And I never forgot that because that was instrumental in me being the best I could be at a young age.

During his time in New York, Sebastian continued to expand his versatility on the drum set. One of the styles that he immersed himself in was Brazilian music, and finding the right "feel" was essential to the process. He would often go to hear a Brazilian band performing in a restaurant near his Soho loft and sit next to the bandstand with a small shaker:

> I'd sit on the side of the stage, at a table next to the stage with that thing and just play along with 'em. It wasn't loud enough to, you know, distract anybody in the band, but it enabled me to get the feel of what the drummer is doing, and I remember the night something just clicked [*snaps fingers*], and I just had it. I had the feel with that shaker, and the next thing I tried to transfer it over to the hi-hat with sticks. And, I don't know why it didn't take me that long to get it. The only thing I can figure is that I was from here.

Ricky Sebastian (*center*) with Heritage School of Music students. In addition to teaching at the University of New Orleans, Sebastian works with younger musicians: "I have couple young drummers, more than a couple, several at the Heritage School that are really gonna be something else; they already are." Photo by Zack Smith. Courtesy of the Heritage School of Music.

He recognizes his grounding in the New Orleans beat connects him to the rhythmic legacy of the African diaspora: "Let's face it, when you look at a map, I look at New Orleans and where it's located, more from water perspective, and we're just the northernmost point of the Caribbean, and we just happen to be in the United States [*laughs*]. And, the vibe here really reflects that. People come here from Cuba, Puerto Rico, Brazil, Haiti, they say, 'Ah, I feel like I'm home here,' in so many ways." There was another essential step in the process of learning the "feel" of new rhythms: "Now, I've been with Brazilians. I learned how to dance the samba, I have done that. That's my philosophy about drumming. Okay, first you learn the beat, then you learn how to dance to it. When your body gets that flow in the dance that's when it lets you know how to really play that beat."[63] His mastery of those rhythms is reflected in the many Brazilian artists with whom he has performed, including Romero Lubambo, Thiago De Mello, Luiz Simas, Steve Barta, and Tania Maria.

In 1998, Sebastian moved back to New Orleans, and his drumming, as a leader and a sideman, continues to enrich Drumsville. He has performed live and recorded with such artists as Donald Harrison, Harold Battiste, Los Hombres Calientes, George Porter, ¡Cubanismo!, and Stephanie Jordan. Sebastian released his first album as a leader, *The Spirit Within* (2001), which features his own compositions along with selections from jazz masters like Duke Ellington, Wayne Shorter, Jaco Pastorius, and Herbie Hancock. One of the highlights is "Don't Trip the Monkey," originally conceived as a showcase during his live performances with Harry Belafonte. It's a rhythmic journey that travels through New Orleans, Cuba, Brazil, and West Africa featuring Sebastian along with fellow percussionists Kenyatta Simon and Bill Summers: "But really that piece represents the journey in my career as far as playing different styles go."[64] He teaches at the University of New Orleans, where he also directs the World Music Ensemble and the Percussion Ensemble. Organizing and augmenting his notes from years of teaching, he created a highly regarded instructional book, *Independence on the Drumset: Coordination Studies for Drummers in All Styles* (2005). In addition to teaching private lessons, Sebastian helps to keep the Drumsville legacy alive and well by working with young drummers in a program run by the Jazz and Heritage Foundation:

I mean I have couple young drummers, more than a couple, several at the Heritage School that are really gonna be something else; they already are. This one ten-year-old kid, Jamie Jones, he's still so little, he almost has to stand up to sit on the drum seat. His feel and his time are just amazing for his age. And, I've been teaching him for years, but I didn't teach him those things. He already had that, just like I did when I was his age. So, particularly after Katrina, I'm so glad to see something like that didn't just wipe out the culture here. It's probably stronger now than it was before.

Joe Lastie Jr.: "I Kept That with Me"

During the early 1970s, Joe Lastie Jr. (b. 1958) moved with his family from the Lower Ninth Ward to Long Island. One of the ways the young drummer maintained a connection to New Orleans music was by watching the Preservation Hall Jazz Band's appearances on television. He never actually heard the band before leaving his hometown, but when he watched and listened to their vintage traditional jazz on television, he knew exactly where he wanted to be. And, it certainly never crossed the teenager's mind that he would become a mainstay on drums at the venerable hall on St. Peter Street for over three decades. Like his first cousin Herlin Riley, Lastie's initiation into drumming came through their family's church:

> My name is Joseph Frank Lastie Jr. I was named after my father and my grandfather. My grandfather's name was Frank Lastie. He played drums in the Spiritual Churches around New Orleans. He was one of the drummers responsible for introducing drums into the Spiritual Churches in New Orleans, And that's how I picked up playing the drums, watching, matter of fact both my grandfathers, my grandfather Frank Lastie and my grandfather Emil Desvignes, both of them played drums in church. I used to watch both of 'em play in church when I was a little boy, and that's basically where it all started.[65]

An enduring lesson from Deacon Lastie that has a become a trademark of Lastie's drumming is his initiation into an old-school approach to gripping his drumsticks: "My grandfather, Frank Lastie, he's the one who really stood out because of the way he used to hold his drumsticks with his fingers and play with his fingers a lot. And I picked up on his playing like that, and people look at me and say, 'Wow, you look like you're hardly moving.' I say, 'because I'm not playing with my wrists or my arms.' I play eighty percent with my fingers." Lastie also finds that the rhythms of the Spiritual Church and traditional jazz are closely related:

> You have to realize that songs that we did playing in church, we play those same songs in the trad circuit, and it's around the same feeling . . . I'm gonna give you an example, "When the Saints Go Marching In," we was playing that even before I knew about "When the Saints Go Marching In," in the trad scene. We played that, and the people used to march around the church . . . It's the same beat with a little swing to it. But with my swinging, I got to put my little backbeat in there and my bass drum to have that spiritual sound.

His childhood was immersed in music. In addition to his grandfathers, his uncles David, Melvin, and Walter "Popee" Lastie were widely respected R&B and jazz players, his aunt Betty Ann Lastie Williams was a gospel singer and pianist, and his cousin Herlin Riley

Joe Lastie Jr. Lastie on playing at Preservation Hall: "You don't have to be Cie Frazier, but you can sound like Cie Frazier, and I kept that with me." Photo by Curtis Knapp. Courtesy of the New Orleans Jazz Museum.

was learning trumpet and drums. As a youngster, he played a three-piece drum set—bass drum, snare drum, and cymbal—in the church. When he was about ten, his grandmother Alice Lastie bought him a full-size, red Pearl drum set. The tales his uncle "Popee" brought home from his life on the road with Fats Domino further sparked Lastie's interests in becoming a professional drummer.

Lastie's relocation to Long Island did not sidetrack his journey into the New Orleans beat. A drummer friend of his parents, Clyde Harris, gave him lessons in rudiments and sight reading, and he played in his junior high stage band, making quite an impression behind the set thanks to his early drumming experiences in New Orleans. He missed his hometown, and, in addition to Preservation Hall television appearances, he stayed connected by putting on headphones and playing along with Al Hirt and Pete Fountain albums he borrowed from the library. During that time on Long Island, a new beat emerged, and Lastie encountered the rhythms of early rap music through a friendship with Flavor Flav (William Jonathan Drayton Jr.), who went on to become one of the founders of Public Enemy. That rhythmic influence would surface on Lastie's solo album *Jazz Corner of the World* (2017).

In 1976, Lastie convinced his parents to allow him to return to New Orleans and live with his grandparents. He attended George Washington Carver High School for his senior year and joined the marching band under the direction of Ms. Yvonne Bush. Lastie was still very much in tune with the sounds of gospel music. He went back to drumming at the family church and eventually picked up his first professional gig: "I started playing professionally I would say when I got with the Desire Community Choir, and I went on the road with them. And, as a matter of fact, that's where I did my first recording at." He went to the Los Angeles area with the choir to appear at a series of churches and festivals, and his first recording work in a band that included organist Sammy Berfect, guitarist Detroit Brooks, and bassist Mark Brooks appears on the album *Thank You Lord* (1978) by Alvin Bridges and the Desire Community Choir. He continued his two-pronged journey into both sacred and secular music: "Then, right after that, I was with Willie Metcalf, the Academy of Black Arts. I started with Wynton and Branford [Marsalis] and all of them." Lastie's first paying club date—for five dollars—came when he performed with one of the Academy's bands at the renowned modern jazz club Lu & Charlie's. Playing with his family continued to take him deeper into the New Orleans beat: "I remember there was a time when Professor Longhair used to come to my aunt's house, which is Herlin's mother, and we used to have jam sessions there, and I did something with them Uptown before it was Tipitina's [The 501 Club]. So, I got to do something with Professor Longhair and my uncle Jesse Hill." He also was playing New Orleans R&B with his uncles in the family band A Taste of New Orleans and with Antoine Domino Jr. in the band Creole Cooking. A chance encounter on Bourbon Street with bassist Richard Payne took him immediately from the sidewalk to an empty drum stool on the bandstand at the La Strada club, and the gig playing standards behind a female vocalist lasted four or five months. Lastie also gained valuable experience, especially with reading charts, backing up vocalist Banu Gibson.[66]

Increasingly drawn toward traditional jazz, in the early 1980s Lastie began working with trumpeter Wallace Davenport at the Maison Bourbon, and thanks to its proximity, he began visiting Preservation Hall to hear Drumsville masters like Freddie Kohlman, Cie Frazier, and Frank Parker. He gained more trad jazz experience and even did some brass band work with Scotty Hill and the French Market Jazz Band. In 1989, a recommendation from trumpeter Greg Stafford earned Lastie his first gig at the Hall, working behind trumpeter George "Kid Sheik" Colar. He has been working there on a regular basis ever since. Taking hold of the baton and carrying forward the tradition at Preservation Hall is a serious responsibility for Lastie:

> It's interesting how the drummers in the past influence us how to keep that same feeling because I remember when I first started playing with Preservation Hall. I had to keep that feeling of who? Cie Frazier. When I started playing with Preservation Hall, I kept the Cie Frazier beat. I kept that in my head to remind myself, "You following Cie Frazier." You don't have to be Cie Frazier, but you can sound like Cie Frazier, and I kept that with me.

He strives to maintain many of the hallmark characteristics that were established by the traditional jazz giants who came before him, including that essential role identified by drummers like Baby Dodds: "The drummer is definitely the timekeeper because if he slows down, the whole thing slows down. If he speeds up, the whole thing speeds up, and if the drummer is on the wrong beat, it changes the whole song." Of course, his emphasis was on building grooves from the bottom up with the bass drum: "When I first started at Preservation Hall, now here we go back with this drumming thing again with the old cats. Now, Mr. Percy [Humphrey] must have been eighty or ninety years old; I was in my early thirties. And when I played with Mr. Percy—what you think—he'd reach back and look back there and tell me, 'Alright, hit that bass drum, boom, boom, boom,' So that's why I told you that bass drum is so important." Lastie also plays the drums with the melody in mind: "With my playing, some people tell me they can hear me play the melody. How is that possible? Bear in mind, I'm always humming the melody in my head, and it comes out in my playing." As much as he is dedicated to maintaining the tradition, he has absorbed modern drum approaches and adapts his playing based on who he's supporting:

> Depending on who you're playing with, like if I play with Wendell Brunious, he has modern phrasing that he does on his trumpet. Sometimes I have to back off my trad and go into a swing. Now when I'm playing with Greg Stafford, he definitely doesn't want you to do the swing thing. He wants you to keep it with that trad sound. It depends on who you're playing with and also if someone takes a solo, like say Freddie Lonzo, if he takes a trombone solo, I can stay in my trad thing more. But they got a new kid on the block; his name is David Harris. You try to play that trad stuff behind him, you're not gonna do it because he's playing so many notes where it needs the swing jazz and modern jazz thing. They have another trumpet player around there, his name is Kevin Lewis, and maybe Will Smith, now when I

play with them there's a certain time where I have to come out with my Mardi Gras Indian mood on the bass drum and the snare and the floor tom. See, I'm prepared to get into my little mood with that.

Lastie, who is featured on a number of Preservation Hall recordings, exhibits his dual allegiance on his two recordings as a leader. He digs deep into his past with *The Lastie Family Gospel* (2008), an album that brings together the gospel and trad worlds, featuring both himself and Riley on drums; his aunt Betty on vocals, piano, and organ; the Reverend Leon Vaughn on organ; and the Choir of St. James Methodist Church, along with Preservation Hall colleagues Lucien Barbarin on trombone; Rickie Monie on piano; Dwayne Burns on trumpet; and Elliot "Stackman" Callier on tenor saxophone. The program covers a number of songs such as "I'll Fly Away," "Down by the Riverside," and "Just a Closer Walk with Thee" that are tunes he has played both in church and on the jazz bandstand. The performances are raw, spontaneous, and immediate. On his album *Jazz Corner of the World,* Lastie is accompanied by many of his regular bandmates from Preservation Hall, including Monie, trumpeter Kid Merv Campbell, and clarinetist Louis Ford, on a program that provides a spirited look inside what listeners experience at his weekly showcase at Preservation Hall on New Orleans standards "Basin Street Blues," "Struttin' with Some Barbeque," and "Bourbon Street Parade." He also flashes some versatility and innovation on the Hurricane Katrina elegy "New Orleans in Me," melding traditional jazz; the hip-hop sensibility he picked up all those years ago from Flavor Flav; and Mardi Gras Indian funk from special guest Big Chief David Montana. That blend of traditional jazz,

R&B, hip-hop, and Black Masking Indian grooves also distinguishes his work with vocalist Eddie Burt Sr. on the Nation of Gumbolia's album *Filé* (2020). In 2014, Lastie reached a whole new audience when he jammed with the Foo Fighters, who took up residence at Preservation Hall for their album and HBO series *Sonic Highways*. He even made the pages of *Rolling Stone* magazine, with Foo Fighters drummer Taylor Hawkins acknowledging Lastie's mastery of the New Orleans beat: "We were hanging on for dear life with those guys. To have their drummer Joe Lastie next to me, playing the craziest upside-down stuff—I just tried to keep time. I wanted to hear *him*."[67] Lead guitarist and vocalist (and drummer) Dave Grohl further explains to Keith Spera what it was like to jam with Lastie: "Watching Joe play the drums, I can't imagine that he's thinking too much about what he's doing. He's just feeling it, and it's just coming out of him. It's like going dancing. You don't want to think about dancing; you just want to dance. When I watch that guy play drums, it's like watching someone dancing in a beautiful moment."[68]

From first picking up the drumsticks in the Lower Ninth Ward church to the teenager on Long Island longing for home, from his first tour with the Desire Community Choir to his countless nights at Preservation Hall, Joe Lastie Jr. has become a Drumsville legend: "Number one, it's a pleasure that I'm being named in the company of great drummers from the past. And also, I think the drummers that have been respected from New Orleans, man . . . I really feel that they set the standards for us to keep the New Orleans drumming tradition alive." In the end, it always circles back to his roots in the rhythms of the Spiritual Church: "That backbeat is that foundation where it give you that kick. And, people listen out for that, where the one is and where the two at, they just get that spiritual thing when they hear that backbeat, and it gets 'em in a dance mood. That's another thing, too, they get up dancing when they hear that New Orleans beat."

Joe Lastie's 1970s Rogers drum stool seat. Lastie's vintage drum stool seat survived the floodwaters of Hurricane Katrina in his Ninth Ward home. Photo by Grace Patterson. Courtesy of the New Orleans Jazz Museum.

Shannon Powell: "The Lord Put Everything in My Lap"

During the early 1970s, the Fairview Baptist Church Brass Band, organized by Danny Barker, introduced a generation of young musicians to traditional New Orleans jazz. On the contemporary scene, many of these band members have carried on Barker's mission and play a vital role in passing along the tradition to the new generation. Shannon Powell (b. 1962) is one of those musicians, but his relationship with Barker was unique and took him far beyond the Fairview band experience. Around the age of twelve, Powell regularly was working gigs with Barker *as a duo*—just banjo/guitar and drums: "That was the greatest experience of my life. As a young, upcoming musician to be able to learn from him. I heard people talk about him in the Treme, and to be able to meet him and become his drummer at such a young age, you know that was a big deal in my life."[69] There was nowhere to hide working in a duo format, and musically the experience transformed Powell into a professional drummer:

> Well, I learned how to play. He taught me how to swing on the drums with the four on the floor with the bass drum. Things like that. I mean a lot of little things that you pretty much

learn on the job, play four on the bass drum, play on the cymbal, and sometimes he didn't want me to have no hi-hat, understand because the hi-hat sometimes would fluctuate because I was just learning about that, the two and four on the hi-hat. And, he didn't really care for that much because he came from the old school. He taught me about different tempos, playing full on the drums, making the drums sound full, like you're playing with a whole band, you know. The bass drum is the trick. Drummers from New Orleans were always taught from the bottom on up.

Meeting Danny Barker was transformative, but it was actually only one of the many encounters that made Powell a drummer whose personal journey is perhaps most deeply rooted in the Drumsville tradition. It's almost as if he was destined to be a part of the evolution of the New Orleans beat: "To this day, I'm so blessed. The Lord put everything in my lap. I was hanging with the best people to learn all these different styles."

The origin of Powell's journey into New Orleans drumming couldn't have been more physically or symbolically fitting. At age five, he moved in with grandmother and aunt in the family home on St. Philip Street in Treme—a home in which he still lives. It is directly across the street from Louis Armstrong Park, which encompasses Congo Square, the ultimate source point for New Orleans drumming, and it sits next door to St. Philip Church of God in Christ. The sanctified rhythms he heard coming from the church were magnetic, and as a child he would slip inside during services and was taught to play the tambourine. The church also provided him with his first opportunity to play a drum set. Eventually, he drummed at his aunt's St. James Methodist Church, supporting the one-hundred-member Voices of Triumph choir. The experience taught him about dynamics and how to play with brushes and mallets, and he found another mentor: "The lady that was the director, her name was Ms. Ruby Porter. She was a beautiful person, very elegant and very musical. She was a person that taught at Dillard University, and she taught me so much, and she treated me like I was her son. She spent time with me showing me how to play the drums."

Church was only the beginning for Powell. He was a member of the Joseph S. Clark High School concert band, but in exploring the streets of Treme, he was surrounded by many facets of the Drumsville tradition. Of course, he was fascinated by the second-line parades that moved through the neighborhood and was particularly drawn to the sound of the bass drum. He also encountered the polyrhythmic hand percussion and call-and-response chants of the Mardi Gras Indians. He realized they were playing beats with which he was quite familiar:

All that Mardi Gras Indian stuff, all that come from the Sanctified Church. Because if you listen to it good, and you listen to the pattern of the style they playing, it all comes out the church. That's a church thing that come straight from the spirit that these people came up with. People in the Sanctified Church were born with a natural feeling. So I heard that in church, then when I got in the streets in New Orleans and started hearing the Mardi Gras Indians, it's the same beat.[70]

He was exposed to African rhythms at the St. Marks Community Center, where he met Alfred "Uganda" Roberts, who was playing for a youth drumming and dance group led by flutist and conga drummer Eluard Burt: "I knew Uganda when I was a child. I come up under him . . . Alfred was the *man*. My God, he could play with everybody. He could play some congas, man!" Professor Longhair lived in an apartment above the Caldonia Inn, also just around the corner from Powell's home, and on his way to school he could hear the piano master. He had a chance to witness some of the city's essential funk grooves take shape: "I knew about the Meters. They recorded a block from my house where Allen Toussaint had his first studio. And I used to stand in front of their house and listen to them all during the '70s. I heard all those guys like Zigaboo when I was a kid." He was introduced to modern jazz drumming thanks to a one-on-one lesson with neighbor James Black:

Shannon Powell performing at the 2013 Jazz and Heritage Festival. Powell: "The trad music part is the heartbeat of all of it. That's where all of it comes from." Photo by Golden G. Richards III / High ISO Music.

> I lived around the corner from him, and I always heard the drums come out of there, but it was always some real tricky kind of drum playing, what I used to call tricky, because I wasn't used to what he was playing. I came up playing trad music and playing four on the floor. I wasn't used to that bebop he was playing. So, I just happened to be sitting on his steps one day, and he came to the door and I introduced myself to him, and he introduced himself to me. And, he invited me in, and he turned me on how to play in five [5/4 time signature]. I was a kid, different time meters, and that was another great experience, to get to learn from him.

Like the antebellum musicians of African descent who could hear both the rhythms of Congo Square and European classical music in the French Quarter or during the early twentieth century—jazz drumming pioneer Baby Dodds standing in the hallway of the Tulane Theatre listening to operas and symphonies—Powell also sought to broaden his musical horizons right in his own neighborhood. The Mahalia Jackson Theater for the Performing Arts is directly across the street from his house: "I was frequently going in there, listening to the symphony. I really loved the timpani drums and just meeting the cats, learning different little things about playing percussion instruments . . . Jeff Boudreaux, great drummer lives in Paris now, I used to go in there and sit down and listen and watch him do certain things."[71] The musical influences that Powell absorbed *just in Treme* literally span the entire history of the New Orleans beat.

Powell's musical explorations took him outside of Treme, and it was in the French Quarter at Preservation Hall that he fueled his passion for playing traditional jazz: "I met Mr. [Alan] Jaffe, and he was very kind to me, always invited me to come into the Hall to listen to the old greats, you know, and I was so blessed to be able to sit there night after night and listen to all these great musicians." He listened to and watched such legends of the New Orleans beat as Louis Barbarin, Cie Frazier, and Freddie Kohlman and cer-

Shannon Powell's snare drum. The 14-inch custom, "old school" snare drum was a gift to Shannon Powell from Cie Frazier. Photo by Grace Patterson. Courtesy of the New Orleans Jazz Museum.

tainly took those lessons to heart. The *Drumsville!* exhibit features a video of Powell from the Jazz Fest Allison Miner Music Heritage Stage illustrating stylistic differences in the drumming of Barbarin and Frazier. He explains: "Louis Barbarin was a much more technical drummer than Cie. Cie Frazier played a lot from the heart." His musical horizons also expanded when he was given access, despite being underage, to Lu & Charlie's nightclub, the Mecca of modern jazz in the city during the 1970s: "I was the only kid allowed in the place . . . and I heard some of the best modern, bebop jazz in the world."[72] And, once again, he met an important mentor and employer, pianist Ellis Marsalis: "I was scared to death because I knew this man played another style of music that I wasn't too much into, but I needed a gig and I wanted to learn." Powell broadened his stylistic repertoire as he learned the nuances of playing the city's trademark brand of rhythm and blues and funk. Smokey Johnson was a prime influence: "I heard Smokey in the neighborhood at different clubs, and then I went to different concerts, you know, when he was playing with Fats Domino I used to be at all the concerts, like at Jazz Fest. He didn't play in New Orleans that much, but when he did, I was there." The number of drummers he learned from is truly remarkable: "Herman Ernest was another inspiration to me. I met him as a kid . . . Herman was a good drummer that could read, and Bernard Johnson, another guy, better known as 'Bunchy.' He was another good pocket drummer, could read, could play any style, nice person too. But Herman Ernest was a *bad* man [*laughs*]." His expertise as an R&B/funk drummer was developed and enhanced through working with veterans like bassist George Porter and saxophonist David Lastie: "I was lucky to be around George and learn a lot of things about rhythm and blues and funk. George turned me on to a whole bunch of stuff. Same with Mr. Lastie. I was being taught, man, when I was in these bands. I wasn't taking the gig as, 'Oh, I'm the man. I know what I'm doing.' Every time I played a gig with those guys back then, I was always in school." His ability to get low down and funky with the blues found a tremendous outlet when he worked alongside Porter at the original Rock 'n' Bowl behind guitarist and singer Snooks Eaglin:

> Snooks Eaglin, boy, that was a great experience. Play straight time, play straight rhythm and blues music, play time, you know, nothing extra, nothing out of the ordinary, just groove and play the shuffles and the backbeat, you know what I'm saying. Snooks was a pocket man, you know, he played in the pocket, very talented man. He used to always tell me to watch his feet. He'd say, "Watch my feet, Powell!" [*laughs*]. That's right 'cause he'd keep the time, see, with his feet while he's playing. 'Cause if you watch him, you could never get off the time, you know.

During the 1980s, Powell came into his own as a drummer with trumpeter Leroy Jones's New Orleans Finest, which also featured pianist Edward Frank; trombonist Lucien Barbarin (great-nephew of Paul and Louis Barbarin); and bassist Rusty Gilder: "New Orleans Finest, that was another good band. See, we all came up together, me and Leroy and Lucien, you know. I played with Leroy when he had Lucien, and then he went to a quartet." The band was a prime outlet for Powell to showcase a wide range of material in a jazz context, from a trad homage to Louis Armstrong with "Someday You'll Be Sorry" to a bebop take on "All the Things You Are" to an R&B ballad like "Betcha by Golly Wow." For Jones, Powell lit an authentic New Orleans fire under the band: "Shannon's got the street thing. He's a natural."[73] But, Powell could also bring a sophisticated technical mastery to the performances. Often when he got a chance to solo, rather than pull out all the stops, he would take things down and deliver a finessed, scintillating workout on the hi-hat, a technique that he credited to hearing played by renowned session drummer Jake Hanna—a musician whose style was far removed from the New Orleans beat. This speaks volumes about Powell because at a young age he not only immersed himself in the Drumsville tradition but was aware of what he could learn from drummers beyond New Orleans. Of course, he got some help with that process:

> Mr. Barker turned me on to him. I didn't know nothing about him . . . He used to show me a lot of pictures years ago when I would go to his house. He'd pull out pictures, and he'd pull out music . . . He had a little phonograph that he played all those old wax records on. And he'd tell me, here's a drummer, Jake Hanna, and Louis Bellson, Buddy Rich, he knew 'em all, Gene Krupa, Cozy Cole.

Powell was able to learn more about a technique like that on the home front: "A lot of that stuff I learned from Smokey because I saw Smokey do it. Smokey had picked it up from Philly Joe [Jones]. Smokey Johnson was the only drummer in New Orleans that was playing that hi-hat like that. They call it 'fannin' the hi-hat' . . . I didn't get a chance to see Mr. Jake Hanna do it too many times, but I saw Smokey do it a bunch of times."

By the early 1990s, Powell's mastery behind the drum set took him to audiences far beyond Drumsville. He toured worldwide with his old friend, pianist and vocalist Harry Connick Jr., in both a trio and big band format. His versatility is displayed on his recordings with Connick: the finesse of his brush work and ability to shade with subtlety on the instrumental trio album *Lofty's Roach Soufflé* as well as on the vocal album with the trio and guest soloist saxophonist Branford Marsalis *We Are in Love* (both released on the same day in 1990), and his fiery swing drives the big band on *Blue Light, Red Light* (1991). That big band experience came in handy when he began working with Jazz at Lincoln Center: "They had two big bands back then. Herlin [Riley] was playing with the first band, and I was playing with the second band." His trio work with Connick also earned him a spot touring in pianist Diana Krall's trio.

However, Powell is a Drumsville man through and through. He established his own band at a weekly gig at Donna's on Rampart Street, and things came full circle when he began working weekly at Preservation Hall. Testimony to the lessons he learned there

Shannon Powell. The origin of Powell's journey into New Orleans drumming couldn't have been more physically or symbolically fitting. He grew up in Treme across the street from Louis Armstrong Park, which encompasses Congo Square, and next door to St. Philip Church of God in Christ. Photo by Curtis Knapp. Courtesy of the New Orleans Jazz Museum.

as kid can be found on the Preservation Hall Jazz Band album *Shake That Thing* (2004), particularly the rocking second-line groove on his featured number "Little Liza Jane." One of the highlights of his live sets is frequently a solo segment on bass drum and tambourine where he takes everything back to the rhythms that first drew him into the spiritual church. The influence of Mr. Barker is evident in his shows as he works the crowd, always conscious that his job is to please his listeners, often following a particularly hot solo by a band member or the conclusion of a knockout version of a tune with his patented, joyous, "Wow!" Powell follows a long line of New Orleans drummers, such as Freddie Kohlman, Bob French, Zig Modeliste, and Herlin Riley, who stepped out and added lead vocalist to their resumes. His first solo album, *Powell's Place* (2005), showcases both his traditional and modern playing. Is it any surprise that the lifelong Treme resident has been dubbed the "King of Treme"? He pays homage to his roots in the neighborhood on the album *Treme Traditions* (2011), a collaboration with brass band horn players, Mardi Gras Indians, and drummers Riley, Uncle Lionel Batiste, and Benny Jones Sr. He is one of the Treme artists that is central to the documentary film *Tradition Is a Temple* (2013). An in-demand sideman, he's worked with such leaders as Johnny Adams, Dr. John, Dr. Michael White, Davell Crawford, Nicholas Payton, Irvin Mayfield, the Blind Boys of Alabama, John Scofield, Topsy Chapman, Henry Butler, and Barbara Shorts. One performance that has been preserved on record and that truly must have been fulfilling is his reunion at the 1989 Jazz Fest with his old mentor and his wife on *Blue Lu Barker Featuring Danny Barker and His Jazz Hounds* (1998). Just as he's done since he was that little boy venturing into the St. Philip Church of God in Christ, Powell has explored new contexts for his drumming, joining forces with guitarist Darren Hoffman in a duo they call Uncle Nef. They've released an EP *Blues* (2017) and album *Love Songs* (2019) on which Powell sings and lays down a heavy backbeat behind Hoffman's Jimi Hendrix–influenced guitar work: "People know me as a jazz drummer, but I wanted people to hear me do some other things, and he encouraged me to do these records with him." Powell continues to collaborate with fellow percussionists Herlin Riley and Jason Marsalis in the New Orleans Groovemasters. As far and wide as Shannon Powell's drums have taken him, he remains devoted to the music that was put in his lap all those years ago: "The trad music part is the heartbeat of all of it. That's where all of it comes from."

WOMEN IN DRUMSVILLE: IT'S ABOUT TIME!

The *Drumsville!* exhibit opens with a photo of two women, Sister Bertha Jackson Pooler and Mother Mamie Felix, and the young girl Bonnie Mae Jackson playing drums and tambourine in the St. Philip Church of God in Christ. It's an image that shines a light on women playing an important role in extending the drumming tradition and in creating the spirit-summoning rhythms that are a part of everyday life in New Orleans. Herlin Riley recalls Mother Lewis playing bass drum alongside his grandfather Deacon Frank Lastie in the Guiding Star Spiritual Church. And, Rev. Lizzie Butler, who was the pastor of St. Anne the Divine Spiritual Church, played the drums for services invoking the spirit of Blackhawk or celebrating a St. Joseph's feast until the little building on the corner of North Claiborne Avenue and Lesseps Street was devasted by Hurricane Katrina and the failure of the levees. For years and years, in churches tucked away in neighborhoods throughout the city, women have been beating drums and ringing tambourines in spiritual praise. Certainly, through the years, young women drummers have been in the schools—in stage bands and in marching bands enlivening Carnival parades. In fact, women were observed drumming in antebellum Congo Square. Women have been playing drums, but their presence was not prevalent onstage or in the recording studio throughout the development of the musical forms that brought worldwide attention to the distinctive grooves created by the New Orleans beat. This is evident in the *Drumsville!* exhibit. Once visitors pass by that black-and-white photograph of the church scene, the historical narrative focuses on the contributions of male drummers—until the final "Extensions and Variations" section. Today, women are picking up those sticks, becoming recognized for contributing to the evolution of the New Orleans beat, and making names for themselves in Drumsville. It's about time!

Christie Jourdain: "Did You Hear Her Beating on Them Drums?"

In October 2013, the Original Pinettes Brass Band, New Orleans's only all-female brass band, triumphed over the TBC, the New Breed Brass Band, and the New Creations Brass Band in the final round of the Red Bull Street Kings brass band competition. The band's title quickly was transformed to "Street Queens." Snare drummer Christie Jourdain (b. 1975) is literally the driving force behind the band. From its inception in 1991, when Jeffrey Herbert organized the original band at St. Mary's Academy, the emphasis was on musicianship over gender: "Mr. Herbert didn't treat us like females. He treated us like musicians. And that's the same kind of attitude I have today in the Original Pinettes. We are musicians. I don't want people to look at us as females."[74]

Although she was drawn to drumming at an early age, Jourdain's journey to becoming the snare-drumming leader of a top-flight brass band was circuitous and sometimes reluctant. Jourdain and her sister grew up in the 1980s watching MTV, and along with megastars like Michael Jackson and Prince, they were seeing emerging female artists like Sheila E, the Bangles, the Go-Go's, and Klymaxx. Her aunt's boyfriend was a member of the city's most prestigious marching band, the St. Augustine Marching 100, and he brought his drumsticks over, encouraging Jourdain to beat out rhythms on pillows: "He would say if you wanna be like Sheila E, you have to practice . . . He started putting the sticks in my hand and would always make me do certain things, and I got a love for it . . . He was teaching me the basic, 'pop-pop-one-two,' drum roles, you know, the basic rudiments. I was young. I had to be maybe nine, ten around that. And that really sparked my interest." By the time she got to St. Mary's, Jourdain was ready to join the marching band: "I fell in love with the snare drum because I felt that was the most complicated drum. So, I was like, 'Oh, let's try to learn that.' I was like telling myself, 'I know it's not going to be easy.' You know that drum seems like it's the most busiest. And when I got on

Christie Jourdain performing at the 2015 Jazz and Heritage Festival. Her mantra for the Original Pinettes: "We're not blood related; we're love related." Photo by Michael Mastrogiovanni. Courtesy of the New Orleans Jazz & Heritage Archive.

it, I learned that it is the instrument that never stops playing in a parade." When Herbert, who played in the Pinstripe Brass Band, formed an all-female Pinettes, Jourdain wasn't that interested but agreed to be an alternate, playing occasional gigs. After high school, she moved to Houston, and when she returned to New Orleans after two years, an old bandmate called and asked her to play with the band. Once again, the educator/mentor played a crucial role: "It was like in 2000 with Mr. Herbert when I hooked back up with the Pinettes. When I walked up, I was like, 'I don't have a drum.' He said, 'Here, here's a drum I have for you.' It was a snare drum for a drum set. In high school, you know, we play with big drums, so I had to transition—remember, I hadn't played marching drums since '94, even though I had little gigs in and out with the Pinettes." A few months later, Herbert moved on from running the Pinettes, and the band was on its own and, like so many other aspects of New Orleans life, was thrown into chaos and uncertainty with Hurricane Katrina.

Based in Houston after the storm, Jourdain found herself increasingly at the heart of trying to revive the band: "Everybody was running around, 'I'm busy right now. Why don't you do it?' One of the tuba players was like, 'You do it. I'll help you.' So, I used my own money and tried to mail out press kits. I'm just taking a shot in the dark because I've never done this . . . I don't know what I'm doing, but I'm trying to lead. So, I come back home and try to get everybody together." There was a dispute over the use of the Pinettes name as new members joined, so Jourdain and company became the Original Pinettes. As the band began trying to establish a place for themselves, Jourdain found new mentors in Troy "Trombone Shorty" Andrews and Rebirth and Hot 8 snare drummer Derrick Tabb:

So, I went to Troy, and he was like, "Show me what you got." And, Troy is a notorious practicer. I mean Troy practices all day, any instrument, any time, whatever it is, you name it. And, this was before he was touring a lot, so, of course, he had a lot of time. So, I'm showing him the stuff I know, and he's like, "Wrong, wrong, you got somewhere to go?" And, I'm like, "No." "Well, good, you're gonna stay here with me." And, I'll tell you for a good week, maybe, I would go to his studio Uptown, and he was there, and Derrick Tabb was there, and they would sit, but it really was Troy, "Sit. Sit. Sit down. I'm gonna show you how to play the snare." He actually put me behind a set of drums too. He was like, "Look, this is how you do it." And then Derrick Tabb got behind it. And then Troy would call me, "Come on, come up here." And, the basic fundamentals I was learning from him was correct. I was teaching myself by ear incorrectly. From the beginning of trying to play brass band music to meeting Troy, I had to learn how to play all over again.

With her new conception of brass band drumming, Jourdain started to observe the performances of other bands like the Dirty Dozen, Treme, the Soul Rebels, Rebirth, the

Hot 8, and the Stooges to shape her own approach to drumming and a distinctive band chemistry:

> You just have to take everything and make it your own pretty much. You know, I've played with a few different bands, and, oh, my goodness, everyone has their own style, the drumming techniques. And, that was at a time when there wasn't much social media. You know, like now, I can go and watch all the young guys, like Sam [Jackson] with the Young Fellaz and Sammy [Cyrus with Hot 8], all the other guys coming up. I can go and watch them now [on social media] 'cause, don't get me wrong, I'm still learning.

Christie Jourdain's snare drum. Jourdain: "I fell in love with the snare drum because I felt that was the most complicated drum." Photo by Grace Patterson. Courtesy of the New Orleans Jazz Museum.

Hard work and determination paid off, and the Original Pinettes released a debut album, *Finally* (2013), and are considered among the upper echelon of brass bands in the city. Their long-standing Friday-night gig at Bullets Sports Bar is always packed with an enthusiastic and discerning crowd of regulars and out-of-town visitors. Jourdain believes the women in the band have a special bond. Her mantra is, "We're not blood related; we're love related." Although the emphasis is always on musicianship and band chemistry, she recognizes that women musicians face distinctive challenges: "You're talking about wives, you're talking about mothers, work, school." And, maintaining an all-female lineup can be a challenge:

> Yeah, those guys can just pack up a suitcase and go. With women it's kind of hard, and then we go through different things with women things going on. A lot of times we're just not able. I'm not making up excuses because we don't have, just think about it, because if Derrick [Tabb] can't make a gig, Rebirth has five other snare drummers that's real good that they can choose from. We don't have that. And what I said is most important is chemistry. If your back row doesn't have chemistry, then your front row damn sure won't have it.

As a drummer and band leader, Christie Jourdain has added her name to Drumsville legacy, and her drumming clearly has tapped into the ineffable spirit and power that reaches back two centuries to the source in Congo Square:

> We have something real different, we have some kind of spiritual culture going within us . . . We get so into our drums that we done lost the song, and I don't mean lost like messed up. I mean we talk with our drumsticks; we make the crowd listen to us talk with our drumsticks. Our drummers here make you look on the side like, "God damn, did you hear her? Did you hear her beating on them drums?" It's just different to me. We dance with our sticks. We dance with our mallets.

Mayumi Shara: "I Will Change Your Image"

The New Orleans beat had such an impact on Japanese drummer Mayumi Shara that she moved to the city and immersed herself in the history and stylistic nuances of Drumsville. In fact, thanks to the depth of knowledge she has acquired and the enthusiasm she exudes, Shara took part in the conception, planning, and research for the exhibit, and one of her Taiko tom-toms is on display in *Drumsville!*

On her journey to become a part of the New Orleans drumming tradition, Shara faced several gender-based obstacles. In Japan, she was an accomplished Taiko drummer, a term that signifies both a traditional Japanese drum and art form. The drum itself originated in China and was introduced to Japan centuries ago, but Shara found herself drawn to modern jazz and identified her country's two top jazz drummers as possible instructors. Her percussion teacher was a classmate of one of those drummers. The request to teach Shara was met with a definitive reply from the jazz man: "I don't teach females." Angered but undeterred, she approached the second jazz drummer she had identified, renowned musician Motohiko "Toko" Hino:

> He told me, "I don't have an image of a female playing jazz drums in a jazz club. I don't have that image." And, I said, "I will change your image [*laughs*]." Anyway, he started teaching me. He was very disciplined. For six years, eight years, he kept asking me, "When will you give up?" Every time he said it, I said, "No, I'm not going to give up" . . . So, I took lessons from him for about eight years, and he kept asking me, "When will you *give up?*" I kept saying, "No, I will not *give up!*" And, after eight years, he started to say, "You'll probably be able to be the first good jazz female drummer in Japan."[75]

He was right. She established herself as a modern jazz drummer, yet because of the culture in Japan, she still felt that that she was looked down on by male musicians. Shara ultimately decided that to pursue her jazz dreams she would have to move to the United States. New York was her first destination, and she had a very clear focus on how she wanted to play modern jazz drums: "At that time, my god was Elvin Jones, 'Not Tony Williams, *Elvin Jones!*' I was like that." In New York, however, she still met with resistance. She signed a list to sit in at a jam session, and her name was never called. Shara persisted and went to another session: "I went to the band leader, 'I play drums. Can I play?' And the leader said, 'Can you play?' And, I said, 'I think so.' He didn't call my name. The next day I went to that jam session again, and I said, 'I play drums. Can I play tonight?' he said, 'Can you play?' I said, 'YES!' And, he said, 'Okay.' So, he liked my playing, and I didn't have any problem after that. So, I learned that I need to be tough."

Her initial interest in New Orleans drumming came through a clarinet player friend who suggested that some of elements in her Elvin Jones–inspired approach reminded him of swing-era drum great (and Baby Dodds disciple) Big Sid Catlett: "I was like, 'Wait a minute, I need to know this music.' So, I started playing with my friend, and I learned a lot of songs from Big Sid's band. Then, I decided to come here to check out the city. That's kind of the beginning of getting interested in New Orleans." Her jazz mentor back home did not approve: "My jazz drum teacher in Japan, he was so upset when I said, 'Teacher, I go to New Orleans.' He said, 'What? You want to play Dixieland music?' I said, 'no, no, no, no. New Orleans is not like that.'"

In 1998, Shara moved to New Orleans. She didn't speak English or know anyone in the city. Her initiation into the New Orleans music scene came from where so many of the city's greatest grooves get created: "I started playing with musicians on the street. That's my roots in New Orleans. I started playing with Tuba Fats [Lacen]. I joined Tuba Fats and the Chosen Few. I went to see Kermit Ruffins, and I asked him if I could sit in. And he said okay, and he liked my playing. So, after that I didn't have any problems to sit in." She also threw herself into studying the contemporary masters of traditional jazz drumming:

> The first person I got to know was [Japanese pianist] Mari Watanabe at Preservation Hall, so she introduced me, and I went to Preservation Hall every day and I learned. I was listening, watching Shannon Powell, Gerald French, Herlin Riley, Ernie Elly, Joe Lastie, those great, great drummers every night at Preservation Hall . . . I focused on the groove and even little things, like a press roll, and the feeling. That's a kind of really difficult thing, feeling—easy to watch and listen but difficult to play. I kind of realized that I loved this music. I didn't realize it when I was in Japan. I thought of myself as modern jazz player. I started opening my mind when I moved to New Orleans.

Like a true New Orleans drummer, in addition to traditional jazz, she learned to play a wide range of musical styles, including blues, R&B, funk, rock and roll, and country: "I started learning a lot of New Orleans music. I played with [Big Chief] Alfred Doucette and learned about Mardi Gras Indian music. And also, I played with Marva Wright at the Ritz Carlton. I played with Benny Turner, who is the brother of Freddie King, and I learned Chicago blues from him. I still sometimes play with him." She also worked with jazz harpist Patrice Fischer and was a member of the James Rivers Movement for ten years.

Mayumi Shara. Shara: "When I saw a picture of Baby Dodds playing his drum set with a Taiko tom-tom, I was like 'Wow, that tom is from my culture in the Far East!'" Photo by HajiMe. Courtesy of Mayumi Shara.

Shara explores ways to fuse her Taiko background with her jazz drumming. Her research into the history of New Orleans drumming led to a big surprise: "I started to trace back to the drummers in 1920s. When I saw a picture of Baby Dodds playing his drum set with a Taiko tom-tom, I was like, 'Wow, that tom is from my culture in the Far East!' I thought my creation of combining Taiko drums in my drum set is new, but it was part of the origin of the drum set. Interesting cultural fusion!" Today, her playing embodies that "interesting cultural fusion" as she continues to drum in a variety of bands as well as lead her own bands around the city. Shara released a debut CD, *New Orleans Jazz Letter from Mayumi* (2009). Becoming a New Orleans drummer is a testament to both her talents and her tenacity. Through her dedication to drumming, Mayumi Shara has come to learn a central lesson about New Orleans culture: "Music is alive everywhere, not a special thing. It's a natural thing."

It's really not surprising that Cori Walters (b. 1969) wound up in Drumsville. Since she was a nine-year-old girl growing up in Alabama, she's been playing and studying drums and percussion in a remarkable range of styles—from R&B to big band jazz, from rock to reggae, from orchestral percussion to salsa, from twentieth-century avant-garde percussion to traditional jazz. And in 1997, she took up residence, thanks to a visit to the Jazz and Heritage Festival and the lure of the New Orleans beat:

> I was just blown away by the zydeco and the Neville Brothers and the feel of the music here, the funk and the groove and the clave. It was similar to me to Afro-Cuban, and I just had to get down here because I figured from my limited studies that New Orleans is the northernmost point of the Caribbean, and it has more in common with Puerto Rican, Cuban, Haitian, Brazilian, even Brazilian, which is totally different, and so I thought, "This is the place that I want to continue my studies because I know it's different, but it's from the same source." And, I thought, "If I move here, I'm still in this country, but I'm learning this African music that I love and the clave." So, that's why I moved here.[76]

Born in New York, she started to play piano at age seven, and when the family moved to Alabama two years later, she was turned on to the African American popular music of the day: "I heard different music, the R&B and soul music of the Deep South, and I wanted to play, I thought this is so exciting to me I want to play drums because I thought that's what makes people dance." In school, she met resistance to the idea of a girl playing drums: "So, I wanted to play drums, and they did not want me to play drums in the junior high band, but I stood my ground. They thought I had perfect pitch, and I would be more suited to trombone or clarinet or chorus, which is what they put all the girls on. I stood my ground; I played drums in junior high band, and my father bought me a pawn shop drum set at I guess age thirteen, fourteen maybe." She began playing along to R&B records and took lessons from a drummer in Atlanta, who introduced her to "*Stick Control* and *The Rhythm Book* and different exercises to do on the drum set, and I just took it from there." In high school, she played snare drum in the marching and concert band and was the drumline leader and captain: "I would write the drum parts out for the high school band, the whole scores and everything, and I would write cadences for my marching band."

Walters earned a scholarship to the University of Alabama, and it was there that she was introduced to big band jazz under the direction of Steve Sample Sr. The focus, however, was orchestral percussion, including marimba, with a wind ensemble. Her goal was to play in an orchestra, and she was earning her living playing drums in rock bands, underground college bands, and soul bands. She continued her studies in orchestral percussion in the master's program at Wichita State University, and it was there that her journey into the music and drumming styles of the African diaspora really branched out. She was exposed to Brazilian and Afro-Cuban music. Guest instructors included African drumming masters; the inventor of the steel drum, Ellie Mannete; and conga player and Latin percussionist Michael Spiro. She founded a salsa band in which she played timbales, congas, bongos, and piano: "I just fell in love with that music and the clave." In 1995, she attended an Afro-Cuban workshop in Canada called "Afrocubanismo" that opened a whole new door as she saw and heard Cuban musicians, such as Irakere, Changuito, Los Muñequitos de Matanzas, Enrique Pla, and a few of the veterans from the Buena Vista Social Club. The attraction to drumming in African-derived musical forms ultimately made New Orleans her destination: "Congo Square is very deep. You can feel the roots in the music still because it was an unbroken lineage, and the dancing is still the same. It's African dancing, and young kids around New Orleans are doing the bamboula, and they don't even know where it came from. It is almost untouched and unbroken here. That's why I wanted to move here."

Cori Walters. Walters believes New Orleans drumming "rivals the top Cuban percussionists and the top Brazilian percussionists. It is that important." Photo by Grace Patterson. Courtesy of the New Orleans Jazz Museum.

In New Orleans, Walters started sitting in with local bands and eventually began gigging with reggae and Cajun bands. Of course, her academic credentials came in handy, and she performed as an extra with the Louisiana Philharmonic Orchestra for about eleven years. She drummed regularly for blues singer Big Al Carson, which was fortuitous because he was also a veteran traditional jazz tuba player. A number of trad players would stop by the Funky Pirate blues gig, and they were impressed with Walters's drumming: "They used to come see him and see me, and say, 'Man, she's great. Get her down here.' And, I'm like, 'I don't know anything about that music.' They said, 'It doesn't matter. We'll teach you.' So, I did that." Walters had been studying different approaches to drumming for years, so she immersed herself in learning how to play the second-line rhythm. An essential resource was Herlin Riley and Johnny Vidacovich's book *New Orleans Jazz and Second Line Drumming:* "Then I met Herlin and I met Johnny, and I would go listen to Herlin a lot, and that was my study. I learn so much more just by watching these drummers live than you can do from any record or book. It's just when you watch people, then you get to hear how they interact with the musicians that are playing on the stage with them at the time." Other drummers she listened to and observed include Willie Green, Joe Lastie Jr., and Wilbert "Junkyard Dog" Arnold. She started playing trad jazz gigs with players like Rickie Monie, Hank Bartels, John Royen, and Tom Fischer: "They loved my feel because I knew that the traditional jazz was funkier than, say, straight-ahead jazz. I did not major in jazz; I don't play straight-ahead jazz. I play traditional jazz because it has that funk, that groove. It's more like Afro-Cuban or soul music. You know, it's funky; it's dance music."

Despite the success that Walters has achieved drumming in so many different contexts, she has encountered that resistance to a woman behind the drum set:

Of course, you have to be five times better than the men just to get the same chance . . . I have that personality where I can fight through things like that, and, you know, growing up in the South, there's a lot of sexism, racism, and all sorts of stuff. You know, I've walked into studios and had old white musicians, when someone says, "That's the drummer," they walked out of the session. There's nothing I can do about it except be better. I could sit and rail for female musicians; that doesn't do our gender any good. What does our gender good is to be excellent at what you do, and that's it.

Walters also teaches piano, various classes at Delgado Community College, and "gifted and talented" music at a charter school in Gretna. In addition, she works mostly traditional jazz gigs with players like Mark Brooks, Kerry Lewis, Meghan Schwartz, Mark Braud, and occasionally with her own Universe Jazz Band. Cori Walters has spent her life pursuing the art of drumming and has definitely found a home in Drumsville. She describes what continues to be fascinating and distinctive about the New Orleans beat:

Well, the implication of the clave is in everything; whether it's played or not, it's implied. It's there in the music and the mind; the predominance of the bass drums, and also the snare drum rolls. The feel is like no other in the world. It settled, and it continues to evolve, of course. But there's no other feel like the New Orleans feel. And after being here twenty-two years, I feel like a novice. I feel like I just need to immerse myself for the rest of my life. I could say it's a cross between swung and straight, but it doesn't even describe it. It is an attitude and a depth that is not there in other places. It rivals the top Cuban percussionists and the top Brazilian percussionists. It is that important.

Boyanna Trayanova: "This Is What I Was Gonna Do with My Life"

In 1990, after the collapse of the Communist regime in Bulgaria, nine-year-old Boyanna Trayanova and her family immigrated to the United States. After five years in Durham, North Carolina, they relocated to New Orleans, and Trayanova, a fledgling drummer, had quite the revelation when she witnessed her first Carnival parades: "I mean the first time I heard like Mardi Gras marching bands on the street, my first Mardi Gras, my jaw was like just on the floor. I couldn't even believe it, and I knew right then and there that this is what I was gonna do with my life."[77] Little did she know that she had landed in Drumsville, the perfect locale to follow that dream.

Trayanova seemed to be instinctively attracted to the drums during her middle-school years in Durham: "I had no prior anything. My parents aren't musicians. I just wanted to play drums because it looked like fun, and it is fun. I was right." She learned rudiments and played in the school band. Arriving in New Orleans in time to start high school, Trayanova joined the band at Benjamin Franklin: "I didn't have a whole lot of drum-specific instruction. It was just like they put a piece of music in front of me and I'm expected to read it." She must have exhibited a certain level of determination because her parents bought her first drum set in her sophomore year: "My parents just wanted to make sure I was serious before they dished out the money. You know, we were an immigrant family; we didn't have a whole lot of expendable cash laying around, so they wanted to make sure I really wanted to do this." She didn't receive a lot of formal instruction, but she stayed focused on her goal: "I mean as a teenager, I gravitated toward rock and roll, you know, teenagery stuff in the '90s, and just listening to the drums, trying to learn how to play it by ear, stuff like that." She played in bands with her friends and attended Tulane University, where she was in the jazz band.

Living in Drumsville certainly began to make an impact: "The longer I lived in New Orleans, the wider it became, the more wide my scope of it." She had direct access to some of the greatest drummers to be found anywhere:

> Johnny Vidacovich was my number-one drum hero and still is to this day. Yeah, I want to be exactly like him when I grow up, whenever that is. Oh, he's just so fluid when he plays. He plays like water, totally. Willie Green, Russell Batiste, local cats. Because I could go watch them live, you know, I could listen to recordings all I want, but it's a whole other thing. I'm self-taught, so I never had someone like giving me personal direction until I went to Johnny directly to get some lessons, but the best teacher was watching the drummer perform onstage and like going home and trying to emulate that. So, luckily I had like a lot of incredible drummers to look up to and catch live.

As would be expected, Trayanova's immersion in New Orleans drumming led her back to the source point: "I've been studying African rhythms since like 2002 maybe, so that's like eighteen years, so the Congo Square stuff, the African rhythms are totally a part of New Orleans drumming. I can hear it. Clave comes directly from the African music. Yeah, it's like the more I study it, the more I can find parallels in New Orleans music." The New Orleans beat is also something with which she is quite familiar: "The groove, man. It swings, it swings. It's got a very distinct swing flavor to it that other styles of drumming just don't have. It's like super laid-back, like falling out of your seat laid-back, you know. Yeah, yeah, where we put the accent, the big four, which is technically on the end of four, of course." She gets a chance to play that "big four" in brass bands, initially working with the Panorama Brass Band more than fifteen years ago: "Once you get that brass band hat and people start seeing you on the street, they start calling you . . . I do a lot of brass band work, so you know, I'm on a gig with another drummer, and it's really enjoyable. It's not like I feel threatened by another drummer; it's all joyful and wonderful that I get to work with another drummer. It's like we have a good time."

Trayanova embraces the diversity that is demanded of a drummer working in Drumsville, playing what the gig calls for, whether it's blues, jazz, R&B, ska, brass band, or her own Balkan band Blato Zlato:

> Something I really love about living in New Orleans is I have so many opportunities to play like insanely different music. I can do like three gigs in a day, and they're all different. It's a

Boyanna Trayanova. Trayanova: "I feel like in the brotherhood of drummers, they know who I am. They know I can play, and we're buddies." Photo by Zack Smith. Courtesy of Boyanna Trayanova.

great thing . . . Every time you play, it expands your capabilities 'cause it's all about the time you invest into it. So, the more you play, the better you get, and the more you play things outside your comfort zone, and, so, guess what, the more you're going to expand your comfort zone. These are all like great ways to grow as a musician, and New Orleans affords me those opportunities. I'm thankful for that and that's why I still live there.

Trayanova believes she is accepted by the community of drummers in the city: "I feel like in the brotherhood of drummers, they know who I am. They know I can play, and we're buddies, you know, and we enjoy playing with each other, and we enjoy sharing information." However, as a woman drummer, Trayanova definitely has faced resistance from band leaders. She's actually had a band leader call her for gig and tell her because she's a woman they have to rehearse. She turned him down: "I face a lot of discrimination, unfortunately, and I feel I don't get the same opportunities . . . I've always kind of rebelled against norms and stuff like that associated with gender divisions. Got into drumming and liked it and stayed there even though it is a boy's club . . . but I was like, 'So what, I'm gonna do it anyway.'" Teaching drumming is another outlet that she came to through seeing a photo in the *Times-Picayune* of child who was shot at her own birthday party:

> Something about that picture just moved me, and I was like, "Oh my God, I gotta do something about this. What can I do?" Well, the solution I came up with is I can teach kids to play drums, and drumming is a really positive thing that can counteract the negative pull of street life for at-risk youth. If I can show 'em how much fun music is and what kind of amazing opportunities you can have with music, like you can travel the world, you know, it's a legitimate career that you can have, and it's really, really fun, like what kid doesn't want to play drums, and it's like an answer to a life of violence.

Her teaching also provides Trayanova with an opportunity to help address the gender inequity she has experienced: "I make sure to give the girls extra attention and support. I think it's good for them to see a role model who's female who also is a drummer that they can see that this actually is something they can do because if all they see is male drum teachers, they might want to put it down at some point. If they have someone to look up to who is also female, they can see that it's actually possible."

Nikki Glaspie: "I Had to Study That Brand of Funk"

When Nikki Glaspie (b. 1983) joined Ivan Neville's Dumpstaphunk in 2012, she had recently left one of the most high-profile drumming gigs in the world—five years anchoring Beyoncé's all-female band the Suga Mamas. Joining Neville's band gave her a chance to take a deep dive into the intricacies of the New Orleans beat.

Glaspie's first beats were made with spoons and forks on pots and pans. Early on, her family bought her a toy drum set. Her first exposure to drums came through her family's church in the Maryland/DC area, where she emulated the movements of the drummer and began drumming for the church when she was nine or ten: "Church was a great way for me to start because I understood the importance of having a purpose behind the music

Nikki Glaspie. Glaspie on female drummers: "It was like, 'Oh, girls don't play drums.' I was like, 'Yeah, actually we do.'" Photo by Josh Timmermans. Courtesy of Nikki Glaspie.

and like connecting with people's souls, connecting with the spirit in order to be a conduit to connect to people's soul. So, that kind of laid the foundation for what would come next." She poured her energy into drumming in multiple contexts in middle school and high school—marching band, jazz band, pep band, and the pit band for plays: "I moved to Raleigh my freshman year of high school, and it's a pretty big band culture there, like marching band culture. So, I was like fully immersed in that. So that definitely helped my hands out a lot, coordination and what not, and I was reading, but I didn't have actual drum set lessons until I got to college." Glaspie's focus on listening to drummers playing different styles of music began in high school: "That was like a big moment because my dad—I was raised in church so the only thing I listened to was gospel music—but then when I was fifteen, my dad played me like Van Halen *1984* and like Rage Against the Machine and Eve 6 and the O'Jays and the Gap Band, but I think that's kind of when I really started to pick the drums out probably."[78]

A major transition came when the preacher and gospel artist William Becton visited Glaspie's church and suggested she think about attending Berklee College of Music. She visited the school for Percussion Week and decided to enroll. The young drummer discovered whole new worlds of musical possibilities:

When I got there, there was so much music that I had not been exposed to. I just sat in the media library. I actually remember discovering Return to Forever and Pat Metheny, and that really changed my trajectory as well. You know, I'm hearing Return to Forever for the first time, and I'm like, "Oh my God, this is incredible. What is this?" . . . It never really was like specifically about drums. That was just the instrument that honestly was chosen for me. I came out playing the drums, but it was the music itself that really spoke to me. I was like, I want to learn how play this. So, I kind of studied fusion for a while, and that kind of morphed into funk, and it's like the rest is history.

Although she had a few grants, Glaspie didn't have scholarship, so she started doing her first work in clubs:

> I figured out that I could make money gigging around town. So, I played at this place called Wally's, which is kind of where I learned how to play music really, like how to actually play a song and how to comp and how to build solos and things like that, and that was like a fifty-dollar gig. I started out on Sundays, and eventually started playing on Tuesdays and Wednesdays, and then eventually I took over those days. I was the band leader for those days and had different bands. It was just like a natural progression. But that really was like my schooling as far as being able to perform and play music.

She eventually moved to New York and was working a variety of gigs to make ends meet when things took a rather abrupt turn.

After six months in New York, she was told about an open audition for Beyoncé's band. She almost didn't go because she had a conflicting gig and needed the money. In the end, she went, auditioned, and was hired:

> I actually had to change my style of drumming to conform to like what the gig was, to like pop drumming, because the guy that had the gig before me, Gerald Hayward, he had been there for a while. He had played with Destiny's Child, and he also played for Beyoncé, so there was the style established there, and there were tapes, and they told us to study the tapes. So, I studied the tapes and picked up some of things he was doing. Slowly, I started to find my voice in that.

The job, however, required a lot more from the drummer than just playing the music. Beyoncé's performances are major stage productions, and the drummer is often responsible for the timing of different aspects of the show: "I kind of turned into a machine basically, like I had to play the same thing every night because, you know, the lighting director was counting on me for cues, you know what I mean? It was like a big production. So, it's like if he doesn't hear [scats], the lights don't happen." Ultimately, Glaspie found the repetition that was required to support the pop diva's show was not allowing her to grow musically: "I had an amazing experience. I traveled the world, but I wanted to get back to music. So, that's how Dumpstaphunk happened."

A gig with saxophonist Sam Kininger at the New Orleans Jazz and Heritage Festival in 2004 and a return to the festival the following year with guitarist/producer Eric Krasno were Glaspie's introduction to Drumsville. She went back to Jazz Fest after leaving Beyoncé, and Krasno let Ivan Neville know that Glaspie was looking for a gig. Joining Dumpstaphunk required that she learn the nuances of the New Orleans beat, and it certainly looks like she did her homework:

> I had to study that brand of funk, that type of music. So, I studied Zig. I studied Russell, Russell Batiste. He's a big one for me for sure, him and Zig, you know, those are the guys. I mean

Johnny V [Vidacovich], when I first came to Jazz Fest, he was like the first one to let me sit in, like I sat in with him at the Dragon's Den; we did double drums, and it was amazing. It was super cool to be able to sit down and play with him. So these are the guys, Raymond [Weber] too, a big influence. I mean Willie Green, too. There's so many guys down there that were accessible. That was like really amazing to be able to talk to them and see them play and listen to them. It definitely had a huge impact on the drummer that I am today.

She tapped into that ineffable quality that makes the drumming so special: "Whenever I hear New Orleans funk, it's like sloppy, but it's tight. It's greasy, but the groove is impenetrable. You can't deny it, and I think that's probably the characteristic, the thing I would say about it. And, you know it immediately when you hear it. There's not anything else like it." Testimony to her effectiveness playing that funk can be found on tracks like "Raise the House" and the title song on the Dumpstaphunk album *Dirty Word* (2013). Since leaving Dumpstaphunk, Glaspie leads her own band, the Nth Power, and works behind one of the all-time legends of funk, saxophonist Maceo Parker.

When Glaspie was younger, she experienced the resistance to women playing drums: "It was like, 'Oh, girls don't play drums.' I was like, 'Yeah, actually we do.'" Today, she believes those shortsighted perspectives have always been a misconception:

It just hasn't been recognized because I could tell you a story about how a woman invented the djembe. You know, she invented the instrument and gave it to a man to play, but I feel we've always been around. It just hasn't been widely recognized because there's been lots of women drummers before me, even from New Orleans, that have played the drums. I don't know; it's just a matter of people knowing where to look. There's so many unsung heroes.

Jaz Butler: "If You've Got the Gift, Then You Just Have the Gift"

At the 2019 Treme Fest, a tribute to the Neville Brothers was performed by an all-women band called Brown Sugar that was organized by drummer Jazmine Butler (b. 1990), one of the first women born and raised in New Orleans to make a name for herself on the drum set. She's been drumming in bands around the city since she graduated cum laude from Dillard University in 2012, and when she was working behind singer/songwriter Joy Clark, she had a revelation about the magic that New Orleans grooves generate:

Every time we would play something like New Orleans sounds, a Meters type of tune or Neville Brothers type of tune, it would have this whole other energy that just resonated in like such an authentic place that I just started thinking, "Man, we gotta do a Neville Brothers tribute." It was interesting the way it came together because they wanted an all-girl band. I had an opportunity to be like more of a band leader and express what I wanted to or what I didn't want to convey.[79]

Growing up in "the Gap," a neighborhood between the Ninth Ward and New Orleans East, Butler always wanted to be a drummer and recalls as a kid putting markers together to use as drumsticks. It was in her family church, St. Paul the Apostle, that she was first drawn to

drumming, thanks to drummer Shannon Hamilton and bassist Parker Shy: "These guys were in the pocket and funky musicians. That was what kind of directed my ear to how to approach drums. So, my biggest thing was just learning how to play a groove and knowing how to keep a groove and just know what makes people feel good rather than just playing a lot of chops and trying to put a lot of embellishment on the music that wasn't really necessary."[80] Hamilton became her first mentor, and by her teenage years she was regularly behind the drum set in church: "He would basically have me play some songs. Other songs, he would play himself, and eventually he would just have me play the whole service." Butler found her next mentor in band director Carl Baham at St. Mary's Academy, where she played snare in the drum section and kept drumming when she went on to Dillard University to major in music industry studies and to minor in marketing. Butler also played in a jazz group through a Jazz and Heritage Foundation education program that included her debut at Jazz Fest: "That was my introduction to learning something about jazz music. Everything else before that was either like marching band, like southern-style drum section songs, not necessarily drum corps, and at church it was more or less a R&B kind of vibe."[81]

Her earliest influences were classic funk and R&B artists like Curtis Mayfield, Teena Marie, Rick James, Sly & the Family Stone, and Funkadelic, but as she began working around New Orleans, Butler was learning about the city's signature beat. She's found that many veteran drummers recognize her potential and contribute to her development:

Zigaboo and Gerald French and Russell Batiste and Jellybean [Jeffery Alexander], and Herlin Riley especially, are willing to share almost any and everything that they know. And, that's pretty much how they came up. Somebody showed them. Somebody saw what they were doing, and they taught them; they schooled them. They showed them how to do what they're doing. It's beautiful to see something passed along to somebody else, you know, who's in an upcoming generation of playing music.[82]

The support she's received from some of the contemporary Drumsville greats is gratifying: "These living legends have opened up their hearts to me. They check me out. They give me great feedback. They seem like they show a level of respect to me, and I really do appreciate it."[83] She's also come to recognize an essential aspect of working on the Drumsville scene:

> I think to be a drummer in New Orleans, they always stress to be versatile, and that's something that I've always had the experience with playing with bands that play blues or bands that play funk or jazz or trad jazz or gospel. There's so many different facets that you can tap into working in this one culture in New Orleans. In order to work, you've got to be able to bring more than one thing. I spent a lot of time in bands that allowed me to do stuff like that.[84]

Butler has particularly found gratification in her work with her cousin Kirk Joseph's Backyard Groove. Known for his groundbreaking work on sousaphone with the Dirty Dozen Brass Band, Joseph gives Butler a chance to deliver some brass band–inspired funk on the drum set: "It's really an honor to play with family members who have that kind of name."[85] The fact that both Willie Green and Kevin O'Day have occupied that drum chair says a lot about Butler's ability to bring the funk. She played snare for a time with the Original Pinettes, and Christie Jourdain acknowledges how far Butler has advanced on the drum set: "I've seen Jaz go from 'Ehhh' to 'Okay, Jaz is knockin' them drums out!'"[86] And, she's expanded her approach to include second-line and Black Masking Indian grooves with musicians like bassist Earl Nunez, guitarist and vocalist June Victory, and Big Chief from the Black Seminole tribe Kenny "KliK" Young. In addition to mastering established approaches, Butler looks forward in her playing, frequently incorporating an SPD SX drum pad into her set for hip-hop-oriented gigs. Her latest project explores the cutting edge of today's dance music: "People are typically familiar with me as a drum set player. There's been like an evolution from that place to be more like an artist, a recording artist, and producer and songwriter. What I'm doing would be under the artist 'Mookie Butler.' It's basically electronic. It's house music. It's trance. It's like EDM, like in that type of world."[87]

Coming up in New Orleans, Butler really had to create the concept of a female drummer in what must have seemed very much like a "man's world":

> For the longest time, I was the only female drummer I knew in New Orleans. Right now, there's other people, one, her name is Taylor Gordon. She also goes by "Pocket Queen." It's just interesting now to know other female drummers and really see that it's not that whole "You're good for a girl type of thing." There's so many great female drummers out there that it's just like "Are you a great drummer or are you not?" It doesn't necessarily need to be defined with being a woman. I don't really feel like I've had that issue too much. I've had it sometimes but, you know, other people correct them.[88]

Today, she takes inspiration from other women drummers: "I love Nikki Glaspie's drumming because she's so powerful, like, she's like one of my favorites, like, hands down, not from just being a woman, but just how she approaches the drums. It's just really amazing."[89] Butler did have a female mentor, Angelamia Bachemin, a former Berklee College of Music drum instructor whom she met through Glaspie: "She stayed right up in the Seventh Ward, and I would go over there like every Friday and just play some drums and stuff. She would show me some things. I want to give her that respect because she definitely spent some time with me at least like two years straight, every Friday."[90] Jaz Butler is truly extending the reach of the Drumsville tradition, and today she pays it forward by passing along the encouragement and knowledge to the next generation:

> It's always good for any female to have other women around you who do what you're doing or has done something that you're aspiring to do or become. I look at it the same way, you know, when I see young girls now, I think that it's beautiful. And for me, it's just like I need to make sure that they have a chance. They need to be poured into, just like young male drummers need to be poured into, you know, 'cause they may not be nurtured as much or supported as much. There's greatness to be had everywhere. If you've got the gift, then you just have the gift. If God just happened to give it to a young Black female, then great. It's beautiful, so why not nurture it? Why try and chase somebody away and tell them to go play a flute because it's a girl's instrument?[91]

MUSICAL FAMILIES: SUSTAINING AND EXTENDING TRADITIONS

Testimony can certainly be found throughout the *Drumsville!* narrative that musical families play a pivotal role in sustaining and extending traditions in New Orleans. Louis Cottrell Sr. was laying down foundational elements of the New Orleans beat in the final decades of the nineteenth century, and at the close of the twentieth century, his grandson Louis Cottrell III (Louis Chevalier) followed in his footsteps. Likewise, master drummers on the contemporary scene Raymond Weber and Alvin Ford both passed the drumsticks down to their sons Raymond Weber Jr.[92] and Alvin Ford Jr. The Barbarin family alone has had a far-ranging impact on the city's traditional music, and brothers Paul Barbarin and Louis Barbarin are towering figures in the history of New Orleans drumming. There were other pairs of brothers who were crucial contributors and extended the development of the New Orleans beat, including Jules Bauduc and Ray Bauduc; Weedy Morris and Leo Morris (Idris Muhammad); and Paul Staehle and Fred Staehle. The French family spans three generations of music making in the city. Banjo player Albert "Papa" French assumed leadership of the Tuxedo Jazz Band in 1958 and continued in that role until 1977. His sons became musicians, George on bass and Bob on drums, and the latter took over leadership of the band until 2012; today, George's son, drummer Gerald French, has taken over the leadership of that band. He takes great pride in extending the family tradition: "The biggest accomplishment for me was playing with cats who played with my grandfather, and I got a chance to do that at the tail end of their careers. Cats that come out of that lineage of New Orleans cats, it's special."[93] The Marsalis family's contributions to the jazz

tradition are immense, from the patriarch Ellis on piano to four of his sons: Branford on saxophone, Wynton on trumpet, Delfeayo on trombone, and Jason on drums and vibraphone. Of course, the Neville family is known worldwide, and today Cyril, the brother on drums, has passed the torch to his son Omari, who leads a band called The Fuel and plays drums behind his father. In performance, Cyril often goes back to his Wild Tchoupitoulas roots, working his rhythmic magic on the tambourine as Omari provides the funk groove foundation on the drum set. And then there's the Lastie family, with three generations of drummers spanning a century of the New Orleans beat—from Deacon Frank Lastie to his son Walter "Popee" Lastie to his grandsons Herlin Riley and Joe Lastie Jr.

Russell Batiste Jr.: "They Would Bring Me up to Play"

One of the great New Orleans musical dynasties is the Batiste family, whose members have been innovators and educators who have been integral to sustaining and extending New Orleans musical traditions. Today they can be found playing in a myriad of bands on the contemporary scene. David Russell Batiste Jr. (b. 1965) is one of the city's highly regarded masters of the drum set, yet he prefers to see himself as a complete musician, proficient on multiple instruments and as a composer/arranger. His father, keyboard player David Russell Batiste Sr., was the leader of the funk band the Gladiators, whose reputation among locals for their work in the early 1970s rivals that of the Meters. That band evolved into the equally renowned Batiste Brothers Band. Batiste was playing drums by age four, sitting in with the family band by age seven, and mastered the saxophone by the fifth grade. The family provided him with his first musical outlet. He recalls those early performances in an interview with John Swenson:

Left: Walter "Popee" Lastie, ca 1970s. For Joe Lastie Jr., the tales his uncle "Popee" brought home from his life on the road with Fats Domino further sparked his interests in becoming a professional drummer. From *Wavelength Magazine.* Gift of Dr. Connie Atkinson. Courtesy of the New Orleans Jazz Museum. Accession number 2009.030.0717.02.

Right: Gerald French. Three generations of the French family have led the Tuxedo Jazz Band: Albert "Papa" French, banjo (1958–1977); his son Bob French, drums (1977–2012); and Albert's grandson and Bob's nephew Gerald French, drums, who assumed leadership of the band in 2012. Photo by Eliot Kamenitz. Courtesy of the New Orleans Jazz Museum.

Russell Batiste Jr., ca. 1980s. On playing with his family as a young musician: "They would bring me up to play sax on one song, another on bass and another on drums." From *Wavelength Magazine*. Gift of Dr. Connie Atkinson. Courtesy of the New Orleans Jazz Museum. Accession number 2009.030.0510.06.

They would bring me up to play sax on one song, another on bass and another on drums. They were the first funk band I heard and the funkiest band I ever heard, that's where I get all my inspiration from funk-wise. My dad was the one who took me into all these clubs when I was seven. I was playing in barrooms when I was seven. I was eight years old one Carnival and I sat in on this guy's drums and the guy left the gig! Left me there playin' in the barroom. A kid wanna be catching beads and doubloons on Mardi Gras day. I was mad, stuck in the barroom with these old men, they're trippin' out and I'm just playing the beat.[94]

Batiste's rhythmic sophistication is evident in his engagement with the St. Augustine Marching 100. Like Smokey Johnson with his "Ratty #9," which became "It Ain't My Fault," Batiste created new cadences that remain part of the marching band repertoire today. His own band's self-titled debut album *Orchestra from da Hood* (2000), opens with a version of one of those propulsive cadences called "St. Augustine 1983." Batiste studied at Southern University of New Orleans for two years with teachers like Roger Dickerson and Edward Kidd Jordan, and then began working gigs. In 1989, Art Neville, George Porter, and Leo Nocentelli regrouped as the renamed Funky Meters; they tapped Batiste to take over Zigaboo Modeliste's drum chair. Those were some mighty big shoes to fill, but Batiste stepped in and maintained a continuity with what the legend had established and still brought his own signature hard-driving, complex attack to the mix. His family background provided him with an insider's take on how to lay down those grooves. In the late 1970s, his father replaced Neville in the original Meters, and Batiste was able to witness Modeliste's drumming firsthand. He also drew inspiration from the underrecognized funk drumming innovator Stanley Ratcliff and synthesized both drummers' approaches to create something all his own:

When you hear me going off, you hear Stanley. And my father played keyboards in The Meters, so I used to fall asleep right underneath Zig while they were practicing. I got his flavor mixed up with Stanley's flavor, and I came up with a flavor that no one else has. You know what's incredible? Those great players got a chance to watch me, and then went back and practiced the stuff I was doing. That ain't no lie.[95]

His influence can be found throughout Drumsville's younger generation. Jaz Butler describes what draws her to his playing: "I really like that Russell, he has like some of the deepest pockets, some of the deepest grooves that you could ever hear that feel so good and could be very minimal, like four beats, and it's just so phat, you know, and then he can go just completely left field and take these very monstrous solos."[96] Joe Dyson looks on Batiste not only as an innovator who extended the New Orleans beat but also as a personal mentor who encouraged him to carry the tradition forward:

Russell Batiste is an anomaly, in my opinion, within, not just the New Orleans scene, but the international scene of drumming and artistry. He's taking the sound built from like everyone that precedes him, like if you look at Zigaboo Modeliste or if you're looking at Herman "Roscoe" Ernest, all of these guys that come before him, he's able to assimilate that sound, those same rhythms that were played, and actually bring his own approach, and there's so much entrenched in the actual lineage and sound of the playing, but they still sound original. They still sound like there's something very new about it.[97]

Batiste was one of the drummers Nikki Glaspie studied to learn New Orleans funk grooves; she relished the respect and encouragement he gave her: "When I went down there in 2004, Russell was like, 'I want you to come play on my album.' And I was like, 'What, you're a drummer'—and you know like a ridiculous drummer—'What are you talking about?' He was like, 'Well, I want you to come play on my album.' I was like, "Alright.' It's kind of the New Orleans way for sure."[98]

Batiste's thundering grooves were a perfect fit when guitarist Brian Stolz replaced Nocentelli and brought a blues-rock edge to the Funky Meters. Porter, Batiste, and Stolz carried on as the blues rock/funk power trio PBS when Neville was dealing with health issues, and the drummer has also worked regularly in a trio with guitarist Walter "Wolfman" Washington and organist Joe Krown. Over the years, he has joined forces with Phish keyboard player Page McConnell and Allman Brothers/Dead & Company bassist Oteil Burbridge in the jam band trio Vida Blue, and he was the engine that propelled the band Papa Grows Funk. His credits as a sideman point to his versatility and mastery behind the drum set, including work with the Big Chief Bo Dollis and the Wild Magnolias, Allen Toussaint, Harry Connick Jr., Champion Jack Dupree, Robbie Robertson, and Maceo Parker. Russell Batiste Jr. continues to lead Orchestra from da Hood, and his innovative, signature grooves are a testament to how musical families have extended the New Orleans beat.

TEACHING THE BEAT: "IT WAS ALWAYS SOME GUY WHO WAS A LITTLE OLDER OR A LITTLE BETTER THAN ME"

Reaching back into the nineteenth century, music education has played a central role in passing on and carrying forward musical traditions in New Orleans. Al Kennedy's *Chord Changes on the Chalkboard: How Public School Teachers Shaped Jazz and the Music of New Orleans* (2005) is a remarkable study of public school music education that reveals just how crucial that role has been. As Kennedy asserts: "Teachers within the public schools pushed an oftentimes unwilling urban institution to become an important institutional structure that transmitted both jazz musicianship and other New Orleans music to future musicians."[99] That is certainly the case for many members of Drumsville. School stage and marching bands are a major starting point for the careers of countless drummers. In fact, look at how many drummers profiled in this book give credit to the training they received from band director and music instructor Ms. Yvonne Bush alone! Recent decades have also seen the emergence of university-level programs that can boast of cream-of-the-crop professional musicians teaching on their faculty. Then there are the programs that have sprung from the efforts of artists within the community. Think of the impact that Danny Barker had with the Fairview Baptist Church Brass Band. Think of how the drum circles led by Alfred "Uganda' Roberts contributed to extending the New

Learning about Congo Square, 2019. New Orleans Jazz Museum Summer Enrichment, run by educational specialist Lisa McLendon (*center right*), includes a Congo Square program for children who learn the history of the gatherings, carry on the tradition of creating their own improvised percussion instruments from everyday materials, and learn drumming. Photo by Travis Waguespack. Courtesy of the New Orleans Jazz Museum.

Orleans beat. In recent years, the Jazz Museum honors the roots of Drumsville by hosting a Congo Square–themed summer program for children who learn the history of the gatherings, carry on the tradition of creating their own improvised percussion instruments from everyday materials, and learn drumming. Today, programs that pass the music on include the New Orleans Center for the Creative Arts (NOCCA); the Jazz and Heritage Foundation's Don "Moose" Jamison Heritage Music School; the Ellis Marsalis Center After-School and Summer Programs; the New Orleans Jazz Orchestra School of Music (NOJOSOM); the Roots of Music; the Trombone Shorty Academy; the Louis Armstrong Educational Foundation's Music Academy and Summer Camp; and the New Orleans Jazz Museum's Jazz Education Center with its Ruth U. Fertel Jazz Lab and its Music Outreach Program in partnership with the Louis Armstrong Educational Foundation. Education certainly has been central to adding musicians to the ranks of Drumsville and the development of the New Orleans beat.

Of course, as the history in this book illustrates, drummers teach each other how to drum. New Orleans drummers always have been a tight-knit community, exhibiting a willingness to share and pass things on to the next generation. Often it has been a mentor/protégé relationship—Louis Cottrell and Freddie Kohlman, or Louis "Bob" Barbarin and Earl Palmer, or Charlie Suhor and Johnny Vidacovich, or Johnny Vidacovich and Stanton Moore. Vidacovich explains: "It was always some guy who was a little older or a little better than me. He would say, 'Do this or do that, listen to this, listen to that . . .' And I would do it."[100] That willingness to pass things on is evident in John Boudreaux's story of how he and Smokey Johnson were introduced to rudiments when Weedy Morris heard them drumming in the street or in Shannon Powell recalling how as a youngster, he was invited into James Black's house and taught to count different time signatures. Drummers would practice together to develop their craft—from Smokey Johnson and Uganda Roberts to David Lee Jr., John Boudreaux, and Mickey Conway to Cyril Neville and Zig Modeliste.

In the innovative spirit of improvising instruments from found and everyday objects and developing the drum set itself, New Orleans drummers have extended the reach of the beat through their inventiveness in creating educational resources. Drumsville artists have published a number of instructional books, including Ray Bauduc's *Dixieland Drumming* (1936) and *150 Progressive Drum Rhythms* (1940); Johnny Vidacovich and Herlin Riley's *New Orleans Jazz and Second Line Drumming*—which includes a CD illustrating the techniques and music discussed (1995); Vernel Fournier's *Drum Techniques:*

Intermediate–Advanced Exercises and Etudes (1997); and Ricky Sebastian's *Independence on the Drumset: Coordination Studies for Drummers in All Styles* (2006). In addition, they have created audio/video educational resources. In the 1940s, Baby Dodds recorded albums on which he demonstrates and explains elements of his pioneering approach to the drum set for Moses Asch and Frederic Ramsey on Folkways Records, *Talking and Drum Solos: Footnotes to Jazz, Vol. 1* (1951) and for Bill Russell's label American Music, much of which is compiled on the CD *Baby Dodds* (1993). Barry Martyn worked with Russell to produce a film, *Baby Dodds: New Orleans Drumming,* that documents the styles of Dodds, Cie Frazier, Alfred Williams, Abbie "Chinee" Foster, and Milford Dolliole. The video series *New Orleans Drumming* is comprised of three instructional volumes: *Johnny Vidacovich/Street Beats: Modern Applications; Herlin Riley/Ragtime and Beyond: Evolution of a Style;* and *Earl Palmer and Herman Ernest/From R&B to Funk* (compiled on DVD 2004). Zigaboo Modeliste documents his history and drum techniques on the DVD *Zigaboo: The Originator of New Orleans Funky Drumming* (2012).

Stanton Moore: "You Have to Do Your Homework"

Stanton Moore (b. 1972) has applied that innovative spirit to creating educational resources, extending the reach of the New Orleans beat to cutting-edge, twenty-first-century technology. It began with writing a column on New Orleans drumming for *Drum* magazine and the recognition that he was good at explaining the ins and outs of drumming. This led to his first book/DVD *Take It to The Streets: A Study in New Orleans Street Beat and Second-Line Rhythms as Applied to Funk* (2005). Subsequently, Moore released a digital download of a companion recording—featuring the Dirty Dozen Brass Band, bassist George Porter Jr., and keyboard player Ivan Neville—that demonstrates his lessons. For *Groove Alchemy* (2010), which focuses on the grooves constructed by funk masters Zigaboo Modeliste and James Brown–associated drummers Jabo Starks and Fred Stubblefield, Moore created a second book, a CD recorded with his trio, and a DVD—which is also available as a digital download with the book. *Groove Alchemy* won the 2011 *Modern Drummers* readers' poll for best educational book and DVD. But Moore was impatient with the composition and production time involved in those kinds of projects. He wanted to share his insights with a greater immediacy, so in 2017 he launched the online learning platform the Stanton Moore Drum Academy. The website provides resources that are applicable to drummers from the basic to highly advanced levels through a series of sections including "Academy Lessons," a video library with over 260 lessons; three levels of lessons that move from "Beginner Fresh Approach" to "Intermediate Fresh Approach" to "Advanced Fresh Approach"; "Interviews" in which he sits down "with some of my favorite drummers and human beings to discuss drums, drumming, music and life"; "Guerrilla Lessons" that provide more spontaneous responses to questions that arise; "Written Lessons"; "Play Alongs"; and "Community," a Facebook-like forum dedicated to creating a sense of an online learning community. In addition to his online academy, in December 2019 Moore hosted his sixth SONO (Spirit of New Orleans) Drum Camp—

Stanton Moore. In 2017, Moore launched the online learning platform the Stanton Moore Drum Academy, extending the reach of the New Orleans beat to cutting-edge, twenty-first-century technology. Photo by Marc Pagani. Courtesy of Stanton Moore.

three days of workshops and lessons at the Jazz Museum and other venues around the French Quarter with guest instructors like Shannon Powell, Johnny Vidacovich, Herlin Riley, and John Wooten. For his 2020 edition, he took the drum camp online thanks to the Covid-19 pandemic.

Teaching is only one aspect of Moore's absolute dedication to drumming. He's also a historian of the drums and the stylistic evolution of the New Orleans beat *and* a versatile, fiery, and inventive player. Moore was raised in nearby Metairie, and it was the drums he heard in Mardi Gras parades that first inspired him to pick up a pair of sticks. Moore's earliest educational experiences came at Brother Martin High School in the band and drumline under the direction of Marty Hurley: "He gave me a solid rudimental, fundamental foundation to work with. The discipline that I learned from that I think has carried over into my career." Another formative experience for Moore was hanging out at Ray Fransen's Drum Center in Kenner: "I used to go to the shop at least once a week as a teenager coming up, always hoping that maybe I would bump into Johnny Vidacovich or Russell Batiste or Jeffery Alexander or Raymond Weber or Willie Green or Shannon, Herlin, or any of those guys. I definitely learned a lot going there." In addition, Moore met the store's manager and repair man, Frank D'Arcangelo: "There should be a plaque somewhere in New Orleans dedicated to Frank D'Arcangelo because Frank has been informing and fixing things for New Orleans drummers for over thirty to thirty-five years . . . If it weren't for Frank, New Orleans drummers and their gear would be in a heap of trouble." D'Arcangelo encouraged Moore, predicting the teenager would be on the cover of *Modern Drummer* magazine:

I said, "What are you talking about? Of course, I would love that, but why do you say that about me?" And he said, "Every drummer in town comes through these doors, and there's nobody who is more passionate, more obsessed, and works harder than you do. Just keep doing what you're doing." Frank recognized that at a very young age and because he told me that, then I believed I could do it. So then I made that my goal. And I have been on the cover *Modern Drummer* twice.[101]

His initial efforts were playing rock, but when he began to explore the New Orleans music scene, he was drawn to the Drumsville tradition. Moore enrolled in the music program at Loyola University and started studying under Vidacovich, who introduced him to both traditional and modern jazz. In an interview with Bunny Matthews, Vidacovich recalls:

All of his fundamental stuff was very much solid. He just came in here and then we grew together. I said, "This is Miles, this is Charlie Parker, this is Baby Dodds, this is Philly Joe, this is Paul Motian, this is Tony Williams. Here's a poem. Let's play a poem. Let's be abstract."

I taught him all the necessary things. As soon as I would introduce an idea to Stanton, he would come back a week later, have that way mastered and then say, "Look what else I figured out how to do." So, in effect, he was teaching me just as quickly as I was teaching him.[102]

Moore's incredibly nuanced knowledge of New Orleans drumming styles is on display in the *Drumsville!* exhibit with a video from his *Groove Alchemy* DVD in which he demonstrates the evolution of the backbeat from Civil War martial drumming through the brass bands to traditional jazz, from swing to Earl Palmer's R&B/rock-and-roll innovations to 1970s funk. In a few minutes, he pretty much delineates most of the *Drumsville!* narrative. Drawing upon his Drumsville heroes to synthesize his own approach, Moore thrives among the community of drummers in the city: "It's all part of the very communal spirit of New Orleans, whether it's the Mardi Gras Indians or brass bands or drumming, you know, it's a very hand-it-down culture."[103]

One of his first outlets for what he was learning about the New Orleans beat was with the New Orleans Klezmer All Stars, but his deep dive into the funk came with the founding of Galactic. Almost three decades and a dozen albums later, they are a mainstay on the jam band circuit and known for the collaborations with such guest vocalists as Cyril Neville, Corey Glover, Maggie Koerner, and Erica Falls. Just as his teaching is high-tech, Moore has used a phrase sampler to create loops of rhythms that he interacts with on his drum set to build dynamic, driving grooves. Holding down a weekly spot at Snug Harbor when he's not on the road, he broadens his stylistic approach through his jazz-oriented work in a trio with bassist James Singleton and pianist David Torkanowsky. It's a setting that allows him to explore the approach to jazz soloing he learned from his mentor. He describes the essence of masterful soloing as part of a panel with Vidacovich and Powell at the Jazz Museum's "Improv Conference: A Festival of Ideas":

You have to do your homework away from the situation. You need to know the songs. You need to know the styles. You need to know as much about it as possible, and as Johnny V used to teach me, you know, you can do all the analytical stuff and thinking about stuff, but when you get to the gig and you start to play music, and in this case, when you start to improvise, as Johnny would say to me, "Bro, it's got to be from the neck down." And what he means by that is that you've got to have prepared, and you've gotta have done all your figuring and configuring and conceptualizing up here, but when you get to the gig and you're playing music or improvising, you've got to react; you've got to be in the moment, and it's gotta be a very visceral, guttural thing. It can't be so cerebral, right?[104]

On his album *With You in Mind: The Songs of Allen Toussaint* (2017), Moore's trio is augmented by horn players like Maceo Parker, Donald Harrison, Trombone Shorty, and Nicholas Payton, along with Cyril Neville on lead vocals, affording him the opportunity to bring together his masterful approach to both funk and jazz.

At his Uptown studio, Moore is surrounded by racks and stacks of drums. He even designed his own signature snare drum. Modeled on an old snare given to him by Vidacovich that was stolen, Moore's drum—the prototype is on display in *Drumsville!*—is made from

Stanton Moore Drum Company's Spirit of New Orleans snare drum. Designed by Moore to replicate a vintage snare given to him by Johnny Vidacovich that was stolen, it features a 4.5" × 14" titanium shell and a logo adapted from the iconic New Orleans Sewerage and Water Board meter cover. Loaned by Stanton Moore. Photo by Grace Patterson. Courtesy of the New Orleans Jazz Museum.

titanium and is emblazoned with his logo, inspired by the iconic New Orleans Sewerage and Water Board meter cover. He is an enthusiastic student of the drum set history detailed in the exhibit: "Dee Dee [Chandler] was the guy who really first started utilizing a bass drum pedal and in 1909, Ludwig made the first workable, marketable, saleable, bass drum pedal, and that's when the drum set really started to take off." Of course, he's a collector of vintage drum equipment, and his 1909 Ludwig bass drum pedal is also displayed. Moore recognizes the pivotal role New Orleans played in that development of the instrument: "How come the drum set didn't happen in Africa, but it happened here? It's because, I think, you have all these cultures being put together. And there's quote unquote American ingenuity. We talk about jazz as the only truly American art form. Well, the drum set is a truly American instrument." And as much as he admires the inventive spirit that created the drum set, he is also a tireless advocate for drummers—even those who lost their gigs thanks to the new contraption: "People have been trying to cut poor drummers out of a job for years."[105] Teaching drumming history or beats or techniques—in person or in cyberspace or sitting behind his set driving the big-time funk jams with Galactic or working with his brushes on a jazz standard with the trio, Stanton Moore is a tireless advocate of the New Orleans drumming tradition.

EXTENDING THE BEAT: "THERE'S A LOT OF THINGS THAT CAN BE EXPRESSED WITH THE DRUMS"

The New Orleans beat is thriving today because a direct lineage can be traced back to drummers who laid the foundation for the tradition at the turn of the twentieth century.

As demonstrated by *Drumsville!*, that lineage leads directly to so many drummers on the current scene who are building on what came before to create something new *and* sustain that impulse to keep passing it on to future generations. Like all the previous sections of the exhibit and this book, this section is intended to be representative rather than comprehensive. This survey of the contemporary scene looks at a selection of drummers. Some of them have achieved renown in New Orleans and beyond; others are like the "blue collar musicians" whom Zig Modeliste observed when he was coming up, drummers "who know their craft." Certainly, there are many others, but they are all contributing their variations to extending the beat.

Kevin O'Day: "The Whole Progression of It"

Kevin O'Day (1973–2022) stands at the front of the line when it comes to new variations and possibilities in drumming. The contexts in which he drums stylistically range from traditional brass band second-line rhythms to hip-hop beats, from modern jazz to alt-rock, and from freeform jazz to funk—to name a few. He came to the city to study jazz and wound up establishing himself on the scene and expanding the scope the New Orleans beat.

His attraction to New Orleans was inspired by one of the city's contemporary drumming masters: "I came to New Orleans to study jazz with Johnny V. at Loyola, and that's why I wanted to go to Loyola, not for any other reason but to study with Johnny." Vidacovich is certainly conscious of the impact he has on the young musicians who, inspired by his drumming and nurtured by his teaching, find their way to Drumsville. Like a proud parent, he recalls: "I taught Kevin O'Day since he was seventeen. He was a Loyola student; I was his instructor, but he came to me when he was in high school. So, I taught him for about five or six years. The same time I taught Stanton [Moore], the same exact years, and prior to that Brian Blade. Yeah, I taught all them boys."[106] O'Day first heard Vidacovich's distinctive approach to the New Orleans beat as a teenager in Baton Rouge:

> When I would see Johnny Vidacovich play, I would just love the looseness when he would play those second-line beats on the drum set. I just loved the looseness and the interplay he would have with the bass, and then when soloists would improvise, he would be interactive with them too, still keeping that incredible second-line greasy feel that he had. And man, I just loved that shit. That really got me.[107]

He certainly learned a lot about the technical aspects of drumming and improvisation from Vidacovich, but based on the myriad directions that O'Day has taken his drumming, it's likely that his mentor's openness to spontaneity and the creative process had just as profound an impact.

O'Day was born in Houston, Texas, and raised in Lafayette, Louisiana, and he believes that the impulse to become a drummer was always there: "When I was a kid, I was grabbing the furniture. We had an ottoman that had a nice floor-tom type of sound. Then I had a couple of chairs in front of me. I would use that for a drum set. Even younger, I would set up in the kitchen with the pots and pans, and my mom would let me play those with

Kevin O'Day. O'Day: "The drum set started here, and now you can't go anywhere in the world without hearing music with a drum set." Photo by Christopher Senac. Courtesy of Kevin O'Day.

like the wooden spoons. I think if you're gonna be a musician, there's a desire there. I think early on you see it." And though the wires may have been slightly crossed, he ultimately got that first drum set he seemingly was destined to have: "When I was eleven, a drum set was a Christmas present to my brother. I got a computer because I was supposed to be an accountant. But I was digging the drum set, so within a week I had traded him the computer for the drum set, and now my brother is an accountant and I'm the drummer." The trajectory of all the bands he has propelled began as a teenager: "The very first gig I had was in Baton Rouge, and it was with a little rock cover band that we had put together with some kids in high school." One of his earliest influences was the legendary Baton Rouge drummer Herman Jackson, an instructor at Southern University and veteran who has played behind countless band leaders, including B.B. King, Count Basie, Al Green, Clark Terry, Ellis Marsalis, and Allen Toussaint. O'Day recalls: "Herman Jackson was definitely one. When I was living in Baton Rouge for high school. I saw him play pretty often over at Gino's, which is a little place in Baton Rouge." That club would also provide his first window into Drumsville: "And, every Thursday, [pianist] Larry Sieberth would lead a band there. So, I saw Herman Jackson, John Vidacovich, Russell Batiste, Herman Ernest. Those guys were big influences in the very beginning. That little scene at Gino's was so cool. You know, he brought in musicians from New Orleans with a different band every week." Once he got to Drumsville, O'Day immersed himself in the tradition:

> I had seen Herman Ernest play also, and then he started playing with Dr. John, and that was a really big deal. I loved what he was doing. He also had that parade rhythm too. And Russell Batiste, I saw these guys play kind of young, and the next thing you know, he's playing with the Funky Meters, so I'm going to those shows with Stanton [Moore] when we were at Loyola together watching Russell Batiste play . . . I definitely started checking out Zigaboo. I started checking out the earlier drummers too like Zutty Singleton and Baby Dodds and tried to get a good feel of the whole progression of it.

Not only did he get the whole progression, but O'Day's drumming has been at the forefront of extending that progression. Modern jazz was his starting point: "The Café Brazil was my first gig in New Orleans, and it was like fourteen dollars, and I did a bunch of little trio things. I met [saxophonist] Rob Wagner around that time, and we were playing together at Kaldi's with [bassist] Andy Wolf."

The extensions and variations took off from there. That trio somehow eventually morphed into the band Iris May Tango that mixed edgy jazz, rock, and funk and eventually worked with two hip-hop MCs. He led his own funky roots rock band, Kevin O'Day and the Animals. Perhaps the project that exemplifies O'Day's openness to possibility and his dedication to extending the New Orleans beat where it had not gone before was the zany mix of diverse styles in Royal Fingerbowl, a trio he joined with guitarist Alex McMurray and bassist Wolf. During the recovery from Hurricane Katrina, O'Day and Moore cooked up a brass band supergroup, the Midnight Disturbers, that has included drummer Mike Dillon and horn players from the Dirty Dozen, Rebirth, Galactic, Big Sam's Funky Nation, and Bonerama. His brass band credentials also include a Jazz at Lincoln Center "Thank You" all-star tour of Middle Eastern countries that had sent aid after the storm. O'Day contributed second-line funk to Kirk Joseph's Backyard Groove, and he followed both Willie Green and Moore in the drumming chair for the New Orleans Klezmer All Stars. Some of the albums on which he's appeared testify to his stylistic range—blues-rock on Anders Osborne's *Ash Wednesday Blues* (2001); traditional jazz on trumpeter James Andrews's *Hear No Evil* (2005); R&B on Walter "Wolfman" Washington's *Doin' the Funk Thing* (2008); and funk on Russell Batiste's Orchestra from da Hood's *Follow Your Dreams* (2010).

Kevin O'Day is clearly engaged in the progression of the Drumsville tradition and the evolution of the New Orleans beat: "The drums mattered so much to this new music that emerged here. It's such a cool thing that happened here. The drum set started here, and now you can't go anywhere in the world without hearing music with a drum set. It's really incredible . . . It's something that's passed along. It really is. I would say every drummer has another drummer like that they pass something on to, a few probably."

Andre Bohren: "What's the Deal, Kid?"

During the early 1990s, while Andre Bohren (b. 1979) was exploring the explosion of live bands that were playing on Frenchmen Street, he came into contact with an older drummer who reached out and welcomed him to Drumsville: "Kevin O'Day was playing with most of the bands I was going to see, and at some point he was like, 'What's the deal, kid? I see you everywhere giving me the eye.' And I told him I was a drummer back in town, and he was like, 'Well, come play a song.' I sat in for a song, and the band leader got my number and I started getting calls for gigs."[108]

Bohren grew up connected to New Orleans music through his father, Spencer Bohren, a blues and folk singer/guitarist who, along with bands like the Radiators and Little Queenie and the Percolators, was part of the scene during the late 1970s and early 1980s around the original Tipitina's. The New Orleans beat was extended by the bands on that scene as it was incorporated into the mix of blues, roots rock, R&B, and funk they were playing. Today, Bohren carries on the spirit of that scene as the drummer in Johnny Sketch and the Dirty Notes and in Rory Danger and the Danger Dangers. Bohren is unique in that he's talented both as a funk/rock drummer *and* a classical pianist. He ul-

Andre Bohren. Ray Bonneville recording session, King Electric Studio, Austin, Texas, 2018. Photo by Justin Douglas. Courtesy of Andre Bohren.

timately received his degree in classical piano studies at Loyola University. In the 1980s, the Bohren family, to put it mildly, moved around quite a bit. When they returned to New Orleans after ten years–plus on the road, Spencer resumed his career there, just as Andre was about to start his. He found a perfect home for an up-and-coming drummer. In addition to O'Day, Bohren was observing lots of great role models on Frenchman Street:

> When we got back to New Orleans, it was such a different scene and there were so many things to keep me from focusing on classical piano music in the form of George Porter and Runnin' Partners and Stanton Moore. Galactic was still playing small rooms . . . One of the guys I would seek out, go watch was Carlo Nuccio, who, at the time, was playing with the Royal Fingerbowl . . . He's the guy I probably steal more from him in my drumming, some of it in the way I play, some of it's the way I approach songs. He's one of the most musical drummers I've ever seen.

Bohren put together his first drum set when the family was living in Fort Collins, Colorado, and it was a longtime friend from back in the Tipitina's days that stepped in to encourage the young drummer:

> For me, my first big drum influence is Frank Bua from the Radiators . . . I grew up watching the Radiators with the guitar players in mind. Then I started piecing together a drum set when I was maybe twelve, and the next time I saw the Radiators, I was all about Frank. He'd been playing on a couple of my dad's records at the time, and when my dad told him I

was interested in drums, he sent me my first cymbals and sticks, which were these big tree trunk sticks he uses and some old, cracked cymbals that he had.

Bohren continued the pursuit of classical piano when the family moved to Casper, Wyoming, but was also playing drums in bands with his high school friends. One of the resources he found that put him in touch with Drumsville was Johnny Vidacovich and Herlin Riley's book and CD *New Orleans Jazz and Second Line Drumming:*

> What was cool to me about that is they're both coming from the same New Orleans second line, but the results of each of their second lines are so different. Herlin's got this really tight, more military march kind of thing going on. And Johnny's just like, he's Johnny, he's just fluid. For me, with Johnny, you know he's got the chops, but it sounds like he's just kind of playing the drums. He's certainly not thinking about, "Okay, I'm gonna do a double stroke roll here that leads into a paradiddle" . . . Those are two of the guys I really dug in on for second-line stuff.

Bohren's exposure to his father's associates passed along a lot of essential lessons about drumming. He recalls his father talking about a time when he was working with Vidacovich that illustrates the classic Drumsville emphasis on the drummer playing melodically and in the service of the band, enhancing the performance of a song:

> You know my dad tells a story about when he had a gig that Johnny Vidacovich was on. And they were doing soundcheck, and Johnny said, "No, I don't need bass in the monitor; I know what he's doing. I don't need any guitar in the monitor; I know what he's doing. All I need is lots and lots of vocals." My dad asked why he didn't want any of the other instruments, why he wanted so much vocals. And Johnny said, "I gotta know what the song is about." You know, he's playing the song; he's not just playing music. He plays the story of the song.

During his earliest years in New Orleans, his family lived right next door to keyboard player and singer John Magnie, so Bohren certainly grew up hearing Little Queenie and the Percolators. Drummer Kenneth Blevins, who also played with his father, made a lasting impression: "My favorite just funky, jankey-ass second-line groove that I've heard on a recording is Kenny Blevins from Lil Queenie and the Percolators on 'My Darling New Orleans.' Half the time it sounds like he's kind of kicking the drum kit down the stairs, but it grooves. And that second line is something that I'm sure in some way is in the back of my head every time I play a second-line groove." Bohren also recalls that Blevins reflected the spirit of the "thinker-tinkers" who improvised their instruments from everyday objects: "He had a hubcap on his setup. It was like from a '57 Buick or something like that." Similarly, Bohren points out that same impulse in the percussionist from the Subdudes, another band that emerged from that Tipitina's scene: "The Subdudes first gig, Steve Amadee just brought whatever he had in the house, and he had a tambourine, and he had a spatula. And that's what he played with on the first couple gigs." Three decades later, Amadee still drives that band primarily by beating a tambourine resting on his knee with a drumstick or brush. Bohren is no stranger to introducing everyday objects to create a new sound: "In the studio, I use all kinds of stuff on my snare. I like putting keys and nuts and bolts [on it], stuff to make it rattle." He definitely has a conception of what he's looking for in a set of drums: "I've always been a less is more kind of player. If I can't get it done with a bass drum, a snare drum, and hi-hat, then it's probably not the right gig for me . . . But for me there's a sweet spot like where you hit the drum that can really make a huge difference to get the good sound that you want."

Like a true Drumsville disciple, Bohren knows all about that emphasis on the bass drum: "I want my bass drum to sound like the St. Aug. marching band, like just a big cannon drum with no—like a lot of rock drummers especially put a pillow in the drum or a blanket or something to muffle it, and to me a drum is supposed to ring." Bohren is a remarkably versatile drummer. He can lay down raucous rock and funk grooves with Johnny Sketch and the Dirty Notes, and he can subtly color and shade performances like he does on his father's recordings, such as *Blackwater Music* (2011) and *Makin' It Home to You* (2018), using his drumming to shape and define a song, just like Vidacovich did all those years ago.

Jason Marsalis: "All the Possibilities of Rhythm"

Like so many other musicians, drummer and vibraphonist Jason Marsalis (b. 1977) found himself without live music venues or audiences due to the Covid-19 pandemic lockdown. But that didn't stop him from performing, and in mid-May 2020, he put together a livestream YouTube concert billed as *The Jason Marsalis One Man Drums Show*. For about an hour and a half, he delivered a solo drum set show that stylistically and conceptually ranged far and wide. He peppered the drum performances with commentary on the selections and his thoughts on the nature of rhythm. Kicking things off with what he calls a "drum fanfare," Marsalis launched into the familiar martial beats of a brass band snare drumming, gradually slid into a funky second-line groove, and culminated with a driving backbeat that would have made Earl Palmer proud. At the conclusion of the fanfare, he explained that it was inspired by the recent passing of Little Richard, who had recorded hits like "Tutti Frutti" in New Orleans in the 1950s with Palmer on drums. Marsalis articulated the agenda for the evening:

> Tonight, with the *One Man Drums Show* you will see showcased all of the different moods in sounds and tempo that can be displayed on the drums. Normally, when a person thinks of the drum solo they think of the loud climax at the end of a song. And then, once you've played it, that's it. There's nowhere to go. But in reality, there's a lot of things that can be expressed with the drums. It's a very emotional instrument, and there's a lot of colors and moods that can be displayed.[109]

He went on to deliver a program of solo drum set variations that moved from the "swinging, grooving rhythms" on "Riffin'" to the "Evolution of a Slow Jam"; from "Cecil's Jitney," an evocation of pianist Cecil Taylor's abstract rhythmic conception, to "The Punk

Rock Rag," illustrating rhythmic similarities across genres. He played two impressionistic "descriptive" pieces that sonically and rhythmically capture "Paris Traffic" and "A Day at the Office." Then he mused on how Zigaboo Modeliste might play funk in an odd time meter on "Zig 7." With "E's Surrey Ride," he paid tribute to his late father, pianist Ellis Marsalis, based on the pianist's version of "Surrey with the Fringe on Top," an arrangement that was inspired by an insistent rhythm he heard his son practicing.

Possibility has been central to Marsalis's life coming up in Drumsville. His father was an elder statesman of both jazz piano and music education, and Jason is the youngest of four brothers who all have become major figures in the jazz world. While Marsalis has been playing drums since he was a child, his early formal musical training was on violin. Yet, the drums remained constant. He was instructed by some of the giants of the New Orleans beat, including James Black and David Lee Jr., both of whom had performed with his father. In an interview with Anthony Brown, recorded for the Smithsonian Jazz Oral History Program, Marsalis describes Black's early influence: "My first teacher was a drummer by the name of James Black who I later found out was my father's partner in crime as far as music goes. At that time, what I learned from James was fundamentals, such as the book, which I later discovered was the bible of drum books, or the J. S. Bach [of] drum books, if you will, a book called *Stick Control.*"[110] Later on, Lee impacted Marsalis when he had a more sophisticated awareness of drumming: "As far as New Orleans, also I did study with David Lee, who was a fabulous drummer. He was somebody that I got a lot of information out of in terms of different exercises, what to play on drums and how to approach solos and form."[111] At some point between the ages of six and eight, Marsalis began sitting in at his father's gig, and by his early teens he was working in the band. He continued his formal studies on violin and eventually found himself drawn to the orchestral percussion instruments. It was through the suggestion of his father that Marsalis began to learn the vibraphone: "And after a while I started to hear more and more music and more possibilities of what I wanted to do. And when I saw that there were many things that could be done with the instrumentation of vibraphone with a rhythm section, that's what inspired me to want to pursue it even more."[112] He has brought that vision to fruition leading a band and recording regularly as a vibraphonist.

Jazz drumming increasingly became his focus, but he continued to pursue studies in classical music and composition both at the New Orleans Center for the Creative Arts (NOCCA) and Loyola University. His initial drumming experiences that came through

Jason Marsalis performing at the 1993 New Orleans Jazz and Heritage Festival. Photo by Sydney Byrd. Courtesy of the New Orleans Jazz Museum. Accession number 1994.003.337.

his father and his brothers immersed him in modern jazz, but he was always expanding his approach to the instrument. He played Brazilian music with Casa Samba and was a founding member of the Afro-Cuban/Caribbean band Los Hombres Calientes with trumpeter Irvin Mayfield and percussionist Bill Summers. He explored funk, and a performance with sousaphonist Kirk Joseph led to a very helpful tip from his father:

> I was playing this funk tune on the gig, and my father looks at me and says, "You're not playing the snare drum right." "Excuse me?" "No. You're not playing it right. See, you're lifting the stick off the drum. You have to lay the stick into the drum.'" "Oh." So I was, okay. I didn't have any concept of how to play funk or any of that. So, after hearing these records, I thought, I'm going to really make an effort to practice this stuff, because I don't really know how to play it.[113]

He went to work and began practicing with James Brown recordings. Marsalis received advice on how to approach traditional jazz drumming from clarinetist and educator Dr. Michael White: "We started to meet. We didn't meet a lot, but we'd meet here and there. I didn't do a performance with him until, I think, four years later . . . We were playing some trad, and I remember trying to do some of the more basic things we talked about, and it worked."[114] He eventually recorded with White and is featured on his album *Blue Crescent* (2009). Over the years, in addition to playing traditional jazz, he's been able to incorporate elements of that music into a modern context as evidenced by his album with his vibes quartet, *The 21st Century Trad Band* (2017). Marsalis stepped into the spotlight as a jazz drummer through his tenure in pianist Marcus Roberts's trio. He has performed and recorded extensively with his father and three brothers—all of them were presented with the National Endowment for the Arts Jazz Master Award in 2011. Marsalis has released albums leading bands both as a drummer and a vibraphonist, and over the past few years, he's collaborated with Herlin Riley and Shannon Powell as the New Orleans Groovemasters.

Jason Marsalis has a remarkably expansive view of what's possible on vibraphone, drums, and percussion. He clearly brings a thematic and compositional approach to his instruments. As he was about to sign off the livestream of his *One Man Drums Show,* Marsalis began clicking his sticks together in a steady pulse as the "theme music" for his show, explaining that he was borrowing the theme from the "iconic stopwatch" on the television show *Sixty Minutes:* "I thought it was apropos to use that theme music for this show because this show demonstrates not only all the possibilities of rhythm and the possibilities of time but also the fact that rhythm is a universal element that is everywhere."[115]

Vernon Severin: "You Better Teach Him Because He's a Drummer"

Vernon Severin (b. 1954) grew up in Treme immersed in second-line culture, but his focus was on the drum set rather than brass band drumming: "I'm a trap drummer, but I took on the brass band thing seriously. Well, 'Uncle' Lionel [Batiste] and Benny [Jones Sr.] used to come by my gigs. I was playing with group called BRW, a funk group, and

'Uncle' Lionel was always after me; he kept on saying, 'Man, you need to play some brass band music, you need to play some brass band music.'[116] In recent years, Severin has fulfilled Batiste's request to play "some brass band music," lighting a fire under the Treme Brass Band with his snare drum since Jones switched over to bass drum after the passing of Batiste. Severin's father, Wilfred "Crip" Severin Jr., was a drummer who played with Dave Bartholomew, the Dooky Chase band, Jesse "Ooh Poo Pa Do" Hill, among others. All three of his sons learned to play the drums. Gerald stopped playing at an early age; Chris went on to become one of the most in-demand and versatile bass players in the city; and Vernon is still at it— and he's passed it along to his son, Adonis Rose. Wilfred Severin always had drums in the house: "His gold set of Premiers, this was the ones he used all the time. Because we lived in the Lafitte projects, they like stood at the foot of the stairs. We better not touch those . . . He had a set of drums upstairs in our, me and Chris's closet, so we used to beat on 'em all the time." His father showed him the basics on the drum set, but Severin went in a different direction with the music: "Mostly my dad used to teach me different things, you know, rudiments and how to swing, you know, different little things. He didn't like me to play funk, but I wanted to play funk. He didn't. 'Don't play no funk.' But, I couldn't work, if I didn't want to play funk because that was the thing that young people was doing."

Wilfred "Crip" Severin Jr., ca. 1975. The patriarch of a New Orleans musical family, Severin Jr. played with Dave Bartholomew, the Dooky Chase Band, and Jesse Hill, among others. Photo courtesy of Vernon Severin.

His formal studies began around fourth grade at Phillis Wheatley Elementary School, and he continued to play in junior high and high school in both the marching band and stage band. In the late 1960s, he had a day job in a muffler shop and was playing in a funk band called LSD. He needed new drums, so his father took him to Werlein's Music, where he bought his first drum set: "It was a Ludwig, transparent green, and it had Zildjian cymbals, oh man, that was the shit! Everybody was like, 'Oh man, look at them drums he got.' You know how much them drums cost me? Fourteen hundred dollars. And I was paying like twenty-five dollars a month, so you know I had to be paying for that forever. I paid for 'em. My daddy made sure I paid for 'em. He didn't pay not one note." Severin passed those green transparent Ludwig drums on to Rose, who played them up until he left for college. Today, the drum set is back with Severin. Those payments to Werlein's may have been tough, but talk about a long-term investment!

Severin continued his music education at SUNO, including the chance to study piano with Edward Kidd Jordan, but when it came to advancing his drumming skills, he went right to the source and took lessons from *both* James Black and Smokey Johnson. His relationship with Black had been somewhat contentious, but Severin recognized a true drum master: "When Mason's Las Vegas Strip was open, I was playing with a funk band at one of the clubs because we used to play there almost every night, and James Black and them with the jazz thing was playing at the smaller club . . . So, I used to go check him out all the time, say 'Damn, that dude. I can learn some drums from this cat,' you know." Severin worked with Black for five or six weeks, but he wasn't satisfied: "He really wasn't teaching me what I really needed. I know now that he was teaching me some things that I didn't understand in my drumming. As I done got older, I learned the concept of it. But, it was basically, what he was teaching me was rudiments." Severin told Black that he wanted to the lessons to go deeper:

> He started showing me different things. I already had the swing thing [*scats groove*]. I already had the shuffle [*scats groove*]. I already had that. But it was a certain way that he do it and he approach it that made it so effective. You know, and he told me the things to practice on, but this one thing, this one beat, it's actually two beats that James Black taught me that I use, and they are very effective. And, it's not many people that do it.

In some ways, the lessons were as philosophical as they were musical: "He was such a smart guy, you know, you see him, he was always like he got a boot in his mouth, but he was so intelligent, like when we used to do the lessons, he used to relate the Bible and all that with my drum lessons, you know, it was like a serious educational thing based on life, not just the drums." Severin applied and received a grant to study drums with the renowned Boston-based drummer Alan Dawson, but with a family to raise, the travel was too expensive. Instead, he took lessons from Johnson: "So, Smokey Johnson and my daddy was real, real close. He was another one that I'd see all the time. The difference in Smokey's playing and James Black's playing, I would say that Smokey was more, I'd say, a New Orleans–type drummer, more second-line flavor . . . but he could swing, and he had some chops, but James Black was more on the exotic side. And that's how I learned 'It Ain't My Fault,' everything through Smokey. And me and him got tight."

When Severin first brought his baby son Adonis to meet his grandfather, Wilfred Severin made sure the drumming legacy was going to be passed on to a third generation: "He looked at him and he say, 'Man, this is a drummer. You better teach him because he's a drummer. Can't you see? He counting off, look at him. He has got it all in him.' I was like, 'Alright Daddy, whatever.' But Severin's house was Drumming Central. With band practices every day and James Black and Smokey Johnson dropping by regularly, the child was already deeply immersed in Drumsville. Finally, when Severin was practicing one day, he had a revelation:

> Remember the green set of Ludwigs I was telling you about, transparent? I'll never forget this, when Adonis was a little baby. He was crawling. So, I'm playing. Back in the days in the '70s, we used to cut the bass drum head off, the surface, just leave the rim where you can tighten the thing that hold the shell on . . . So, man, I'm just practicing, boy, I'm just wailing. It feels good, boy, just wailing, wailing. Lady gone. She at work, and I'm babysitting. I'm just tearing it up all day, loud, just banging on the drums, having a ball. I'm looking, saying, "Where is Adonis?" I'm just looking 'cause I'm babysitting. Guess where he was? Guess where he was? In the bass drum! In the bass drum! Boy just setting there.

He began teaching the child the fundamentals that his father had passed along to him, the lessons he had learned from years of experience, and eventually the lessons from Black, Johnson, and other associates: "I put drumsticks in his hand when he was like one. See, by the time he was three, he could play a paradiddle; see, by the time he was ten, I couldn't even mess with him." Today, Rose has earned a worldwide reputation as a master drummer and teacher. Rose's students sometimes show up to sit in with the Treme Brass Band: "And, you know what I notice about them little cats, man, their ear is so good, and they catch on so fast. I mean they play everything I play. I say, 'Bro, get off my drum, get out of here' [*laughs*]. So much speed, man, especially Joe Dyson, goodness gracious. Yeah, I've done a couple gigs where Joe Dyson showed up. He say, 'I see now.' I say, 'What you see?' 'I see where Adonis get it from' [*laughs*]."

Adonis Rose: "It Comes with Responsibility"

Adonis Rose (b. 1975) may not remember that day back in the mid-1970s when his father, Vernon Severin, was practicing and found Rose as an infant sitting inside a green transparent Ludwig bass drum; however, the instruction, support, and encouragement Rose received from family, musical mentors, and educators on his journey to becoming a third-generation master of New Orleans drumming attained fulfillment in January 2017 when he became artistic director for the New Orleans Jazz Orchestra. It almost seems like he was destined to play such a role. His grandfather Wilfred Severin sensed he was a drummer the first time he met the child and encouraged his son to begin teaching Rose: "So, my dad did that, really took the time, made an investment to teach me how to play. So, I started out maybe at three or four years old, literally, with a little drum set, and it was set up on the porch in the projects, and I would play every day, practice. And then eventually, maybe a couple years later, my dad started to teach me my rudiments." Within a short time, he would be playing drums for folks in the neighborhood: "My friends used to crowd around me and watch me play. Some of my family members have photos from when I was like four years old playing on the center court out in the St. Bernard Projects with kids kind of gathering around and watching me play."[117]

Rose learned his rudiments from his father, just as he had learned them from his father. He went to Edward H. Phillips Elementary School and played in the concert band there. At Capdau Junior High, he played snare in the marching band and became a section leader marching in Mardi Gras parades. Rose earned a full scholarship to St. Augustine, but his father had other ideas, insisting he attend the New Orleans Center for Creative Arts (NOCCA). It was a prescient decision:

> Being there with my peers and being under the direction of Clyde Kerr, I dug deep into the study. Once I saw people like Mark Chatters and Nicholas Payton, who were all in the class, and we had to play and perform every day, I really became interested in being a jazz musician. I took it serious. I really fell in love with it. All I did was listen to music, study music. I was taking lessons with David Lee. At the time, he was one of the drummers that would come in and work with the students, the student drummers.

During his junior and senior years at NOCCA, Rose was working gigs around New Orleans almost nightly. He had deep roots in the Drumsville tradition, and his family ties provided him with a unique window into the local scene:

Adonis Rose (*left*) and Vernon Severin with Green Ludwig drum set. When Severin was practicing on his green Ludwig set, he looked around and couldn't find his infant son Adonis. He recalls: "Guess where he was? In the bass drum! In the bass drum! Boy just setting there." Rose also played the Ludwig drum set before he went to Berklee College of Music. Photo by Grace Patterson. Courtesy of the New Orleans Jazz Museum.

I was familiar with drummers in New Orleans and drummers outside New Orleans. You know, Ed Blackwell, Zigaboo, my dad was friends with Zigaboo and a lot of these drummers. I didn't know a whole lot about them and what they did, but because dad was a musician and my uncle [bassist Chris Severin] was a musician, I mean they had rehearsals at the house every week. We stayed next door to my uncle, who was playing with Diane Reeves and Dr. John, and all of their rehearsals, a lot of the times, would be in my uncle's studio in the backyard behind the house.

Rose earned a full Presidential Scholarship to Berklee College of Music in Boston, but before he even headed off to college, his drumming was in demand: "I got a call from Terence Blanchard about going on tour with him before I went to college. So when I graduated from high school, a couple days later I hit the road with Terence and toured with him all summer until I started Berklee."

The signature beat that has evolved from the Sunday-afternoon gatherings in Congo Square all the way to the twenty-first century represents a legacy that permeates New Orleans culture. For Rose, that legacy is integrally linked to everyday life:

Here, I can grab the average guy, I mean, my mom can pull out a triangle and beat on a beer bottle and play a second-line groove or some type of Indian six groove [*claps groove*]. I mean everybody around here can hear that, and for us, again, you gotta go back to the process; it's just the way we do things. I mean we can take anything and make music out of it, and that's what I love about people like Herlin Riley and Shannon Powell, Smokey Johnson. It didn't matter what they played because it was from within. So, yeah, I think the culture dictated how the process, how we did it.

Thanks to both family and education, Rose is steeped in the entire history of jazz drumming. Riley is one of the drummers who helped broaden his perspective: "You have musicians that are stepping-stones to other musicians. So, for me, that musician was Herlin Riley. You know, Herlin was playing with Wynton [Marsalis], playing with Jazz at Lincoln Center, and he was on the road. Herlin studied the entire history of the drum set; he knows it all. For me, he was the gateway to understanding what everybody else was doing." He recognizes that "bottom up" orientation is one of the elements that makes the New Orleans beat so distinctive: "I think the thing that separates my drumming from somebody that's not from here, Herlin's or Joe Dyson's or Shannon's or Gerald French's playing, is the way we fill the bottom of the drum set." Whether he is drumming behind artists from his hometown, such as Ellis Marsalis, Nicholas Payton, Terence Blanchard, Wynton Marsalis, and Harry Connick Jr., or artists from outside New Orleans, such as Betty Carter, Diane Reeves, Marcus Roberts, Nnenna Freelon, and Kurt Elling, Rose believes the conception of the drums in which he was reared characterizes his approach: "It's just always there, so it informs us, the way we approach the drum kit, so we may play the drum kit from the top down, if we're playing jazz, but we're always thinking about the bottom." Rose recognizes the special bond that exists in the New Orleans drumming community, a bond that he clearly first experienced through the drummers who hung out together and performed in his father's home:

> I think it's special to the drummers here because of our history. You can't get away from the history. The first form of the jazz band had two drummers in it. It was a marching band; it was a brass band. Drummers have always had to work together. African drummers, it was groups of them in the hundreds. It's communal, and it's a brotherhood, and I think it's different than other instruments because it's a supportive instrument . . . We have to make everybody sound good, including ourselves.

Making everybody sound good was the role of the drummer that Baby Dodds articulated more than a century ago, and Adonis Rose understands what writer Albert Murray calls the "ancestral imperative,"[118] the duty of each generation to take the baton to both extend the efforts and accomplishments of previous generations and ensure that the next generation can keep that legacy going, just as his grandfather and father did:

> I'm doing this partly because I love to do it, and it's fun, but it comes with responsibility. You know, it's almost like Earl Palmer. He was out here doing this for a reason. It was to keep the tradition of great New Orleans drum set playing alive, and that's just as important to me as getting up onstage and performing because I'm having fun. I would never want to go out and give a bad reputation of what New Orleans drumming is. I would never, ever want to do that. We have good nights, and we have bad nights, but you're supposed to be consistent and get out here and play on a high level regardless of how you feel or what

you have going on, and I would not take all of the hours and years and days of investment of people like Bob French and Ernie Elly and all these drummers gave to me. I would not waste their time by not taking this seriously.

Rose has broadened that sense of responsibility in his position as artistic director of the New Orleans Jazz Orchestra. He plans the programming; conducts and performs with the big band; leads small combos; passes on the tradition through the NOJO School of Music; and oversees the state-of-the-art facility the New Orleans Jazz Market. Projects under his leadership range from performing Duke Ellington's "Nutcracker Suite" to an ambitious big band recording, *Songs—The Music of Allen Toussaint* (2019) featuring guest vocalist DeeDee Bridgewater. It seems like his grandfather knew what he was talking about all those years ago:

> We're here to give back to the community and preserve the art, our art, New Orleans's art and music. So, again, a great opportunity, a great way for me to be able to have artistic expression, not only sitting behind a drum kit but being a leader, being able to produce shows and curate events, and artistic planning and working with funders and partnerships and come up with concepts for records and tours. It's another way of being a complete musician.

Joe Dyson: "I Want to Touch the Heart. I Want Them to Be Able to Move"

Joe Dyson (b. 1989) is a perfect example of how both the influence of family and community-based education contribute to the development of an artist dedicated to extending the legacy of the New Orleans beat. His initial experiences with drums were centered in his family and church. His grandmother sang; his father, Dr. Joseph J. C. Dyson Sr., is an organist and bassist; his uncle John Dyson Jr., is a drummer; and he grew up with "a slew of cousins" who play music: "So, my earliest interaction with the music was first from home, seeing the family and experiencing the family, and, of course, going to church, not just my church, but following my father around at different churches, sitting next to him while he was playing the organ, and also performing in church." Drawn to the drums, he started on pots and pans, moved to a toy kit, and got his first drums from a family friend and pastor, who gave him an old Rogers set when he was buying new drums for his church. Dyson was also engaged in the cultural milieu of New Orleans that he calls a "start in the music from the folkloric position": "A lot of times in New Orleans there are Super Sundays. You have a second line every other Sunday, so I would always see a second line passing . . . and also see different brass bands practicing in the neighborhood and participating in school with different friends and playing in different brass bands and marching bands . . . so that was like my earliest forms of interacting within the music in New Orleans culture."[119]

Soon Dyson found himself advancing through education at McDonogh 15 Elementary School, where he started developing the technical aspects of drumming—learning how to read music and play rudiments—with instructor Jerry McGowan. His growth as a drummer continued through summer programs, both the Prodigy Project and the Louis "Satchmo" Armstrong Jazz Camp, where he met musician/educators like Jonathan Bloom, Herman Jackson, and his mentor, Donald Harrison: "I started to see really talented young artists emerge in the city, and I was able to witness how to actually develop your artistry and be around masters in the city who were teaching these young artists and also teaching you how to become masters like them." As his educational experiences advanced, he came into contact with role models who took him right to the heart of New Orleans beat: "I was studying at the New Orleans Center for Creative Arts with Adonis Rose, and he's a very serious technician when it comes to playing, so I really started to model myself, when I first started getting serious about it, I started modeling myself after that." His experiences are illustrative of how these generational relationships extend a continuum as Dyson also connected with the mentor who initially helped Rose find his voice on the drums: "But I think some of my stylistic and conceptual approach was coming more out of Herlin Riley at the time, just because that was one of the first drummers that was touring on an international basis actually from New Orleans that I was able to be around." That communal sharing of the mentor/protégé relationship has played a significant role in extending the legacy of the New Orleans beat. Even though Dyson has made a name for himself in the broader jazz world, performing with such artists as Harrison, Ellis Marsalis, Dr. Lonnie Smith, Christian Scott aTunde Adjuah, Nicholas Payton, Esperanza Spalding, and Paquito D'Rivera, he is still benefiting from those relationships with his drumming elders: "In the airport a few weeks ago, I ran into Shannon Powell, and we sat down and talked for a long time. He was just telling me about everything that was going on at the time that he was coming up . . . how James Black would give him a lesson and how he got him to open up more to playing more obtuse rhythms and being able to still imply his personality over the drums." Russell Batiste was another drummer who supported Dyson when he was developing his craft and instilled in him that impulse to pass it on: "I was around him when I was a kid, and he would come to my band practices and look after me, but that's one of the influences that I would like to have in terms of my playing, being able to assimilate the sound that comes before me within the lineage."

All those influences helped to shape Dyson into a distinctive representative of Drumsville. One of the characteristics that he believes defines the New Orleans beat is the ability and impulse to "have a sense of playing the heart of the groove." He grew up consistently guided by the mantra "from the bottom up":

This is a phrase that I've always heard other drummers use, but now, being a drummer and being able to tour in different parts of the world, and also being in New York at the mo-

Joe Dyson. Dyson: "We have a way of making sure that the low end of the drums itself actually speaks more; part of the low end is actually where the groove somewhat lives." Photo courtesy of Joe Dyson.

ment, I truly understand what they mean from that. We have a way of making sure that the low end of the drums itself actually speaks more; part of the low end is actually where the groove somewhat lives, so you can instantly tell when someone is coming out of the sound of New Orleans and how they're actually pushing it.

Dyson also believes that the current generation's up-and-coming musicians can take advantage of digital age technology to enhance and expand their knowledge and understanding of the historical and stylistic development of the music:

> If they're diligent enough, and someone says I want you to check out Philly Joe Jones, and I want you to check out what he does throughout all the records with Miles Davis and what he does with Stan Getz and with all these other people, and you can actually go directly to whatever your medium is, whether it's YouTube, iTunes, or Spotify, you can directly pull up that whole discography and listen to it.

During his time at NOCCA, Dyson connected with fellow students, pianist Conun Pappas Jr. and bassist Max Moran, to form the Bridge Trio. In addition to working on their own, they backed Donald Harrison and Alvin Batiste, releasing two albums, *The Bridge Trio featuring Donald Harrison & Davell Crawford* (2012) and *The Search: Departure* (2015). In preparing to record his debut solo album, *Look Within* (2021), Dyson listened to drummers like Paul Barbarin, Idris Muhammad, James Black, Herlin Riley, Russell Batiste, and Terrence Higgins, "all those guys that are actually composing music and able to create on top of that and set up a great lane for themselves to be able to work and set up a platform and hold the torch high that this is the New Orleans sound, and we're the presenters of this." Joe Dyson is living proof of the vitality of the New Orleans beat. He has learned his lessons well and applied his formidable talents to engage fully in the tradition of Drumsville with a solid foundation built on the generations that came before him and a clear vision of where he wants to take the beat. He knows what the drums have always been and always will be all about:

> I think I'm always trying to make sure that from a subconscious place that the intent behind what I'm playing, the energy, is not lost to the audience, no matter what the complexity of what I'm playing. I still want it to have the certain fundamentals of what a drummer actually is. For one, I want to touch the heart. I want them to be able to move. That's part of the natural inhabitants of the instrument itself. We animate the body instantly; as soon as you hear a rhythm that you like, in some ways, you can't help but move.

Peter Varnado: "It Felt Good to Pass on Information and Actually Explain It"

That impulse to "pass it on" that sustains the New Orleans drumming tradition manifested very early for Peter Varnado (b. 1993). He taught his first drum lesson at fourteen: "It was to one of my friends that stayed around the corner who was maybe three or four years younger than me, and I gave him a drum lesson at my house, and that was like the first drum lesson I ever gave, and that's when I knew I had a knack for it or it felt good to pass

on information and actually explain it, explain the things that I'm doing."[120] A working drummer, he pursues his teaching avocation at Tulane University as an adjunct jazz drum instructor and at Hynes Charter School as an elementary/middle-school music teacher.

Varnado's own musical journey began one day in church around age six when he decided to sit behind the drums. Things accelerated rather abruptly. His father went out *that* night and bought him a drum set: "Yeah, huge investment. He purchased a seven-piece drum kit that was on sale that he just figured, well you know, it's more drums, I guess a bigger bang for your buck or whatever, so he got a seven-piece kit." His father, who is a pianist and did some drumming in high school, got him started with the basics: "First my dad showed me whatever he knew, some rudiments and a few grooves on the kit." He started playing in church the following year when the regular drummer left, and he was definitely learning by the seat of his pants:

> Oh, it was terrible [*laughs*]. It wasn't too good. I only knew how to play a few a grooves, and, you know, with gospel music there's many different sections and parts, a groove will change, dynamics, slow songs. I didn't know how to play any of that. I just knew how to play one groove, and I was still learning my rudiments and everything else. Yeah, that first year was a lot of blood, sweat, tears, crying behind the kit . . . But, after that it was pretty much I got the hang of it.

Varnado began reading drum music at age seven, once again, thanks to his father: "My dad, he actually purchased these flash cards, and it would be like fifty flash cards and he

Peter Varnado with Roots of Music students. The students toured the *Drumsville!* exhibit and participated in a drum clinic with Varnado: "I'm a part of the history too, and I can change the history for the better." Photo by Ann Cobb.

would lay 'em out on the floor, and I would just read 'em from top to bottom. One to fifty without stopping. Then you switch it up, and you start again from the bottom. You start slow, and then you go fast, different tempos. Then from there, I kind of morphed into doing it all on the snare drum to doing it on the kit."

Since church was the primary outlet for his drumming, Varnado found his first role models in gospel music: "Listening to the gospel music at the time, so that's like John P. Kee, Fred Hammond, Hezekiah Walker, and I was listening to those drummers, which was Kelvin Rogers, I forget the other drummers' names at the time, but those I was really checking out, and then from there, that's when I started going into more of the funk drumming because those drummers were taking from the funk world and bringing it to gospel." Those drummers also impacted his drum setup: "Well, you know, it was the music I was listening to. Gospel music back then, I would say the '90s, early 2000s, it was a lot of drums. It was three drums at the top, three floor toms, an auxiliary snare drum on the side, and there's a few drummers that still do that nowadays, just to get that type sound, going from that high drum all the way down to that low drum, I mean just playing a bunch of notes." His initial interest in jazz drumming also came through gospel drummer Terreon Gully: "His playing style at the time was mixed with gospel and jazz. And that's what introduced me to jazz music, and that's what really got me interested in it" Of course, growing up in New Orleans, he was hearing the city's signature beats and rhythms at parades and second lines in the community. He drummed in the band at Mc-Donough 35 and also attended both NOCCA Academy and NOCCA. His journey into jazz and New Orleans drumming accelerated in NOCCA under the direction of instructors such as Clyde Kerr, Jonathan Bloom, Herman Jones, and Keith Hart: "We studied a few of the drummers, the pioneers, who started it all, and, you know, who was on which album, and how one drummer influenced another drummer and changed that drummer's playing style and even drummers that are not from New Orleans who listened to New Orleans drummers and tried to implement that somewhere else." This also impacted his drum setup: "The music that I was listening to eventually turned into, 'Okay, maybe I should have less drums. I'm not hearing three, four floor toms; I'm only hearing one. I'm not hearing three high toms; I'm only hearing one. I'm not hearing fifteen cymbals; I'm only hearing two." He went on to earn both his bachelor's and master's degrees at UNO, and along the way he took private lessons with some Drumsville masters, including Shannon Powell, Ricky Sebastian, Herlin Riley, Herman LeBeaux, and Jason Marsalis. Tuned into teaching drums from an early age, he approached those one-on-one lessons with a specific focus: "From those lessons, I mainly would ask them about different ideas or different approaches to certain songs or to a groove, and I would show them a groove that either I'd been working on or a groove from a record and ask them if it was a groove that they played, I'd ask them what made you think of this groove when you heard this song or how did you come up with this groove?" Varnado considers the second-line and bamboula rhythms "a New Orleans language" and is conscious of his position in extending the tradition of the New Orleans beat:

I definitely see myself as a part of that, being from here and growing up here and being around all those drummers, especially being around Herlin and Shannon, just them calling you "nephew" [*laughs*]. As soon as you meet 'em, they ask you where you're from, as soon as they know you're from New Orleans, "Oh, okay, you're related." You know, you're family. And so, just that, growing up hearing that, learning about that and learning that I'm a part of the history too, and I can change the history for the better. I can take my own route from this history, so I do feel like a part of the family and the great lineage, too.

Varnado is ready to play whatever the gig calls for: "It's like the gig tomorrow is a funk gig, but it has some swing in there; that's that gig, and then Friday, it's nothing but straight ahead, and then Saturday is R&B/soulful, so it switches a lot."

Teaching the drums, however, remains his top priority: "Right now, I'm really focusing on teaching, teaching higher education, and so mainly understanding everything that I'm playing and making sure I can explain it to someone close to my age and also making sure that it's interesting to them with what I'm doing." In July 2018, the Jazz Museum hosted a group of middle-school drum students and their instructor Shoan Ruffin from the Roots of Music program for a guided tour of the *Drumsville!* exhibit and a drum workshop taught by Varnado. He talked about his experiences coming up and opportunities that open up by studying music. Sitting behind the drum set, he concisely explained and demonstrated some rhythmic patterns and patiently guided each of them as they sat at the drums and gave it a shot. He sees their generation as having a tremendous advantage in that they can learn firsthand from instructors like himself, Ruffin, and program artistic director Derrick Tabb, *and* they have access to all the resources that come with the digital age: "It just makes things easier, which is why musicians are advancing younger now: "Wow, you're only eighteen years old, and you sound like you're thirty-five years old."

Derrick Tabb: "I Think about These Young Kids Coming up Now"

Opening night for the *Drumsville!* exhibit began with the Roots of Music Marching Crusaders entering through the front gate into the courtyard of the Jazz Museum. As the sun set, the exhibit was launched by this group of more than one hundred young musicians, including around twenty drummers. The opening-night reception crowd surrounded the band, enraptured by the boisterous exuberance of the brass and reeds and pulsing grooves generated by the drummers. The Roots of Music program was founded by snare drummer Derrick Tabb and Allison Reinhardt in 2007. Since that time, hundreds of young people between the ages of nine and fourteen have participated in this program that not only teaches them how to play an instrument and work together as a marching band, particularly in all the bigtime Carnival parades, but also provides them with year-round academic support, healthy meals, and transportation home to their neighborhoods.

Derrick Tabb (b. 1975) grew up in Treme, and his first mentor was sousaphonist Anthony "Tuba Fats" Lacen. As a kid, Tabb wanted to follow in Lacen's footsteps and play sousaphone, despite the fact that he was being urged to play drums. Lacen finally made his case when he got his protégé to walk about three blocks carrying the sousaphone. A

Derrick Tabb. Tabb: "I found a way to connect both styles together, the marching band being more straight and brass band being more calypso, more syncopated. It worked because nobody had heard anybody play like that." Photo by Chelsea Dunn. Courtesy of the New Orleans Jazz & Heritage Archive.

drummer was born: "I was like, 'No, I'm going back to drums. I want to play the drums,' so I started with 'Uncle' Lionel [Batiste], Benny [Jones], and Andrew 'Big Daddy' [Green], and those were the cats I was around that were playing the brass band drumming." By age eight, he was going on gigs with Lacen: "I never would get paid, but I was a young cat that was getting to know a lot of the musicians that other cats didn't have the opportunity—the professionals didn't have the opportunity to be around these musicians." Finally, when Tabb was around eleven, they went to perform in Switzerland, and Lacen put him on the payroll: "And from there I was just like the kid—I called myself the first free agent because I played with every brass band."[121]

As experienced as he was, when Tabb went to Andrew J. Bell Junior High, he had a lot to learn about the technical aspects of drumming. He found that life-changing influence of a musical educator/mentor in band director Donald Richardson:

> This program Roots of Music is really dedicated to and like a carbon copy of his. He took a special interest in me. My grandmother passed away right before I went to Bell school, and I went through a really hard time just dealing with the changes that happened in my life, and I started being real rebellious and started hanging out with the wrong cats. And, Mr. Richardson taught me the technical side of drumming. He taught me how to read. He taught me the dynamics, the discipline of playing the drums.

By the time Tabb got to high school, he was forming a succession of his own brass bands— the High Steppers, the Hot 8 Brass Band, and the Night Bird Brass Band: "From there I went to the professional league. I was already pretty much a professional. Then I started playing with the Olympia Brass Band and then the Rebirth Brass Band. I've been with the Rebirth for twenty-four years now." Tabb did some set drumming in his church but found gigs were scarce because there were so many topflight musicians on the drum set. His snare drumming, however, was increasingly in demand because of his unique approach and the innovative rhythms he was creating:

> On the snare drum I opened up new doors. The stuff I was doing had never really been heard on the brass band side. The brass band drumming didn't play marching band music, didn't have the technical side on the snare drum in the brass band. So, I started getting a lot of work being different. I found a way to connect both styles together, the marching band being more straight, and brass band being more calypso, more syncopated. It worked because nobody had heard anybody play like that. I started getting more and more work.

In 1998, Tabb joined Rebirth and saw it as a validation of his mastery of the drums, but, once again, he found that he still had to develop his approach, particularly that ineffable rhythmic sensibility that drives and maintains a groove that New Orleans drummers prize—playing in the pocket:

> And when Phil [Frazier] with the Rebirth hired me, I was like, "Whoa, I had reached the epitome. I was up there at the top." And Phil was like, "Man, you need a lot of work. You have it, but you don't have it." I didn't understand that at first. I wasn't in the pocket. I had

Roots of Music drum section. Tabb (*far right,* with instructor Shoan Ruffin in green) cofounded the Roots of Music program in 2007. Tabb: "If I came in the late '80s, and I'm able to bring so much that I'm able to change the music, I think about these young kids coming up now." Photo courtesy Roots of Music.

to really learn how to be a pocket drummer. And that's something that New Orleans musicians do naturally. But I wanted to play so much that I heard and learned that I was taking myself out of the pocket.

Tabb figured it out, and his inventiveness *and* consummate pocket playing place him in the forefront of the city's snare drummers. For Christie Jourdain, leader and snare drummer for the Original Pinettes, he is the ultimate role model:

> If you ask anybody here, *anybody here,* and I'll put all my money on it, any snare drummer, or not even a snare drummer, a trumpet player, saxophone player, trombone player, if you ask anybody in this city who's the number-one snare drum player, everybody, I'm telling you, they're gonna say Derrick Tabb. He has his own style. His DNA is in all of us, from Jenard Andrews, who is Trombone Shorty's nephew, in Glen Andrews, his DNA is in all of us.[122]

Tabb's goal in founding the Roots of Music was to bring to his students that same drive to constantly improve that Donald Richardson instilled in him: "I wanted to take care of every kid that comes into this program, and I wanted to give them the best opportunity. I wanted to show 'em love. I wanted to give them the time. I wanted to be that person that they can come talk to in any situation." Tabb may provide nurturing and guidance to these young people, but he and his staff, like band director Darren Rogers and senior music and percussion instructor Shoan Ruffin, are all about disciplined, serious, hard work. This is testified to in *The Whole Gritty City* (2013), the documentary film that examines the city's marching band culture as they exhibit total engagement in each student's development with the focus on the band working together. For Tabb, the program is crucial because it helps to fill in for some of the interactions that had passed the music between generations. He finds that its harder for young musicians to come into contact with established artists because there's an increased economic need to tour since Hurricane Katrina:

> When I was coming up, I could walk out my door and see Willie Green on the corner. I could see "Uncle" Lionel [Batiste] coming up the street. If you look at New Orleans, passing on the music, Treme was so culturally rich because the musicians was there, and the kids looking up to the musicians were there, and they got the opportunity to talk to somebody they were looking up to and who inspired them to play that horn or that drum, mostly that drum out of Treme. I used to walk around the corner and go to Shannon Powell's house . . . I sat out in front of Shannon's house a thousand times just listening to him. I used to go sit on the steps and just listen, didn't see nothing that he did, but I got to listen to one of the baddest drummers in the world practice.

Tabb finds the advancements in technology help enhance the learning process: "The oral way of teaching is never gonna go out, but they have so many different ways of teaching these days to keep kids' attention." He'll often use YouTube to reinforce lessons: "'Hey man, I want you to such and such,' and before you know it, they're not just learning one thing that you told them to learn, they're learning five other things." He is also a big advocate for the use of apps that provide students with resources like a metronome: "It's simple. It's free, and it opens up a different world for kids. When they're just playing patting their feet, they don't get the same understanding as hearing that click and understand that that click doesn't stop. Time doesn't stop, so if you mess up, it's still going." For Tabb, who was honored as a 2009 CNN Top Heroes Finalist, the Roots of Music program is about teaching the musical skills and history, but it's also about keeping the tradition vital and moving forward: "A lot of people don't understand when you look at the brass bands, they're not really that old . . . so I believe brass bands still have a lot to learn, so many different styles that can be incorporated. If I came in the late '80s, and I'm able to bring so much that I'm able to change the music, I think about these young kids coming up now.

During the Roots of Music student drummers' tour of the *Drumsville!* exhibit, while they were standing at the front end of the exhibit next to Baby Dodds's drum set, the video screen down at the far end of the room began playing a clip of Tabb drumming with Rebirth as they made their way through the streets of Treme in the 2011 Treme Side Steppers second-line parade. It's a stunning performance, and the drumming is a perfect example of the enlivening spirit of the New Orleans beat. Within seconds of the video's start, every one of the students had turned their heads toward the screen that was not visible from where they were standing and immediately began exclaiming, "That's Mr. Tabb! That's Mr. Tabb!" Adonis Rose is not surprised that the students recognized their mentor after only a few drumbeats: "That's right. The instruments are only extensions of who we are. We have our own voices and personalities on the instrument. When I hear Herlin, I know its him. When I hear Elvin Jones, there's no question about who it is, or

Philly Joe or Max Roach. It was an extension of their personalities. It's clear."[123] When the students reached the final section of the exhibit, "Extensions and Variations," they beamed with pride when they saw a portrait of themselves with the full Roots of Music drum section next to a bass drum head sporting the program's logo hanging on the wall along with the drummers who paved the way for them, from Baby Dodds, Earl Palmer, Ed Blackwell, and Joseph "Zigaboo" Modeliste to Johnny Vidacovich, Herlin Riley, Shannon Powell, and, of course, Derrick Tabb. They represent the future of the legacy that began back in Congo Square.

CODA: "GET BACK"

In June 2020, in the midst of the Covid-19 lockdown, Shannon Powell posted a grainy, cell phone video on Facebook. He and Herlin Riley—both wearing masks—are on the sidewalk dancing in front St. Philip Church of God in Christ in Treme. Riley is playing a conch shell, and Powell is beating out a groove on his tambourine—the same groove he learned as little boy sneaking into that same church directly next door to his family home. Riley also learned that groove as a child in his grandfather's spiritual church. The two Drumsville masters are engaged in a call-and-response chanting, "Don't let Corona get up on ya." Directly across the street from Congo Square, their performance features the same building blocks that people of African descent employed for their Sunday gatherings three hundred years ago—call-and-response, rhythmic sophistication, and improvisation, and like the musical expressions back in Congo Square, it's both aesthetic and functional. It's a seductive groove that makes dancing irresistible; it's artistic and creative. At the same time, it serves a purpose; it does a job; it's a warning about the dire consequences posed by Covid-19 to the community. A few days later, they were joined by drummer and vibraphonist Jason Marsalis—the New Orleans Groovemasters—and headed into the studio to record a funky, hip-hop-flavored version of the chant, now developed into a full-fledged song, "Get Back," for which Riley wrote the lyrics and created an arrangement. Powell explains:

> We were right in front of the church where I learned to play the tambourine. We did the first thing out there on the street, and then we decided to take it into the studio. Oh, I'm playing the drum set, Jason's playing the vibes, and we're all playing different percussion instruments. Herlin played congas; he played timbales, he played the shell, he played a lot of percussion. He played tambourine. He played the bass track on a keyboard. We overdubbed everything. Just the three of us, and June Yamagishi played a little guitar on it.[124]

Shortly thereafter, the single was available for download and a video of the new version featuring the three drummers was posted. In the hands of these Drumsville masters, twenty-first century technology meets a centuries old tradition. "Get Back" testifies to the vitality and continuing evolution of the New Orleans beat.

Herlin Riley (*left*) and Shannon Powell performing "Get Back," 2021. On the street in front St. Philip Church of God in Christ in Treme, Riley and Powell improvised a call-and-response, polyrhythmic warning about the dire consequences posed by COVID-19 to the community. Shortly thereafter, a single they recorded with Jason Marsalis was available for download, and a video of the new version was posted. In the hands of these Drumsville masters, twenty-first-century technology meets a centuries old tradition. Photo by R. Cataliotti.

Afterword

HISTORY, POWER, ECSTASY, AND EXISTENTIAL FUNK

After all that you have read before, you should know there is something more to the drumming and drummers of New Orleans. Most aspects of life here in New Orleans have a rhythm to them. The way people walk, talk, bike, drive, eat, drink, play sports, garden, sing—there is a rhythm to it and often a dance. Each of the drummers portrayed in the *Drumsville!* exhibit and the book have a way of interpreting that. Like all artists, they are taking what they feel and see and hear and experience, and they are putting it into the way they snap the snare, pound the bass, clip the hi-hat, bounce the cymbals, and hit the tambourine. However, in New Orleans they are interpreting a rhythmic uniqueness only the Crescent City possesses. When you hear Herlin Riley or Shannon Powell or Smokey Johnson, there is something so organic about what they play. It connects you to this place in a profound way. It grounds you in the beats of New Orleans, which are inherent to the identity of the city, so it also grounds you to the history of New Orleans and what the people and place have been through: the Middle Passage and slavery, the liberation of Congo Square rituals that lead to the Sunday second line, the improvised and homemade percussion of the Black Masking Indians and their tales of legend and song, the European marching parades, the Mardi Gras parades, the high school marching bands at football games and Carnival routes, street cars' surging wheels and the clink and thump of freight unloading at the port, street peddler cries, the metal-on-metal ping in the making of the intricate gallery posts and fences, and wooden spoons scraping cast-iron cookware and mixing ingredients. It's all in there with the spirits and people who created it. That's heady stuff when you are just listening to Stanton Moore hit it with his song "Tchefunkta," but it is also booty stuff and foot stuff. When you are hearing this in the right place at the right time, when the set and setting are calibrated correctly or even just close, when the rhythms and timbres and vibrations are sympathetic, these drummers can erase the mind/body/spirit dichotomies and combine them all into a joyous dance. It can become positively synergistic, an elevation beyond words that makes you connect to the sum total of our humanity.

I remember a moment in the early 2000s. It was a beautiful Sunday, and the second line had been making a stop at the Magnolia Super Market on Jackson Avenue and Magnolia Street. I was standing in the street remembering a black-and-white photo I had seen of Paul Barbarin's Onward Brass Band on the same corner sometime in the 1960s. I started looking around. The social aid and pleasure club members organizing the parade began to line up and the Rebirth Brass Band with their relentless rhythm section of Keith "Shorty" Frazier on bass drum, his brother Philip Frazier on sousaphone, and tough-as-nails Derek Tabb on snare began to get down. As I continued to look around, I realized that except for the electric wires, this could be 2003 or 1953 or 1913 or 1893. The music was basically the same that had been echoing off these shotguns houses and asphalt and cobblestones and dirt potholes for at least a century. My feet and hips dipped and stuttered of their own accord. I had never felt anything like this before. I was dancing steps I didn't know how to do. The idea of past, present, and future melted before me. This rhythm and music had existed before me, right now in me, and would continue to exist all at the same time in this continuum. It was all combined, happening now, and would never stop with its history, power, ecstasy, and existential funk. This is the stuff of shamans and speaking in tongues. It's still there now. It's in you too, and in all that encompasses the rhythms, inhabitants, and essences of New Orleans. I know it's still in me, and on any given day I can feel it, and my toes start to tapping.

I hope somehow this book and the exhibit from which it derives got you to that place, or right up next to it. It's a joy we all deserve.

David Kunian
Music Curator, New Orleans Jazz Museum

Acknowledgments

My deepest thanks go to my dear friend the late Spencer Bohren. He brought me to the New Orleans Jazz Museum in 2017 and introduced me to museum director Greg Lambousy. It was at that first meeting that Greg mentioned his idea for an exhibit tracing the evolution of the drum set and New Orleans drumming. I am indebted to Greg for entrusting me with the concept, allowing me to shape the exhibit, and working with me in the development of this book. I also must acknowledge the crucial role museum curator (and exhibit cocurator) David Kunian played in transforming my research and outline into a vibrant exhibit. Thanks also to David for providing an afterword and for his help in putting the book together.

I am grateful for the support this book has received from Louisiana State University Press, especially acquisitions editors Margaret H. Lovecraft and Jenny Keegan as well as senior editor Neal Novak and copy editor Susan Murray. I also thank the LSU Press peer reviewer, who provided such great feedback, knowledge, and commentary. My deepest gratitude to Michelle Neustrom for the design of this book.

I am also indebted to the New Orleans Jazz and Heritage Foundation, which supported my research with a 2019 Archive Fellowship and a 2020 Media and Documentation Grant to help fund the creation of the book. Thank you to the Threadhead Cultural Foundation for awarding a grant to the museum to assist our review committee—which included Ann Cobb, Ricky Sebastian, J. J. Juliano, Bruce "Sunpie" Barnes, and Melissa A. Weber—that reviewed the first draft of the manuscript. Their insights, suggestions, and corrections were invaluable. I must give special thanks to J. J. for sharing his extensive knowledge of drumming history with me as I developed the exhibit.

Special thanks to Herlin Riley for his input throughout the development of the exhibit and the writing of the book. I can never thank him enough for the tremendous foreword. Ricky Sebastian also deserves acknowledgment for his insights and encouragement, and especially for the great transcriptions that he made to illustrate the evolution of the New Orleans beat. I truly appreciate drum maker Margo Rosas, who donated her hand drum and beater to the exhibit and for sharing her knowledge of the Native American traditions of Louisiana.

James Brown famously declared "Give the drummer some!" And I extend heartfelt thanks to the drummers who agreed to be interviewed: Andre Bohren, Jaz Butler, Joe Dyson, Nikki Glaspie, Luther Gray, "Mean" Willie Green, Vernel Fournier, William "Dan" Isaac, Christie Jourdain, Joe Lastie, "Washboard" Chaz Leary, Joseph "Zigaboo" Modeliste, Stanton Moore, Kevin O'Day, Grayhawk Perkins, Shannon Powell, Herlin Riley, Alfred "Uganda" Roberts, Adonis Rose, Ricky Sebastian, Vernon Severin, Mayumi Shara, Fred Staehle, Derrick Tabb, Boyanna Trayanova, Peter Varnado, Johnny Vidacovich, and Cori Walters. Special thanks to my old friend Titos Sompa, who taught me so much about rhythm all those years ago. And I am grateful for the encouraging words from the late great Charlie Watts, who spent an afternoon at the exhibit in July 2019.

I'm truly indebted to all the photographers whose work enhances this book, including JS Makkos/Intelligent Archives for his AI-enhanced images on historic photos. Special thanks to Grace Patterson for her images of the exhibit.

The New Orleans Jazz Museum has provided invaluable help. Thank you to Baylee Badawy, Ilyanette M. Bernabel, Rennie Buras, Maria Burns, Patrick Burns, Adrienne Byrd, Chloe Cosgrove, Kerianne Ellison, Cassandra Erb, Mindy Jarrett, Penelope Jenkins, Danny Kadar, Curtis Knapp, Jennifer Long, Danielle Maurer, Lisa McLendon, Lt. Governor Billy Nungesser, Glinda "Gee Gee" Powell, Bryanne Schexnayder, Caitlin Sheehan, Valerie Vindici, and Travis Waguespack.

My thanks must go out to those who helped me with my research: Lynn Abbott, retired associate curator of Recorded Sound Collection at the Hogan Archive of New Orleans Music and New Orleans Jazz at Tulane University; Connie Zeanah Atkinson, PhD, Professor Emeritus, University of New Orleans, and editor of *Wavelength* magazine; LaTrice Curtis-Istance, head of reference, research, instruction at Parlett L. Moore Library, Coppin State University; Dr. Agnieszka Czeblakow, head of research services, Tulane University Special Collections; Leslie Eames, Maryland Center for History and Culture; Dr. Haitham Eid, director of museum studies, Southern University at New Orleans; Rachel Lyons, archivist for the New Orleans Jazz and Heritage Foundation, as well as her assistants, Dolores Hooper and Joe Stolarick; Lisa Moore, Amistad Research Center; Dr. Ibrahima Seck, director of research at the Whitney Plantation; Lori Schexnayder, Tulane University Special Collections; Rebecca Smith, the Historic New Orleans Collection; and Melissa A. Weber, curator of the Hogan Archive of New Orleans Music and New Orleans Jazz at Tulane University.

I must acknowledge the groundbreaking work of Gwendolyn Midlo Hall's *Africans In Colonial Louisiana* and Freddie Williams Evans's *Congo Square: African Roots in New Orleans,* which have enhanced our understanding of the African presence in New Orleans.

I have to thank my musical compadres for sharing their insights and years of musical memories: Marilyn Bohren, Ray Bonneville, Don DeBacker, Jamie Dell'Apa, Sal Fallica, Paul Gass, Ken "Snakebite" Jacobs, Erik Johnson, Jessica Jones, J. J. Juliano, Chaz Leary, Joe McLerran, Rob McLerran, Dexter Payne, Paula Rangell, Gerard "The Guvna" Rigney, David Scott, Pres Speulda, Doug Sutherland, Karren Turgeon, and those who are no longer with us—Spencer Bohren, Terry Kelsey, Candy McLerran, and Peter Fassoulis.

Last but certainly not least, I owe my sincerest gratitude to Ann Cobb for all her support and feedback, and for bearing with four years of endless drum talk.

Notes

1. WELCOME TO DRUMSVILLE!

1. "Improv Conference: A Festival of Ideas," drum panel: Shannon Powell, Johnny Vidacovich, Stanton Moore; moderator: David Kunian, November 9, 2019, New Orleans Jazz Museum.

2. Herlin Riley, interview by author, December 17, 2019.

2. LEGACY OF CONGO SQUARE

1. Freddi Williams Evans, *Congo Square: African Roots in New Orleans* (Lafayette: University of Louisiana at Lafayette Press, 2011), 63.

2. The list of African nations appears on the "Transatlantic Slave Trade to Louisiana" marker, which was dedicated in July 2018 in the Moonwalk Riverfront Park on the Mississippi River levee.

3. See Evans, *Congo Square,* 47–48; and Gwendolyn Midlo Hall's *Africans in Colonial Louisiana* (Baton Rouge: Louisiana State University Press, 1992), 347–48.

4. See Lawrence Levine, *Black Culture and Black Consciousness* (Oxford: Oxford University Press, 1977), chap. 1, "The Sacred World of Black Slaves," and chap. 2, "The Meaning of Slave Tales."

5. See Samuel Floyd, *The Power of Black Music: Interpreting Its History from Africa to the United States* (New York: Oxford University Press, 1995). These building blocks could be considered an example of what Floyd calls "cultural memory," which he defines as "a repository of meanings that comprise the subjective knowledge of a people, its immanent thoughts, its structures, and its practices; these thoughts, structures, and practices are transferred and understood unconsciously but become conscious and culturally objective in practice and perception" (8).

6. Hall, *Africans in Colonial Louisiana,* 200.

7. Evans, *Congo Square,* 9.

8. John Smith Kendall, *History of New Orleans,* 3 vols. (New Orleans: Lewis, 1922), 2:979.

9. Grayhawk Perkins, interview by author, July 2018, New Orleans Jazz Museum.

10. Quoted in Shane Lief and John McCusker, *Jockomo: The Native Roots of Mardi Gras Indians* (Jackson: University of Mississippi Press, 2019), 33.

11. Ibid.

12. William "Dan" Isaac, conversation with author, May 2021.

13. Perkins, interview.

14. David I. Bushnell Jr., *The Choctaw of Bayou Lacomb, St. Tammany Parish, Louisiana* (Washington, DC: Government Printing Office, 1909), 22. See also Fred B. Kniffen, Hiram F. Gregory, and George A. Stokes, *The Historic Indian Tribes of Louisiana: From 1542 to the Present* (Baton Rouge: Louisiana State University Press, 1987), 145.

15. Jerah Johnson, *Congo Square in New Orleans* (New Orleans: Louisiana Landmarks Society, 1995), 38.

16. George J. Joyaux, ed., "Forest's *Voyage aux États-Unis de l'Amérique en 1831,*" *Louisiana Historical Quarterly* 39, no. 4 (October 1956): 488.

17. See Lief and McCusker, *Jockomo.*

18. *Rumble: The Indians Who Rocked the World,* dir. Catherine Bainbridge, DVD (Canada: Rezolution Pictures, 2017).

19. Evans asserts that most of these writers "documented a group of people whom they did not understand linguistically, spiritually, culturally and whom they considered inferior" (Evans, *Congo Square,* 6).

20. Anthologized in Reuben Gold Thwaites, ed., *Early Western Travels, 1748–1846,* vol. 4 (Cleveland: A. H. Clark, 1904), 363.

21. Christian Schultz, *Travels on an inland voyage through the states of New-York, Pennsylvania, Virginia, Ohio, Kentucky and Tennessee, and through the territories of Indiana, Louisiana, Mississippi and New-Orleans; performed in the years 1807 and 1808; including a tour of nearly six thousand miles* (New York: Isaac Riley, 1810), 197.

22. Quoted in Henry Kmen, *Music in New Orleans* (Baton Rouge: Louisiana State University Press, 1966), 227.

23. "Interrogatoire, procès et jugement des nègres arrêtés pour cause d'insurrection et recensement des nègres absents de leurs habitations respectives. Procès-verbal N° 2, 13–18 janvier 1811 [St. Charles Parish Courthouse, Original Acts, Book 41, 1811. Examination, trial and judgment of the negroes arrested for insurrection]," document and translation provided by Dr. Ibrahima Seck, director of research, Whitney Plantation.

24. Evans, *Congo Square,* 7.

25. Benjamin Latrobe, *The Journals of Benjamin Henry Latrobe 1977–1820,* vol. 3: *From Philadelphia to New Orleans* (Baltimore: Maryland Historical Society, 1980), 203–4.

26. Ibid.

27. Ibid.

28. John Joyce, "Notes on the Drawings of Benjamin Latrobe," in *Congo Square in New Orleans* (New Orleans: Louisiana Landmarks Society, 1995), 31–32.

29. Ilyanette M. Bernabel, communication with author, October 2018.

30. Luther Gray, interview by author, June 2018, Ashe Cultural Center.

31. "Manuscript Louisiana slave narratives from Francis Doby, 1817 St. Ann Street," recorded December 6, 1938, by Flossie McElwee and Arguedas. The quote appears on a stone marker in the "Field of Angels" children's memorial at the Whitney Plantation Museum. Thanks to Dr. Ibrahima Seck, director of research.

32. George Washington Cable, "The Dance in Place Congo," *Century Magazine* 31 (February 1886): 519. Jerah Johnson explains that Cable's article was not drawn from personal observation: "For his descriptions of the Congo Square dances Cable relied heavily on Mederic Moreau de Saint-Mery's *Description topographique de l'Isle Saint Domingue,* 2 vols. (Philadelphia, 1797–1798) and the same author's *De la danse* (Parma 1801), both of which were second-hand descriptions of the Saint-Domingue dances. However carefully Cable used these works, probably to fill in details lacking in the descriptions of Congo Square dances he gleaned from elderly New Orleanians, the fact remains that he was writing long after the dances ceased in Congo Square and using some materials from a questionable source. Thus while Cable's descriptions are probably not misleading in their essentials, they have to be used with care" (Johnson, *Congo Square in New Orleans,* 38n). Likewise, Johnson asserts that the spires on St. Louis Cathedral in the background of Kemble's *Bamboula* sketch may be anachronistic, given that the spires were added in 1851, "long after the heyday" of the dances (ibid., 32).

33. James R. Creecy, *Scenes in the South: And Other Miscellaneous Pieces* (Washington, DC: Thomas McGill, 1860), 20–21.

34. Kmen, *Music in New Orleans,* 227.

35. Scott K. Fish, "Back Home with James Black," *Modern Drummer,* December 1982.

36. Alfred "Uganda" Roberts, interview by author, November 11, 2019, Roberts's home.

37. Ned Sublette, *The World That Made New Orleans: From Spanish Silver to Congo Square* (Chicago: Lawrence Hill Books, 2009), 124.

38. Gray, interview.

39. S. Frederick Starr, *Bamboula: The Life and Times of Louis Moreau Gottschalk* (Oxford: Oxford University Press, 1995), 30, 42.

40. Ibid., 184.

41. Gary A. Donaldson, "A Window on Slave Culture Dances at Congo Square in New Orleans, 1800–1862," *Journal of Negro History* 69, no. 2 (Spring 1984): 67.

42. Sidney Bechet, *Treat It Gentle* (1960; Boston: Da Capo, 2002), 6–7.

43. Floyd calls Bechet's story of Omar an example of "cultural memory" (see note 5 above). He says, "For Bechet, although he did not see or experience it, slavery was a 'memory': of New Orleans's Congo Square, where Omar had participated as a musicians and dancer" (Floyd, *The Power of Black Music,* 9).

44. See Bryan Wagner, "Disarmed and Dangerous: The Strange Career of Bras-Coupé," *Representations* 92, no. 1 (Fall 2005): 117–51.

45. Gray, interview.

46. Herlin Riley, interview by author, July 2018.

47. The song was written by guitarist Sonny Landreth and harmonica player Mel Melton. Neville's intro to the song can be heard on the recording *Live on Planet Earth* (A&M, 1994).

3. EUROPEAN INFLUENCE

1. Ann Ostendorf, "Music in the Early American Republic," *American Historian,* https://tah.oah.org/february-2019/music-in-the-early-american-republic/.

2. *Daily Picayune,* December 28, 1856, p. 2, col. 1; quoted in Warren Keith Kimball's "Northern Music Culture in Antebellum New Orleans" (Ph.D. diss., LSU, 2017), 8, LSU Doctoral Dissertations, 4119. 8, https://digitalcommons.lsu.edu/gradschool_dissertations/4119.

3. Henry Kmen, *Music in New Orleans* (Baton Rouge: Louisiana State University Press, 1966), 214.

4. Larry Gara, *The Baby Dodds Story as Told to Larry Gara* (1959; Alma, MI: Rebeats Publications, 2002), 3.

5. Kmen, *Music in New Orleans,* 234–36.

6. Ibid., 21.

7. Benjamin Latrobe, *The Journals of Benjamin Henry Latrobe 1977–1820,* vol. 3: *From Philadelphia to New Orleans* (Baltimore: Maryland Historical Society, 1980), 185.

8. Alan Lomax, *Mister Jelly Roll* (1950; Berkeley: University of California Press, 2001).

9. Caroline Vézina, "Jazz À La Creole: The Music of the French Creoles of Louisiana and Their Contribution to the Development of Early Jazz at the Turn of the Twentieth Century" (master's thesis, Carleton University Ottawa, Ontario, August 11, 2014), 60.

10. Ibid.

11. William J. Schafer, *Brass Bands & New Orleans Jazz,* with Richard B. Allen (Baton Rouge: Louisiana State University Press, 1977), 3.

12. Kmen, *Music in New Orleans,* 203.

13. James R. Creecy, *Scenes in the South: And Other Miscellaneous Pieces* (Washington DC: Thomas McGill, 1860), 35.

14. Henry Didimus, *New Orleans as I Found It* (New York: Harper and Brothers, 1845), 34.

15. Ibid., 36.

16. May 28, 1839, quoted in Kmen, *Music in New Orleans,* 202.

17. Ibid., 208.

18. Jerry Brock. "Jordan Noble: Drummer, Soldier, Statesman," *64 Parishes,* https://64parishes.org/jordan-noble.

19. "Jordan B. Noble," National Park Service, www.nps.gov/people/jordan-noble.htm.

20. Ned Hémard, "Noble Drummer," *New Orleans Nostalgia,* New Orleans Bar Association, www.neworleansbar.org/uploads/files/NobleDrummerArticle.pdf.

21. "Story behind the Sound: Rare Battle of New Orleans Drum on Auction Block," www.wwltv.com/article/news/local/story-behind-the-sound-rare-battle-of-new-orleans-drum-on-auction-block/355069246.

4. IMPROVISED PERCUSSION INSTRUMENTS

1. Ralph Ellison, *Invisible Man* (1952; New York: Vintage, 1995), 7.

2. Ibid., 8.

3. Lafcadio Hearn, "The Scenes of Cable's Romances," in *"Old Creole Days" together with "The Scenes of Cable's Romances"* (New York: Heritage, 1943), xxvii. See also Henry A. Kmen, "The Roots of Jazz and the Dance in Place Congo: A Re-Appraisal," *Anuario Interamericano de Investigación Musical* 8 (1972): 12–15.

4. Washboard Chaz Leary, interview by author, July 2018, New Orleans.

5. Harold Courlander, liner notes, *Sonny Terry's Washboard Band* (FA 2006, Folkways Records, 1954).

6. Herbert Asbury, *The French Quarter* (1936; New York: Thunder's Mouth, 2003), 437.

7. Papa Jack Laine, interview by William Russell, March 26, 1957, Hogan Jazz Archive, Tulane University.

8. Bill Russell, *New Orleans Style,* comp. and ed. Barry Martyn and Mike Hazeldine (New Orleans: Jazzology Press, 1994), 171–72.

9. Danny Barker, *A Life in Jazz,* ed. Alyn Shipton (New York: Oxford University Press, 1986), 35.

10. Ibid., 40–41.

11. "Danny Barker," Louisiana Digital Library, Accession Number 1978.118(B).00396.

12. Professor Longhair (Henry Roeland Byrd), interview by Eddie Kurtz, in *Fess Up,* dir. Stevenson J. Palfi, DVD (NEPO LLC, 2018).

13. Mimi Read, "New Orleans Jazz Journal: Adieu to a Band of One," *New York Times,* December 5, 1990, A24.

14. Amy Meaney, "New Orleans Jazz Artist Identified in Fox Movietone New Collection," Moving Image Research Collection, March 3, 2014, https://digital.library.sc.edu/blogs/mirc/2014/03/07/new-orleans-jazz-artist-identified/.

15. Norbert Susemihl, New Orleans Jazzband, www.susemihljazzband.com.

16. Shane Lief and John McCusker, *Jockomo: The Native Roots of Mardi Gras Indians* (Jackson: University of Mississippi Press, 2019) provides a richly detailed and documented analysis of the native sources for the Mardi Gras Indians as a "cultural system."

17. Ibid., 92–107

18. "Guardians of the Flame (Group)," Amistad Research Center, http://amistadresearchcenter.tulane.edu/archon/?p=creators/creator&id=702.

19. Donald Harrison Jr. and Charles Henry Rowell, "Donald Harrison, Jr. with Charles Henry Rowell," *Callaloo* 29, no. 4 (Autumn 2006): 1298.

20. Ibid., 1297.

21. Sublette, *The World That Made New Orleans,* 280.

22. Alan Lomax, prod., *Jazz Parade: Feet Don't Fail Me Now,* documentary (Association for Cultural Equity, 1990).

23. Alan Lomax, *Mister Jelly Roll* (1950; Berkeley: University of California Press, 2001), 4.

24. Russell, *New Orleans Style,* 55.

25. Benny Jones and Uncle Lionel Batiste, interview by David Kunian, May 2011, Allison Miner Music Heritage Stage, New Orleans Jazz & Heritage Festival.

26. Ibid.

27. Derrick Tabb, interview by author, June 2018, Roots of Music facility.

28. Russell, *New Orleans Style,* 16.

29. Scott K. Fish, "Singin' on the Set," *Modern Drummer,* November 1981, www.moderndrummer.com/article/november-1981-ed-blackwell-singin-set/.

30. Scott K. Fish, "Back Home with James Black," *Modern Drummer,* December 1982, www.moderndrummer.com/article/december-1982-back-home-james-black/.

31. Leary, interview.

5. BRASS BAND DRUMMING AND THE EMERGENCE OF THE DRUM KIT

1. Matt Sakakeeny, "New Orleans Music as a Circulatory System," *Black Music Research Journal* 31, no. 2 (Fall 2011): 306.

2. Ibid.

3. William J. Schafer, *Brass Bands & New Orleans Jazz,* with Richard B. Allen (Baton Rouge: Louisiana State University Press, 1977), 5.

4. Richard H. Knowles, *Fallen Heroes: A History of New Orleans Brass Bands* (New Orleans: Jazzology Press, 1996), 20

5. James M. Trotter, *Music and Some Highly Musical People* (Boston: Lee and Shepard, 1878), 351 (scan of original work).

6. Barker, *A Life in Jazz,* 49.

7. Michael G. White, liner notes, *Through the Streets of the City: New Orleans Brass Bands* (Smithsonian Folkways, SFW40212, 2014).

8. Michael G. White, "The New Orleans Brass Band: A Cultural Tradition," in *The Triumph of Soul: Cultural and Psychological Aspects of African American Music,* ed. Ferdinand Jones and Arthur C. Jones (Westport, CT: Praeger, 2001), 78.

9. Arthur "Zutty" Singleton, interview by Bob Greene, February 1969, Hogan Jazz Archive, Tulane University.

10. Bill Russell, *New Orleans Style,* comp. and ed. Barry Martyn and Mike Hazeldine (New Orleans: Jazzology Press, 1994), 18.

11. Sakakeeny, "New Orleans Music as a Circulatory System," 310.

12. Russell, *New Orleans Style,* 53.

13. Ibid., 73.

14. Ibid., 59.

15. Louis Cottrell III, interview by Dr. Michael White, April 1998, Allison Miner Music Heritage Stage, New Orleans Jazz & Heritage Festival.

16. Barker, *A Life in Jazz,* 51. "Trepagnier" is the more commonly accepted spelling.

17. For use of the term "Dixieland" as a "disrespectful usurpation of the music created by New Orleans Black musical artists," please see Michael White, "Dr. Michael White: The Doc Paulin Years," *Jazz Archivist* 23 (2010): 6, along with my discussion in chapter 6 of this work.

18. Scott K. Fish, "Back Home with James Black," *Modern Drummer,* December 1982, www.moderndrummer.com/article/december-1982-back-home-james-black/.

19. Herlin Riley, interview by Tom Morgan, May 2010, Allison Miner Music Heritage Stage, New Orleans Jazz & Heritage Festival.

20. Herlin Riley, interview by author, July 2018.

21. Joseph Lastie Jr., interview by author, August 2018.

22. Louis Armstrong, *Satchmo: My Life in New Orleans* (1954; New York: DaCapo, 1988), 91.

23. Knowles, *Fallen Heroes,* 7.

24. Sakakeeny, "New Orleans Music as a Circulatory System," 307.

25. Barker, *A Life in Jazz,* 27.

26. Russell, *New Orleans Style,* 44.

27. John Doheny, "The Spanish Tinge: Afro-Caribbean Characteristics in Early New Orleans Jazz Drumming," *Jazz Archivist* 19 (2005–6): 11.

28. Lawrence Gushee, "The Nineteenth-Century Origins of Jazz," *Black Music Research Journal* 14, no. 1 (Spring 1994): 172.

29. Although Robichaux was a bass drummer, he switched to violin because Chandler could now handle both drums.

30. Eothen Alapatt, "The Idris Muhamad Interview," *Wax Poetics,* www.wax poetics.com/blog/features/articles/idris-muhamad-interview/.

31. See Adam Perlmutter, "A Brief History of the Drum Set," *Gear History,* Reverb.com, December 30, 2015; Paul Archibald, "Searching for the First Bass Drum Pedal: Rock Harmonicas to Viennese Pianos," *Popular Music History* 9, no. 3 (2014): 285–305; and Dennis Brown, "The Bass Drum Pedal: In the Beginning," *Percussive Arts Society* 21, no. 2 (1983): 28–32.

32. Samuel B. Charters, *Jazz: New Orleans 1885–1963,* rev. ed. (San Francisco: Oak, 1963), 6.

33. Dr. Karl Koenig, *Sonic Boom: Drums, Drummers & Drumming in Early Jazz,* pdf (1990), 7, basinstreet.com.

34. Riley, interview by author.

35. T. Dennis Brown, "Drum Set," in *New Grove Dictionary of Jazz,* ed. Barry Kernfeld (New York: St. Martin's, 1991), 308–15.

36. Freddie Kohlman, interview by David Thress, in *New Orleans Jazz and Second Line Drumming* by Herlin Riley and Johnny Vidacovich (Van Nuys, CA: Alfred Music Publishing, 1995), 65.

37. Ibid., 64.

38. Russell, *New Orleans Style,* 58–59.

39. Larry Gara, *The Baby Dodds Story as Told to Larry Gara* (1959; Alma, MI: Rebeats, 2002), 27.

40. Ray Bauduc, interviews by Dick Allen, 1985, Hogan Jazz Archive, Tulane University, transcribed by author, September 2019.

41. Herlin Riley, interview by Ashley Kahn, April 2013, Allison Miner Music Heritage Stage, New Orleans Jazz & Heritage Festival.

6. TRADITIONAL JAZZ

1. Ricky Sebastian, communication with author, November 2020.

2. Herlin Riley, interview by author, July 2018.

3. William J. Schafer, *Brass Bands & New Orleans Jazz,* with Richard B. Allen (Baton Rouge: Louisiana State University Press, 1977), 9.

4. Bruce Raeburn, "Traditional New Orleans Jazz," *64 Parishes,* https://64par ishes.org/entry/traditional-new-orleans-jazz.

5. Wynton Marsalis, quoted in "Gumbo," pt. 1 of *Jazz,* dir. Ken Burns, prod. Burns and Lynn Novick, 2000.

6. Ned Sublette, "Interview with Bruce Raeburn," *Afropop Worldwide Hip Deep* program, October 14, 2009.

7. John Doheny, "The Spanish Tinge: Afro-Caribbean Characteristics in Early New Orleans Jazz Drumming," *Jazz Archivist* 19 (2005–6): 10.

8. Alan Lomax, *Mister Jelly Roll* (1950; Berkeley: University of California Press, 2001), 62.

9. Doheny, "The Spanish Tinge," 15.

10. Richard H. Knowles, *Fallen Heroes: A History of New Orleans Brass Bands* (New Orleans: Jazzology Press, 1996), 27.

11. Bill Russell, *New Orleans Style,* comp. and ed. Barry Martyn and Mike Hazeldine (New Orleans: Jazzology Press, 1994), 30.

12. Ibid., 50.

13. Larry Gara, *The Baby Dodds Story as Told to Larry Gara* (1959; Alma, MI: Rebeats, 2002), 39.

14. Derrick Tabb, interview by author, June 2018.

15. Herlin Riley and Johnny Vidacovich, *New Orleans Jazz and Second Line Drumming,* (Van Nuys, CA: Alfred Music Publishing, 1995), 13.

16. Gara, *The Baby Dodds Story as Told to Larry Gara,* 26.

17. George Wettling. "A Tribute to Baby Dodds," *Down Beat,* March 29, 1962, 21.

18. Russell, *New Orleans Style,* 44.

19. Gara, *The Baby Dodds Story as Told to Larry Gara,* 64.

20. Samuel Charters, *A Trumpet around the Corner: The Story of New Orleans Jazz* (Jackson: University Press of Mississippi, 2008), 58.

21. Louis Armstrong, *Louis Armstrong in His Own Words: Selected Writings,* ed. Thomas Brothers (New York: Oxford University Press, 1999), 116.

22. "Arthur 'Zutty' Singleton: True Jazz Drumming Pioneer," www.modern drummer.com/2009/12/arthur-zutty-singleton/.

23. Ibid.

24. Martin T. Williams, *Jazz Masters of New Orleans* (New York: Macmillan, 1967), 191.

25. Sidney Bechet, *Treat It Gentle* (1960; Boston: Da Capo, 2002), 197.

26. Trevor Richards, "Paul Barbarin," *64 Parishes,* https://64parishes.org /entry/paul-barbarin.

27. Armstrong, *Louis Armstrong in His Own Words* 125.

28. Russell, *New Orleans Style,* 58.

29. Scott Fish, "Singin' on the Set," *Modern Drummer,* November 1981, www.moderndrummer.com/article/november-1981-ed-blackwelll-singin-set/.

30. "Death of Louis Barbarin, 94, Cuts Link with Jazz's Past," *Times Picayune,* May 14, 1997, http://files.usgwarchives.net/la/orleans/newspapers/00000338.txt.

31. Ibid.

32. "Louis Barbarin," Music Rising at Tulane, https://musicrising.tulane.edu /discover/people/louis-barbarin/.

33. Shannon Powell, interview by author, August 3, 2020.

34. Cie Frazier, interview by William Russell and Ralph Collins, December 1960, Hogan Jazz Archive, Tulane University.

35. Powell, interview.

36. William Carter, *Preservation Hall: Music from the Heart* (New York: Norton, 1991), 255.

37. Ibid., 209.

38. Russell, *New Orleans Style,* 60.

39. Jason Berry, Jonathan Foose, and Tad Jones, *Up from the Cradle of Jazz* (Athens: University of Georgia Press, 1986), 42. For additional background on the Spiritual Church, see Berry's *The Spirit of Blackhawk* (Jackson: University of Mississippi Press, 1995); and Andrew J. Kaslow, *The Spiritual Churches of New Orleans* (Knoxville: University of Tennessee Press, 1991).

40. Dr. John (Mac Rebennack) with Jack Rummel, *Under a Hoodoo Moon* (New York: St. Martin's, 1994), 165.

41. Joe Lastie Jr., interview by author, August 2018.

42. Ray Bauduc, "Smoky Mary," in "The Bible," handwritten personal reminiscence, Hogan Jazz Archive, Tulane University.

43. Ray Bauduc, interview by Dick Allen, June 26, 1984, Houston, Texas, transcribed by the author, September 2019.

44. Ibid.

45. Ibid.

46. "Ray Bauduc," *Drummerworld,* www.drummerworld.com/drummers/Ray_Bauduc.html.

47. Bauduc, interview.

48. Michael White, "Dr. Michael White: The Doc Paulin Years," *Jazz Archivist* 23 (2010): 6. Thanks to Chris Thomas King's *The Blues: The Authentic Narrative of My Music and Culture* (2021) for the reference to this article.

49. Bauduc, "Smoky Mary."

50. Ray Bauduc, "South Rampart Street Parade," in "The Bible," handwritten personal reminiscence, Hogan Jazz Archive, Tulane University.

51. Ray Bauduc, "Big Noise from Winnetka," in "The Bible," handwritten personal reminiscence, Hogan Jazz Archive, Tulane University.

52. Adonis Rose, interview by author, July 2018.

7. MODERN JAZZ, RHYTHM & BLUES, AND FUNK

1. Ricky Sebastian, communication with author, November 2020.

2. Kohlman, in an interview by Val Wilmer, quoted in *New Orleans Jazz and Second Line Drumming* by Herlin Riley and Johnny Vidacovich (Van Nuys, CA: Alfred Music Publishing, 1995), 63.

3. Ibid., 62.

4. Ibid., 65.

5. Ibid., 64.

6. Earl Palmer, interview by Michael Tisserand, April 24, 1999 (001.1999.007), Allison Miner Heritage Stage, New Orleans Jazz & Heritage Festival.

7. Joseph "Smokey" Johnson, interview by David Thress, in *New Orleans Jazz and Second Line Drumming* by Riley and Vidacovich, 97.

8. Vernel Fournier, interview by author; portions of this interview appeared in "From Treme to the Big Apple," *Wavelength,* May 1985, 43.

9. Ibid.

10. Ibid.

11. Ibid., 44.

12. Ibid., 43.

13. Vernel Fournier, interview by David Thress, in *New Orleans Jazz and Second Line Drumming,* by Riley and Vidacovich, 46.

14. Jamal quoted in Eugene Holley Jr.,"Pianist Ahmad Jamal Charted a New Popularity for Jazz," *Wax Poetics,* www.waxpoetics.com/blog/features/articles/pianist-ahmad-jamal-charted-new-popularity-jazz/.

15. Fournier, interview by Thress, 47.

16. From "Talking Drums," Tom Dent Lecture Series, March 18, 2000, New Orleans Center for Creative Arts, 2000 Chartres Street, New Orleans, New Orleans Jazz & Heritage Foundation (catalogue number 030.2000.009).

17. Miles Davis, *Miles: The Autobiography,* with Quincy Troupe (New York: Simon and Schuster, 1989), 178.

18. Ben Ratliff, "Vernel Fournier, 72, Jazz Drummer Revered for Precision and Understatement," *New York Times,* November 10, 2000, www.nytimes.com/2000/11/10/arts/vernel-fournier-72-jazz-drummer-revered-for-precision-and-understatement.html.

19. Vernel Fournier, in a 1990 interview by Ted Panken, aired on *Today Is the Question: Ted Panken on Music, Politics and the Arts,* WKCR, July 3, 2011, https://tedpanken.wordpress.com/2011/07/03/vernell-fournier-on-ahmad-jamal-wkcr-1990/.

20. Fournier, interview by author, "From Treme to the Big Apple," *Wavelength,* May 1985, 43.

21. Ibid., 44.

22. Randy Weston and Willard Jenkins, *African Rhythms: The Autobiography of Randy Weston* (Durham, NC: Duke University Press, 2010), 128.

23. Valerie Wilmer, "The Drummer: Street Parade Fan," *Melody Maker,* March 9, 1968, 10.

24. Robert Palmer, "Crescent City Thumper," *Down Beat* 44, no. 12 (June 16, 1977): 18.

25. Bill Mikowski, "Masters of the Free Universe," *Modern Drummer,* December 1992, 35.

26. Ed Blackwell, in an interview by *Jazzset,* National Public Radio, September 9, 1993, quoted by David Thress in *New Orleans Jazz and Second Line Drumming* by Riley and Vidacovich, 50.

27. Scott K. Fish, "Ed Blackwell—Singin' on the Set," *Modern Drummer,* November 1981, www.moderndrummer.com/article/november-1981-ed-blackwelll-singin-set/.

28. Robert Palmer, liner notes, *Beauty Is a Rare Thing: The Ornette Coleman Quartet's Complete Atlantic Recordings* (Rhino Records, 1993), 14.

29. Bill Milkowski, "Masters of the Free Universe," *Modern Drummer,* December 1992, 114.

30. Harold R. Battiste Jr., *Unfinished Business: Memories of a New Orleans Music Man* (New Orleans: Historic New Orleans Collection, 2010), 33–34.

31. Valerie Wilmer, *As Serious as Your Life* (London: Serpent's Tail, 1992), quoted in Milkowski, "Masters of the Free Universe," 36–113.

32. Palmer, liner notes, *Beauty Is a Rare Thing,* 14.

33. LeRoi Jones (Amiri Baraka), "The Jazz Avant-Garde" (1961), in *Black Music* (New York: William Morrow, 1968), 76.

34. Milkowski, "Masters of the Free Universe," 115.

35. Fish, "Ed Blackwell—Singin' on the Set."

36. Kalamu ya Salaam, "The Original American Jazz Quintet: It Just Gets Better with Time," *Wavelength* 86 (December 1987): 6.

37. Idris Muhammad, *Inside the Music: The Life of Idris Muhammad* (Bloomington, IN: Xlibris, 2012), 161.

38. Ibid., 59.

39. R. J. Deluke, "Idris Muhammad: Coming to Grips with His Greatness," All about Jazz, August 6, 2014, www.allaboutjazz.com/idris-muhammad-coming-to-grips-with-his-greatness-idris-muhammad-by-rj-deluke.php?pg=2.

40. Art Neville, Aaron Neville, Charles Neville, Cyril Neville, and David Ritz, *The Brothers* (Boston: Little, Brown, 2000), 98.

41. Ibid., 82.

42. Ibid., 108.

43. Ibid., 149.

44. Eothen Alapatt, "The Idris Muhammad Interview," *Wax Poetics,* www.waxpoetics.com/blog/features/articles/idris-muhammad-interview/.

45. Muhammad, *Inside the Music,* 186.

46. Ibid., 187.

47. Alapatt, "The Idris Muhammad Interview."

48. Harold Battiste, liner notes, *New Orleans Heritage Jazz 1956–1966* (Opus 43, 1976), 11.

49. James Black, interview by Pat Jolly, April 9, 1983, WWOZ, Jazz & Heritage Archive (catalogue number 005.100.0024).

50. Michael Hurtt, "Best of the Beat Lifetime Achievement in Music Award: Eddie Bo," *Offbeat,* February 1, 2004, www.offbeat.com/articles/lifetime-achive ment-performer-eddie-bo/.

51. Scott K. Fish, "Back Home with James Black, *Modern Drummer,* December 1982, 66, www.moderndrummer.com/article/december-1982-back-home-james -black/.

52. Black, interview by Jolly.

53. Battiste, liner notes, *New Orleans Heritage Jazz 1956–1966,* 12.

54. Ernie Elly, interview by David Thress, in *New Orleans Jazz and Second Line Drumming,* by Riley and Vidacovich, 67.

55. Alfred "Uganda" Roberts, interview by author, November 2019.

56. Johnny Vidacovich, interview by David Thress, in *New Orleans Jazz and Second Line Drumming,* by Riley and Vidacovich, 101.

57. Ricky Sebastian, communication with author, November 2020.

58. Vernon Severin, interview by author, July 2019.

59. Jason Marsalis, interview by Anthony Brown, November 2010, Smithsonian Jazz Oral History Program, NEA Jazz Master interview, 17.

60. Kalamu ya Salaam, "James N. Black, Jr. Is Dead." *Wavelength,* October 1988. 7.

61. David Lee Jr., interview by David Thress, in *New Orleans Jazz and Second Line Drumming,* by Riley and Vidacovich, 104.

62. Ibid., 103.

63. Ibid., 104.

64. Ibid.

65. Fred Staehle, interview by author, June 12, 2020.

66. Lee, interview by Thress, 104.

67. Tony Scherman, *Backbeat: Earl Palmer's Story* (Washington, DC: Smithsonian Institution Press, 1999), 79.

68. Earl Palmer, interview by Michael Tisserand, April 24, 1999, Allison Miner Heritage Stage, New Orleans Jazz & Heritage Festival (catalogue number 001.1999.007), transcribed by author, 2019.

69. Ibid.

70. Ibid. Earl Palmer's assertion that Paul Barbarin could not read music may be incorrect because Barbarin composed a number of songs and likely would have needed some ability to read in order to compose.

71. Ibid.

72. Daniel Glass, ed., *The Roots of Rock Drumming: Interviews with the Drummers Who Shaped Rock 'n' Roll Music* (New York: Hudson Music, 2013), 167.

73. John Broven, *Rhythm and Blues in New Orleans,* rev. and updated ed. (Gretna, LA: Pelican, 2016), 141.

74. Ibid., 141–42.

75. Jim Payne, *Give the Drummers Some: The Great Drummers of R&B, Funk & Soul,* ed. Harry Weinger (Katonah, NY: Face the Music Productions, 1996), 5.

76. Ibid.

77. Ibid., 6.

78. Scherman, *Backbeat,* 85.

79. Palmer, interview by Tisserand.

80. For a more extensive listing of his work, see the appendix in Scherman, *Backbeat.*

81. Scherman, *Backbeat,* 80.

82. Earl King, interview by author, May 8, 1981, Sea-Saint Studios.

83. Charles "Hungry" Williams, interview by Tad Jones (and Mac Rebennack), "Charles 'Hungry' Williams," *Wavelength,* November 1983, 21.

84. Ibid.

85. Ibid.

86. Ibid., 22.

87. Payne, *Give the Drummers Some,* 8

88. Williams, interview by Jones, 22–23.

89. Ibid., 23.

90. Broven, *Rhythm and Blues in New Orleans,* 143.

91. Ibid., 124.

92. Ibid., 143.

93. Ibid., 130.

94. Williams, interview by Jones, 23.

95. Broven, *Rhythm and Blues in New Orleans,* 143.

96. Johnson, interview by Thress, 91.

97. Bunny Matthews, "Joseph 'Smokey' Johnson," *Offbeat,* July 1, 2000, https://web.archive.org/web/20170601174433/http://www.offbeat.com/articles/joseph -smokey-johnson/.

98. Ibid.

99. Johnson, interview by Thress, 94.

100. Matthews, "Joseph 'Smokey' Johnson."

101. Geraldine Wyckoff, "Obituary: Joseph 'Smokey' Johnson," *Offbeat,* October 25, 2015, www.offbeat.com/articles/obituary-joseph-smokey-johnson/.

102. Matthews, "Joseph 'Smokey' Johnson."

103. Michael Hurtt, "Best of the Beat Lifetime Achievement Sideman Award: Smokey Johnson," *Offbeat,* February 1, 2004, www.offbeat.com/articles/lifetime -achievement-sideman-smokey-johnson/

104. Jeff Hannusch (Almost Slim), *I Hear You Knockin': The Sound of New Orleans Rhythm and Blues* (Ville Platte, LA: Swallow, 1985), 201.

105. Matthews, "Joseph 'Smokey' Johnson."

106. Broven, *Rhythm and Blues in New Orleans,* 260.

107. Hurtt, "Best of the Beat Lifetime Achievement Sideman Award."

108. Matthews, "Joseph 'Smokey' Johnson."

109. Herlin Riley, interview by author, March 2021.

110. John Nova Lomax, "Rotation: Smokey Johnson, *It Ain't My Fault,*" Houston Press, January 24, 2008, www.houstonpress.com/music/rotation-smokey -johnson-it-aint-my-fault-6500674.

111. Hurtt, "Best of the Beat Lifetime Achievement Sideman Award."

112. Johnson, interview by Thress, 96–97.

113. Riley, interview by author, March 2021.

114. Wyckoff, "Obituary: Joseph 'Smokey' Johnson."

115. Almost Slim (Jeff Hannusch), "Gentleman June Gardner," *Wavelength,* July 1985, 22.

116. Ibid., 22.

117. Ibid., 23.

118. Ibid., 24.

119. Peter Guralnick, *Dream Boogie: The Triumph of Sam Cooke* (Boston: Little, Brown, 2005), 347.

120. Ibid., 591–92.

121. Almost Slim, "Gentleman June Gardner," 23.

122. Ibid., 24.

123. Dr. John, liner notes, *N'Awlinz Dis Dat or D'Udda* (EMI, 2004).

124. Dr. John (Mac Rebennack), *Under a Hoodoo Moon,* with Jack Rummel (New York: St. Martin's, 1994), 187. Charles Williams claims he is the drummer on "Working in a Coal Mine" (see Almost Slim, "Gentleman June Gardner," 23).

125. Hammond Scott, "Dr. John on Mac Rebennack," *Wavelength,* November 1981, 13

126. Dr. John, liner notes, *Gumbo* (Atlantic, 1972).

127. Payne, *Give the Drummers Some,* 21–22, 53, 55; Alexander Stewart, "'Funky Drummer': New Orleans, James Brown and the Rhythmic Transformation of American Popular Music," *Popular Music* 9, no. 3 (2000): 293–318.

128. James Brown, "Funky Drummer," single (King Records, 1970).

129. Scott, "Dr. John on Mac Rebennack," 14.

130. Jeff Hannusch, "John Boudreaux," *Offbeat,* March 1, 2002, www.offbeat .com/articles/john-boudreaux/.

131. Ibid.

132. Harold Battiste, liner notes, *New Orleans Jazz Heritage—Jazz: 1956–1966* (Opus 43, 1976), 12–13.

133. Leo Morris (Idris Muhammad), interview by Dan Thress, in *New Orleans Jazz and Second Line Drumming,* by Riley and Vidacovich, 8.

134. Glass, *The Roots of Rock Drumming,* 169.

135. "Mambo Kings," *Gambit,* February 10, 2004.

136. Bart Bull, "The Absent Professor," *Spin Magazine,* May 1987, 52.

137. Dr. John, *Under a Hoodoo Moon,* with Rummel, 212–13.

138. Bart Bull, "The Absent Professor," 53.

139. Battiste, liner notes, *New Orleans Jazz Heritage—Jazz: 1956–1966,* 13.

140. Glass, *The Roots of Rock Drumming,* 168.

141. Broven, *Rhythm and Blues in New Orleans,* 218.

142. Battiste, liner notes, *New Orleans Jazz Heritage—Jazz: 1956–1966,* 12.

143. Dr. John, *Under a Hoodoo Moon,* with Rummel, 84–85.

144. Ibid., 155.

145. Val Wilmer, "John Boudreaux," in *The New Grove Dictionary of Jazz,* 2nd ed., ed. Barry Kernfeld (Oxford: Oxford University Press, 2003).

146. Hannusch, "John Boudreaux."

147. Fred Staehle, interview by author, June 12, 2020. The quotations of Staehle in this section are drawn from this interview.

148. Michael Hurtt. "Mac's Wild Years," *Offbeat,* May 1, 2007, www.offbeat .com/articles/macs-wild-years/.

149. Dr. John, *Under a Hoodoo Moon,* with Rummel, 186.

150. Dr. John, liner notes, *Gumbo.*

151. Dr. John, *Under a Hoodoo Moon,* with Rummel, 51.

152. Dr. John, *Trippin' Live,* promo-only interview disc (Surefire, 1997).

153. Keith Spera, "Herman Ernest, Longtime Dr. John Drummer, Dies of Cancer," NOLA.com, *Times-Picayune,* March 7, 2011, updated June 25, 2019, www.nola.com/entertainment_life/music/article_46057082-f544-5152-aa94 -67f3f84f5211.html.

154. Michael Swindle, "On the One with Herman the German," *Wavelength,* July 1989, 29.

155. Ibid.

156. Debra Devi, "Language of the Blues: Second Line," *Amer- icanbluesscene,* March 18, 2016, www.americanbluesscene.com/ language-of-the-blues-second-line/.

157. Herman Ernest, interview by Dan Thress, in *New Orleans Drumming,* dir. Stevenson J. Palfi, DVD (Warner Bros., 2004).

158. Shannon Powell, interview by Ben Sandmel, "A Tribute to Herman Ernest," April 2011, Allison Miner Music Heritage Stage, New Orleans Jazz & Heritage Festival.

159. Ibid.

160. Ernest, interview by Thress.

161. Dan Phillips, "The Importance of Herman Ernest, Part 1 and Part 2," *Home of the Groove,* April 3, 2011 and May 15, 2011, https://homeofthegroove.blogspot .com.

162. Ernest, interview by Thress.

163. Ibid.

164. Ibid.

165. Spera, "Herman Ernest, Longtime Dr. John Drummer, Dies of Cancer."

166. Ernest, interview by Thress.

167. Joseph "Zigaboo" Modeliste, interview by author, December 12, 2019. The quotations of Modeliste in this section are drawn from this interview.

168. Neville Brothers and Ritz, *The Brothers,* 98.

169. *Zigaboo: The Originator of the New Orleans Funky Drumming,* DVD (Drumchannel.com. 2012).

170. Neville Brothers and Ritz, *The Brothers,* 187.

171. *Zigaboo: The Originator of the New Orleans Funky Drumming.*

172. Robert Christgau. "Cissy Strut Compilation Album Review," robertchrist gau.com, archived from the original on March 28, 2012, retrieved July 9, 2017, www.robertchristgau.com/get_artist.php?name=The+Meters.

173. Ibid.

174. Ibid.

175. Keith Richards, *Life,* with James Fox (Boston: Little, Brown, 2010), 416.

176. "100 Greatest Drummers of All Time," *Rolling Stone,* March 31, 2016, www.rollingstone.com/music/music-lists/100-greatest-drummers-of-all-time -77933/christian-vander-30083/.

177. Jon Cohan, Rick Mattingly, and Andy Doerschuk, "50 Most Important Drummers of All Time," *Drum!,* August 16, 2011, https://Drummagazine.Com /50-Most-Important-Drummers-Of-All-Time/.

178. Dominic Massa, "The Meters to Receive Grammy Lifetime Achievement," WWL, January 9, 2018, www.wwltv.com/article/news/local/the-meters-to -receive-grammy-lifetime-achievement-award/289-506667106.

179. Alfred "Uganda" Roberts, interview by author, November 22, 2019. The quotations of Roberts in this section are drawn from this interview.

180. "The Cyril Neville Interview," *The Jake Feinberg Show,* April 27, 2019, www.jakefeinbergshow.com/2019/04/neville-the-cyril-neville-interview/.

181. Shannon Powell, interview by author, August 3, 2020.

182. "Mean" Willie Green, interview by author, July 2019. The quotations of Green in this section are drawn from this interview.

8. EXTENSIONS AND VARIATIONS

1. Joe Watkins's birth name was Mitchell Watson, according to Larry Borenstein and Bill Russel, *Preservation Hall Portraits* (Baton Rouge: Louisiana State University Press, 1968).

2. *Goldmine,* December 2017, 61.

3. Stanton Moore, interview by author, July 2018.

4. Ricky Sebastian, interview by author, July 2019.

5. Barry Marytn, *Walking with Legends: Barry Martyn's New Orleans Jazz Odyssey,* ed. Mick Burns (Baton Rouge: Louisiana State University Press, 2007), 31.

6. Barry Martyn, interview by Dr. Bruce Raeburn, May 1999, Allison Miner Music Heritage Stage, New Orleans Jazz & Heritage Festival.

7. Nat Hentoff, liner notes, John Coltrane, *Kulu Se Mama* (Impulse, 1967).

8. Juno Lewis, "JUNO SE MAMA," liner notes, John Coltrane, *Kulu Se Mama* (Impulse, 1967).

9. Christopher Porter, "Juno Lewis Dies at 70," *Jazz Times,* April 22, 2002, https://jazztimes.com/archives/juno-lewis-dies-at-70/.

10. Harold R. Battiste Jr., *Unfinished Business: Memories of a New Orleans Music Man* (New Orleans: Historic New Orleans Collection, 2010), 114.

11. Ibid., 115.

12. Porter, "Juno Lewis Dies at 70."

13. Ernie Elly, interview by Holly Hobbs, February 22, 2016, "Ernie Elly Oral History," Preservation Hall Foundation, www.preshallfoundation.org/oralhistories.

14. Ibid.

15. Ibid.

16. Joe Lastie Jr., interview by author, August 2018.

17. Herlin Riley, interview by author, July 2018.

18. *Zigaboo: The Originator of the New Orleans Funky Drumming,* DVD (Drumchannel.com, 2012).

19. Ted Panken, "Two Interviews with Drummer Brian Blade," *Today Is the Question: Ted Panken on Music, Politics and the Arts,* https://tedpanken.wordpress.com/2011/07/28/two-interviews-with-drummer-brian-blade/.

20. Ibid.

21. Ibid.

22. Keith Spera, "Easy Beat: New Orleans Drummers Roundtable," *Drum!* magazine, December 2011, https://drummagazine.com/easy-beat-new-orleans-drummers-roundtable/.

23. Johnny Vidacovich, interview by Michael Vosbein, *Drummer Nation,* January 9, 2018, www.facebook.com/stantonmooremusic/posts/new-interview-with-my-mentor-johnny-vidacovich-shot-at-my-son05-drum-camp-last-m/10155542975181185/.

24. "Improv Conference: A Festival of Ideas," drum panel: Shannon Powell, Johnny Vidacovich, Stanton Moore; moderator: David Kunian, November 9, 2019, New Orleans Jazz Museum.

25. Geraldine Wycoff, "Lifetime Achievement in Music: Johnny Vidacovich," *Offbeat,* December 28, 2016, www.offbeat.com/articles/lifetime-achievement-music-johnny-vidacovich-2/.

26. Johnny Vidacovich, interview by author, July 6, 2018.

27. Ibid.

28. Johnny Vidacovich, interview by Bruce Raeburn, April 24, 2009, Allison Miner Heritage Stage, New Orleans Jazz & Heritage Festival (001.2009.004).

29. Charles Suhor, *Jazz in New Orleans: The Postwar Years through 1970* (Lanham, MD: Scarecrow, 2001), 11.

30. "The Charlie Suhor Interview," *The Jake Feinberg Show,* www.jakefeinbergshow.com.

31. Johnny Vidacovich, interview by David Thress, in *New Orleans Jazz and Second Line Drumming,* by Herlin Riley and Johnny Vidacovich (Van Nuys, CA: Alfred Music Publishing, 1995), 97.

32. Ibid., 101.

33. Ibid., 102.

34. Bunny Matthews, "Johnny Vidacovich," *Offbeat,* March 1, 2002, www.offbeat.com/articles/johnny-vidacovich/.

35. Yorke Corbin, "Johnny Vidacovich: Fess's Drummer Is a Jazz Master," *Wavelength,* December 1980, 4–6.

36. Vidacovich, interview by Raeburn.

37. "Improv Conference: A Festival of Ideas."

38. Tony Dagradi, interview by Larry Englund, KFAI Radio Without Borders, September 22, 2009, Astral Project, https://astralproject.com/interview-with.

39. Jonathan Tabak, "Astral Project," *Offbeat,* June 1, 1999, www.offbeat.com/articles/astral-project-2/.

40. "Improv Conference: A Festival of Ideas."

41. Herlin Riley, interview by author, originally appeared in "Herlin Riley Keeps Time," *Wavelength,* August 1984, 20.

42. Herlin Riley, interview by David Thress, in *New Orleans Jazz and Second Line Drumming,* by Riley and Vidacovich, 32.

43. Herlin Riley, interview by author, December 17, 2019.

44. Herlin Riley, interview by author, July 11, 2018.

45. Riley, interview by Thress, 36.

46. Riley, interview by author, *Wavelength,* August 1984, 21.

47. Herlin Riley, interview by Ted Panken, "Herlin Riley: New Orleans Drummer," 1999/2005, Wordpress.com, July 22, 2011, https://tedpanken.wordpress.com/2011/07/22/herlin-riley-new-orleans-drummer-1999-interview/.

48. Riley, interview by author, *Wavelength,* August 1984, 21.

49. Ibid.

50. Ibid.

51. Ibid.

52. Ibid.

53. Riley, interview by Panken.

54. Riley, interview by author, July 11, 2018.

55. Ibid.

56. Ibid.

57. Riley, interview by author, December 17, 2019.

58. Ibid.

59. Ricky Sebastian, interview by author, July 17, 2019. Unless otherwise indicated, the quotations of Sebastian in this section are drawn from this interview.

60. Ricky Sebastian, interview by author, originally appeared in "You Can't Play It If You Can't Dance to It," *Wavelength,* no. 73 (November 1986), 10.

61. Ibid.

62. Ibid., 11.

63. Ibid.

64. Bill Milkowski, liner notes, *The Spirit Within* (STR Digital Records, 2001).

65. Joe Lastie Jr., interview by author, August 2018. Unless otherwise indicated, the quotations of Lastie in this section are drawn from this interview.

66. From Lastie, interview by author, August 2018, and an interview by Gabe Soria, "Joe Lastie Oral History," February 23, 2016, Preservation Hall Foundation, www.preshallfoundation.org/oralhistories.

67. David Fricke, "Inside the Foo Fighters' Wildly Ambitious New Album and HBO Series," *Rolling Stone*, June 4, 2014, www.rollingstone.com/music/music-news /inside-the-foo-fighters-wildly-ambitious-new-album-and-hbo-series-86456/.

68. Keith Spera, "Dave Grohl Recounts the Foo Fighters' Excellent 'Sonic Highways' Adventure in New Orleans," NOLA.com, *Times-Picayune*, October 31, 2014, www.nola.com/entertainment_life/festivals/article_c97541a1-7496-55aa-b077-c8a0ddcf5c5c.html/.

69. Shannon Powell, interview by author, August 3, 2020. Unless otherwise indicated, the quotations of Powell in this section are drawn from this interview.

70. Shannon Powell, interview by Tom Morgan, "Shannon Powell: New Orleans Drumming," May 2, 2010, Allison Miner Heritage Stage. Jazz & Heritage Festival (catalogue number 001.2010.028).

71. "Improv Conference: A Festival of Ideas."

72. Ibid.

73. Leroy Jones, interview by author (originally appeared in "Has N.O. Produced a New Satchmo?," *Times-Picayune/States-Item*, July 27, 1984, 23.

74. Christie Jourdain, interview by author, June 2020. The quotations of Jourdain in this section are drawn from this interview.

75. Mayumi Shara, interview by author, June 2018. The quotations of Shara in this section are drawn from this interview.

76. Cori Walters, interview by author, July 2019. The quotations of Walters in this section are drawn from this interview.

77. Boyanna Trayanova, interview by author, July 2020. The quotations of Trayanova in this section are drawn from this interview.

78. Nikki Glaspie, interview with author, October 2019. The quotations of Glaspie in this section are drawn from this interview.

79. Jaz Butler, interview by author, August 2020.

80. Jaz Butler, interview by author, July 2018.

81. Butler, interview, August 2020.

82. Butler, interview, July 2018.

83. Butler, interview, August 2020.

84. Ibid.

85. Butler, interview, July 2018.

86. Christie Jourdain, interview by author, June 2020.

87. Butler, interview, August 2020.

88. Ibid.

89. Butler, interview, July 2018.

90. Butler, interview, August 2020.

91. Ibid.

92. Sadly, Raymond Weber Jr. passed away on September 24, 2020.

93. LBJ, "Drummer Gerald French Blends Family and New Orleans Music Traditions," WGNO.com, August 15, 2019, https://wgno.com/news-with-a-twist /music/drummer-gerald-french-blends-family-and-new-orleans-music -traditions/ https://wgno.com/news-with-a-twist/music/drummer-gerald -french-blends-family-and-new-orleans-music-traditions/.

94. John Swenson, "Russell Batiste," *Offbeat*, August 1, 2000, www.offbeat .com/articles/russell-batiste/.

95. "Drummers: Russell Batiste," *Modern Drummer*, www.moderndrummer .com/2005/06/russell-batiste/.

96. Butler, interview, July 2018.

97. Joe Dyson, interview by author, July 2018.

98. Nikki Glaspie, interview by author, October 2019.

99. Al Kennedy, *Chord Changes on the Chalkboard: How Public Teachers Shaped Jazz and the Music of New Orleans* (Lanham, MD.: Scarecrow, 2005), xx.

100. "Johnny Vidacovich," interview by Bunny Matthews, *Offbeat*, March 1, 2002, www.offbeat.com/articles/johnny-vidacovich/.

101. Stanton Moore, interview by author, December 2020.

102. "Johnny Vidacovich," interview by Matthews.

103. Stanton Moore, interview by author, July 2018.

104. Improv Conference: A Festival of Ideas."

105. Moore, interview, July 2018.

106. Vidacovich, interview by author, July 2018.

107. Kevin O'Day, interview by author, July 2018. The quotations of O'Day in this section are drawn from this interview.

108. Andre Bohren, interview by author, July 2018. The quotations of Bohren in this section are drawn from this interview.

109. *The Jason Marsalis One Man Drums Show*, May 14, 2020, www.youtube .com/watch?v=Eaiw957kk5E.

110. "Jason Marsalis, NEA Jazz Master Interview," interview by Anthony Brown, November 7, 2010, 7, Smithsonian Jazz Oral History Program. Archives Center, National Museum of American History.

111. Ibid., 18.

112. Jason Marsalis, interview by Anita Malhotra, April 14, 2013, https://arts mania.ca/2014/04/30/interview-with-jason-marsalis/.

113. "Jason Marsalis, NEA Jazz Master Interview," interview by Brown, 27.

114. Ibid., 28.

115. *The Jason Marsalis One Man Drums Show*.

116. Vernon Severin, interview by author, July 2019. The quotations of Severin in this section are drawn from this interview.

117. Adonis Rose, interview by author, July 2019. The quotations of Rose in this section are drawn from this interview.

118. Albert Murray uses the term in book 2, *The Spy Glass Tree*, of his four-book series on the coming-of-age of a jazz musician: "an ancestral imperative to do something and become something and be somebody" (1974; New York: Vintage, 1998), 23.

119. Joe Dyson, interview by author, July 2018. The quotations of Dyson in this section are drawn from this interview.

120. Peter Varnado, interview by author, July 2018. The quotations of Varnado in this section are drawn from this interview.

121. Derrick Tabb, interview by author, June 2018. The quotations of Tabb in this section are drawn from this interview.

122. Christie Jourdain, interview by author, June 2020.

123. Adonis Rose, interview by author, July 2019.

124. Shannon Powell, interview by author, August 2020.

Index

A. J. Piron and his Novelty Orchestra, *43*

Adams, Johnny, 95, 115, 148, 162

Academy of Black Arts, 154

Adams, Justin, 99

Adderley, Nat, 81

African musical traditions, 1–22, 78, 84, 121, 199, 209

Alexander, Jeffery "Jellybean," 176, 184

All For One (A.F.O.), 77, 104–105, *102*

Allman Brothers, 108, 141

Allen, Henry "Red," Jr., 61, 62, 71

Allen, Henry "Red," Sr., 48, 71

Allison, Mose, 141

Allison Miner Music Heritage Stage, 35, 133, 141, 160

Alvin Bridges and the Desire Community Choir, 154, 157

Amadee, Steve, 191

American Jazz Quintet, 77, 79

American Music label, 183

Americo, Tony, 106

Ammons, Albert, 72

Ammons, Gene, 81

Anderson, E. M., 48

Andrews, Glen, 207

Andrews, James, 189

Andrews, Jenard, 207

Andrews, Revon, 2

Andrews, Troy "Trombone Shorty," 164, 207; Trombone Shorty Academy, 182

Apollo Theater, 80

Ardrey, Robert, 135

Armstrong, Louis "Satchmo," ix, 22, 29, 44, 57, 59, 60, 61, 62, 65, 72, 92, 147, 149, 160

Arnold, Wilbert "Junkyard Dog," 169

Asch, Moses, 183

Astral Project, 138, 141, 143

Ayers, Roy, 86

Bachemin, Angelamia, 178

Bachemin, Johnny, 145

Backbeat (rhythm), 87, 88, 90, 94, 98, 104, 113, 115, 121, 133, 153, 160, 162, 185, 192

Badie, Peter Chuck, *102,* 104

Badu, Erykah, 102

Baker, Chet, 86

Bamboula dance, 3, 20, 30, 169; bamboula drum, *18,* 20; bamboula rhythm, 3, 20, 30, 169

Bamboula, The (engraving) *8, 18;* "Bamboula," (composition), 20–21, *21*

Bamboula 2000, 18

Baraka, Amiri (LeRoi Jones), 78

Bangles, The, 163

Barbarin, Adolphe Paul, *25,* 35, 42, 43, *44,* 49, 54, 61–62, *62,* 65, 72, 74, 80, 88, 132, 137, 160, 178, 202; "Paul Barbarin's Second Line," 35, 44, 54, 62, 96; "Bourbon Street Parade," 35, 62, 96, 156

Barbarin, Isidore, 45, 51, 61

Barbarin, Louis "Bob," *42,* 62–63, *63,* 88, 159–160, 178, 182

Barbarin, Lucien, 156, 160

Barber, Chris, 72

Barefield, Eddie, 75

Barker, Blue Lu, 31, 162

Barker, Danny, 31, *32,* 41, 44, 65, 87, 145, 147, 157, 158, 161, 162

Barnes, Emile, 64

Barard, David, 111

Barrett, Sweet Emma, 54

Barron, Ronnie, 101, 115

Barta, Steve, 152

Bartels, Hank, 169

Basie, William Count, 50, 188

Baham, Carl, 176

Baptiste, Tene, *27*

Barthelemy, Joseph "CoCoMo Joe," 32–33, *33*

Bartholomew, Dave, 88–90, 95, 107, 195

Bascomb, Paul, 99

Bass drum pedal, 38, *47, 49,* 45, 54, 63–65, 67, 73, 76, 194–195, 199, 209, 269

Batiste, Alvin, 77, 79, 144, 202

Batiste, "Uncle" Lionel, 35–36, 162, 194, 208

Batiste, Quentin, 71

Batiste, David Russell, Jr., 171, 174, 177, 179–181, *180,* 184, 188, 189, 201, 202

Batiste, David Russell, Sr., 179

Batiste Brothers Band, 259

Battiste, Harold, 37, 77, 79, 82, 83, 101, *102,* 110, 135, 137, 152

Bauduc, Jules, Jr., 66, 69, 178

Bauduc Sr, Jules, 66–67

Bauduc, Ray, 50, 66–69, *67,* 106, 178, 182–183

Bayersdorffer, Johnny, 67

Bazzle, Germaine, 85, 87, 137, 148–149

Beach Boys, 90, 134

Beastie Boys, 122

Beatles, 101, 131–132

Bechet, Sidney, ix, 21–22, 61, 62

Becton, William, 173

Belafonte, Harry, 151

Belletto, Al, 140, 143

Bellson, Louis, 68, 161

Benson, George, 81, 148

Berfect, Sammy, 128, 154

Berger, Karl, 79

Berklee College of Music, 150–151, 173, 178, 198

Berry, Jason, 65

Beyoncé, 172, 174

Bienville, Jean-Baptiste Le Moyne, sieur de, 11, 19

Bichini Bia Congo Dance Theater Company, *6*

Big Chief Jolly (George Landry), 118

Big four (rhythm), 44, 52, 53, 60, 90, 96, 171

Big Maybelle (Smith), 143

Big Sam's Funky Nation, 273

Black Masking Indians (Mardi Gras Indians), 11, 14, 19, 20, 29, 33–35, *34, 35,* 37, 53, 55, 76, 79, 82, 112,-113, 118, 126–127, 130, 149, 156, 158, 162, 167, 177, 185, 198

Black, James, 19, 37, 44, 82–85, *83, 84,* 86, 94, 100, 101, 102, 107, 109, 115, 130, 140, 141, 150, 159, 182, 193, 195–196, 201

Blackwell, Ed, 36–37, 62, 74–79, *77,* 87, 98, 106, 116, 120, 130, 133, 135, 141, 198

Blade, Brian, 87, 133, 137–138, 143, 187

Blakey, Art, 74, 81, 87, 102, 135, 150

Blanchard, Edgar, 98

Blanchard, Terence, 79, 198, 199

Blato Zlato, 171

Blevins, Kenneth, 191

Blind Boys of Alabama, 162

Bloom, Jonathan, 127, 201, 204

Bo Diddley (Ellas McDaniel), 99

Bo, Eddie (Edwin Bocage), 83, 85, 97, 102, 140

Bohren, Andre, 189–192, *190*

Bohren, Spencer, 189–192

Bolden, Buddy, 22, 52, 90

Boleros (dance rhythm), 25

Bolton, Red Happy, 63

Bond, Graham, 105

Bonerama, 189

Bonfá, Luiz, 136

Bonney, Robert "Bulldog," 111

Bontemps, Willie, 59

Booker T and the MGs, 120

Booker, James, 99, 105, 109, 141

Boudreaux, Jeff, 159

Boudreaux, John, 85, 88, 95, 100, 101–105, *102,* 107, 108, 109, 111, 115, 130, 149, 182

Boudreaux, Joseph, Jr., *35*

Bourbon Street, 49, 71, 85–86, 87, 88, 107, 110, 111, 115, 132, 145, 151, 154

Brackeen, JoAnne, 151

Bras-Coupé, 21–22

Brass bands, 35–36, 36–50, *38, 83, 84,* 86, 94, 100, 101, 102, 107, 109, 115, 130, 140, 141, 150, 159, 182, 193, 195–196, 201

Braud, Mark, 170

Brazilian music, 53, 127, 136, 147, 151, 152, 168, 170, 194

Brecker, Michael, 151

Bridge Trio, 202

Bridgewater, DeeDee, 200

Brooks, Detroit, 154

Brooks, Mark, 154, 170

Brooks, Wayne, *106*

Broom, Bobby, 111

Broven, John, 103

Brown, Anthony, 193

Brown, Charles, 102

Brown, Clarence "Gatemouth," 151

Brown, Clarence "Junie Boy," 100, 116

Brown, Gary, 119

Brown, James, 90, 101, 128, 183, 194

Brown, Jimmy, *27*

Brown, Maxine, 80

Brown, Roy, 98

Brundy, Walter, 56

Brunious, Wendell, 155

Bua, Frank, 190–191

Buena Vista Social Club, 169

Burbridge, Oteil, 181

Burns, Dwayne, 156

Burt, Eddie, Sr., 155

Burt, Eluard, 159

Bush, Dolores, 95

Bush, Yvonne, 94–96, 135, 144, 154, 181

Bushnell, David I., Jr., 13

Butera, Sam, 71

Butler, Frank, 134

Butler, Henry, 162

Butler, Jazmine "Jaz," 175–178, *176,* 180

Butler, Jerry, 80

Butler, Rev. Lizzie, 162

Butterbeans and Susie, 49

Byrd, Henry Roeland. *See* Professor Longhair

Cable, George Washington, *8, 18*

Callier, Elliot "Stackman," 156

Calloway, Cab, 31

Carey, Mutt, *52*

Carson, Big Al, 169

Carter, Betty, 81, 199

Casa Samba, 194

Catlett, Big Sid, 61, 166

Celestin, Oscar "Papa," 62, 64, 72

Cha Wa, *35*

Chambers, Joe, 86

Chandler, Dee Dee, 26, 46–48, *47,* 60, 137, 147, 186

Changuito, 169

Chapman, Topsy, 162

Charles, Ray, 77, 90, 135–136

Charles, Erving, 97

Charters, Samuel, 47

Chase, Dooky, Jr., 73, 87, 195

Chatters, Mark, 197

Cherry, Don, 77, 78

Chichicois, 11, 19

Chief Bey (James Hawthorne), 20

Chief Jake, 126

Chinese tom-tom, 49, 57, 60, *60, 167. See also* Taiko drums

Choctaw Nation, 11–13; Choctaw drum, 11–12, *12*
Christgau, Robert, 121
Cinquillo (rhythm), 53
Clapton, Eric, 105
Clark, Dee, 80
Clark, Joy, 175
Clave (rhythm), 52, 110, 168–170, *171*
Cleary, Jon, 122
Cobham, Billy, 81
Colar, George "Kid Sheik," 155
Cole, William Cozy, 166
Coleman, Cornelius "Tenoo," 92
Coleman, George, 81
Coleman, Ornette, 37, 62, 77–79
Collins, Lee, 72
Colored Waifs' Home for Boys (Municipal Boys Home), 65, 92
Coltrane, John, 78, 134–135
Colvin, Shawn, 138
Congo Square, x, 3, 4, *6*, 7–22, *18*, 24, 25, 26, 29, 30, 31, 33, 34, 41, 43, 48, 53, 56, 58, 78, 94, 97, 110, 121, 123–124, 127, 134, 135, 137, 148, 158, 159, 163, 165, 169, 171, 182, 198, 209, 211; "Congo Square" (song), 22
Connick, Harry, Jr., 72–73, 148, 161, 181, 199
Contradanza, 20–21
Conway, Mickey, 85, 102, 182
Cooke, Sam, 80, 90, 97–99, 134
Corbin, Yorke, 140
Corea, Chick (Return To Forever), 86, 137, 150, 173
Coryell, Larry, 86
Costello, Elvis, 1330
Cottrell, Louis, III (Louis Chevalier), 42–43, 178
Cottrell, Louis, Jr., 72
Cottrell, Louis, Sr., 42–43, *43*, 49, 60, 72, 178, 182
Cox, Ida, 88
Cole, William "Cozy," 105, 161
Cranshaw, Bob, 86
Crawford, Davell, 123, 162, 202
Crawford, James "Sugar Boy," 95
Crawford, Ralston, 4, 22
Creecy, James, 19, 26
Creole Wild West, 33
Christen's Brass Band, *40*
Crosby, Bob, 67–68
Crosby, Israel, 74
Crusto, Manuel, 72
Cruz, Celia, 123
Cummings, Fortescue, 14
Cuba, 8, 17, 19, 20, 21, 53, 54–55, 83, 93, 99, 108, 123, 124, 126, 147, 148, 152, 168, 169, 170, 194
Cubanismo, 152

Cuber, Ronnie, 111
Cypress Hill, 122
Cyrus, Sammy, 165

da Costa, Paulinho, 114–115
Dagradi, Tony, 137, 141–143, *141*
D'Arcangelo, Frank, 184
Davenport, Wallace, 155
Davilla, Sid, 71
Davis, Eddie "Lockjaw," 105
Davis, George, 85, 86, 94–95, 110
Davis, Miles, 75, 202
Davis, Peter, 92
Davis, Quint, 123, 125
Dawson, Alan, 196
Day, Bobby, 90
Dejan, Harold, 45; Dejan's Olympia Brass Band, *88*
DeJohnette, Jack, 75
deKay, Colman, 115
DeLeo, Carl, 150
De Mello, Thiago, 152
Derek and the Dominoes, 105
Destiny's Child, 174
Desvigne, Sidney, 62
Desvignes, Emil, 153
Devi, Debra, 112
Dew Drop Inn, 95, 98, 102
Dickerson, Roger, 180
Didimus, Henry, 26
Dion (DiMucci), 99
Dillon, Mike, 189
Dirty Dozen Brass Band, 35, 100, 129, 164, 177, 183, 189
Doby, Francis, 89
Dodds, Johnny, 36, 59, 133
Dodds, Warren "Baby," ix, 1, 24, 25, *33*, 36, 41, 42, 46, 49, 50, *52*, 56, 57–59, *57*, *58*, *59*, 60, 61, 62, 66, 69, 72, 74, 75, 86, 89, 116, 133, 141, 155, 159, 166, 167, 183, 184, 188, 199, 208, 209
Dolliole, Milford, 183
Dollis, Big Chief Bo, 126, 127, 181
Dolphy, Eric, 78, 79
Donaldson, Lou, 81, 88
Doheny, John, 53
Domino, Antoine "Fats," 65, 88, *89*, 92, 93, 97, 116, 144, 154, 160, 179
Domino, Antoine, Jr., 154
Dorsey, Lee, 83, 99, 100, 103, 114, 119
Doucette, Big Chief Alfred, 167
Drum set development, 19, 24, 28, 35–37, 39, 46–50, 139, 147–148, 186, 189
D'Rivera, Paquito, 201
Drummer's Collective, 151
Duffy, Mike, *36*
Dumpstaphunk, 172, 174, 175
Dunc's Honky Tonks, 140
Dupree, Champion Jack, 181

Duvernay, Miss, 74
Dylan, Bob, 130, 138
Dyson, Joe, 180, 197, 199, 200–202, *201*
Dyson, John, Jr., 200
Dyson, Dr. Joseph J. C., Sr., 200

Eaglin, Snooks, 95, 115, 119, 160
Eckstine, Billy, 74, 87
Eddy, Duane, 99
Edegran, Lars, 63
Eighth Calvary Mexican Band, 53
Eldridge, Roy, 61
Ellington, Edward Duke, 115, 147, 152, 200
Ellis Marsalis Center After-School and Summer Programs, 182
Ellison, Ralph, 29
Emerson, Lake and Palmer, 150
Eminem, 122
EPMD, 122
Ernest, Herman "Roscoe," III, 101, 111–115, *112*, 129, 160, 180, 183, 188
Elling, Kurt, 199
Elly, Ernie, 83, 133, 135–136, *136*, 137, 140, 167, 200
Esquerita (Eskew Reeder), 95
Eureka Brass Band, *39*, 64
European musical traditions, 23–28, 159
Exuma, 151
Evans, Freddi Williams, 1
Evans, Neal, 122
Evans, Samuel "Sticks," 98
Excelsior Brass Band, 61

Fairview Baptist Church Brass Band, 145, 157, 181
Faithful, Marianne, 138
Falls, Erica, 185
Feinberg, Jake, 125, 140
Felix, Mother Mamie, 162
Fillmore West, 65
Fields, Frank, 99
Filhe, George, *21*
Fillyau, Clayton, 101
Fisher, Andre, 114
Fischer, Patrice, 167
Fischer, Tom, 169
Flack, Roberta, 81
Flavor Flav (William Johnathan Drayton, Jr.), 154, 156
Fogerty, John, 122
Folkways record label, 59, 143
Foo Fighters, 167
Foose, Jonathan, 65
Ford, Alvin, 178
Ford, Alvin, Jr., 178
Ford, Frankie, 93
Forest, P., 13–14

Foster, Abbie "Chinee," 42, 56, *56*, 183
Foster, George "Pops," 92
Foundation of Funk, *120*, 122
Fountain, Pete, 154
Fournier, Vernel (Amir Rushdan), 73–76, *74*, 87, 99, 100, 135, 141, 145, 182
Framboise, Chief, 11
Frank, Edward, 97, 160
Frazier, Cie, I, 62–65, *64*, 132–133, *132*, 155
Frazier, Phil, 206, 211
Freelon, Nnenna, 199
French, Albert "Papa," 178, 258
French, Bob, 63, 162, 200
French, George, 85, 95, 178
French, Gerald, 167, 176, 178, *179*, 199
Funkadelic, 176
Funky Meters, 180, 181, 188

Gadd, Steve, 114
Galactic, 185, 186, 189, 190
Gap Band, 173
Gara, Larry, 59
Garcia, Jerry, 127
Gardner, Albert June, 97–100, *98*
Garland, Ed "Montudie," *52*
Garrett, Donald, 134
Garrison, Jimmy, 134
Gavotte (dance rhythm), 25
Gayten, Paul, 93
Gendron, Lorraine, 15
German Coast Uprising (1811 Revolt), *15*
Germania Hall, 140
Getz, Stan, 74, 202
Gibson, Banu, 155
Gilder, Rusty, 160
Gillespie, John Birks Dizzy, 61, 73, 85, 86, 90
Gilman, Michael, *106*
Gilmore, Patrick, 39
Gladiators, The, 179
Glaspie, Nikki, 172–175, *173*, 178, 181
Glover, Corey, 185
Go-Go's, The, 163
Golden Comanche Mardi Indians, *34*
Goodman, Shirley, 101, *101*, 105, *106*. *See also* Shirley and Lee
Gondoliers, 98
Gordon, Dexter, 105
Gordon, Jim, 105
Gordon, Taylor ("Pocket Queen"), 177
Gordon, Wycliffe, 148
Gordy, Berry, 131–132
Gottschalk, Louis Moreau, 20–21, *21*
Grateful Dead, 65, 127–128
Gray, Luther, 18, *18*, 20, *20*, 22, 180, 127

Green, Al, 188
Green, Lil, 98
Green, Andrew "Big Daddy," 206
Green, Grant, 81
Green, Millard, *18*
Green, Mean Willie, 127–130, *129*, 169, 171, 175, 184, 189, 208
Greer, Sonny, 68
Grohl, Dave, 157
Groovesect, 127
Gruenwald School of Music, 88
Guerineau, Henry, 106
Gully, Terreon, 204

Habanera (rhythm), 20, 21, 53
Haden, Charlie, 77, 79
Haggart, Bob, 68
Hair: The American Tribal Love-Rock Musical, 79, 80, 81
Haiti (Saint-Domingue), 8, 19, 20, 21, 152, 168
Hall, Gwendolyn Midlo, 7, 10
Hall, Tony, 122
Hamilton, Shannon, 176
Hammond, Fred, 204
Hampton, Lionel, 83, 99
Hancock, Herbie, 150, 152
Handy, W. C., 20
Hanna, Jake, 161
Hannusch, Jeff, 105
Harris, Betty, 120
Harris, Clyde, 154
Harris, David, 155
Harrison, Donald, Jr., 34, 79, 82, 126, 152, 185, 201, 202
Harrison, Donald, Sr., 34, 82
Hart, Billy, 86
Hart, Keith, 296
Hart, Mickey, 127
Havens, Richie, 114
Hawketts, 80, 102, 116, 119
Hawkins, Taylor, 157
Hayward, Gerald, 174
Hearn, Lafcadio, 30
Heath, Jimmy, 136
Hendricks, Jon, 147
Hendrix, Jimi, 84, 162
Henry, Clarence "Frogman," 116, 145
Hentoff, Nat, 134
Herbert, Jeffrey, 163
Heritage Hall Jazz Band (All Stars), 72, 145
Heritage Music School, 152–153, *153*, 182
Hermann, Jojo, 122, 127
Herring, Jimmy, 122
"Hey Pocky A-Way" ("Hey Pocky Way"), 54, 114
Hicks, John, 82

Higgins, Billy, 37, 77–78, 135
Higgins, Terrence, 202
High Steppers Brass Band, 206
Hill, Jessie, 101, 102, 105
Hill, Scotty, 155
Hines, Earl, 60, 61, 72
Hino, Motohiko "Toko," 166
Hirt, Al, 107, 145, 154
Hodes, Art, 72
Hoffman, Darren, 232
Hogan, Wilbur, 76, 98
Holiday, Billie, 21, 72
Hot 8 Brass Band, 126, 164–165, 206
Houma Nation, 11, 20
Howard, Kid, 64
Hubbard, Freddie, 135
Humphrey, Percy, 64, *136*, 155
Humphrey, Willie, 71
Hurley, Marty, 184
Hurricane Katrina, *153*, 156, 163, 164, 189, 208

Ice Cube, 122
Imperial Orchestra, *27*
Isaac, William "Dan," 12, *12*
Impressions, The, 72, 81
Irakere, 169
Iris May Tango, 189
Irving Fields Biggest Show of Stars, 99
Ivanhoe club, 115, 116

J&M Recording Studio, 82, 87, 89, 94, 99, 101, 107
Jackson, Andrew, 27–28
Jackson, Bonnie Mae, 4, 162
Jackson, Herman, 188, 201
Jackson, Mahalia, 22
Jackson, Michael, 119, 136, 163
Jackson, Sam, 165
Jacksons, 136
Jaffe, Alan, 159
Jagger, Mick, 105
Jamal, Ahmad, 68, 74, 82, 100, 145
James, Etta, 114
James, Rick, 176
Jahnz, Janhein, 19
Jan and Dean, 90
Jefferson, Andrew, 116
Jefferson, Thomas (trumpeter), 71
Jiles, Albert, 44
Jimmy Ryan's club, 61
Johanson, Jai Johanny "Jaimoe," 108
John, Elton, 119, 136
Johnny Sketch and the Dirty Notes, 189, 192
Johnson, Al "Carnival Time," *97*, 115
Johnson, Bernard "Bunchy," 116

Johnson, J. J., 74
Johnson, Joseph "Smokey," 55, 73, 91, 94–97, *95, 97,* 99, 100, 102, 107, 109, 111, 116–117, 120, 124, 130, 140, 149, 160, 161, 180, 182, 195, 196, 199, 211; "It Ain't My Fault," 55, 96
Johnson, Lonnie, 62
Johnson, Plas, 77, 101
Johnson, Ronald, 77
Jolly, Pat, 83
Joplin, Scott, 21
Jones, Benny, 35–36, *36,* 162, 194–196, 206
Jones, Elvin, 81, 134, 166, 208
Jones, Eugene, 107, 116
Jones, Herman, 204
Jones, Jamie, 152–153
Jones, Papa Jo, 50, 68
Jones, Joe, 80, 83, 95, 99
Jones, Philly Joe, 150, 161, 184, 202, 209
Jones, Joenie, *106*
Jones, Leroy, 145, 160
Jones, Norah, 160
Jones, Tad, 65, 91
Jordan, Clifford, 75, 77
Jordan, Edward Kidd, 95, 97, 144, 180, 195
Jordan, Stephanie, 152
Joseph, Kirk, 177, 189, 194
Jourdain, Christie, 163–165, *164, 165,* 177, 207
Joseph, Waldron "Frog," 71
Joyce, John, 17

K-Doe, Ernie, 103, 107, 112, 119
Kaslow, Andy, *141*
Kee, John P., 204
Kemble, Edward. W., 18; *The Bamboula,* 18
Kemp, Fred, 97
Kendall, John Smith, 15
Kennedy, Al, 181
Kenner, Chris, 93, 103, 119
Keppard, Freddie, 61
Kerr, Clyde, 197, 204
King, B. B., 188
King, Earl, 90, 91, 93, 94, 95, 115, 119
King Curtis (Ousley), 98
King Floyd, 113
Kininger, Sam, 174
Klemm & Brother, *28*
Klezmer All Stars, 185, 189
Klymaxx, 163
Kmen, Henry, 24, 25, 27
Knox, Emile, *45*
Koenig, Dr. Karl, 48
Koerner, Maggie, 185
King Kolax (William Little), 74
Kohlman, Freddie, 42, 49, 71–73, *72,* 74, 145, 155, 159, 162, 182

Krall, Diana, 161
Krasno, Eric, 122, 174
Kreutzmann, Bill, 127
Krown, Joe, 181
Krupa, Gene, 61, 68, 105, 161

La Havana club, 123
Labelle, 113–114
Lacen, Anthony. *See* Tuba Fats
Lacoume, Emile "Stalebread," 31, 87
Laine, Alfred, *48*
Laine, Papa Jack, 1, 31, 48, *48, 49*
Lamare, Nappy, 69
Lambousy, Greg, 32
Landry, George. *See* Big Chief Jolly
Lanois, Daniel, 130, 137
Larsen, Neil, 114
Lastie, Alice, 154
Lastie, Betty, 65, 143, 153, 156
Lastie, Deacon Frank, 4, 65–66, *66,* 92, 100, 143, 153, 162, 179
Lastie, Melvin, 65, '*102,* 104, 143
Lastie, Walter "Popee," 65, 144, 153, *179*
Lastie, Joseph, Jr., 65, 136, 138, 163, 170, 180, 184, 197, 211
Lastie, Joseph, 65, 136, 138, 144, 153–157, *154, 156,* 157, 167, 169, 179
Lastie, David, Sr., 65, 97, 105, 143, 160
Lateef, Yusef, 83
Latrobe, Benjamin Henry, 16–17, *17,* 25
Leary, Washboard Chaz, 30, *31,* 37
LeBeaux, Herman, 204
Lee, David, Jr., 85–87, *86,* 102, 110, 137, 140, 141, 182, 193, 197
Leedy, Ulysses G., 49
Lesh, Phil, 127
Levine, Stewart, 109
Lewis, Barbara, 72
Lewis, George, 62, 131–135
Lewis, Juno, 133–135
Lewis, Kerry, 170
Lewis, Kevin, 155
Lewis, Mother, 8, 162
Lewis, Ramsey, 114
Lewis, Smiley (Overton Amos Lemons), 107
Lief, Shane, 11, 34
Lincoln Center, 143, 146, 161, 189, 199
Lindor, 15, *15*
Little, Booker, 78
Little Queenie and the Percolators, 189, 191
Little Richard (Penniman), 89, 90, 100, 192
Lomax, Alan, 35, 53
Lonzo, Fred, 72, 147, 155
Lopez, Ricardo, 93

Los Hombres Calientes, 152, 194
Louis Armstrong Educational Foundation's Music Academy and Summer Camp, 112, 182
Louisiana Philharmonic Orchestra, 169
Lovano, Joe, 79
Lu & Charlie's (club), 83, 84, 154, 160
Ludwig Company, 1, 48, *49,* 50, 132, 186, 195, 196, 197, *198*
Lynn, Tami, 101, 104
Lyric Theatre, 77, 82, 95

MacAulay, Don, 133
MacDermot, Galt, 81
MacMurray, John, *27,* 49
Madonna, 119, 136
Magnie, John, 191
Mahalia Jackson Theater for the Performing Arts, 159
Mannete, Ellie, 168
Manetta, Manuel "Fess," *71*
Marable, Fate, 57, 60
Mardi Gras (Carnival), 26, 33, 34, 41, 62, 72, 79, 82, 85, 101, 103, 115, 118, 127, 137, 149, 163, 170, 180, 184, 197, 211
Mardi Gras Indians. *See* Black Masking Indians
Mamas & the Papas, 134
Mann, Herbie, 148, 151
Maria, Tania, 152
Marie, Teena, 176
Marley, Ziggy, 130
Marquis, Don, 63
Marsalis, Branford, 85, 154, 161, 179
Marsalis, Delfeayo, 148, 179
Marsalis, Ellis, 72, 77, 79, 82, 84, 85, 87, 108, 137, 145, 147, 160, 188, 193, 199, 201
Marsalis, Jason, 87, 162, 192–194, *193,* 204, 209
Marsalis, Wynton, 52, 65, 85, 143, 154, 179, 199
Martin, Chink, *48*
Martinez, Pedrito, 148
Martyn, Barry, 132–133, *132,* 183
Masakowski, Steve, 141
Matassa, Cosimo, 82, 89, *89,* 96, 103
Matthews, Bunny, 94, 140, 184
Mayall, John, 114
Mayfield, Curtis, 108, 254
Mayfield, Irving, 99
Mazurkas ("mazooka") dance rhythm, 25, 46
McBride, Christian, 137
McConnell, Page, 181
McCusker, John, 11, 34, *63*
McFerrin, Bobby, 151
McGowan, Jerry, 200
McLachlan, Sarah, 138

McLean, Ernest, 101
McLendon, Lisa, *182*
McMurray, Alex, 189
Medeski, John, 122
Mele, Joe, 98
Mello, Leonce, *48*
Mello, Manuel, *48*
Metaire Lodge, 149–150
Metcalf, Willie, 154
Meters, The, 54–55, 96, 100, 109, 113–114, 119–123, *117,* 126, 129, 133, 159, 179, 180
Metheny, Pat, 173
Midnight Disturbers, 189
Militia bands, 11–12, 16, 23, 26–28, 39, 134
Miller, Charlie, 110
Miller, Glenn, 73
Mitchell, Bobby, 93
Mitchell, Joni, 138
Modeliste, Joseph "Zigaboo," 54–55, 80, 96, 100–101, 109, 114, 115–123, *116, 117, 119, 120,* 137, 180, 182, 183, 187, 193, 209; "Hey Pocky A-way," 55
Moffett, Jonathan "Sugarfoot," 119, 133, 136–137
Monk, Thelonious, 147
Monkees, 90
Montana, Big Chief David, 156
Montana, Big Chief Tootie, 22
Monie, Rickie, 156, 169
Montegue, Sydney, 74
Montgomery, Robbie, *101*
Montrell, Roy, *102*
Mooney, John, 126, 127
Moore, Deacon John, 119
Moore, Stanton, 1, 48, 131, *142,* 143, 182, 183–186, *184, 186,* 187, 188, 189, 190, 211
Moore, Tom, 98
Moran, Max, 202
Morgan, Lee, 136
Morgan, Sam, 72
Morgan, Oliver, 112
Morgan, Red Morgan, 135
Morgan, Sam, 95
Morris, Leo. *See* Idris Muhammad
Morris, Weedy, 79, 102, 178, 182
Morton, Jelly Roll Morton (Ferdinand Joseph LaMothe), ix, 20, 21, 25, 35, 53, 59, 61, 62
Motian, Paul, 140, 184
Motown Records, 95–96, 100, 104
Mouzon, Alphonse, 81
Muhammad, Idris (Leo Morris), 79–82, *80,* 99, 102, 178, 202
Muldaur, Maria, 179, 210
Muñequitos de Matanzas, Los, 163

Municipal Boys Home. *See* Colored Waifs' Home for Boys
Murray, Albert, 199
Murray, David, 79
Muskogean Nation, 11
Mydland, Brent, 127

Narcisse, Jules, 134
Nasser, Jamil, 75
Nation of Gumbolia, 157
Naughty by Nature, 122
Negro Philharmonic Society, 24
Nelson, "Big Eye" Louis, 27
Nelson, Ricky, 90
Nelson, Walter "Papoose," 91
Nelson, Willie, 130
Neville, Aaron, 119, 128–129
Neville, Art, 113, 116, *117,* 119, 120, 130
Neville, Charles, 19
Neville, Cyril, 22, *22,* 80, 109, 118–119, 120, 122, 125, 182, 185
Neville, Ian, 122
Neville, Ivan, 122, 129, 174, 183
Neville, Omari, 179
Neville Brothers, 14, 22, 99, 114, 118, 128–130, 168, 175
Neville Sounds, 116, 119
New Barbarians, 122
New Breed Brass Band, 163
New Creations Brass Band, 163
New Orleans Center for Creative Arts (NOCCA), 127, 182, 193, 197, 201, 202, 204
New Orleans Groovemasters, 162, 194, 209
New Orleans Jazz and Heritage Festival (Jazz Fest), 22, 35, *98,* 116, 120, 123, 125, *126,* 133, *144, 156, 159,* 160, 162, 168, 174–175, 176, *193*
New Orleans Jazz and Second Line Drumming, 56, 169, 182, 191
New Orleans Jazz Collective, 85
New Orleans Jazz Market, 200
New Orleans Jazz Museum, ix, 1, 3, 18, 31, 32, 63, 133, 138–139, *182,* 182, 184, 185; Ruth U. Fertel Jazz Lab, 182
New Orleans Jazz Orchestra, 69, 197, 200; School of Music (NOJOSOM), 182
New Orleans Suspects, 130
Night Bird Brass Band, 206
Nite Cap Lounge, 119
Noble, Jordan B., 27–28, *28*
Nocentelli, Leo, 113, 116, 119, 180, 181
Noone, Jimmy, 61
Nth Power, 175

Nuccio, Carlo, 190
Nunez, Alcide, *48*
Nunez, Ear, 177
NWA, 122

O'Day, Kevin, 139, 177, 187–189, *189*
O'Jays, 173
Old and New Dreams, 79
Oliver, Joe "King," 57, 58, 61
Olympia Brass Band, *45,* 206
One Mo' Time, 145
O'Neill, Leo, *106*
Onward Brass Band, *44,* 61, 62, 63, 72, 211
Opera, 23–24, *24*
Original Pinettes Brass Band, 163–163, *164,* 177, 207
Ory, Edward "Kid," 31, *52*
Osborne, Anders, 122
Ostendorf, Ann, 23
Owens, Chris, 123

PBS (band), 181
Palao, James A., *27*
Palmer, Earl, 1, 5, 63, 73, 87–91, *88, 89, 90,* 92, 93, 94, 99, 100, 101, 107, 109, 111, 116, 120, 136, 149, 182, 183, 192, 199, 209
Palmer, Robert (singer), 122
Palmer, Robert (writer), 77–78
Panken, Ted, 137
Panorama Brass Band, 171
Papa Grows Funk, 181
Pappas, Conun, Jr., 202
Parker, Charlie, 31, 61, 74, 76, 184
Parker, Frank, 155
Parker, Maceo, 175, 181, 185
Pastorius, Jaco, 151, 152
Patitucci, John, 137
Paul, Clarence, 95
Pavageau, Alcide "Slow Drag," 131, *132*
Payne, Richard, 77, 79, 154
Payton, Nicholas, 162, 182, 197, 199, 201
Payton, Walter, Jr., 72, 128
Pénigaut, André, 11
Peraza, Armando, 124
Perez, Manuel, *27*
Perrilliat, Nat, 82, 94, 103
Perkins, Grayhawk, 11, *11,* 13
Phillips, Bill, 89
Phish, 181
Pichon, Walter "Fats," 87
Pierce, Billie and DeDe, 64–65
Pinstripe Brass Band, 164
Piron, A. J., *43*
Pla, Enrique, 169
Polkas dance rhythm, 3, 46
Pollak, Ben, 67
Pooler, Sister Bertha Jackson, 4, 162
Poppa Stoppa (Clarence Hayman), 106

Porter, George, 113, 116, *117*, 118, *120*, 143, 151, 152, 160, 180, 183, 190

Porter, Ruby, 158

Powell, Benny, *74*

Powell, Shannon, 4, *5*, 44, 63, 73, 113, 125, 138, *142*, 148, 157–162, *159, 160, 161*, 167, 182, 184, 194, 199, 201, 204–205, 208, 209, *210*

Pratz, Antoine-Simon Le Page du, 11, 19

Preservation Hall, 49, 62, 63, 64, 65, 72, 136, 153–157, 159, 161, 162, 167

Price, Lloyd, 89

Prima, Louis, 8

Prince, 163, 234

Prince La La (Lawrence Nelson), 104

Prodigy Project, 201

Professor Longhair (Henry Roeland Byrd), 32, 76, 91, 92, 94, 99, 102, 103, 107, 119, 123, 125, *126*, 127, 137, 138, 140–141, *141*, 143, 144, 154, 159

Public Enemy, 122, 154

Puente, Tito, 123

Purdie, Bernard "Pretty," 81

Quadrilles dance rhythms, *25, 27,* 46

Queen Latifah, 122

Quezergue, Wardell, 94, 95, 96, 99

Radiators, The, 130, 189, 190

Radle, Carl, 105

Raeburn, Dr. Bruce, 52–53, 133, 141

Rage Against the Machine, 173

Ragtime, x, 19, 21, 46, 57, 183

Ramsey, Frederic, 183

Rankin, Leroy "Batman," 99

Ratcliff, Stanley, 180

Ray Fransen's Drum Center, 184

Rebennack, Mac "Dr. John," 65, 72, 90, 91, 93, 100–101, *101*, 102, 103, 104, 105, 106, *106*, 107, 108, 109, 110, 111, 112, 114, 115, 125, 126, 129, 148, 151, 162, 188, 198

Rebirth Brass Band, 36, 164, 165, 189, 206, 208, 211

Redman, Dewey, 79

Redman, Joshua, 137

Reed, Arthur, 94

Reels (dance rhythms), 25

Reeves, Diane, 148, 198, 199

Reinhardt, Allison, 205

Reliance Band, *48*

Rich, Buddy, 88, 230

Richards, Keith, 121

Richards, Trevor, 64

Richardson, Donald, 206, 207

Ricks, Chief "Smiley," 111, 130

Ridgely, Tommy, 93

Riley, Herlin, ix–x, *1, 2, 3*–4, 22, 37, 44, 48, 50, 51, 56, 65, 73, 96, 97, 101, 136, 137, 138, 143–148, *144, 146*, 154, 156, 161, 162, 167, 169, 176, 179, 183, 184, 194, 199, 201, 202, 204, 209, *210*

Riley, Teddy, 72, 99, 147

Rivers, James, 167

Rivers, Sam, 151

Roach, Max, 76, 77, 105, 125, 135, 140, 150, 209

Roberts, Alfred "Uganda," 19–20, *20*, 84, 97, *97*, 100, 123–127, *124, 126*, 159, 181, 182

Roberts, Eddie, 122

Roberts, Linda, 124

Roberts, Marcus, 65, 148, 199

Roberston, Robbie, 122, 181

Robichaux, John, 12, 46–47, *47*, 60, 63, 147

Robichaux, Joseph, 72

Robicheaux, Coco, 126

Robinson, Alvin "Shine," 105

Robinson, Smokey, 95

Robredo, Manuel Saumell, 21

Rock & Roll Hall of Fame, 91

Rogers, Darren, 207

Rogers, Kelvin, 204

Rolling Stones, 121, 133

Rollins, Sonny, 86

Ronnie Scott's club, 111

Ronson, Mark, 122

Roots of Music, 36, 182, *203*, 205–209, *207*

Rory Danger and the Danger Dangers, 189

Rosas, Margo A., 12, *12, 13*

Rose, Adonis, 195–200, *198*, 201, 208

Ross, Diana, 95

Rouse, Charlie, 86

Royal Fingerbowl, 189, 190

Royen, John, 169

Ruffin, Shoan, 205, 207, *207*

Ruffins, Kermit, 148, 167

Romero, Lubambo, 152

Run DMC, 122

Russell, Bill, 183

Russell, Luis, 61

Rydell, Bobby, 99

St. Augustine Marching, 100, 163, 180, 192, 197

Saint-Domingue. *See* Haiti

St. Mary's Academy, 163, 176

St. Philip Church of God in Christ, 4, 158, 162, *209*

St. Cyr, Johnny, 42

Salaam, Kalamu ya, 79, 85

Salt N' Pepa, 173

Sample, Steve, Sr., 122

Sanchez, Paul, 115

Sanders, Pharoah, 82, 134

Santamaria, Mongo, 123, 124

Santana, 130

Santería, 19

Santino, Edward, 99

Schafer, William J., 26

Scherman, Tony, 90

Schexnayder, Carl, 150

Schottisches (dance rhythm), 48

Schultz, Christian, 14–15

Schwartz, Meghan, 170

Scofield, John, 151, 162

Scott aTunde Adjuah, Christian, 201

Scott, Shirley, 81

Sea-Saint Studio, 113, 125

Seals, Mother Catherine, 65

Sebastian, Ricky, 51, 54–55, 70, 84, 132, 138, 148–153, *149, 152*, 183, 204

Second line, x, 3, 9, 20, *36*, 37, 39, 41, 42, 44, 45, *46*, 53, 54–55, 59, 65, 68, 74, 82, 86, 94, 96, 97, 98, 99, 100, 103, 104, 105, 107, 108–109, 110, 112, 118, 122, 128, 130, 140, 147, 148–149, 158, 162, 169, 177, 183

Sehorn, Marshall, 116

Severin, Chris, 195, 198

Severin, Vernon, 2, *2*, 84, 194–197, 198, *198*

Severin, Wilfred "Crip," 195, *195*, 197, 199

Shara, Mayumi, 165–167, *167*

Shearing, George, 75

Sheila E, 163

Shirley and Lee (Shirley Goodman and Leonard Lee), 89, 102

Shorter, Wayne, 137, 152

Shorts, Barbara, 162

Shy, Parker, 76

Sieberth, Larry, 188

Silver, Horace, 83

Simas, Luiz, 217

Simon, Kenyatta, 100, 127, 152

Simon, Paul, 130

Sinatra, Frank, 90

Singleton, Arthur Zutty, 33, 41–42, *50*, 59–60, *60*, 62, 63, 66–67, 69, 72, 74, 132, 133, 138

Singleton, James, 141, 142, 185

Sly & the Family Stone, 176

Smith, Bessie, 49

Smith, Hezekiah "Stuff," 72

Smith, Huey "Piano" 93, 100

Smith, Jessie, *101*

Smith, Dr. Lonnie, 1, 48

Smith, Marshall, 82

Smith, Will, 155

Smithsonian Jazz Oral History Program, 193

Snug Harbor (club), 148

Social aid and pleasure clubs (benevolent associations), 41, *46*, 211

Sompa, Titos, *6*

Sonny and Cher, 135

Sousa, John Philip, 39

Southern University at New Orleans's Center for African and African American Studies, 17–18

Spalding, Esperanza, 201

Spasm bands, 29–33, *30, 33*, 48, 58, 103, 110, 135, 137

Spector, Phil, 134

Spellman, Benny, 107

Spera, Keith, 111, 115

Spiro, Michael, 168

Spitelera, Joseph "Peewee," 107

Spivey, Victoria, 61

Sperling, Jack, 140

Staehle, Fred, 86, 101, 105–110, *106, 107*, 115, 140, 178

Staehle, Paul, 105–107, 108, 178

Stafford George, 57

Stafford, Greg, 155

Stanley, Earl, 106

Starks, John "Jabo," 101, 183

Starr, Ringo (Richard Starkey), 131–133

Stevens, Mike, *48*

Stevens, Milton, 91

Stitt, Sonny, 74, 81

Stolz, Brian, 181

Stooges Brass Band, 165

Storyville, 53, 71

Streisand, Barbara, 90

Stubblefield, Clyde, 101, 183

Subdudes, 191

Sublette, Ned, 20

Suhor, Charlie, 139–140

Summers, Bill, 152, 194, 217, 280

Swenson, John, 179

Taiko (Chinese) drums, 49, 57, *60, 60*, 166–167, *167*

TBC brass band, 163

Tabb, Derrick, 36, 56, 164, 165, 205–209, *206, 207*, 211

Tango (rhythm), 20, 109

Taylor, Art, 135

Taylor, Cecil, 192

Taylor, Creed, 82

Tee, Willie (Wilson Turbinton), 82, 126

Terry, Clark, 188

Tervalon, Clement, 71, *72*

Tharpe, Sister Rosetta, 131

Theolphile, Thelma and Nita, 87–88

Thomas, Irma, 83, 99, 102, 107, 115, 127

Thomas, Leon, 86

Thompson, Emory, 145

Thornton, Big Mama, 105

Thress, Dan, 112–114, 143

Tijuana (club), 92–93, 95

Tio, Mario, *18*

Torkanowsky, David, 99, 141, 185

Tough, Dave, 57, 61

Toussaint, Allen, 83, 99, 103, 109, 113, 114, 116, 118, 119, 120, 122, 125, 159, 181, 185, 188, 200

Trappanier, Ernest, 44

Trayanova, Boyanna, 170–172, *171*

Treme Brass Band, *2*, 3, 38–39, *39*, 195, 197

Treme Side Steppers, 206

Tresillo (rhythm), 53

Tribe Called Quest, A, 122

Trombone Shorty. *See* Andrews, Troy "Trombone Shorty"

Trotter, James M., 40

Troy, Doris, 105

Tuba Fats (Anthony Lacen), 37, 145, 167, 205

Turbinton, Earl, 79, 85, 87, 110

Turner, Benny, 167

Turner, Ike and Tina, 90

Turner, Big Joe, 89

Tuxedo Brass Band, 61, 62

Tuxedo Jazz Band, 178, *179*

Tyler, Alvin "Red," 61, 88, 94, 95, 97, 99, *102*, 104, 111, 137

Uncle Nef, 162

Universe Jazz Band, 170

Valens, Richie, 90

Van Halen, 173

Varnado, Peter, 202–205, *201*

Vaughn, Reverend Leon, 156

Veal, Reginald, 147

Vézina, Carol, 23–24

Victor, Professor Valmont, 98

Victory, June, 177

Vidacovich, Johnny, 127, 137, 138–143, *139, 141, 142*, 150, 171, 175, 182, 183, 184, 185, 187, 189, 191, 192

Vinson, Eddie "Cleanhead," 105

Vosbein, Michael, 138

Vodou/Voudou, 19

Wagner, Rob, 188

Waits, Tom, 90

Walker, Hezekiah, 204

Waller, Thomas Fats, 61

Walters, Cori, 168–170, *169*

Waltz (dance rhythm), 25, 46, 56, 68

Watanabe, Mari, 167

Water drum, 11

Ward, Michael, 127

Washington, Walter "Wolfman," 181, 189

Watkins, Joe, 131–132, *132*

Watson, Dave, *141*

Watts, Charlie, 122, 133, *133*

Webb, Chick, 57

Weber, Raymond, 175, 178

Weber, Raymond, Jr., 178

Webster, Ben, 74

Webster-Modeliste, Kathy, 122

Weir, Bob, 127

Werlein's Music, 195

Werner, Kenny, 137

Weston, Randy, 76, 78

Wettling, George, 57–58, 61

Whaley, Wade, *52*

Whitfield, Mark, 148

White, Clifton, 98

White, Danny, 107

White, Dr. Michael, 41, 62, 67, 147, 162, 194

White Eagles, 34

Whitlock, Bobby, 105

Wild Magnolias, 118, 126, 130, 181

Wild Tchoupitoulas, 14, 118, 179

Wilder, Joe, 75

Williams, Alfred, 132, 183

Williams, Black Benny, 44

Williams, Charles "Hungry," 91–94, *92*, 100, 109, 111, 132, 1149, 183

Williams, Kenneth "Afro," *18*

Williams, Larry, 89

Williams, Martin, 60–61

Williams, Tony, 86, 140, 150, 166, 184

Wilson, Cassandra, 148

Wilson, Nancy, 75

Wilson, Shadow, 140

Wilson, Theodore Shaw "Teddy," 74

Wolf, Andy, 188

Wonder, Stevie, 96

Wood, Ronnie, 121

Woods, Eddie "Face-o," 63

Wooten, John, 184

Works Progress Administration, 16

Wrecking Crew, 90

Wright, Marva, 167

Wycoff, Geraldine, 95, 139

Yamagishi, June, 143, 209

Yes, 128

Young, Kenny "KliK," 177

Young, Lester "Pres," 74

Young Fellaz Brass Band, 165

Young Swingsters, 73, 87

Young Tuxedo Band, 64

Zawinul, Joe, 86

Zildjian company, 50, 57, 195

Zydeco, x, 3, 151, 168

Robert H. Cataliotti is a music critic and historian who teaches courses in American and African American literature at Coppin State University in Baltimore. He is the winner of a 1983 ASCAP Foundation Deems Taylor Award for excellence in writing on music. A contributing writer for *Living Blues* magazine, he has published two books, *The Music in African American Fiction* and *The Songs Became the Stories: The Music in African American Fiction, 1970–2005.* He produced and annotated the Smithsonian Folkways CDs *Classic Sounds of New Orleans, On My Journey: Paul Robeson's Independent Recordings,* and *Every Tone a Testimony: An African American Aural History.* He is the annotator of *A Voice Ringing O'er the Gale! The Oratory of Frederick Douglass Read by Ossie Davis,* and his essay "It Feels Good to Call Something Yours" appears in the fiftieth anniversary book/box set *Jazz Fest: The New Orleans Jazz and Heritage Festival.* He is the cocurator of the *Drumsville! The Evolution of the New Orleans Beat* exhibit at the New Orleans Jazz Museum.

David Kunian serves as the curator for the New Orleans Jazz Museum, where he has assembled exhibits on women in New Orleans music, a history of New Orleans drumming and drummers, painters Emilie Rhys and Noel Rockmore, Louis Prima, Professor Longhair, Pete Fountain, and 300 years of New Orleans music. His writing has appeared in the *Oxford American, Downbeat, Offbeat, Gambit Weekly,* and *Beat Street.* He has participated in numerous radio documentaries on New Orleans music icons and institutions such as James Booker, Earl King, Lee Dorsey, Everette Maddow, the Dew Drop Inn, and Jonathan Freilich. He also hosts the *Freaknologist Lunatique* program on WWOZ-FM New Orleans on Tuesday nights at 10 p.m., where his varied musical taste is on full display.

Greg Lambousy is the director of the New Orleans Jazz Museum. Prior to accepting this position, he served as the director of curatorial services for the National World War II Museum. He began his career at the New Orleans Museum of Art and later moved to the Louisiana State Museum (LSM). During his twenty-year tenure at the LSM, Lambousy managed the institution's collections of more than 500,000 artifacts and other historical items, directed improvements to collections storage at the New Orleans Mint, developed conservation and digitization projects across collections and within the Louisiana Historical Center archives, conducted oral histories, and guided the selection and accession of materials related to Hurricane Katrina. At the Jazz Museum, he has led efforts to further the museum's mission to celebrate the history of jazz with educational programming, exhibitions, research projects, digitization, and by engaging musical performances and developing Gallatin Street Records.

Herlin Riley is a preeminent drummer on the contemporary New Orleans music scene. Early on, he was mentored by the guitarist, banjo player, and singer Danny Barker in the Fairview Baptist Church Brass Band. In 1982, he began the first of two tenures in the Ahmad Jamal Quartet. Six years later, Riley launched a seventeen-year collaboration with Wynton Marsalis in his quintet/septet and as a member of the Lincoln Center Jazz Orchestra, becoming the first jazz drummer on a Pulitzer Prize–winning recording of the oratorio *Blood on the Fields* (1997). His versatility is evident in the roster of artists with whom he has recorded, including Harry Connick Jr., Marcus Roberts, Cassandra Wilson, Wycliffe Gordon, Dr. John, Maria Muldaur, Diane Reeves, Dee Daniels, Delfeayo Marsalis, Kermit Ruffins, Dr. Lonnie Smith, George Benson, McCoy Tyner, Ron Carter, and many more. He has released four albums as a leader that focus on his original compositions, including *Watch What You're Doing* (2000), *Cream of the Crescent* (2005), *New Direction* (2016), and *Perpetual Optimism* (2019). Riley is the coauthor (with Johnny Vidacovich) of *New Orleans Jazz and Second Line Drumming* (1995) and an adjunct drum instructor at the University of New Orleans, Northwestern University, and The Juilliard School.